Lecture Notes in Computer Science 9766

Commenced Publication in 1973
Founding and Former Series Editors:
Gerhard Goos, Juris Hartmanis, and Jan van Leeuwen

More information about this series at http://www.springer.com/series/7409

Silvio Ranise · Vipin Swarup (Eds.)

Data and Applications Security and Privacy XXX

30th Annual IFIP WG 11.3 Conference, DBSec 2016
Trento, Italy, July 18–20, 2016
Proceedings

 Springer

Editors
Silvio Ranise
Fondazione Bruno Kessler
Trento
Italy

Vipin Swarup
The Mitre Corp
McLean, VA
USA

ISSN 0302-9743   ISSN 1611-3349 (electronic)
Lecture Notes in Computer Science
ISBN 978-3-319-41482-9   ISBN 978-3-319-41483-6 (eBook)
DOI 10.1007/978-3-319-41483-6

Library of Congress Control Number: 2016942496

LNCS Sublibrary: SL3 – Information Systems and Applications, incl. Internet/Web, and HCI

This Springer imprint is published by Springer Nature
The registered company is Springer International Publishing AG Switzerland

Preface

These proceedings contain the papers selected for presentation at the 30th IFIP WG 11.3 Conference on Data and Applications Security (DBSec16), held in Trento, Italy, July 18–20, 2016.

DBSec16 received 54 submissions that were evaluated on the basis of their significance, novelty, technical quality, and appropriateness to the DBSec audience. Each paper was reviewed by at least three members of the Program Committee. After intensive reviewing and electronic discussions, 17 full papers and 7 short papers were selected for presentation at the conference. Their topics cover a wide range of data and application security and privacy problems including those of mobile devices, collaborative systems, databases, big data, virtual systems, cloud computing, and social networks. The program also included two invited talks.

We would like to thank all the people who invested their time and energy to make this year's edition of DBSec happen. In particular, we thank the authors for submitting their manuscripts and the attendees for contributing to the conference discussion. We are also very grateful to the members of the Program Committee and to the external reviewers for carefully reviewing and discussing the submissions, and for their commitment to meeting the strict deadlines.

We thank the people at Springer for their assistance in publishing these proceedings. Last but certainly not least, our thanks go to everybody involved in the organization of the event, most notably to Sabrina De Capitani di Vimercati (IFIP WG 11.3 Chair) for her guidance and support, Alessandro Armando (Conference Chair), Giovanni Livraga (Publicity Chair), Roberto Carbone (Local Organization Chair), and Federico Sinigaglia (Web Master).

We hope you find the proceedings of DBSec16 interesting, stimulating, and inspiring for your future research.

July 2016

Silvio Ranise
Vipin Swarup

Organization

Program Committee

Program Chairs

Silvio Ranise   Fondazione Bruno Kessler, Trento, Italy
Vipin Swarup   The MITRE Corporation, USA

Members

Vijay Atluri	Rutgers University, USA
Joachim Biskup	Technische Universität Dortmund, Germany
Achim D. Brucker	The University of Sheffield, UK
Soon Ae Chun	CUNY, USA
Frédéric Cuppens	Telecom Bretagne, France
Nora Cuppens-Boulahia	Telecom Bretagne, France
Jun Dai	California State University, Sacramento, USA
Sabrina De Capitani di Vimercati	Università degli Studi di Milano, Italy
Josep Domingo-Ferrer	Universitat Rovira i Virgili, Spain
Carmen Fernández-Gago	University of Malaga, Spain
Simon Foley	University College Cork, Ireland
Sara Foresti	Università degli Studi di Milano, Italy
Joaquin Garcia-Alfaro	Telecom SudParis, France
Ehud Gudes	Ben-Gurion University, Israel
Yuan Hong	University at Albany, SUNY, USA
Florian Kerschbaum	SAP, Germany
Ram Krishnan	University of Texas at San Antonio, USA
Adam J. Lee	University of Pittsburgh, USA
Yingjiu Li	Singapore Management University, Singapore
Peng Liu	The Pennsylvania State University, USA
Javier Lopez	University of Malaga, Spain
Sjouke Mauw	University of Luxembourg, Luxembourg
Charles Morisset	Newcastle University, UK
Martin Olivier	University of Pretoria, South Africa
Stefano Paraboschi	Università di Bergamo, Italy
Günther Pernul	Universität Regensburg, Germany
Indrakshi Ray	Colorado State University, USA
Kui Ren	State University of New York at Buffalo, USA
Pierangela Samarati	Università degli Studi di Milano, Italy
Ravi Sandhu	University of Texas at San Antonio, USA
Scott Stoller	Stony Brook University, USA
Tamir Tassa	The Open University of Israel, Israel

Mahesh Tripunitara	University of Waterloo, Canada
Jaideep Vaidya	Rutgers University, USA
Lingyu Wang	Concordia University, Canada
Meng Yu	University of Texas at San Antonio, USA
Nicola Zannone	Eindhoven University of Technology, The Netherlands
Shengzhi Zhang	Florida Tech, USA

Additional Reviewers

Ahmed, Tahmina
Al Lail, Mustafa
Blanco-Justicia, Alberto
Carmichael, Peter
Casas-Roma, Jordi
Chang, Bing
Chen, Bo
Cheng, Yao
Fuchs, Ludwig
Ghosh, Sudipto
Hachana, Safaa
Hassan, Sabri
Herzberg, Michael
Hummer, Matthias
Idrees, Sabir
Imran-Daud, Malik
Iovino, Vincenzo
Kywe, Su Mon
Moataz, Tarik

Mulamba, Dieudonne
Nieto, Ana
Nuñez, David
Pieczul, Olgierd
Ren, Chuangang
Ribes-González, Jordi
Ricci, Sara
Rizzo, Nicholas
Romero-Tris, Cristina
Sprissler, Ethan
Sun, Xiaoyan
Sural, Shamik
Trujillo, Rolando
Xie, Xing
Yoon, Eunjung
Yu, Xingjie
Zang, Wanyu
Zhang, Yang
Zhao, Mingyi

IFIP WG 11.3 Chair

Sabrina De Capitani di Vimercati   Università degli Studi di Milano, Italy

Contents

Protection and Privacy of Data and Big Data

Security and Privacy in Social Networks and Collaborative Systems

Reasoning about Security and Its Cost

Trust and Zero-Day Vulnerabilities

Mobile Security and Privacy

Deciphering Text from Touchscreen Key Taps

Haritabh Gupta[1], Shamik Sural[1(✉)], Vijayalakshmi Atluri[2],
and Jaideep Vaidya[2]

[1] Department of Computer Science and Engineering, Indian Institute of Technology,
Kharagpur, India
{haritabh,shamik}@sit.iitkgp.ernet.in
[2] Management Science and Information Systems Department, Rutgers University,
Newark, USA
{atluri,jsvaidya}@rutgers.edu

Abstract. Exploiting acoustic emanations from electronic as well as mechanical devices as a means for side channel attack has recently emerged as a topic of security concern. In this paper, we present an attack methodology that can be used to extract the text typed by a user from the sound recorded by the built-in microphones of a mobile phone. We use signal processing techniques to initially extract a likely set of characters per tap on the touchscreen and then use natural language processing algorithms to find the most probable words and sentences that can be constructed from a given tap sequence. We also discuss the causes that result in this vulnerability and briefly present some countermeasures.

Keywords: Acoustic emanation · Touchscreen · Side-channel attack · Time Difference of Arrival (TDoA) · NLP

1 Introduction

In recent times, mobile phones have almost become a necessity rather than a luxury for a large section of people throughout the world. Reports show that mobile phone penetration will reach approximately 70 % of the global population by the year 2020. With increased reliance on mobile phones, especially for personal and confidential information exchange like mobile-commerce applications, the level of security ensured by these devices is an important topical issue.

Many users have started using phones for doing almost all of the work that they used to do on computers even a few years back. Although these mobile devices are yet to replace computers in their entirety, still a majority of the work has now shifted to the mobile devices due to various reasons such as mobility, portability, etc. Tasks range from composing e-mails, editing documents and accessing e-banking sites to surfing the net, using various applications (apps) like cab and hotel booking, chatting and participating in online social networking. All these tasks involve text input using a keypad, which is typically touchscreen in nature. In this paper, mobile phones (including smartphones and tablets) are

© IFIP International Federation for Information Processing 2016
Published by Springer International Publishing Switzerland 2016. All Rights Reserved
S. Ranise and V. Swarup (Eds.): DBSec 2016, LNCS 9766, pp. 3–18, 2016.
DOI: 10.1007/978-3-319-41483-6_1

hereinafter referred to simply as phones and they represent mobile devices that have a touchscreen user interface and have features like Internet access, support for recording and storing media files.

Most phones today are equipped with at least two microphones. Since these microphones are attached to the phone body, they pick up even the slightest sound produced on the surface of the phone. As a user taps on the touchscreen while typing, it produces a sound that may not be quite audible to the human ear due to the presence of ambient noise. Such tap sounds can, however, be captured using the microphones of the phone itself. A user hardly ever denies microphone use permission and Internet access to an app while installing the same. Also, an app is not considered to be suspicious unless it asks for some unusual combination of permissions. We show that even the above two seemingly innocuous permissions can be maliciously exploited to extract the text typed on the device and thus cause a security breach.

In the past, there has been some limited work that shows ways to recover text using acoustic emanations from mechanical keyboards [7]. They use external microphones to capture the sound and the recorded sound is used to train classifiers that differentiate between the sounds produced by different keys. It has also been shown that the sensors equipped with mobile phones such as accelerometer and gyroscope can be used for text extraction [8,10,11]. While such an approach uses the sensors attached to the phone, still it requires supervised learning. The possibility of exploiting the audio signal captured by the built-in microphones of a phone to decipher the typed text has never been studied, to the best of our knowledge.

This paper presents a novel methodology for carrying out a side-channel attack using acoustic emanations from the touchscreen keypad of a phone and that too using readily available tools. The approach is based on phone geometry and keypad layout, while using signal processing and natural language processing (NLP) techniques.

The rest of the paper is organized as follows: Sect. 2 describes our methodology and the associated algorithms in detail. Section 3 provides the complete workflow of an implemented system. Section 4 presents the results obtained in terms of accuracy of the proposed methodology. Related work is reviewed in Sect. 5. Some preventive measures are discussed in Sect. 6. Finally, Sect. 7 concludes the paper and presents some directions in which this work can be carried forward in future.

2   Attack Methodology

The complete methodology of the attack can be divided into two phases. The first phase, which is described in Subsect. 2.1, uses signal processing techniques to determine the probability of different characters that might have been entered with each tap using the audio signal received by the two microphones. It exploits the phone geometry and touchscreen keypad layout. In the second phase (Subsect. 2.2), NLP techniques are used to extract the probable word sequence that has been typed by processing the output of the first phase.

2.1 Character Sequence Extraction Using Microphone Data

Most of the phones nowadays are equipped with at least two microphones with stereo recording capability. As a user types on the phone touchscreen, it produces a sound for each tap. The microphones, which are quite close to the touch surface, capture this sound. There is hardly any damping as the microphones are solidly attached to the phone body. The two microphones are almost invariably positioned at unequal distances from the point of touch. As a result, from the recorded sound of key taps, the time difference of arrival (TDoA) of peaks in the two microphones can be computed. For each TDoA, the locus of the touch point such that the difference of its distance from the two microphones is constant, forms a hyperbola, with the two microphones at its two foci. Depending on the sign of TDoA, it can be inferred which half of the hyperbola is meaningful for a given key tap. We compute TDoA using cross correlation [2] between the two audio signals recorded at the two microphones as explained below.

The co-ordinate system is defined such that the top left corner of the phone, while holding it upright and facing front, coincides with the origin and the left edge is parallel to the x-axis. As a result, one microphone (denoted as m_1) lies on the y-axis and the other (denoted as m_2) is in the first quadrant. Let the coordinates of the microphones be $(0, p)$ and (l, q), respectively. Then the phone can be represented as shown in Fig. 1a. Thus, the vertex of the hyperbola, as mentioned above, also lies in the first quadrant. Hence, we use the general equation of a hyperbola with vertex at (x_0, y_0). The equation to represent this hyperbola from the obtained TDoA is as follows:

$$\frac{(x - x_0)^2}{a^2} - \frac{(y - y_0)^2}{b^2} = 1 \tag{1}$$

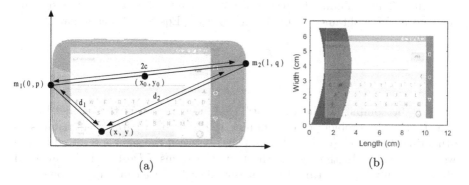

(a)   (b)

Fig. 1. (a) Hyperbola coverage on keyboard with $k = 3$. (b) Hyperbola coverage on keyboard with $k = 6$.

In Eq. 1, (x, y) represents any arbitrary tap point while a and b denote parameters of the desired semi-hyperbola. The following equations are used to compute these parameters in terms of other known and measurable quantities.

$$a = \frac{\Delta d}{2}, \text{ where } \Delta d = |d_1 - d_2| \tag{2}$$

Here, d_i is the distance of the ith microphone from the tapped point on the touchscreen, $i \in \{1, 2\}$. From Fig. 1a, it is seen that

$$c = \frac{\sqrt{(l - 0)^2 + (q - p)^2}}{2} \tag{3}$$

Here, l, p, q are phone parameters of which l denotes the length of the phone (dimension of the longer edge). p and q denote the distances of the microphones m_1 and m_2, respectively from the base of the phone. Hence, we can write:

$$b = \sqrt{c^2 - a^2} \tag{4}$$

$$x_0 = c \tag{5}$$

$$y_0 = min(p, q) \tag{6}$$

Simplifying and solving for x in terms of y from Eq. 1, we get:

$$x = x_0 \pm \left(\frac{a}{b} \sqrt{b^2 + (y - y_0)^2} \right) \tag{7}$$

We use this equation to obtain the values of x corresponding to the values of y, where $y = [0, w]$, w being the width of the phone. Δd is computed using the TDoA obtained and the parameters of the recorded sound, namely, the sampling frequency f_s and the sample offset Δs. Sample offset is the value by which one of the audio signals needs to be shifted so that the correlation between the two signals is maximum. The rest of the parameter values are computed using Eqs. 2 to 7. Δd is obtained from Δs and f_s using Eqs. 8 and 9 as follows:

$$TDoA = \frac{\Delta s}{f_s} \tag{8}$$

$$\Delta d = v_{sound} \cdot TDoA \tag{9}$$

Thus, by computing the value of TDoA, we can obtain the desired hyperbola. Hence, the problem of determining the hyperbola parameters reduces to estimating the TDoA (or sample offset Δs) between the signals received by the two microphones. In the rest of the text, the terms $TDoA$ and Δs are used interchangeably because from Eq. 8, it is evident that we can compute one from the other as f_s is kept constant.

From the recorded audio signals of the microphones, the first task is to detect the tap instants (peaks in the signal). We present an automated scheme for peak detection, which is shown as the *Detect_Peak_Intervals* algorithm (Algorithm 1). It takes the audio signals as input and returns a set of time intervals, each containing only one tap. A detailed description of the algorithm follows.

Algorithm 1. *Detect_Peak_Intervals*

Input: Sound signal $x_i(t)$ where $i \in \{1, 2\}$, half window size w_h, threshold θ
Output: Set of intervals containing taps: *intervals*
  1: **for** t=1 to n **do**   ▷ Calculate Energy
  2:      $A_i(t) = \sum_{n=t}^{t+10} x_i^2(n)$, where $i \in \{1, 2\}$
  3: **end for**
  4: **for** $t = 1$ to $A.length$ **do**   ▷ $A \in \{A_1, A_2\}$
  5:    s_k and e_k store beginning and end of a window around the selected time t
  6:    $[M, I] \leftarrow max(A_i(s_k : e_k))$ where $i \in \{1, 2\}$ ▷ I : index of the maximum value
  7:    **if** $t = I + s_k$ **and** $M > \theta \cdot max(A)$ **then**
  8:        $tmpIntr \leftarrow tmpIntr \cup (s_k : e_k)$
  9:    **end if**
10: **end for**
11: *intervals* contains time readjusted and center positioned peaks
12: **return** *intervals*

In Algorithm 1, the *for loop* of Lines 1–3 computes the energy levels of the signal by accumulating 10 sample points together. Next, in the *for loop* of Lines 4–10, for each sample point, first the beginning and end points of the interval window are set in variables s_k and e_k for the kth sample point. Lines 6–9 compute the maxima of the signal in the interval. If this value is greater than the threshold computed according to θ, then the corresponding interval is added to the set *tmpIntr*. Finally, the computed time intervals are readjusted so that the peaks are positioned at the center of each interval.

Algorithm 1 runs in $O(n)$ time as there are three loops in the algorithm of complexity $O(n)$, $O(n)$ and $O(k)$, respectively. Here, n is the number of sample points of the audio signal, k is the number of taps in the recording and $n \gg k$.

The output of Algorithm 1 is a set of intervals, each of which contains a tap. These intervals are further processed to get the TDoA corresponding to each tap. We next propose an algorithm (*Compute_TDoA*) to find the sample offset Δs of the two signals in a given interval, which is shown in Algorithm 2. It takes the audio signals (x_1 and x_2) from the two microphones (m_1 and m_2) and for each of the intervals obtained from Algorithm 1, finds their cross-correlation. Then it takes the median of the top p peaks.

The *for loop* of Lines 3–13 in Algorithm 2 selects each interval from the set of intervals one at a time. Next, the *for loop* of Lines 7–11 selects the top p peaks (empirically set to a value of 3) from the cross correlation. Line 12 adds the computed median to the set *lagMedian*. The final *lagMedian* set is returned by the algorithm.

The set of time lags thus obtained is used to determine the hyperbola corresponding to each tap. The locus of the valid semi-hyperbola obtained using Eq. 7, when overlayed on the keyboard layout as shown in Fig. 1b, returns the shortest distance of each key from the semi-hyperbola. The probability with

---

Algorithm 2. *Compute_TDoA*

Input: Set of intervals *intervals* each containing one peak, audio signal $x_i(t)$ where $i \in \{1, 2\}$

Output: Set of TDoA corresponding to each peak: *lagMedian*

1: $lagMedian \leftarrow \phi$
2: $p \leftarrow 3$ ▷ Median of p peaks is computed
3: **for** $n = 1$ **to** *intervals.length* **do**
4:       $s_i = x_i(s_n : e_n)$, where $(s_n, e_n) = interval[n]$ and $i \in \{1, 2\}$
5:       $[acorr, lag] \leftarrow xcorr(s_1, s_2)$ ▷ Compute cross-correlation
6:       $lagTemp \leftarrow \phi$
7:       **for** $i = 1$ **to** p **do**
8:            $[M, I] \leftarrow max(\|acorr\|)$ ▷ I is the index of the maximum value
9:            $acorr[I] \leftarrow 0$
10:           $lagTemp \leftarrow lagTemp \cup M$
11:      **end for**
12:      $lagMedian \leftarrow lagMedian \cup median(lagTemp)$
13: **end for**
14: **return** *lagMedian*

---

which a key is pressed, i.e., the individual character entered by the user, is considered to be inversely proportional to the shortest distance of the key from the semi-hyperbola. Thus, we obtain the top k most probable characters for each TDoA and hence, for each key tap.

2.2   Word and Sentence Inferencing from Probable Character Sequence

This subsection describes the methodology used to construct sentences from the sequence of characters obtained using Algorithm 2 of Subsect. 2.1.

To carry out the attack, uni-gram, bi-gram and tri-gram probabilities are used. The character-level n-grams as well as word-level n-gram counts are learned from the e-mail corpus[1] in a pre-processing step.

The probability of occurrence of an n-gram is the count of that n-gram divided by the total number of n-grams. However, since the number of n-grams is very large, the probability value comes out to be too small. To compute the probability of a string, we need to multiply these n-gram probabilities. If we use the actual probability values, the product might cause an underflow. On the other hand, taking the product of the count of n-grams results in an overflow. Hence, to avoid both underflow and overflow, instead of using the probabilities directly, we introduce the notion of *pseudo − probability*, which is the *log* of the count of n-grams. The steps for computing pseudo-probability are shown in Algorithm 3 (*Compute_pseudo-probability_of_a_string*).

---

[1] Enron Mail corpus: https://www.cs.cmu.edu/~./enron/.

Algorithm 3. *Compute_pseudo-probability_of_a_string*

Input: Candidate string str, weight factor ω, maximum n-gram length $nGrams$
Output: Pseudo-probability of string: $prob$
1: $prob \leftarrow 0$
2: **for** $l = 1$ **to** $nGrams$ **do**
3:     **if** $l > str.length$ **then**
4:          **break**
5:     **end if**
6:     $prob_t \leftarrow 0$
7:     **for** $i = 1$ **to** $str.length$ **do**
8:          $subStr \leftarrow str[i : i + l]$
9:          $prob_t \leftarrow prob_t + \log(gramCount(subStr)) + 1$
10:    **end for**
11:    $prob \leftarrow prob + (prob_t) \cdot \omega^l$ $\triangleright$ weighted sum of n-gram pseudo-probabilities
12: **end for**
13: **return** $prob$

In this algorithm, the outer *for loop* of Lines 2–12 runs the inner loop considering i-grams in its ith iteration. The inner *for loop* of Lines 7–10 picks up an i-gram from the string, computes its *pseudo-probability*, and adds it to the temporary variable $prob_t$. Finally, Line 11 adds the temporary probability ($prob_t$) to the total probability variable $prob$ of the string after multiplying it with the appropriate weight factor.

There are two loops in Algorithm 3. The outer loop runs n times if n-grams are used for the computation, while the inner loop runs in the order of the length of the string, denoted here as l. Hence, the overall time complexity is $O(n \cdot l)$

From the computed score of strings, we build an inference tree to determine the most probable text that was typed. The language model is based on n-gram and inference based tree [4,13]. The character-level n-grams are used to construct a word-level inference tree. At each level, we include the next set of probable characters and recompute the probabilities of the strings thus obtained. At every level, only the top k nodes are retained and the rest are pruned. This prevents the tree from expanding exponentially. In the last level of the tree, we are left with k most probable words that can be constructed using the character sequences obtained from the algorithms presented in Subsect. 2.1.

The node used to create the tree in Algorithm 4 is a three-tuple represented as $node = \langle string, prob, children \rangle$, where $string$ is the partial word that is stored in the node. $prob$ stores the *pseudo-probability* of this partial word computed using Algorithm 3. The children for this node is stored in the list $children$. In this tree, for any child node c, if p is its parent node, then $p.string$ is a prefix of $c.string$ (*Property 1*). Also, the tree is constructed in such a way that at any level l of the inference tree, the maximum number of nodes does not exceed n, where n is a user-defined input parameter (*Property 2*).

We propose an algorithm (*Generate_Word − level_inference_tree*) that builds the word-level inference tree whose properties and node structure are defined in the previous paragraph. It is shown in Algorithm 4.

Algorithm 4. *Generate_Word − level_inference_tree*

Input: Probable characters of a word in 2-d array *aplha*, child count *c*

Output: set of *c* most probable words: *words*

  1:   initialize *root* node and set all parameters to ϕ

  2:   **for** $i = 1$ **to** *alpha.length* **do**

  3:      *allLeaves* ← *getLeaves(root)*

  4:      *trLeaves* ← *truncateLeaves(allLeaves, c)*

  5:      **for all** *curr* $\in$ *trLeaves* **do**

  6:         **for all** *ch* $\in$ *alpha[i]* **do**

  7:            $t \leftarrow \phi$

  8:            *t.string* ← *curr.string* · *ch*   ▷ append *ch* to the string of parent node

  9:            *t.prob* ← *stringProb(t.string)/t.string.length*   ▷ Compute
pseudo-probability of string *t.string* and normalize by string length

10:             *curr.children* ← *curr.children* $\cup$ *t*

11:         **end for**

12:      **end for**

13:   **end for**

14:   **return** *getLeaves(root)*

This algorithm builds the inference tree one level at a time. Each level of the tree adds to the tree, the set of probable characters corresponding to the next tap. The outermost *for loop* of Lines 2–13 selects the set of characters corresponding to the ith tap in the ith iteration. Next, the leaf nodes in the tree are pruned so that the tree retains Property 2. The *for loop* of Lines 5–12 selects each of the remaining leaves one at a time. Pruning of leaves is done using the *Truncate_leaves* procedure as shown in Algorithm 5. The *for loop* of Lines 6–11 adds new child nodes to the current node and sets the *string* so that they satisfy Property 1. The *prob* value in new nodes (denoted as *t*) is computed using Algorithm 3. Algorithm 4 terminates when all the probable characters corresponding to all the key taps have been added to the tree.

There are three nested *for loops* in Algorithm 4, with time complexity of $O(n)$, $O(c)$ and $O(k)$, respectively. Here, *n* is the total number of taps, *k* is the number of probable characters returned per tap and *c* is the number of allowed child nodes per level. Invocation of *Truncate_leaves()* contributes to $O(l)$ time, where *l* is the number of nodes at a level prior to pruning. So, the time complexity of Algorithm 4 is $O(n \cdot (O(l) + (c \cdot k)))$. *c* and *k* being fixed parameters and independent of the input size *n*, the time complexity becomes $O(n \cdot l)$.

A similar approach is used to build a sentence-level inference tree based on the most probable word sequence. As in the word-level inference tree, at each level, we prune all the nodes except the top *k* (based on the pseudo-probability value). In the last level, we are then left with the top *k* most probable sentences that can be constructed from the set of probable words and hence from the set of probable characters.

Both the word-level as well as sentence-level inference trees use leaf pruning to prevent exponential expansion of the tree. The pruning algorithm

(*Truncate_leaves*) first takes the list of all children at the current level as shown in Algorithm 5. It then deletes all nodes except the top c nodes and returns the modified list. The time complexity of this algorithm is $O(n \cdot c)$, where n is the number of leaves prior to pruning and c is the desired number of leaves after pruning. Since c is a constant, the overall time complexity is $O(n)$.

Algorithm 5. *Truncate_leaves*

Input: List of leaves l_o, maximum number of child nodes c
Output: Set of c most probable leaves: l_t
1: $d.prob \leftarrow -1$ ▷ d is a dummy node
2: **for** $i = 1$ **to** c **do**
3:      $max.prob \leftarrow -1$
4:      **for all** $t \in l_o$ **do**   ▷ Node with maximum pseudo-probability is stored in max
5:          **if** $t.prob > max.prob$ **then**
6:              $max \leftarrow t$
7:              $index \leftarrow l_o.indexOf(t)$
8:          **end if**
9:      **end for**
10:     $l_t \leftarrow l_t \cup max$ ▷ Add max to modified set of leaves
11:     $l_o[index] \leftarrow d$ ▷ Replace max by dummy node d
12: **end for**
13: **return** l_t

In this section, we have described the two phases of the proposed attack methodology and the algorithms used to carry out the attack. The next section presents the details of implementation of a complete system for carrying out such an attack.

3   Implementation Details

This section presents an implementation flow of the attack starting from the recording of sound to the extraction of estimated typed text. A trojan app is installed on the victim's phone that creates audio files from the recorded tap sounds. It needs only microphone permission during installation and Internet access permission so that the audio files can be sent to the attacker's server for further processing. The processing of audio files needs information extracted from preprocessed text corpus which is quite large to store in the phone and the word extraction will be quite computation expensive for the phone processor. Hence, we propose to perform all computations on the server rather than on the phone.

The first module at the server end processing in the overall block diagram of Fig. 2 takes the raw audio file as input and generates the list of time intervals that contain peaks (taps on the touchscreen). Our recording environment emulated any quiet room like library, office, conference room, etc., typical places where

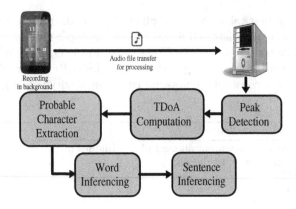

Fig. 2. Block diagram of attack flow implementation

a user is likely to reveal personal information or carry out online transactions. During the experiments, the source of ambient noise was ceiling fan and air conditioner.

The list of peaks is given as input to the next module along with the audio file. This module, as described in Algorithm 2, computes the cross correlation between the sound waves from the two microphones. Figure 3a shows the energy spectrum of the audio signals as captured by the two microphones corresponding to a tap. It is seen in the figure that there are sharp peaks during the tap, preceded and followed by periods of silence. This property of the microphone captured signal is used to extract peaks from the audio files.

The time domain representation of the two audio signal amplitudes in Fig. 3b shows that there is a noticeable shift between them. Figure 4a presents a detailed view of the two audio signals corresponding to a tap. Cross correlation is computed between these two signals. The cross correlation peak is the actual TDoA between the signals. The computed TDoA is used as a parameter for the hyperbola that corresponds to the probable region of tap. It is also observed from Fig. 3a and b that out of the two signals, one has higher amplitude than the other. This difference in amplitude is used to select the valid semi-hyperbola. As an example, if signal from microphone m_1 has higher amplitude, then the tap sound must be emanating from the left half of the keyboard (the half that is closer to microphone m_1).

Note that, the sign of TDoA can also be used to select the correct half of the hyperbola. For example, if the peak in the signal from microphone m_1 occurs before the peak in the signal from microphone m_2, it can be concluded that the click originated from that half of the keypad which is closer to microphone m_1.

The magnitude of the TDoA is used next to obtain the probable region on the keyboard layout where the tap occurred. This is shown in Fig. 4b. In this example, the key a was tapped. The computed TDoA was used to plot the hyperbola and depending upon the sign of the TDoA, the other half of the hyperbola was discarded. We see that the maximum probability region passes over a.

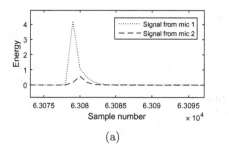 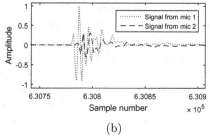

(a)   (b)

Fig. 3. (a) Energy spectrum of the input signal corresponding to a single tap. (b) Input signals in time domain corresponding to a tap.

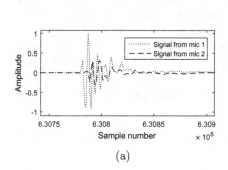 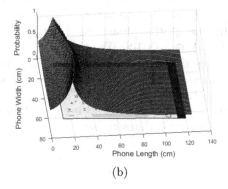

(a)   (b)

Fig. 4. (a) Shift between two signals captured by the two microphones in time domain. (b) Overlay of hyperbola region on phone keyboard.

Thus, for every tap, we determine the most probable region of the tap. To get the k most probable characters, we set the width of the band in such a way that k number of keys fit into the band of the hyperbola. The *Probable Character Extraction* module of Fig. 2 then returns the k characters that have the highest intersection area with the plotted region.

Text inferencing from the probable sequence of letters is done by building the inference tree and pruning leaves at each level as explained in Algorithms 4 and 5. This approach is used for both word level as well as sentence level inferencing of Fig. 2.

4   Experimental Results

We carried out detailed experiments with our system implementation described in Sect. 3. In this section, we present several important observations that were made during the experiments as well as quantitative result on accuracy. The results consist of two parts. Subsection 4.1 presents the results obtained till the extraction of the probable characters from the audio signal captured by the microphones. Subsection 4.2 then presents the results of the stages related to inferencing of words from probable characters and that of sentences from the probable set of words.

The dataset that we used to test the hypothesis and proposed methodology has following statistics. On average, the audio encoding of each character takes $\approx$82 kB per character, while the average typing speed was $\approx$2 characters per second. Moreover, the complete methodology presented in Sect. 2, takes about 70 s to decipher text from a recording containing $\approx$100 taps.

4.1   Audio Processing Results

Figure 5 shows the plot of various TDoAs measured in number of sample points and the character set that are returned corresponding to each TDoA. In one of the phones used for experimentation (layout shown in Fig. 1b), $TDoA \in [-8, 10]$. We plot each TDoA over the keyboard layout keeping $k = 3$ as described in Sect. 3 and return the character set corresponding to that TDoA. A linear trend is seen in the values of TDoA and the characters returned also shift from the left end of the keypad to the right end. For example, for $TDoA = 10$, the returned character set is $\{q, w, a\}$ and for the minimum value of $TDoA = -8$, the returned character set is $\{p, l, o\}$.

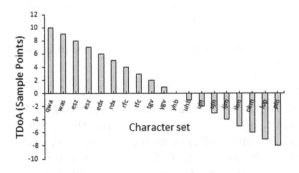

Fig. 5. Character sets for different values of TDoA

In Fig. 6a, we plot the distribution of the computed value of TDoA for one particular letter (clicked letter is a). The set of top k most probable characters containing the typed character can be extracted with quite good accuracy. From Fig. 6b it is seen that, using $k = 3$, the character that was actually typed is present in the set of probable characters 90 % of the time. For the rest 10 %, the computed TDoA deviates only by 1. Hence, it can be concluded that TDoA is a robust feature to be used for the proposed attack methodology. This set of probable characters is used as input for the NLP module, the results of which are presented in the next subsection.

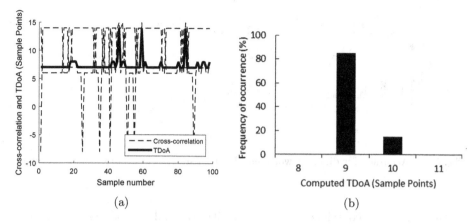

Fig. 6. (a) Computed values of TDoA obtained from cross-correlation for 100 taps of a. (b) Distribution of the computed TDoA.

4.2   Text Extraction Results

Figure 7a shows the variation in word occurrence frequency and word level accuracy with change in word length. We took a test set of 30 messages of varying sizes. The text was deciphered using the proposed attack methodology from the tapping sounds picked up by the two microphones and compared with the actual typed text. The bars in the graph show the fraction of the count of occurrences and the fraction of the number of times they were recovered correctly. The piecewise continuous line represents the accuracy and a linear trend line is also plotted in the graph for reference. From the figure, it is observed that accuracy approaches 1.0 when the word length is 1 *or* 2. This is because these are usually stop words like a, an, be, at, etc. Such words are quite common and thus can be inferred accurately. The next peaks occur at word lengths 3, 4 and 5. This is due to the fact that, in the English language, the average word length is 5.1 letters [3]. Words with greater length occur rarely, as a result of which, there are less number of samples with longer length to train the language model. Therefore, while inferring, the accuracy decreases with increasing word length beyond 5. The average word level accuracy is 0.81.

Figure 7b shows the variation in accuracy of complete text with message size. For this study, we use the same data set as in Fig. 7a. It is seen from the figure that the accuracy lies in the range of 0.57–0.95, with an average of 0.88. It is also observed that accuracy tends to increase with increasing length of the text. The NLP algorithm assumes that the text is composed of English words only. Hence, such a trend is observed, because with increase in message size, the ratio of valid English words to the total number of words increases.

A few local variations are also seen in the figure. This point was further investigated. It was found that our assumption that the user would be typing in English, i.e., using words from the valid English vocabulary did not always hold.

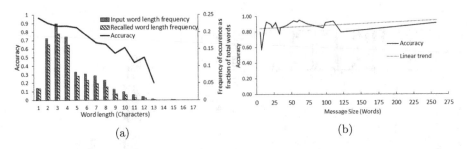

Fig. 7. (a) Accuracy for different word lengths (b) Variation in accuracy with message size

Often the message contained certain words like URLs, dates, proper nouns, etc., that are not there in the English dictionary, which caused some degradation in performance.

5   Related Work

It has been shown in the literature that emanations from devices can be exploited in ways to reveal information associated with the source, thereby breaching security. There are several variations of this type of attack based on the type of emanation [6,9]. Particularly, acoustic emanations from various devices is an important field of research.

Asonov et al. [1] show that the keyboard strokes can be recovered using the acoustic emanations from mechanical keyboards. They argue that although the emanations from different keys sound similar to human ear, they are actually different and a classifier can be trained to distinguish between the keys. Fast Fourier Transform is used as the feature set of the sound and backpropagation neural network is used for classification.

The above issue was readdressed by Zhuang et al. [14], who presented a novel technique using which even random keystrokes can be recovered. Unlike the attack methodology of [1], which requires labeled data to train the neural network before it can be used as a classifier, this attack uses the statistical constraints of the English language to train a model by unsupervised learning. They use cepstrum features, which were shown to be superior to FFT. Another related work [5] provides a brief explanation and analysis of the possible attacks that can be carried out using mobile phones. It presents a nomenclature for various attacks. Some preventive measures are suggested that can be implemented to minimize the risk from the identified possibilities of attack.

Since our work is aimed at deciphering text from touchscreen mobile phones, we next present some work in this field. Miluzzo et al. [10] discuss the possibility of use of the accelerometer and gyroscope sensors of phones and present a method to recover the tap position as well as the typed text. They propose that each point on the screen, when tapped, produces different values of linear and angular acceleration, which can be captured using the phone sensors.

Zhu et al. [12] present a context-free attack technique to recover keystrokes using phones as recording devices placed in the vicinity of the keyboard being typed on. With enough number of such external microphones, the keystroke region can be pinpointed with good accuracy. To make the attack even more general, the keyboard orientation is also assumed to be unknown beforehand. Keyboard reconstruction is formulated as an optimization problem and the most likely keyboard layout is taken as the orientation of the keyboard. Finally, the keystrokes are recovered.

There is, however, no work that recovers key taps from touchscreen keypads using built-in microphones of a mobile phone as reported in this paper. Such an attack is more realistic than the ones mentioned above since the previous attacks require external hardware to record the sound of key presses. Setting up of extra hardware in the vicinity of the victim while he is typing is susceptible to detection. Since the proposed methodology uses the microphone already attached to the device, it can silently record and transmit the audio signals to the attacker's server.

6   Preventive Measures

There are a few basic preventive measures, which however, might reduce the impact of such an attack, even though it cannot be eliminated fully. For instance, if the user keeps the key-press tone ON, then with each tap, an additional sound will be generated masking the actual sound created by the tap to a certain extent. A similar effect may be achieved if the vibration on each key-press is kept ON. However, both of these counter-measures are inconvenient for the user and they drain the battery as well.

Another approach that may be adopted by the operating system developers is that the OS can display notifications (using icons) to depict which devices are currently being used in the background. Thus, the user will be notified if the microphone or any other sensor is running in the background. The OS may also display the apps which are currently using that sensor data. In this way, the user can become aware of any background app trying to eavesdrop and possibly terminate it to prevent the attack. However, such measures demand a certain level of maturity and knowledge on the part of the user.

7   Conclusion

The primary goal of this paper was to bring to light the vulnerabilities of touchscreen phones, which we have exploited and devised an attack methodology that is reasonably accurate. It may be noted that, any form of encryption will not help to prevent this attack as the proposed methodology records the tap sounds generated at the time of typing itself.

The direction for future work on improving the attack methodology is threefold: (i) improving accuracy of the signal processing unit (ii) use of other NLP techniques to enhance the performance of the text inferencing phase and also to detect special characters and numerals. This would allow the attack to detect passwords as well. (iii) Fusion of data from more number of sensors. Sensors such as gyroscope and accelerometer are also present in almost all smartphones. For each key tap, the accelerometer and gyroscope values would vary. Although this data is a bit more difficult to make use of as compared to the microphone data, still it is a possibility that is worth exploring to see how the attack performs.

References

1. Asonov, D., Agrawal, R.: Keyboard acoustic emanations. In: Proceedings of IEEE Symposium on Security and Privacy, pp. 3–11 (2004)
2. Benesty, J., Chen, J., Huang, Y.: Time-delay estimation via linear interpolation and cross correlation. IEEE Trans. Speech Audio Process. **12**(5), 509–519 (2004)
3. Bochkarev, V.V., Shevlyakova, A.V., Solovyev, V.D.: Average word length dynamics as indicator of cultural changes in society. arXiv preprint (2012). arXiv:1208.6109
4. Brown, P.F., Desouza, P.V., Mercer, R.L., Pietra, V.J.D., Lai, J.C.: Class-based n-gram models of natural language. Comput. Linguist. **18**(4), 467–479 (1992)
5. Dagon, D., Martin, T., Starner, T.: Mobile phones as computing devices: the viruses are coming! Pervasive Comput. **3**(4), 11–15 (2004)
6. Halevi, T., Saxena, N.: Acoustic eavesdropping attacks on constrained wireless device pairing. IEEE Trans. Inf. Forensics Secur. **8**(3), 563–577 (2013)
7. Hussain, M., Al-Haiqi, A., Zaidan, A., Zaidan, B., Kiah, M.M., Anuar, N.B., Abdulnabi, M.: The rise of keyloggers on smartphones: a survey and insight into motion-based tap inference attacks. Pervasive Mob. Comput. **25**, 1–25 (2015)
8. Liu, X., Zhou, Z., Diao, W., Li, Z., Zhang, K.: When good becomes evil: keystroke inference with smartwatch. In: Proceedings of the 22nd ACM SIGSAC Conference on Computer and Communications Security, pp. 1273–1285. ACM (2015)
9. Meng, W., Lee, W.H., Murali, S., Krishnan, S.: Charging me and i know your secrets!: towards juice filming attacks on smartphones. In: Proceedings of the 1st ACM Workshop on Cyber-Physical System Security, pp. 89–98 (2015)
10. Miluzzo, E., Varshavsky, A., Balakrishnan, S., Choudhury, R.R.: Tapprints: your finger taps have fingerprints. In: Proceedings of the 10th International Conference on Mobile Systems, Applications, and Services, pp. 323–336 (2012)
11. Ping, D., Sun, X., Mao, B.: Textlogger: inferring longer inputs on touch screen using motion sensors. In: Proceedings of the 8th ACM Conference on Security & Privacy in Wireless and Mobile Networks, pp. 1–12. ACM (2015)
12. Zhu, T., Ma, Q., Zhang, S., Liu, Y.: Context-free attacks using keyboard acoustic emanations. In: Proceedings of the ACM Conference on Computer and Communications Security, pp. 453–464 (2014)
13. Zhu, Z., Bernhard, D., Gurevych, I.: A monolingual tree-based translation model for sentence simplification. In: Proceedings of the 23rd International Conference on Computational Linguistics, pp. 1353–1361 (2010)
14. Zhuang, L., Zhou, F., Tygar, J.D.: Keyboard acoustic emanations revisited. ACM Trans. Inf. Syst. Secur. **13**(1), 1–26 (2009)

The Fréchet/Manhattan Distance and the Trajectory Anonymisation Problem

Christof Ferreira Torres[1] and Rolando Trujillo-Rasua[1,2]($\boxtimes$)

[1] University of Luxembourg, CSC, Luxembourg, Luxembourg
rolando.trujillo@uni.lu
[2] Interdisciplinary Centre for Security, Reliability and Trust,
Luxembourg, Luxembourg

Abstract. Mobile communication has grown quickly in the last two decades. Connections can be wirelessly established from almost any habitable place in the earth, leading to a plethora of connection-based tracking mechanisms, such as GPS, GSM, RFID, etc. Trajectories representing the movement of people are consequently being gathered and analysed in a daily basis. However, a trajectory may contain sensitive and private information, which raises the problem of whether spatio-temporal data can be published in a private manner.

In this article, we introduce a novel distance measure for trajectories that captures both aspect of the microaggregation process, namely clustering and obfuscation. Based on this distance measure we propose a trajectory anonymisation heuristic method ensuring that each trajectory is indistinguishable from $k - 1$ other trajectories. The proposed distance measure is loosely based on the Fréchet distance, yet it can be computed efficiently in quadratic time complexity. Empirical studies on synthetic trajectories show that our anonymisation approach improves previous work in terms of utility without sacrificing privacy.

1 Introduction

Not long ago, visual identification was the only mean to collect spatio-temporal data from people. Nowadays this task is far easier since there is no need of direct human intervention for monitoring and tracking. Instead, surveillance cameras, social networks, credit card transactions, and many other worldwide adopted technologies and services, automatically collect this type of data. Today's pervasiveness of location-aware devices like mobile phones and GPS receivers helps even further companies and governments to easily collect huge amount of information about people's movement.

Analysing and mining this type of information, also known as trajectories, might reveal new trends and previously unknown knowledge to be used in traffic, sustainable mobility management, urban planning and supply chain management. By doing so, resources might be optimised and business and government

© IFIP International Federation for Information Processing 2016
Published by Springer International Publishing Switzerland 2016. All Rights Reserved
S. Ranise and V. Swarup (Eds.): DBSec 2016, LNCS 9766, pp. 19–34, 2016.
DOI: 10.1007/978-3-319-41483-6_2

decisions can be solid and well-founded. In this sense, both companies and citizens profit directly from the publication and analysis of databases of trajectories.

Despite of all these benefits, there are obvious threats to people's privacy if their movement data are published in a way which allows re-identification of the person behind a trajectory. Just considering the locations visited by a trajectory, it may reveal sensitive information about users like religious, political, or sexual preferences. The privacy threat grows when the time information exposes user's habits that may be used for unauthorized advertisement and user profiling.

A tentative solution to achieve anonymity is de-identification by means of removing identifying attributes of individuals. However, this is often insufficient to preserve privacy due to other type of attributes called *quasi-identifiers*, which are non-identifying attributes that together with external information might uniquely identify the individual behind a record. Unfortunately, in the case of spatio-temporal data, every location can be regarded as a quasi-identifier [25]. Therefore, just knowing some locations visited by an individual could be enough to identify his trajectory in a database. As an example, let's consider a GPS application recording trajectories of citizens. Daily routine indicates that an early morning trajectory is likely to begin at the user's home and end at the user's workplace. This simple assumption might be enough to accurately re-identify a user's trajectory.

The above problem has been addressed relying on k-anonymity [18,19], a widely used privacy notion. A set S is said to satisfy k-anonymity if each combination of quasi-identifier attribute values is shared by at least k records in S. Therefore, considering that all identifying attributes have been removed, k-anonymity ensures that no anonymised record can be correctly linked to an individual with probability higher than $1/k$. In microdata, the set of quasi-identifiers is typically considered small and known in advance. In spatio-temporal data, however, a similar assumption can hardly hold; any location can be regarded as a quasi-identifier. As a result, anonymisation methods aimed at achieving k-anonymity on microdata cannot be directly applied on spatio-temporal data and vice versa.

Contributions. In this article we propose a distance measure for trajectories specially suited for clustering and obfuscation. The distance is loosely based on the Fréchet distance [3], yet it is efficiently computable. The novel construction has significant advantages: (i) it can deal with non-overlapping trajectories, (ii) it outputs, in addition to a distance value, a set of matching points that are exploited later in the obfuscation process, and (iii) it considers the shape of the trajectories due to the very nature of the Fréchet distance. We use the proposed distance measure as the basis of a trajectory anonymisation technique that releases datasets satisfying k-anonymity, regardless of the adversary knowledge. We show, through experiments on synthetic spatio-temporal data, that our approach outperforms previous comparable work in terms of utility.

Outline of the Paper. This paper is structured as follows. Section 2 next provides related work. Section 3 introduces a novel distance measure based on the

Fréchet distance and the Manhattan norm. A microaggregation-based method for trajectory anonymisation is proposed in Sect. 4, which is empirically evaluated in Sect. 5. Finally, Sect. 6 draws conclusions and future work.

2   Related Work

Trajectory k-anonymity is aimed at hiding a single trajectory into a crowd of at least $k - 1$ other trajectories. The idea is that every trajectory in the published dataset be indistinguishable from $k - 1$ other trajectories and, as a consequence, an adversary cannot identify the individual behind a trajectory with probability higher than $1/k$.

An approach to achieve k-anonymity is by means of suppression of attribute values, which is generally used on discrete and/or semantic data where perturbation methods are not well suited. One of the first suppression-based methods for trajectory anonymization is due to Terrovitis and Mamoulis [20]. They consider trajectories to be sequences of addresses taken from an address domain $\mathcal{P}$. The adversary controls subsets of addresses of $\mathcal{P}$, and thus his knowledge is represented as projections of original trajectories over the addresses in $\mathcal{P}$ that are in the adversary's knowledge. A greedy algorithm aimed at guaranteeing that no address unknown by the adversary can be linked with an user with probability higher than a given threshold is proposed in [20]. The main problem with this approach is that dealing with all possible adversary's knowledge becomes harder than the original k-anonymity problem, which is already known to be NP-Hard [13]. There exist other suppression-based methods in the literature, e.g., [6]. However, they target privacy notions different to k-anonymity.

Like Terrovitis and Mamoulis in [20], Yarovoy et al. also consider an adversary controlling a subset of user's locations or quasi-identifiers [25], with the distinction that such a subset may differ for different users. Trajectory k-anonymity is defined in terms of a bipartite attack graph relating original trajectories with the anonymised trajectories. The authors propose to create anonymised groups through generalisation with respect to the joint set of quasi-identifiers from the users within the group. K-anonymity is thus achieved by creating anonymised groups such that the bipartite attack graph is symmetric and the degree of each vertex representing an anonymised trajectory is at least k. It is worth remarking that the privacy model considered in this article is different, as any user's location is regarded as a quasi-identifier.

Another generalisation-based approach was proposed by Monreale et al. [14]. As in [20], they ignore the time information. Therefore, k-anonymity is achieved if the generalisation of every original trajectory is a sub-trajectory of the generalisation of $k - 1$ other trajectories. In order to preserve the utility of the original dataset, a Voronoi tessellation of the geographical area is created so that each location is transformed into the Voronoi cell that contains it. Utility is measured by simply comparing clustering results.

In [8,9], Domingo-Ferrer et al. propose a different approach based on microagrregation and permutation rather than on generalisation. First, they introduce a novel distance measure that consider both spatial and temporal aspects of trajectories. The distance measure is flexible enough to be used either for spatio-temporal data or time series. Based on this distance measure, the authors propose to create clusters of trajectories so as to minimise the intra-cluster distance. Within a given cluster, locations are randomly swapped with other $k - 1$ unswapped close locations. Locations that cannot be swapped are removed and so are the trajectories without swapped locations.

Abul et al. [1,2] proposed two trajectory anonymisation methods: Never Walk Alone (NWA) and Wait For Me (W4M). Both are partially based on microggregation [7]. The microggregation technique works as follows. The dataset of trajectories is partitioned into several clusters of size at least k and at most $2k - 1$. To do so, NWA relies on the Euclidean distance while W4M uses on the edit distance on real sequences (EDR) [5]. Trajectories within a cluster are perturbed by using space translation. The claimed privacy of these proposals has proven to be flawed [22], though.

In [15,16], Nergiz et al. consider a trajectory to be a sequence of square geographical areas where a user moves randomly within a given time frame. For clustering, the authors use the log cost metric that balances the spatial and temporal distortion with user-provided weights. Since the log cost metric is based on point matching, the anonymisation process is directly inferred from the clustering process, which improves efficiency.

Recently, Gao et al. proposed a privacy-preserving technique that does not target trajectory k-anonymity directly, as most previous work do, but a trade-off between privacy and utility [12]. Privacy is measured in terms of anonymity sets that are created based on a similarity measure that takes the angles and directions of the trajectories into account. Utility relies on the classical Euclidean distance.

In the literature we can find a variety of distance measures for trajectories and time-series. Vlachos et al. proposed two distance measures based on the Longest Common Subsequence problem (LCSS) [24]. The first one matches only points that are within a given spatio-temporal region. Unmatched points are discarded and taken as outliers. This criterion for outliers detection is smoothed in their second distance measure by using a weighted matching function that considers the distance between points. Another distance measure that has been designed to cope with noise is the Edit Distance on Real sequences (EDR) [5]. The problem is that it requires a fixed and global distance threshold that defines whether a location is too far from another location. A survey on distance measures for trajectory clustering can be found in [27].

3   A Distance Measure for Trajectory Microaggregation

We consider trajectories describing the movements of objects on the surface of the earth. Even though a movement is assumed to be continuous, it is typically described by a finite polyline. Formally, a trajectory is defined as a sequence of time-stamped locations $\tau = \ell_1 \cdots \ell_n$ such that $\ell_i.t < \ell_{i+1}.t \; \forall i \in \{1, \cdots, n-1\}$ where $\ell.t$, $\ell.x$, and $\ell.y$, denote the time, latitude, and longitude of the location ℓ, respectively. In general, trajectories can be recorded at different and irregular sampling rates, are not noise-free, and the velocity between two consecutive locations is assumed to be constant. A collection of trajectories is called a spatio-temporal database. For large databases, the size of a trajectory is considered to be significantly smaller than the size of the database.

The choice of the distance measure is critical in microaggregation. It influences the way trajectories are clustered and usually it also impacts on the anonymisation process. There exist different factors that characterise a trajectory distance measure. For example, a distance measure may consider only trajectories within a given timespan, or look for spatial similarity regardless of direction and sampling rate, or take into account trajectory's features such as speed and angle.

The distance measure we propose in this article is loosely based on the Fréchet distance [11]. The Fréchet distance, also known as the *dog-leash* distance, assumes that a person walks over one trajectory and his dog over the other trajectory. Both may travel at independent but positive speed. The Fréchet distance outputs the minimum-length leash required for that person to walk his dog. Intuitively, the shorter the leash the closer the two curves.

Alt and Godau proposed in 1995 an algorithm to compute the Fréchet distance for two polylines [3] with computational complexity $\mathcal{O}(pq \log(p+q))$ where p and q are the size of the polylines. To the best of our knowledge, this computational complexity has not been improved significantly without making assumptions on the curves. We thus consider variations of the Fréchet distance such as the Coupling distance [10] and the Dynamic Time Warping (DTW) distance [26], which are significantly simpler and run in $O(pq)$ time complexity.

We say that a sequence $L = (u_{a_1}, v_{b_1}) \cdots (u_{a_n}, v_{b_n})$ is a coupling between two trajectories $U = u_1 \cdots u_p$ and $V = v_1 \cdots v_q$ if the following conditions are satisfied:

- $a_1 = 1$ and $b_1 = 1$
- $a_n = p$ and $b_n = q$
- For every $i \in \{1, \cdots, n-1\}$ it holds that $a_{i+1} = a_i$ or $a_{i+1} = a_i + 1$, and $b_{i+1} = b_i$ or $b_{i+1} = b_i + 1$

A coupling can be seen as sequence of matching points, as defined in the Edit Distance on Real sequences (EDR) [5]. The difference, however, is that a coupling respects the order of the locations and also ensures that all points are considered.

Definition 1 (Coupling distance). *Let $U = u_1 \cdots u_p$ and $V = v_1 \cdots v_q$ be two trajectories and let $\mathcal{L}$ be the set of all couplings between U and V. Let $\|.\|$ denote a norm on $\mathcal{L}$. The coupling distance is defined as follows:*

$$coupling\_dist(U, V) = \min\{\|L\| | L \in \mathcal{L}\}$$

The coupling distance can be computed by a simple dynamic algorithm. The norm that directly relates to the original discrete Fréchet distance is the Infinite norm. Given $L = (u_{a_1}, v_{b_1}) \cdots (u_{a_n}, v_{b_n})$, the Infinite norm $\|L\|_\infty$ is the longest distance between a pair of linked locations in L, i.e., $\|L\|_\infty = \max_{i \in \{1, \cdots, n\}} d(u_{a_i}, v_{b_i})$. Another relevant norm, which we use in this article, is the Manhattan norm, defined as $\|L\|_1 = \sum_{i \in \{1, \cdots, n\}} d(u_{a_i}, v_{b_i})$.

Using the Infinite norm in the coupling distance has a clear interpretation in microaggregation of trajectories, that is, the longest distance that ought to be covered in order to spatially translate a trajectory into another one. However, accounting for the longest distance may lead to non-robust behaviors, because small variations in the trajectories can cause large variations in the distance function. For this reason, we propose to use the infinity norm to compute the optimal coupling between trajectories, yet we consider the average Manhattan norm to represent the actual distance between them. We claim that the average Manhattan norm approximates better the required distortion to microaggregate trajectories. Formally, the distance measure used in the present article is defined as follows.

Definition 2 (Fréchet/Manhattan coupling distance). *Let $U = u_1 \cdots u_p$ and $V = v_1 \cdots v_q$ be two trajectories and let $\mathcal{L}$ be the set of all couplings between U and V. Let $L \subseteq \mathcal{L}$ such that for every $l \in L$ it holds that $\|l\|_\infty$ is minimum amongst the couplings in $\mathcal{L}$. The average coupling distance is defined as:*

$$\min_{l \in L} \frac{1}{|l|} \|l\|_1$$

Computing the Fréchet/Manhattan distance is a bit more elaborated than computing the coupling distance. Nevertheless, it can still be computed in $\mathcal{O}(pq)$ time complexity as shown by Algorithm 1. Given two trajectories $U = u_1 \cdots u_p$ and $V = v_1 \cdots v_q$, we create a matrix I of size $p \times q$ where we store the optimal coupling with respect to the Infinite norm. Such computation is performed by the standard dynamic approach proposed in [10]. In order to determine the Fréchet/Manhattan distance, we consider another matrix M where we store the optimal coupling distance with respect to the Manhattan norm among those optimal couplings with respect to the Infinite norm. To do so, we need to find where those optimal couplings with respect to the Infinite norm come from. Let us analyse what is the impact of having the pair (u_x, v_y) in an optimal coupling l. First, we should notice that if $(u_x, v_y) \in l$ then $\|l\|_\infty \geq d(u_x, v_y)$. Indeed, if $d(u_x, v_y) < \min\{I[x-1, y], I[x-1, y-1], I[x, y-1]\}$ then $\|l\|_\infty = \min\{[x-1, y], [x-1, y-1], [x, y-1]\}$, otherwise $\|l\|_\infty = d(u_x, v_y)$. We thus store in a set C all pairs that lead to an optimal coupling with respect to the Infinite norm amongst the pairs $\{I[x-1, y], I[x-1, y-1], I[x, y-1]\}$. Finally, $M[x, y]$ is computed as $\min\{M[x, y]/L[x, y]|[x, y] \in C\}$ where $L[x, y]$ is the size of the optimal coupling with respect the Manhattan norm for the subtrajectories $u_1 \cdots u_x$ and $v_1 \cdots v_y$.

Algorithm 1. Average coupling distance

Require: Two trajectories $U = u_1 \cdots u_p$ and $V = v_1 \cdots v_q$
1: Let I, M, L be three matrices of size $p \times q$. Intuitively, I and M represent the
   Infinity and Manhattan norms, respectively, while L is the length of the optimal
   coupling
2: Let d represent the Euclidean distance.
3: $I[1,1] = M[1,1] = d(u_1, v_1)$
4: $L[1,1] = 1$
5: **for** $i = 2$ to p **do**
6:     $I[i,1] = \max\{I[i-1,1], d(u_i, v_1)\}$
7:     $M[i,1] = M[i-1,1] + d(u_i, v_1)$
8:     $L[i,1] = i$
9: **end for**
10: **for** $j = 2$ to q **do**
11:     $I[1,j] = \max\{I[1,j-1], d(u_1, v_j)\}$
12:     $M[1,j] = M[1,j-1] + d(u_1, v_j)$
13:     $L[1,j] = j$
14: **end for**
15: **for** $i = 2$ to p **do**
16:     **for** $j = 2$ to q **do**
17:        Let R be the set $\{[i-1,j], [i-1,j-1], [i,j-1]\}$
18:        Let $C \subseteq R$ such that for every $[x,y] \in C$ it holds that $I[x,y] \leq d(u_i, v_j)$
19:        **if** C is empty **then**
20:           Let $[a,b] \in R$ such that for every $[x,y] \in R$ it holds that $I[a,b] \leq I[x,y]$
21:           $I[i,j] = I[a,b]$
22:           Add to C every element $[x,y]$ in R such that $I[x,y] = I[a,b]$
23:        **else**
24:           $I[i,j] = d(u_i, v_j)$
25:        **end if**
26:        Let $[x,y] \in C$ such that $M[x,y]/L[x,y] \leq M[a,b]/L[a,b]$ for every $[a,b] \in C$
27:        $M[i,j] = M[x,y] + d(u_i, v_j)$
28:        $L[i,j] = L[x,y] + 1$
29:     **end for**
30: **end for**
31: **return** $M[p,q]/L[p,q]$

---

4   A Microaggregation-Based Approach

The anonymisation method proposed in this article is based on k-microaggregation, that is, a process whereby clusters of at least k *homogeneous* trajectories are anonymised independently. A usual homogeneity criterion is the sum of squared pairwise distances between trajectories within a cluster (intra-cluster distance). Hence, an optimal microaggregation can be intuitively defined as the one maximising the within-groups homogeneity.

The optimal microaggregation problem for multivariate points, like trajectories, has proven to be NP-hard [17]. That justifies the use of heuristics in microaggregation-based approaches for trajectory anonymisation [23]. An additional challenge to be addressed is that distance measures between trajectories tend to be computationally expensive. This implies that computing all pairwise distances between trajectories in a large database may not be feasible.

Below, we detail the two main components of our microaggregation-based approach, namely the proposed heuristic for trajectory clustering and the obfuscation technique.

4.1   Clustering

We use a greedy approach to address the k-microaggregation problem explained above. Each cluster is represented by a *pivot* trajectory, and contains $k-1$ other trajectories that are close to the pivot trajectory. In other words, we consider as homogeneity criterion the sum of squared distances between the pivot trajectory and the other trajectories in the cluster. Once a cluster C is created from a pool D of trajectories, all trajectories in C are removed from D. As shown by Algorithm 2, this process is repeated until D contains less than k trajectories.

Algorithm 2. Trajectory clustering

Require: $D = \{\tau_1, \ldots, \tau_N\}$ a set of trajectories; a distance measure $d : D \times D \to \mathbb{R}$; a natural number δ representing the number of clusters generated at each iteration; and an anonymisation parameter k

1: Let $\mathcal{C}$ be an empty set of clusters of trajectories
2: **while** $|D| \geq k$ **do**
3:    Let τ_1' be a random trajectory in D
4:    Let τ_δ' be the farthest trajectory to τ_1' with respect to d
5:    Let $\tau_1', \tau_2', \cdots, \tau_\delta'$ be δ trajectories in D that minimises the sum of squares $\sum_{i \in [1..\delta-1]} d(\tau_{i+1}', \tau_i')^2$
6:    Let C_0 be an empty set of trajectories and $d_0 = \infty$
7:    **for all** $i = 1$ to δ **do**
8:       Create the cluster of trajectories C_i containing τ_i' and the closest $k-1$ trajectories to τ_i'
9:       Compute $d_i = \sum_{\tau \in C_i} d(\tau_i', \tau)^2$
10:       **if** $d_i < d_0$ **then**
11:          $C_0 = C_i$ and $d_0 = d_i$
12:       **end if**
13:    **end for**
14:    $\mathcal{C} = \mathcal{C} \cup \{C_0\}$
15:    Remove all trajectories in C_0 from D
16: **end while**
17: **return** $\mathcal{C}$

In our approach, depicted in Algorithm 2, finding the optimal set of clusters is equivalent to finding the optimal sequence of pivot trajectories. The most effective greedy solution to this problem is to choose the best cluster amongst the $|D|$ clusters that can be created considering each trajectory in D a pivot trajectory.

However, that requires the computation of all pairwise distances between the trajectories in D. As a trade-off, given a natural number $\delta \ll |D|$, we choose a random trajectory τ'_1 in D and find the sequence $\tau'_1, \tau'_2, \cdots \tau'_\delta$ such that: (i) τ'_δ is the farthest trajectory to τ'_1 and (ii) the sum of squares $\sum_{i \in [1..\delta-1]} d(\tau'_{i+1}, \tau'_i)^2$ is minimum. We thus choose the best cluster amongst the δ clusters that can be built considering either τ'_1, or τ'_2, $\cdots$, or τ'_δ, as pivot. Note that, if $\delta = |D|$ then we actually find the optimal set of clusters.

4.2   Obfuscation Technique

Our privacy-preserving method for the publication of trajectories is based on the clustering technique and the Fréchet/Manhattan coupling distance described above. Even though the coupling distance deals well with trajectories recorded at different sampling rates, the lower is the sampling rate the better it approximates the classical Fréchet distance. We thus use linear interpolation to decrease and homogenise the sampling rate of two trajectories as follows. Let $U = u_1 \cdots u_p$ and $V = v_1 \cdots v_q$ be two trajectories. For every $i \in \{1, \cdots, p\}$, we insert in V by using linear interpolation a new point at time $v_1.t + \frac{(v_q.t - v_1.t)(u_i.t - u_1.t)}{u_p.t - u_1.t}$. An analogous procedure is used to increase the sampling rate of U with respect to V. Note that, the trajectories U' and V' resulting from re-sampling U and V, respectively, have equal size.

We use the Fréchet/Manhattan distance in Algorithm 2 to partition a collection of trajectories $\{\tau_1, \cdots, \tau_N\}$ into a set of homogeneous clusters $\{C_1, \cdots, C_m\}$. For every $i \in \{1, \cdots, m\}$, let X be the pivot trajectory in the cluster C_i as considered in Algorithm 2. For each $Y \in C_i$ $(X \neq Y)$, let $(u_{a_1}, u_{b_1}) \cdots (u_{a_n}, v_{b_n})$ be the optimal coupling between X and Y with respect to the Fréchet/Manhattan distance, where $U = u_1 \cdots u_p$ and $V = v_1 \cdots v_q$ are the re-sampling of X and Y, respectively. For each $j \in \{1, \cdots, n\}$ and if $u_{a_j} \in X$, i.e., if u_{a_j} is an original location of X rather than an interpolated location added during the re-sampling procedure, we add to the set $S(u_{a_i})$ the location v_{b_i}. Once this process is finished for all trajectories in C_i, we consider, for every location $x \in X$, the set $S(x)$ containing those locations from other trajectories in C_i that formed a pair with x in an optimal coupling. We always include x into $S(x)$ whenever $S(x)$ is not empty. The anonymised trajectory for the cluster C_i will be that formed by the average locations obtained from the sets $\{S(x) | x \in X, S(x) \neq \emptyset\}$. A pseudo-code description of this procedure is given in Algorithm 3.

4.3   Privacy Analysis

Several notions of trajectory k-anonymity exist. For example, in [14,20], the adversary ignores the time dimension. In [1,2], an adversary is considered unable to distinguish two locations if their distance is below a predefined threshold. In [9], the model is defined considering that original locations must be preserved, which means that random spatial distortion is disallowed.

Algorithm 3. Trajectory anonymisation algorithm

Require: $\{\tau_1, \ldots, \tau_N\}$ a collection of original trajectories; a number δ to be used in the clustering process; the Fréchet/Manhattan distance d; an anonymisation parameter k

1: Use the clustering technique defined by Algorithm 2 on input $\{\tau_1, \ldots, \tau_N\}$, the distance measure d, δ, and k, to obtain a set of clusters $\{C_1, \cdots, C_m\}$
2: Let $D^\star$ be an empty set of trajectories
3: **for** $i = 1$ to m **do**
4:     Let X be the pivot trajectory in C_i as defined in Algorithm 2
5:     Let $S(x)$ be an empty set for every $x \in X$
6:     **for** $Y \in C_i$ and $X \neq Y$ **do**
7:         Let $(u_{a_1}, v_{b_1}) \cdots (u_{a_n}, v_{b_n})$ be the optimal coupling between X and Y with respect to the Fréchet/Manhattan distance d, where $U = u_1 \cdots u_p$ and $V = v_1 \cdots v_q$ are the re-sampling of X and Y, respectively
8:         **for** $j = 1$ to n **do**
9:             **if** $u_{a_j} \in X$ **then**
10:                 $S(u_{a_j}) = S(u_{a_j}) \cup \{v_{b_j}\}$
11:             **end if**
12:         **end for**
13:     **end for**
14:     Let τ be an empty trajectory
15:     **for** $x \in X$ and $S(x) \neq \emptyset$ **do**
16:         $S(x) = S(x) \cup \{x\}$
17:         Add to τ the average location formed by the locations in $S(x)$
18:     **end for**
19:     $D^\star = D^\star \cup \underbrace{\{\tau, \ldots, \tau\}}_{k}$
20: **end for**
21: **return** $D^\star$

In this article we consider trajectory k-anonymity as a property of the anonymised dataset regardless the adversary capabilities. Our notion of k-anonymity is indeed similar to that presented in [15, 16] for generalised trajectories.

Definition 3 (Trajectory k-anonymity). *Let $D^\star$ be a collection of trajectories. $D^\star$ meets trajectory k-anonymity if every trajectory in $D^\star$ is equal to other $k - 1$ trajectories in $D^\star$.*

Theorem 1. *Let D be a collection of original trajectories and $D^\star$ the output of Algorithm 3 on input D. $D^\star$ satisfies trajectory k-anonymity.*

Proof. The proof trivially follows from the fact that Algorithm 3 produces k equal trajectories for each cluster (see Step 19 in Algorithm 3).   □

5   Empirical Evaluation

As the privacy-preserving anonimisation technique introduced in this article replaces a cluster of k close, but potentially different, trajectories by k identical trajectories, it is of paramount importance to evaluate utility loss in this method. Next, we introduce spatial-range queries as a measure of utility loss. We finally compare our anonymisation approach with other state-of-the-art privacy preserving techniques.

5.1 Trajectory Analysis and Utility Measures

There exist a plethora of trajectory analysis techniques developed within the Geographic Information Science and Data Mining fields. These techniques may look for movement patterns such as flocking, leadership, commuting, and encounter, or may be aimed at answering basic queries such as nearest neighbor or range queries.

In this article we mainly focus on queries that are used for aggregate statistics. This queries are typically measurable, and thus they can be defined as functions on the domain of all spatio-temporal databases ranging over a metric space. Let $\mathcal{D}$ be the universe of all possible collections of trajectories and let (M, d) be a metric space. A spatio-temporal query Q is formally defined as a function $Q : \mathcal{D} \rightarrow M$. Examples of measurable queries are traffic density, travel time, peak hours, amongst many others.

Measurable queries can be naturally used to define utility measures for anonymisation techniques as follows. Let $D \in \mathcal{D}$ be an original spatio-temporal database and $D^\star \in \mathcal{D}$ its anonymised version. Given a measurable query $Q : \mathcal{D} \rightarrow M$, we measure utility loss by the formula $d(Q(D), Q(D^\star))$. The closer this measure to zero the better $D^\star$ approximates D with respect to Q.

A well-known type of measurable query in trajectory analysis is *spatio-temporal range queries*, which were introduced by Trajcevski et al. in [21] in 2004. In particular, we consider the two following queries.

- *Sometime_Definitely_Inside(T, R, t_b, t_e)* is *true* if and only if there exists a time $t \in [t_b, t_e]$ at which trajectory T is inside region R.
- *Always_Definitely_Inside(T, R, t_b, t_e)* is *true* if and only if at every time $t \in [t_b, t_e]$, trajectory T is inside region R.

At a first sight, it may seem that the query *Always_Definitely_Inside*(AI) is stronger than *Sometime_Definitely_Inside*(SI). However, with the later we can formulate questions at a local level like: how many users pass through the Grand Place in Belgium?, whilst with AI the shape of trajectories becomes more relevant and might be useful for questions like: how many users take the toll highway placed between Barcelona and Tarragona cities?

Other important points to be remarked are the area of R and the time interval $[t_b, t_e]$. Both provide flexibility when dealing with uncertain or perturbed trajectories. Asking for trajectories passing through a single location at a given time-stamp is meaningless in this type of imprecise data. The size of the area and the time interval should not be too large either, though.

Similarly to [1,2,9], we used both queries to define a distortion metric of the anonymised dataset $\mathcal{T}^\star$ with respect to original dataset $\mathcal{T}$. The idea is to define a large set of queries according to some distribution of regions and time intervals.

The same set of queries is applied to both datasets $\mathcal{T}^*$ and $\mathcal{T}$ and the number of trajectories satisfying SI and AI are counted as shows the following SQL style code.

- Query $\mathcal{Q}_1(\mathcal{T}, R, t_b, t_e)$:
    ```
    SELECT COUNT (*) FROM T WHERE SI(T.traj, R, tb, te)
    ```
- Query $\mathcal{Q}_2(\mathcal{T}, R, t_b, t_e)$:
    ```
    SELECT COUNT (*) FROM T WHERE AI(T.traj, R, tb, te)
    ```

Two different *range query distortions* $SID(\mathcal{T}, \mathcal{T}^*)$ and $AID(\mathcal{T}, \mathcal{T}^*)$ are defined by using the accumulative queries $\mathcal{Q}_1$ and $\mathcal{Q}_2$, respectively.

- $SID(\mathcal{T}, \mathcal{T}^*) = \frac{1}{|\xi|} \sum_{\forall <R, t_b, t_e> \in \xi} \frac{|\mathcal{Q}_1(\mathcal{T}, R, t_b, t_e) - \mathcal{Q}_1(\mathcal{T}^*, R, t_b, t_e)|}{\max(\mathcal{Q}_1(\mathcal{T}, R, t_b, t_e), \mathcal{Q}_1(\mathcal{T}^*, R, t_b, t_e))}$ where ξ is a large set of SI queries.
- $AID(\mathcal{T}, \mathcal{T}^*) = \frac{1}{|\xi|} \sum_{\forall <R, t_b, t_e> \in \xi} \frac{|\mathcal{Q}_2(\mathcal{T}, R, t_b, t_e) - \mathcal{Q}_2(\mathcal{T}^*, R, t_b, t_e)|}{\max(\mathcal{Q}_2(\mathcal{T}, R, t_b, t_e), \mathcal{Q}_2(\mathcal{T}^*, R, t_b, t_e))}$ where ξ is a large set of AI queries.

Both metrics SID and AID are bounded by 0 and 1. The minimum is achieved when $\mathcal{Q}_i(\mathcal{T}, R, t_b, t_e) = \mathcal{Q}_i(\mathcal{T}^*, R, t_b, t_e)$, and the maximum if $\mathcal{Q}_i(\mathcal{T}^*, R, t_b, t_e) = 0$, where $i \in \{1, 2\}$. Therefore, the lower the range query distortion the lower the utility loss of the anonymised dataset.

5.2   Implementation Details of the Considered Methods

We compare our method with the generalisation-based and permutation-based approach proposed in [9, 16], respectively. The generalisation-based method relies on a distance threshold, which allows the Log-cost distance measure to discard outlier locations. Because in this section we only consider noiseless synthetic data, we have set up such a distance threshold to its maximum value. The permutation-based method, instead, discard outlier locations during the obfuscation process by considering both a distance and a time threshold. Again, we set up both thresholds to their maximum values so as to avoid outlier removal in a noiseless dataset. The permutation-based method considered in this article is the one named *SwapLocations* in [9].

5.3   Results on Synthetic Trajectories

We compare our anonymisation method with other approaches by using a synthetic dataset generated with Brinkhoff's framework [4], which is used often to evaluate privacy-preserving approaches. Synthetic data generated with Brinkhoff's generator have the advantage of being easily transferable and reproducible. We thus provide next the parameters used to generate the dataset of trajectories considered in our experiments.

The generation parameters over the map of Oldenburg were: 6 moving object classes and 3 external object classes; 5 moving objects and 3 external object generated per time-stamp; the maximum lifespan of a trajectory was set up to 1,000 time-stamps; speed 10; and report probability 1,000. This resulted in 5,000 synthetic trajectories provided by Brinkhoff's generator [4], which contain a total of 492,105 locations in the German city of Oldenburg and 98.421 locations per trajectory in average.

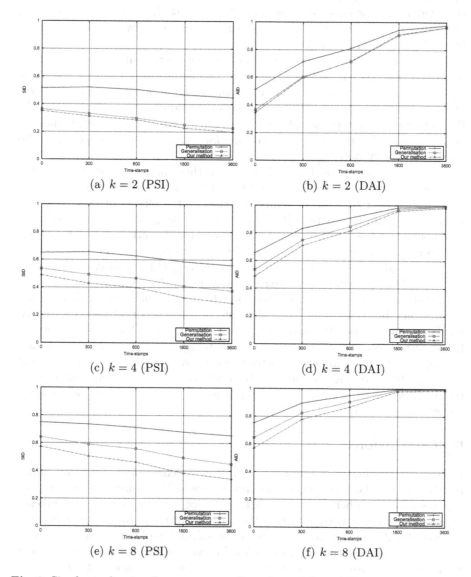

Fig. 1. Six charts showing the range query distortions of three different anonymisation methods. Charts on the left depict the SI query distortion (SID), while charts on the right show the AI query distortion (AID). (Color figure online)

In order to generate spatial-range queries, we considered regions whose radius randomly distributes over the interval of natural numbers $[0, 500]$. The maximum of this interval is a small fraction of the average length of each trajectory, which is 7284. Remark that the smaller the spatial interval the tighter is the spatial-range query and the harder become for an anonymisation technique to apply spatial distortion without bringing down utility. We respect to the time dimension we considered different time intervals $[0, 0], [0, 300], [0, 600], [0, 1800], [0, 3600]$. For a given time interval $[0, t]$, we generate a spatial-range query by choosing a random interval $[t_b, t_e]$ such that $0 \leq t_b \leq t_e \leq t$.

We generated for each time interval $100,000$ spatial-range queries of both types: Q_1 and Q_2. Armed with these set of queries, we computed the range query distortions SID and AID of the anonymised data sets provided by three different anonymisation methods: the Generalisation-based approach [16], the Permutation-based approach [9], and our method. Each anonymisation method provided three different datasets satisfying k-anonymity with $k \in \{2, 4, 8\}$. The results are depicted in Fig. 1.

It can be seen from Fig. 1 that our method performs better than the approaches proposed in [9,16] for every cluster size and every time interval. The improvement in terms of utility increases as the offered privacy increases. For $k = 2$, our method is just slightly better than the generalisation-based approach, while for $k \in \{4, 8\}$ our method performs significantly better. This means that our technique clusters and anonymises trajectories more efficiently.

Figure 1 also shows that more research on trajectory anonymisation techniques ought to be conducted. The ideal range query distortion is zero, and none of the three considered techniques gets close to this optimal value. This issue can be overcome by considering larger datasets of original trajectories. Intuitively, the larger the dataset the easier is to find clusters with low intra-cluster distance. Other solution approach consists in removing outlier trajectories, that is, trajectories that cannot be clustered with other $k - 1$ trajectories without dramatically increasing the intra-cluster distance. The study and evaluation of these solution approaches, as well as reporting on results over real-life datasets, are left as future work.

6   Conclusions

In this article we have introduced a novel distance measure for trajectories, which is well suited for both clustering and anoymisation. The proposed distance measure resembles to other types of coupling distance measures, such as the Fréchet distance, with the particularity that the Infinite norm and the Manhattan norm are considered together. To demonstrate the suitability of our distance measure, we presented a trajectory-anonymisation heuristic method that creates cluster with low intra-cluster distance and satisfies trajectory k-anonymity. Empirical results show that our method offers better utility than other state-of-the-art methods, such as the generalisation-based and permutation-based approaches. Future work will be directed towards reaching optimal range-query distortion values.

References

1. Abul, O., Bonchi, F., Nanni, M.: Never walk alone: uncertainty for anonymity in moving objects databases. In: Proceedings of the 24th International Conference on Data Engineering, ICDE 2008, Cancun, Mexico, 7–12 April 2008, pp. 376–385. IEEE (2008)
2. Abul, O., Bonchi, F., Nanni, M.: Anonymization of moving objects databases by clustering and perturbation. Inf. Syst. **35**(8), 884–910 (2010)
3. Alt, H., Godau, M.: Computing the Fréchet distance between two polygonal curves. Int. J. Comput. Geom. Appl. **5**, 75–91 (1995)
4. Brinkhoff, T.: A framework for generating network-based moving objects. Geoinformatica **6**(2), 153–180 (2002)
5. Chen, L., Tamer Özsu, M., Oria, V.: Robust and fast similarity search for moving object trajectories. In: Proceedings of 2005 ACM SIGMOD International Conference on Management of Data, Baltimore, Maryland, USA, 14–16 June 2005, pp. 491–502. ACM (2005)
6. Chen, R., Fung, B.C.M., Mohammed, N., Desai, B.C., Wang, K.: Privacy-preserving trajectory data publishing by local suppression. Inf. Sci. **231**, 83–97 (2013)
7. Domingo-Ferrer, J., Mateo-Sanz, J.M.: Practical data-oriented microaggregation for statistical disclosure control. IEEE Trans. Knowl. Data Eng. **14**(1), 189–201 (2002)
8. Domingo-Ferrer, J., Sramka, M., Trujillo-Rasúa, R.: Privacy-preserving publication of trajectories using microaggregation. In: Proceedings of the 3rd ACM SIGSPATIAL International Workshop on Security and Privacy in GIS and LBS, SPRINGL 2010, pp. 26–33. ACM, New York (2010)
9. Domingo-Ferrer, J., Trujillo-Rasua, R.: Microaggregation- and permutation-based anonymization of movement data. Inf. Sci. **208**, 55–80 (2012)
10. Eiter, T., Mannila, H.: Computing Discrete Fréchet Distance. Technical report, Christian Doppler Laboratory for Expert Systems, TU Vienna, Austria. Technical report CD-TR 94/64 (1994)
11. Fréchet, M.: Sur quelques points du calcul functionnel [On some points of functional calculus]. Rendiconti del Circolo Matematico di Palermo **22**, 1–74 (1906)
12. Gao, S., Ma, J., Sun, C., Li, X.: Balancing trajectory privacy and data utility using a personalized anonymization model. J. Netw. Comput. Appl. **38**, 125–134 (2014)
13. Meyerson, A., Williams, R.: On the complexity of optimal k-anonymity. In: Proceedings of the Twenty-Third ACM SIGMOD-SIGACT-SIGART Symposium on Principles of Database Systems, PODS 2004, pp. 223–228. ACM, New York (2004)
14. Monreale, A., Andrienko, G., Andrienko, N., Giannotti, F., Pedreschi, D., Rinzivillo, S., Wrobel, S.: Movement data anonymity through generalization. Trans. Data Priv. **3**(2), 91–121 (2010)
15. Nergiz, M.E., Atzori, M., Saygin, Y.: Towards trajectory anonymization: a generalization-based approach. In: Proceedings of the SIGSPATIAL ACM GIS 2008 International Workshop on Security and Privacy in GIS and LBS, SPRINGL 2008, Irvine, California, USA, 4 November 2008, pp. 52–61. ACM (2008)
16. Nergiz, M.E., Atzori, M., Saygin, Y., Guc, B.: Towards trajectory anonymization: a generalization-based approach. Trans. Data Priv. **2**(1), 47–75 (2009)
17. Oganian, A., Domingo-Ferrer, J.: On the complexity of optimal microaggregation for statistical disclosure control. Stat. J. Unit. Nations Econ. Comm. Eur. **18**, 345–354 (2001)

18. Samarati, P., Sweeney, L.: Protecting privacy when disclosing information: k-anonymity and its enforcement through generalization and suppression. Technical report SRI-CSL-98-04, SRI Computer Science Laboratory (1998)
19. Sweeney, L.: k-anonymity: a model for protecting privacy. Int. J. Uncertain. Fuzz. **10**(5), 557–570 (2002)
20. Terrovitis, M., Mamoulis, N.: Privacy preservation in the publication of trajectories. In: IEEE International Conference on Mobile Data Management, Los Alamitos, CA, USA, pp. 65–72. IEEE Computer Society (2008)
21. Trajcevski, G., Wolfson, O., Hinrichs, K., Chamberlain, S.: Managing uncertainty in moving objects databases. ACM Trans. Database Syst. **29**, 463–507 (2004)
22. Trujillo-Rasua, R., Domingo-Ferrer, J.: On the privacy offered by (k, δ)-anonymity. Inf. Syst. **38**(4), 491–494 (2013)
23. Trujillo-Rasua, R., Domingo-Ferrer, J.: Privacy in spatio-temporal databases: a microaggregation-based approach. In: Navarro-Arribas, G., Torra, V. (eds.) Advanced Research in Data Privacy. SCI, vol. 567, pp. 197–214. Springer, Switzerland (2015)
24. Vlachos, M., Gunopulos, D., Kollios, G.: Robust similarity measures for mobile object trajectories. In: Proceedings of the 13th International Workshop on Database and Expert Systems Applications, pp. 721–726, September 2002
25. Yarovoy, R., Bonchi, F., Lakshmanan, L.V.S. Wang, W.H.: Anonymizing moving objects: how to hide a mob in a crowd? In: Proceedings of the 12th International Conference on Extending Database Technology, EDBT 2009. ACM International Conference Proceeding Series, vol. 360, Saint Petersburg, Russia, 24–26 March 2009, pp. 72–83. ACM (2009)
26. Yi, B.-K., Jagadish, H.V., Faloutsos, C.: Efficient retrieval of similar time sequences under time warping. In: Proceedings of the Fourteenth International Conference on Data Engineering, ICDE 1998, Washington, DC, USA, pp. 201–208. IEEE Computer Society (1998)
27. Zhang, Z., Huang, K., Tan, T.: Comparison of similarity measures for trajectory clustering in outdoor surveillance scenes. In: Proceedings of the 18th International Conference on Pattern Recognition, ICPR 2006, vol. 3, Washington, DC, USA, pp. 1135–1138. IEEE Computer Society (2006)

Security and Privacy in Databases

Guaranteeing Correctness of Bulk Operations in Outsourced Databases

Luca Ferretti$^{(\boxtimes)}$, Michele Colajanni, and Mirco Marchetti

Department of Engineering "Enzo Ferrari",
University of Modena and Reggio Emilia, Modena, Italy
{luca.ferretti,michele.colajanni,mirco.marchetti}@unimore.it

Abstract. The adoption of public cloud services, as well as other data outsourcing solutions, raises concerns about confidentiality and integrity of information managed by a third party. By focusing on data integrity, we propose a novel protocol that allows cloud customers to verify the correctness of results produced by key-value databases. The protocol is designed for supporting efficient insertion and retrieval of large sets of data through bulk operations in read and append-only workloads. In these contexts, the proposed protocol improves state-of-the-art by reducing network overheads thanks to an original combination of aggregate bilinear map signatures and extractable collision resistant hash functions.

Keywords: Database · Outsourcing · Cloud · Integrity · Authenticity · Completeness · Aggregate · Signature · Accumulator · Bilinear map · ECRH · BLS

1 Introduction

The adoption of cloud services and other data outsourcing solutions is often hindered by data confidentiality needs and by limited trust about the correctness of operations performed by the service provider. Data confidentiality issues are addressed by several proposals based on encryption schemes (e.g., [10,12,21]). The correctness may be guaranteed through standard *authenticated data structures* [15,24] based on message authentication codes [1] and digital signatures [19] that are affected by large network overheads and by limited database operations. Recent proposals, such as [13,16,17,20], improve standard protocols but they cannot be adopted to guarantee results correctness in outsourced key-value databases because they incur either in network overheads [13,16,20] or in high computational costs [9,16,17]. For these reasons, we propose Bulkopt, a novel protocol that allows us to detect unauthorized modifications on outsourced data, as well as the correctness of all results produced by a cloud database service. Bulkopt guarantees authenticity, completeness and freshness of results produced by outsourced databases including cloud related services. It is specifically designed

© IFIP International Federation for Information Processing 2016
Published by Springer International Publishing Switzerland 2016. All Rights Reserved
S. Ranise and V. Swarup (Eds.): DBSec 2016, LNCS 9766, pp. 37–51, 2016.
DOI: 10.1007/978-3-319-41483-6_3

to work efficiently in read and append-only workloads possibly characterized by bulk operations, where large amounts of records may be inserted in the key-value database through one write operation. Moreover, Bulkopt supports efficient fine-grained data retrievals by reducing network overhead related to the verification of bulk read operations in which multiple, possibly dispersed, keys are retrieved at once.

Closer cryptographic protocols [8,14] proposed for memory checking data model [5] efficiently support operations on large numbers of records, but they do not support standard database queries and they cannot be immediately extended to database outsourcing scenarios. Bulkopt supports standard insert and read operations on key-value databases and limits communication overhead and verification costs of bulk operations. It recasts the problem of verifying the correctness of results produced by an untrusted database in terms of set operations by leveraging an original combination of *bilinear map aggregate signatures* [7] and *extractable collision resistant* (ECR) hash functions [4,8].

The remainder of the paper is structured as following. Section 2 outlines the system and threat models assumed by the Bulkopt protocol. Section 3 describes the main ideas behind the Bulkopt protocol and outlines the high-level design of the solution. Section 4 proposes the implementation based on aggregate signatures and ECR hash functions. Section 5 outlines the Bulkopt main contributions and compares it with related work. Finally, Sect. 6 concludes the paper and outlines future work.

2   System and Threat Models

We adopt popular terminology for database outsourcing [23]. We identify a data *owner* that stores data on a database *server* managed by an untrusted *service provider*, and many authorized *users* that retrieve data from the server. The server offers a query interface that can be accessed by the data owner and the authorized users to retrieve values by providing a set of keys. We consider a *publicly verifiable* setting [23] and assume that only the data owner knows his private key, that is required to insert data into the database, and that authorized users know the public key of the owner that is required to verify results produced by the server. We note that in this first version of the protocol, we do not consider delete and update operations and focus on efficient insert and read database operations.

Our threat model assumes that the owner and all users are honest, while the server is untrusted. In particular we assume that the server (or any other unauthorized party, that does not have legitimate access to the private key) may try to insert, modify and delete data on behalf of the owner. The Bulkopt protocol allows all users and the owner to verify the correctness of all results produced by the server. We distinguish three types of results violations:

– **authenticity:** results that contain records that have never been previously inserted by the data owner or that have been modified after insertion;

- **completeness:** results that do not include all keys requested by the client but that have been previously inserted by the data owner;
- **freshness:** results that are based on an old version of the database. In the considered operation workload the server can only violate freshness if he returns results that are both authentic and complete, but refer to an old version of the database.

3   Protocol Overview

We describe the formal model used by Bulkopt to represent data and operations (Sect. 3.1) and to express authenticity and completeness guarantees as set operations (Sects. 3.2 and 3.3). We note that since in this version of the protocol we do not consider delete and updates, the server can only violate freshness if he returns results that are both authentic and complete, but that refer to an old version of the database. As a result, clients can detect freshness violations by always using updated cryptographic digest to compute authenticity and completeness proofs. For details about verification operations please refer to the candidate implementation of the protocol described in Sect. 4.

3.1   Data Model

We model the key-value database as a set of tuples $D = \{(k, v)\}$, where k is the key and v is the value associated to k. The owner populates the key-value database by executing one or more insert operations. For each insert operation the owner sends a set of tuples $B_i = \{(k, v)\}$, where i is an incremental counter that uniquely identifies an insert operation. The set B_i contains at least one tuple, and may contain several tuples in case of bulk insertions. Without loss of generality, in the following we refer to each set of tuples B_i as a *bulk*. We define as K_i the set of keys included in B_i, and $D_n = \cup_{i=1}^{n} B_i$ the set of records stored in the database after n bulk insertions.

We assume that the server has access to a lookup function that given a set of keys $\{k\}$ allows him to retrieve the set of insert operation identifiers $\{i\}$ in which these keys were sent by the owner. Such function can be obtained by deploying any standard indexing data structure of preference (e.g., a B-tree).

Any client (including the owner) can issue a *read operation* requesting an arbitrary set of keys $X = \{k\}$. If the server behaves correctly he must return the subset of the database A, defined as:

$$A = \{(k, v) \in D_n \mid k \in X\} \tag{1}$$

We define R as the set of keys included in A, that is:

$$R = \{k \in X \mid (k, v) \in A\} \tag{2}$$

While executing read operations issued by clients, the server distinguishes two different sets of keys: T and $\bar{T}$.

T is the union of all sets K_i that contain at least one key among those requested by a client:

$$T = \bigcup K_i \mid K_i \cap X \neq \emptyset \tag{3}$$

Within each K_i we identify two subsets of keys: $R_i = K_i \cap X$ and $Q_i = K_i \backslash R_i$. We define Q as the union of all sets Q_i, and we note that the union of all sets R_i is equal to set R (see Eq. (2)). Thus, set Q is the complement of R in T.

$\bar{T}$ is the union of all sets K_i that do not contain any key among those requested by a client:

$$\bar{T} = \bigcup K_i \mid K_i \cap X = \emptyset \tag{4}$$

To better explain how these sets are built and the relationships among them, we refer to a simple example shown in Fig. 1. In this example we have a key-value database on which the owner already executed five bulk insert operations, each involving a different amount of tuples. The keys included in the database are represented by sets K_1 to K_5. We assume that a legitimate client executes a read operation, asking to retrieve six keys belonging to three different bulks. The set of keys requested is represented by X. Since X includes keys belonging to bulks K_1, K_3 and K_4, all keys of these bulks belong to T, while $\bar{T}$ includes all keys belonging in the remaining bulks (K_2 and K_5). Sets R_1, R_3 and R_5 include only the keys requested by the client and belonging to K_1, K_3 and K_5, respectively. Set R includes all the keys belonging to the union of R_1, R_3 and R_5. Sets Q_1, Q_3 and Q_5 include only the keys that were not requested by the client and that belong to K_1, K_3 and K_5, respectively. Finally, set Q includes all the keys belonging to the union of Q_1, Q_3 and Q_5.

Sets Q and $\bar{T}$ are the main building blocks that Bulkopt leverages to identify a violation of the security properties or to prove the correctness of results produced by the server.

3.2 Authenticity

Bulkopt builds proofs of authenticity by demonstrating that:

$$R \cup Q \cup \bar{T} = K_D \tag{5}$$

where K_D represents the set of keys included in D_n. We recall from Sect. 2 that authenticity is violated if the server produces a result containing a key that has not been inserted by the owner. Let us assume that R includes a fake key k_f that has been created by the server but does not belong to K_D. Then it is obvious that Eq. (5) does not hold, since R is not a subset of K_D.

An obvious solution to demonstrate that R is a subset of K_D would be for the client to have the complete set K_D. Of course this is not applicable, since it would require all clients to maintain a local copy of the whole key-value database.

To overcome this issue, Bulkopt requires the owner to maintain a cryptographic accumulator $\sigma(K_D)$ that represents the state of the keys stored in the

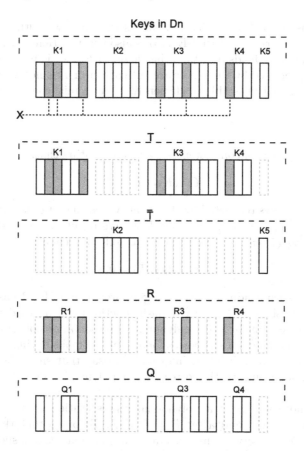

Fig. 1. Example of sets computed over a key-value database.

database D_n. This accumulator is updated after each insert operation and has to be available to all users. Moreover, the server builds two witness data structures W_Q and $W_{\bar{T}}$ that represent the sets Q and $\bar{T}$, and sends them to the client together with its response A. We remark that cryptographic accumulators and witnesses are small and fixed-size data structures, that can be transmitted with minimal network overhead [3,6].

To verify Eq. (5) a client can extract the set of keys R from A, and use two accumulators verification functions. In particular, it checks whether the witness data structures received by the database validates the results with respect to the requested data and the current state of the database that is maintained locally. Intuitively, the client verification process can be represented as following:

$$verify\left(verify\left(\sigma(R), W_Q\right), W_{\bar{T}}\right) \stackrel{?}{=} \sigma(K_D) \qquad (6)$$

where *verify* denotes accumulators verification functions.

If Eq. (6) is verified, then the user knows that the two witnesses produced by the server are correct and that Eq. (5) is also verified. Hence R is a subset of K_D and authenticity holds. On the other hand, if Eq. (6) is not verified, either the witnesses produced by the server are not correct or R is not a subset of K_D. In both cases, the client is able to efficiently detect a misbehavior of the server.

3.3 Completeness

Bulkopt builds proofs of completeness by demonstrating that:

$$X \cap (K_D \backslash R) = \emptyset \tag{7}$$

that is, the set of keys requested by the client X and the set of keys not returned by the server $K_D \backslash R$ share no common keys. We recall that $K_D \backslash R$ is equal to $Q \cup \bar{T}$, hence Eq. (7) can be expressed as the following equation:

$$X \cap (Q \cup \bar{T}) = \emptyset \tag{8}$$

Bulkopt proves such conditions by leveraging properties of ECR hash functions. In particular, as shown by [8], ECR hash functions can be used to efficiently express set intersections by using polynomial representations of sets. That is, an empty intersection between sets correspond to polynomials having *great common divisor* (*gcd*) equal to 1 (that is, informally we say that since the sets do not share any common elements, the corresponding polynomials do not have common roots).

Let us denote as $\mathcal{C}_M(s)$ a polynomial representation of a generic set M w.r.t. variable s [8,11], and a set $P = Q \cup \bar{T}$. To prove that the *gcd* of the polynomials is 1, the server must generate two polynomials $\dot{p}, \dot{x}$ such that:

$$\mathcal{C}_P \cdot \dot{p} + \mathcal{C}_X \cdot \dot{x} = 1, \tag{9}$$

The server sends witnesses W_P, $W_{\dot{p}}$ and $W_{\dot{x}}$ in addition to W_Q and $W_{\bar{T}}$ that were already sent to prove authenticity. A user can now exploit verification functions of the considered cryptographic signature to verify Eq. (9). If Eq. (9) is verified, then the client knows that the witnesses produced by the server are correct and that Eq. (7) is also verified. Hence R includes all keys X requested by the client that are available in the server database, and completeness holds. On the other hand, if Eq. (9) is not verified, either the witnesses produced by the server are not correct or X shares common elements with sets of keys Q or $\bar{T}$ that were not sent by the server, thus violating completeness. In both cases, the client is able to efficiently detect a misbehavior of the server.

4   Protocol Implementation

In this section we describe the Bulkopt protocol by referring to its main three phases: *setup and key generation* (Sect. 4.1), *insert operations* (Sect. 4.2) and *read operations* (Sect. 4.3).

4.1   Setup and Key Generation

Setup. Let g be a generator of the cyclic multiplicative group $\mathbb{G}$ of prime order p, $\mathbb{G}_T$ a cyclic multiplicative group of the same order and $\hat{e} : \mathbb{G} \times \mathbb{G} \to \mathbb{G}_T$ be the pairing function that satisfies the following properties: bilinearity: $\hat{e}(m^a, n^b) = \hat{e}(m, n)^{ab} \; \forall m, n \in \mathbb{G}, a, b \in \mathbb{Z}_p^*$; non-degeneracy: $\hat{e}(g, g) \neq 1$; computability: there exists an efficient one-way algorithm to compute $\hat{e}(m, n)$, $\forall m, n \in \mathbb{G}$.

Let h be a cryptographic hash function and $h_z(\cdot), h_g(\cdot)$ be two full domain hash functions (FDH) secure in the random oracle model [2, 7] defined as following:

$$h_z : \{0, 1\}^* \to \mathbb{Z}_p^* \tag{10}$$

$$h_g : \{0, 1\}^* \to \mathbb{G} \tag{11}$$

Let us denote as $C_M(s)$ the characteristic polynomial that uniquely represents the set M, generated by using as roots of the polynomial the sum opposite of the elements of the set and as variable the secret key s [22]. Polynomial $C_M(s)$ can be computed as following:

$$C_M(s) = \prod_{m \in M} (m + s) \tag{12}$$

Let $F_M = (f(M), f'(M))$ be the output of an extractable collision resistant (ECR) hash function [4] with secret key $(s, \alpha) \in \mathbb{Z}_p^* \times \mathbb{Z}_p^*$ and public key $[g, g^s, \ldots, g^{s^q}, g^\alpha, g^{\alpha s}, \ldots, g^{\alpha s^q}]$, where M denotes a set of values $m \in \mathbb{Z}_p^*$. The output of the function can be computed through two different algorithms depending on the knowledge of the secret key s. For this reason, we denote as $(f_{sk}(M), f'_{sk}(M))$ the computation of $(f(M), f'(M))$ with knowledge of the secret key and $(f_{pk}(M), f'_{pk}(M))$ the computation of $(f(M), f'(M))$ with only knowledge of the public key. We will use notation $F_M, f(M)$ and $f'(M)$ to identify the black-box outputs of the functions when it is indifferent if they were computed with or without knowledge of the secret key. Functions $f_{sk}(M)$ and $f_{sk}(M)$ can be computed by using straightforwardly the polynomial $C_M(s)$ shown in Eq. (12) as following:

$$f_{sk}(M) = g^{C_M(s)} = g^{\prod_{i=1}^{|M|}(m_i + s)}, \tag{13}$$

$$f'_{sk}(M) = g^{\alpha C_M(s)} = g^{\alpha \prod_{i=1}^{|M|}(m_i + s)}, \tag{14}$$

Functions $f_{pk}(M)$ and $f'_{pk}(M)$ can be computed by using the coefficients of the polynomial $C_M(s)$. That is, if we consider the set of the coefficients $\{a_i\}_{i=[1,\ldots,|M|]}$ of the polynomial $C_M(s)$ such that $C_M(s) = \sum_{i=1}^{|M|} a_i \cdot s^i$, $f_{pk}(M)$ and $f'_{pk}(M)$ can be computed as following:

$$f_{pk}(M) = \prod_{i=1}^{|M|} \left(g^{s^i}\right)^{a_i} \tag{15}$$

$$f'_{pk}(M) = \prod_{i=1}^{|M|} \left(g^{\alpha s^i}\right)^{a_i} \tag{16}$$

Although functions $(f_{sk}(\cdot), f'_{sk}(\cdot))$ and $(f_{pk}(\cdot), f'_{pk}(\cdot))$ have the same behavior, computing of $(f_{sk}(\cdot), f'_{sk}(\cdot))$ is more efficient due to the computation of only one exponentiation in the group $\mathbb{G}$. Without knowledge of the secret key, ECR hash functions can be verified as following:

$$\hat{e}(f(M), g^\alpha) \stackrel{?}{=} \hat{e}(f'(M), g) \tag{17}$$

Otherwise, the secret key allows a more efficient verification:

$$f(M)^\alpha \stackrel{?}{=} f'(M) \tag{18}$$

Although knowledge of the secret key improves the algorithm efficiency, it allows one to cheat in the computation of the hash function. Hence, it cannot be given to parties that have advantages in breaking the security of the ECR hash function.

Key Generation. We denote the owner's secret and public keys as sk and pk and generate them as follows:

$$sk = (u, s, \alpha), \quad (u, s, \alpha) \xleftarrow{R} \mathbb{Z}_p^* \times \mathbb{Z}_p^* \times \mathbb{Z}_p^* \tag{19}$$

$$pk = (U, [g^s, \ldots, g^{s^q}, g^\alpha, g^{\alpha s}, \ldots, g^{\alpha s^q}]), \quad U = g^u \tag{20}$$

where $q \in \mathbb{N}$ must be greater than or equal to the maximum number of records involved for each insert or read operation, and u, s and α be different from each other.

4.2   Insert Operations

The owner issues an insert operation by sending the tuple $(B_i, \sigma_i, \Gamma_i)$, where:

- $i \in \mathbb{N}$ is the *operation identifier*, that is the incremental counter maintained locally by the owner and by the server that identifies the insert operation (see Sect. 3);
- $B_i = \{(k, v)\}$ is the set of keys and records inserted in the database at operation i. We also denote as K_i the set of the keys $\{k\}$ inserted in this operation;
- σ_i is the *bulk signature* of the set of keys K_i inserted at operation i. It is computed by the tenant as:

$$\sigma_i(K_i) = \left([h_g(i) \cdot f_{sk}(K_i)]^u, [h_g(i) \cdot f'_{sk}(K_i)]^u\right) =$$
$$= \left(\left[h_g(i) \cdot g^{\prod_{k \in K_i}(k+s)}\right]^u, \left[h_g(i) \cdot g^{\alpha \prod_{k \in K_i}(k+s)}\right]^u\right) \tag{21}$$

- Γ_i is the set of the *record signatures* of the records B_i, computed by using a BLS aggregate signature scheme [7]:

$$\Gamma_i(B_i) = \{\gamma_i(k, v)\}_{(k,v) \in B_i} \tag{22}$$

$$\gamma(k, v) = h_g(k \parallel v)^u \tag{23}$$

where $\parallel$ denotes the concatenation operator. We assume that the concatenation of the values k and v does not compromise the security of $h_g(\cdot)$. If the security of the candidate implementation of $h_g(\cdot)$ in this context, one should apply a collision resistant hash function or a message authentication code algorithm on the value v previous to the concatenation operation [1].

We note that the *bulk signature* σ_i (Eq. (21)) is similar to the computation of a bilinear map accumulator [18]. The original scheme would compute the signature of $f_{sk}(K_i)$ as $f_{sk}(K_i)^u$. Our scheme differs for the factor $h_g(i)^u$, that could be seen as a BLS signature of the operation identifier i. This variant allows us to bind the bulk signature $\sigma_i(K_i)$ to the operation identifier i in which the insert operation is executed. As we describe in Sect. 4.3, this design choice also allows us to verify correctness of the server answers by using security proofs that were originally proposed for the memory checking setting [8].

Both the owner and the server keep track of the operation identifier i locally, without exchanging it in each insert operation. After each insert operation, the server stores all records B_i, the bulk signatures σ_i and the record signatures Γ_i in the database associated to the operation identifier i.

The owner does not store any bulk signature σ_i or record Γ_i, but he maintains a cryptographic structure of constant size to keep track of the state of the database. We call it the *database signature* $\mathcal{D} = (\sigma^{\star}_{last}, F_{D_{last}})$, where *last* is the value of the operation identifier i for the last insert operation executed on the server, and $\sigma^{\star}_{last}$ and $F_{D_{last}}$ are the bulk signature and ECR hash function of all the keys inserted in the database.

The owner computes the bulk signature $\sigma^{\star}_{last}$ as following:

- after the first insertion ($i = 1$) he sets the initial value of the database signature as $\sigma^{\star}_1 = \sigma_1$;
- after any other insert operation ($i > 1$), the owner computes the database signature $\sigma^{\star}_i$ by computing the product of the current version of the database signature $\sigma^{\star}_{i-1}$ and the bulk signature σ_i of the last executed insert operation as $\sigma^{\star}_i = \sigma^{\star}_{i-1} \cdot \sigma_{i-1}$.

As a result, the value of the database signature $\sigma^{\star}_{last}$ is equal to the product of all the bulk signatures σ_i ever sent by the owner to the server:

$$\sigma^{\star}_{last} = \prod_{i=1}^{i=last} \sigma_i \tag{24}$$

The owner computes the database ECR hash function $F_{D_{last}}$ as following:

- after the first operation $(i = 1)$, the database accumulator is equal to the ECR hash function of the keys included in the first bulk of data, that is $F_{D_1} = (f_{sk}(K_1), f'_{sk}(K_1))$;
- after any other operation $(i > 1)$, the database accumulator is computed as $F_{D_i} = F_{D_{i-1}}^{C_{K_i}(s)}$.

As a result, the value of $F_{D_{last}}$ after the last insert operation is the following:

$$F_{D_{last}} = (g^{\prod_{i=1}^{last} C_{K_i}(S)}, g^{\alpha \prod_{i=1}^{last} C_{K_i}(S)}) \qquad (25)$$

4.3   Read Operations

To execute a read operation a client must send a set of keys $X = \{k\}$ to the server. The server returns the following tuple:

$$response\,(X) := (I, A, \pi_{auth}, \pi_{comp}, \pi_{rec}) \qquad (26)$$

where $I = \{i\}$ is the set of the operation identifiers associated to the bulks that include at least one of the keys X requested by the client; $A = \{A_i\}_{i \in I}$ is the set of the key-value records that compose the actual response to the client, grouped by the corresponding operation identifier i from which the server retrieved it; π_{auth}, π_{comp} and π_{rec} are the *keys authenticity proof*, the *keys completeness proof* and the *records authenticity proof* used to prove keys authenticity, completeness for the returned keys and authenticity of the values associated to the keys, respectively. Although from a security perspective keys authenticity and completeness proofs depend on each other, we distinguish them for the sake of clarity. We also observe that guaranteeing records correctness does not require any completeness proof because we are considering a key-value database where projection queries are not allowed. We recall from Sect. 3 that the elements of each set of the response A_i is a key-value tuple (k, v), and we denote as R_i the set of the keys included in the set A_i. In the following we describe separately the generation and the verification processes for keys authenticity proofs, keys completeness proofs and records authenticity proofs.

Keys Authenticity. The keys authenticity proof is a tuple that includes the following values:

$$\pi_{auth} = (\{F_{Q_i}\}_{i \in I}, F_T, W_{\bar{T}}), \qquad (27)$$

where $\{F_{Q_i}\}_{i \in I}$ is the set of the *bulk witnesses*, F_T is the aggregate ECR hash function of bulks that include at least one of the keys requested by the client, $W_{\bar{T}}$ is the aggregate bilinear signature of the bulks that do not include any of the keys requested by the client.

The server generates each bulk witness F_{Q_i} by computing the ECR hash function f_{pk} (see Eq. (16)) on the set complement Q_i of R_i with respect to K_i, as following:

$$F_{Q_i} = \left(f_{pk}(Q_i), f'_{pk}(Q_i)\right) = \left(f_{pk}(K_i \backslash R_i), f'_{pk}(K_i \backslash R_i)\right) =$$
$$= \left(g^{C_{K_i \backslash R_i}(s)}, g^{\alpha \cdot C_{K_i \backslash R_i}(s)}\right), \forall i \in I \tag{28}$$

Moreover, the server computes the aggregate bilinear signature $W_{\bar{T}}$ as the witness for bulks that do not include any keys requested by the client by aggregating the owner signatures as following:

$$W_{\bar{T}} = \prod_{i \in I} \sigma_i(K_i) = \left[\prod_{i \in I} h_g(i) g^{C_{K_i}}\right]^u \tag{29}$$

The client verifies authenticity of the keys $\{R_i\}$ returned by the server by using values included in the authentication proof π_{auth} and the database signature $\sigma^\star_{last}$ stored locally (see Eq. (24)). The client verifies correctness of the ECR hash function F_T by using Eq. (17). Then, the client verifies that the ECR hash function F_T is built correctly with respect to the aggregate bilinear signature $W_{\bar{T}}$ by using the locally maintained database signature $\sigma^\star_{last}$, as following:

$$\hat{e}(F_T, U) \stackrel{?}{=} \hat{e}\left(\frac{\sigma^\star_{last}}{W_{\bar{T}}}, g\right) \tag{30}$$

Finally, the client uses F_T to verify authenticity of the returned records $\{R_i\}_{i \in I}$ by using the bulk witnesses $\{F_{Q_i}\}_{i \in I}$, as following:

$$\hat{e}\left(\prod_{i \in I} h_g(i), g\right) \prod_{i \in I} \hat{e}(f_{pk}(R_i), F_{Q_i}) \stackrel{?}{=} \hat{e}(F_T, g) \tag{31}$$

After this verification process the client is sure about the following guarantees:

- F_T is a valid witness for the bilinear aggregate signature $W_{\bar{T}}$, as the probability of generating or extracting any other owner signature would break the non-extractability guarantees of aggregate bilinear signatures [7];
- all the returned keys $\{R_i\}_{i \in I}$ are authentic, because the server proved existence of the witnesses Q_i with respect to bulks aggregate hash function F_T and generating false witnesses would break extractable collision resistance (ECR) guarantees of the ECR hash function $(f(\cdot), f'(\cdot))$ [8];
- all the operation identifiers $i \in I$ sent by the client are authentic, as generating identifiers that satisfy Eq. (31) would break either the FDH function $h_g(\cdot)$ or the collision resistance guarantees of aggregate bilinear signatures [7].

Keys Completeness. As described in Sect. 3.3, to prove completeness of the response the server must produce witnesses that prove disjunction the requested keys X with respect to the complement sets Q and $\bar{T}$. The completeness proof is a tuple that includes such witnesses, and additional values that allow the client to verify that the server generated them correctly:

$$\pi_{comp} = (F_P, F_{\dot{p}}, F_{\dot{x}}), \tag{32}$$

where F_P is the ECR hash function of the set union including the complement sets Q and $\bar{T}$, $(F_{\dot{q}}$ and $F_{\dot{x}})$ the witnesses that prove disjunction of the set of the requested keys X with respect to sets $\bar{T}$ and Q.

First, the server computes the ECR hash function of $Q \cup \bar{T}$ as:

$$F_P = \left(f_{pk}(Q \cup \bar{T}), f'_{pk}(Q \cup \bar{T}) \right) = \left(g^{C_{Q \cup \bar{T}}(s)}, g^{\alpha \cdot C_{Q \cup \bar{T}}(s)} \right) \tag{33}$$

The two witnesses $F_{\dot{p}}$ and $F_{\dot{x}}$ of polynomials $\dot{x}$ and $\dot{p}$ are generated by the server to show that the gcd between the characteristic polynomials C_X and $C_{Q \cup \bar{T}}$ of sets X and $Q \cup \bar{T}$ is 1, that is equivalent to prove disjunction of sets X, Q and $\bar{T}$, as shown in [8]:

$$\dot{x}, \dot{p} : C_X(s) \cdot \dot{x} + C_P(s) \cdot \dot{p} = 1 \tag{34}$$

$$F_{\dot{p}} = \left(f_{pk}(\dot{p}), f'_{pk}(\dot{p}) \right) \tag{35}$$

$$F_{\dot{x}} = \left(f_{pk}(\dot{x}), f'_{pk}(\dot{x}) \right) \tag{36}$$

The client verifies correctness of the ECR hash functions $F_P, F_{\dot{q}}$ and $F_{\dot{x}}$ sent by the server by using Eq. (17). Then, he verifies whether F_P represents the set complement of R with respect to D by checking the value of F_P against the database accumulator $F_{D_{last}}$ (see Eq. (25)) publicly distributed by the owner:

$$\hat{e}\left(f_{pk}(R), F_P \right) \stackrel{?}{=} \hat{e}\left(F_{D_{last}}, g \right) \tag{37}$$

Now that the client verified the correct generation of the witnesses F_P, he can verify disjunction of X, Q and $\bar{T}$ by testing Eq. (34) as following:

$$\hat{e}(f_{pk}(X), F_{\dot{x}}) \cdot \hat{e}(F_P, F_{\dot{p}}) \stackrel{?}{=} \hat{e}(g, g) \tag{38}$$

Records Authenticity. The server computes the proof of authenticity π_{rec} by aggregating all the record signatures $\gamma_{k,v} = \gamma(k, v)$ previously received by the owner for all the records returned to the client, as following:

$$\pi_{rec} = \prod_{(k,v) \in A_i, \forall A_i \in A} \gamma_{k,v} \tag{39}$$

The client verifies authenticity of the response A given the server integrity proof π_{int} and the owner public key U by verifying the following condition:

$$\hat{e}\left(\prod_{(k,v) \in A_i, \forall A_i \in A} h_g(k \parallel v), U \right) \stackrel{?}{=} \hat{e}(\pi_{rec}, g) \tag{40}$$

This concludes the description of the protocol: any client that is enabled to query the database and that knows the owner's public key pk and the state of the database $\mathcal{D}$ can verify correctness of the results by using the described verification operations. We recall that if a client knows the secret key sk, such as in symmetric settings, he can verify results correctness more efficiently by using the secret exponents u and α.

5 Related Work

Most literature related to security of data outsourcing and cloud services aims to protect data confidentiality of tenant data against malicious insiders of cloud providers. These works typically assume the honest-but-curious threat model where an insider within the cloud provider may access and copy tenant data without corrupting or deleting them. To solve this issue several works already proposed in the literature leverage architectures based on partially homomorphic and property preserving encryptions that allow cloud computations and efficient retrieval on encrypted data (e.g., [10,12,21]). Unlike these works, in this paper we do not trust the cloud provider to behave correctly, but we assume a threat model where the cloud provider can violate authenticity and completeness of tenant data, either due to hardware/software failures or deliberate attacks. The main problem in this context is to combine authenticity and completeness guarantees without affecting the database performance and functionalities. As an example, standard message authentication codes or digital signatures can guarantee authenticity of outsourced data. However, they cannot guarantee results completeness without incurring in great network overhead.

A well-known solution to guarantee results correctness is to adopt Merkle hash trees [9], that allow to build efficient proofs for range queries by authenticating the sorted leafs of the tree with respect to an index defined at design time. However, they do not support efficient queries on arbitrary values and efficient proofs on dispersed key values. Other solutions allow the tenant to verify authenticity and completeness of outsourced data by means of RSA accumulators [13,16,17]. Although RSA accumulators provide constant asymptotic complexity for read and update operations, their high constant computational overhead often prevent their practical application in most scenarios [9]. A different approach is proposed in [25], that relies on the insertion of a number of fake records in the database. These records are then retrieved to verify their presence, and possibly identify completeness violations. However, since no cryptographic verification is executed on the real database, such a solution provides lower security guarantees based on probabilistic completeness verification. The protocols proposed in [8] guarantees authenticity of operations in a memory-checking model by maintaining an N-ary tree of constant height. Since only the values of the nodes change (but not the number of cells), these protocols can produce proofs of constant size with respect to the cardinality of the sets stored in each memory cell. However, their proposal cannot be easily adopted in the data outsourcing scenario because the amount of sets is not constant and the tree structure would require expensive re-balancing operations.

6 Conclusion

This paper proposes Bulkopt, a novel protocol that provides authenticity and completeness guarantees for key-value databases. Bulkopt is specifically designed for providing data security guarantees in the context of cloud-based services subject to read/write workloads, and efficiently support bulk insert operations, as well as read requests that involve the retrieval of multiple and not contiguous keys at once. Efficient verification of bulk operations is achieved by modeling data security constraints in terms of set operations, and by leveraging cryptographic proofs based for set operations. In particular, Bulkopt is the first protocol that combines extractable collision resistant hash functions and aggregate bilinear map signatures to achieve novel cryptographic constructions that allow the verification of authenticity and completeness over large sets of data by relying on small cryptographic proofs. More work is needed to tune the protocol performance by using data structures to cache partial proofs at the server side, as well as further developments to also support update operations.

Acknowledgments. The authors acknowledge the support of HORIZON 2020 FCT-1-2015 project ASGARD "Analysis System for Gathered Raw Data".

References

1. Bellare, M., Canetti, R., Krawczyk, H.: Keying hash functions for message authentication. In: Koblitz, N. (ed.) CRYPTO 1996. LNCS, vol. 1109, pp. 1–15. Springer, Heidelberg (1996)
2. Bellare, M., Rogaway, P.: The exact security of digital signatures - how to sign with RSA and Rabin. In: Maurer, U.M. (ed.) EUROCRYPT 1996. LNCS, vol. 1070, pp. 399–416. Springer, Heidelberg (1996)
3. Benaloh, J.C., de Mare, M.: One-way accumulators: a decentralized alternative to digital signatures. In: Helleseth, T. (ed.) EUROCRYPT 1993. LNCS, vol. 765, pp. 274–285. Springer, Heidelberg (1994)
4. Bitansky, N., Canetti, R., Chiesa, A., Tromer, E.: From extractable collision resistance to succinct non-interactive arguments of knowledge, and back again. In: Proceedings of the 2012 ACM Third International Conference on Innovations in Theoretical Computer Science (2012)
5. Blum, M., Evans, W., Gemmell, P., Kannan, S., Naor, M.: Checking the correctness of memories. Algorithmica **12**(2–3), 90–95 (1994)
6. Boneh, D., Gentry, C., Lynn, B., Shacham, H.: Aggregate and verifiably encrypted signatures from bilinear maps. In: Biham, E. (ed.) EUROCRYPT 2003. LNCS, vol. 2656, pp. 416–432. Springer, Heidelberg (2003)
7. Boneh, D., Lynn, B., Shacham, H.: Short signatures from the weil pairing. In: Boyd, C. (ed.) ASIACRYPT 2001. LNCS, vol. 2248, pp. 514–532. Springer, Heidelberg (2001)
8. Canetti, R., Paneth, O., Papadopoulos, D., Triandopoulos, N.: Verifiable set operations over outsourced databases. In: Krawczyk, H. (ed.) PKC 2014. LNCS, vol. 8383, pp. 113–130. Springer, Heidelberg (2014)
9. Crosby, S.A., Wallach, D.S.: Authenticated dictionaries: real-world costs and trade-offs. ACM Trans. Inf. Syst. Secur. **14**(2), 17 (2011)

10. Ferretti, L., Colajanni, M., Marchetti, M.: Distributed, concurrent, and independent access to encrypted cloud databases. IEEE Trans. Parallel Distrib. Syst. **25**(2), 437–446 (2014)

11. Freedman, M.J., Nissim, K., Pinkas, B.: Efficient private matching and set intersection. In: Cachin, C., Camenisch, J.L. (eds.) EUROCRYPT 2004. LNCS, vol. 3027, pp. 1–19. Springer, Heidelberg (2004)

12. Hacigümüş, H., Iyer, B., Li, C., Mehrotra, S.: Executing sql over encrypted data in the database-service-provider model. In: Proceedings of the 2002 ACM SIGMOD International Conference on Management of Data (2002)

13. Hong, J., Wen, T., Gu, Q., Sheng, G.: Query integrity verification based-on mac chain in cloud storage. In: Proceedings of the 13th IEEE/ACIS International Conference on Computer and Information Science (2014)

14. Kosba, A.E., Papadopoulos, D., Papamanthou, C., Sayed, M.F., Shi, E., Triandopoulos, N.: Trueset: faster verifiable set computations. In: Proceedings of the 23rd USENIX International Conference on Security Symposium (2014)

15. Miller, A., Hicks, M., Katz, J., Shi, E.: Authenticated data structures, generically. ACM SIGPLAN Not. **49**(1), 411–423 (2014)

16. Mykletun, E., Narasimha, M., Tsudik, G.: Authentication and integrity in outsourced databases. ACM Trans. Storage **2**(2), 107–138 (2006)

17. Narasimha, M., Tsudik, G.: Dsac: an approach to ensure integrity of outsourced databases using signature aggregation and chaining. Cryptology ePrint Archive, Report 2005/297 (2005)

18. Nguyen, L.: Accumulators from bilinear pairings and applications. In: Menezes, A. (ed.) CT-RSA 2005. LNCS, vol. 3376, pp. 275–292. Springer, Heidelberg (2005)

19. Nist. Digital signature standard. Technical report, July 2013

20. Popa, R.A., Lorch, J.R., Molnar, D., Wang, H.J., Zhuang, L.: Enabling security in cloud storage slas with cloudproof. In: Proceedings of the USENIX Annual Technical Conference (2011)

21. Popa, R.A., Redfield, C.M.S., Zeldovich, N., Balakrishnan, H.: CryptDB: protecting confidentiality with encrypted query processing. In: Proceedings of the 23rd ACM Symposium Operating Systems Principles, October 2011

22. Preparata, F.P., Sarwate, D.V.: Computational complexity of fourier transforms over finite fields. Math. Comput. **31**(139), 740–751 (1977)

23. Samarati, P., di Vimercati, S.D.C.: Data protection in outsourcing scenarios: issues and directions. In: Proceedings of the 5th ACM Symposium Information, Computer and Communications Security (2010)

24. Tamassia, R.: Authenticated data structures. In: Di Battista, G., Zwick, U. (eds.) ESA 2003. LNCS, vol. 2832, pp. 2–5. Springer, Heidelberg (2003)

25. Xie, M., Wang, H., Yin, J., Meng, X.: Integrity auditing of outsourced data. In: Proceedings of the 33rd International Conference on Very Large Data Bases. VLDB Endowment (2007)

Enhanced Functionality and Confidentiality for Database Search and Publish/Subscribe Protocols

Giovanni Di Crescenzo$^{(\boxtimes)}$, Euthimios Panagos, and Brian Coan

Applied Communication Sciences, Basking Ridge, NJ, USA
{gdicrescenzo,epanagos,bcoan}@appcomsci.com

Abstract. We show a privacy-preserving and performance-preserving approach to provably transform any database search protocol into a (pull-mode or batch-mode) publish-subscribe protocol, and viceversa. This enhances functionality of both protocol types, notably implying practically efficient publish-subscribe solutions for a large class of subscriptions (e.g., index, keyword, range and conjunction). Previous work either missed practicality or focused on customized solutions for specific subscription types. We also show simple padding techniques that enhance the confidentiality of database search and publish-subscribe protocols against communication eavesdroppers. Specifically, these techniques provide optimal hiding of the number of matching database records or publications, while restricted to keeping the communication increase below a specified limit.

1 Introduction

Private information retrieval, in its early results (i.e., [1,8]), showed the surprising possibility of accessing data while provably not leaking undesired information about a database or a query, although at significant applicability restrictions [1] or performance costs [8]. After several advances, more recent literature on provably privacy-preserving database retrieval (DR) protocols contains constructions with practical efficiency (i.e., only a constant factor slower than an analogue non-private solution to the problem) for specific query types, and in a 3-party model. There, a help server facilitates a querying client and a data owner achieve their goal, where the only leakage is to the help server and can be provably characterized as 'access-pattern' over encrypted data. Intriguing questions related to this area include: what other types of protocols are possible with similar (or better) privacy and efficiency guarantees?

In this paper, we answer this question for a large class of publish/subscribe (PS) protocols. We show a general paradigm to transform a class of DR protocols into a related class of (pull-mode or batch-mode) PS protocols, while preserving privacy and practical efficiency. The resulting PS protocols provably protect the privacy of publications and subscriptions, and have efficiency only a constant

Published by Springer International Publishing Switzerland 2016. All Rights Reserved
S. Ranise and V. Swarup (Eds.): DBSec 2016, LNCS 9766, pp. 52–60, 2016.
DOI: 10.1007/978-3-319-41483-6_4

factor slower than an analogue non-private solution to the problem. Moreover, they can benefit from practically efficient 3-party database retrieval protocols, without inheriting their drawbacks ('access pattern' leakage to the matching server). To the best of our knowledge, this is the first example in the area of an application where this combination of properties is achievable. We also show a converse transformation of a class of (pull-mode) publish-subscribe protocols into a related class of database retrieval protocols that have practical latency and provably protect privacy of database and queries. Finally, we show how simple padding approaches can further enhance confidentiality against eavesdroppers for both DR and PS protocols. To capture tradeoffs between privacy and communication, we formulate a restricted padding problem, and define a simple padding algorithm that provably increases the eavesdropper's uncertainty about the number of matched database records or publications. Using entropy, we can then quantify the improved confidentiality, and show that the proposed simple padding algorithm is optimal within the considered restriction model.

Related work. We note that designing PS or DR protocols using general solutions from the area of secure function evaluation protocols in the 2-party [10] or 3-party [4,6] model, would not result in practically efficient solutions. Practically efficient 3-party DR protocols with provable privacy include [3,7,9] for the case of index, keyword, range and conjunction queries. Practically efficient PS protocols with provable privacy in the 3-party model include [2] for the case of subscriptions based on boolean circuits. (See references therein for more related work on DR and PS protocols.)

2   Models and Definitions for DR and PS Protocols

DR protocols. A *database* is an n-row, $(m + 1)$-column matrix $Db = (A_1, \ldots, A_{m+1})$, where each row is associated with a data *record*, denoted as rec_i, for $i = 1, \ldots, n$, each column is associated with an *attribute*, denoted as A_j, for $j = 1, \ldots, m+1$, and each *entry* is denoted as $A_j(i)$. The first m columns are *value attributes*, where entries $A_j(i)$ are values in a *domain* $Dom_j = \{0, 1\}^\ell$ allowing suitable operations, and the last column A_{m+1} is a *payload attribute*, where entries are from a domain $Dom_{m+1} = \{0, 1\}^r$, for integers $\ell, r > 0$. The database *schema*, including all parameters and domain descriptions, is known to all parties. A *query* is a sequence $q = (qv_1, \ldots, qv_s, mc)$, where $s \geq 1$, mc is a boolean *(matching) circuit* and, for $h = 1, \ldots, s$, each *query value* $qv_h \in Dom_j$, for some $j \in \{1, \ldots, m\}$. An *equality query gate* $(A(i), q, j, h)$, for some $j \in \{1, \ldots, m\}$ and $h \in \{1, \ldots, s\}$, is a function that takes as input $A_j(i)$ and qv_h, and outputs 1 if $A_j(i) = qv_h$ and 0 otherwise. An *equality-based query* is a query where $mc = mc'(x_1, \ldots, x_t)$, where mc is a boolean circuit and, for $h = 1, \ldots, t$, each x_h is the output of the h-th equality query gate.

A *secure database retrieval (DR) protocol in the 3-party model* is an interactive protocol between 3 types of efficient parties: a *querier* Q, having as input a query; a *data owner* D, having as input database $Db = (A_1, \ldots, A_{m+1})$; and a *help server* HS, helping Q and D to more efficiently reach their goals. To align with many results in the area, we consider DR protocols with the following 4 subprotocols, as detailed in Fig. 1:

1. (*Key Setup*) D and Q share a key k that is unknown to HS;
2. (*Db Setup*) D sends an encrypted (using k) version of its database to HS;
3. (*Query*) Q sends an encrypted (using k) version of its query value(s) to HS;
4. (*Answer*) HS computes an answer over the received encrypted data, possibly interacting with Q and without involving D, and resulting in Q returning an output.

We define correctness and privacy requirements for DR protocols.

Correctness. The protocol's outcome should be Q's retrieval of the payload(s) $A_{m+1}(i)$ such that C's query is 'matched' by attribute values $A_1(i), \ldots, A_m(i)$. Important examples of queries and matching conditions are as follows:

1. index query: an index $ind \in \{1, \ldots, n\}$; matching condition: $i = ind$;
2. keyword query: a keyword $v \in Dom_j$; matching condition: $A_j(i) = v$;
3. conjunction query: multiple keywords $v_1 \in Dom_1, \ldots, v_t \in Dom_t$; matching condition: $(A_1(i) = v_1) \wedge \ldots \wedge (A_t(i) = v_t)$ for a specific column j;
4. range query: a range $[v_1, v_2] \subseteq Dom_j$; matching condition: $v_1 \le A_j(i) \le v_2$.

Privacy. The protocol communication should not reveal to any efficient adversary Adv corrupting any one among C, S or HS, any information other than system parameters $\sigma, m, s, r, \ell, \kappa, n$, or the following: (a) when Adv corrupts C, the query and the matching payloads which C is entitled to retrieve in the correctness requirement; (b) when Adv corrupts HS, 'access pattern' information relative to when HS accesses encrypted data provided by D. Given this intended leakage, a formal privacy definition can be derived using known approaches frequently used in the cryptography literature [5]. Note that such protocols, even when all communication is encrypted, can leak information to an eavesdropper, such as an upper bound on the number of matching records [3]. We study how to limit this leakage in Sect. 4.

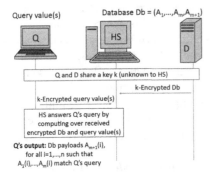

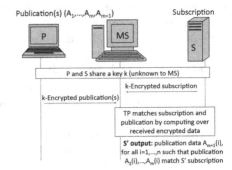

Fig. 1. Structure of 3-party DR protocols   **Fig. 2.** Structure of 3-party PS protocols

PS protocols. We formally define a data model for PS protocols so to exactly mirror the one for DR protocols; that is, publications are defined like database records, subscriptions like queries, and equality-based subscriptions like equality-based queries. A *secure publish/subscribe retrieval* protocol is an interactive protocol between 3 types of efficient parties: a subscriber S, having as input a subscription; a publisher P, having as input a publication; and a *matching server*, denoted as MS, maintaining a repository rp and helping subscribers and publishers to store their subscriptions, publications and carry out their desired functions, including matching publications with subscriptions based on matching circuit mc. To align with some results in the area, we consider publish-subscribe protocols as made of the following 4 subprotocols, with a specific structure, as detailed in Fig. 2:

1. (*Init*): P and S share a key k that is unknown to MS;
2. (*Subscribe*): S sends an encrypted (using k) version of its subscription to MS;
3. (*Publish*): P sends an encrypted (using k) version of its publication to MS;
4. (*Pull-based Match*): Upon S' request, MS determines if there is a match between the subscription and the publication, based on the received encrypted data and matching predicate mc, resulting in S returning an output.

We define correctness and privacy requirements for pull-mode PS protocols.
Correctness. At the end of the protocol S should receive a publication item $data_i$ for all publications issued by S and matching with C's current subscription.
Privacy. The communication transmitted during the protocol should not reveal to any efficient adversary Adv that corrupts any one among S, P or HS, any information other than system parameters $\sigma, m, s, r, \ell, \kappa, n$, and the following: (a) when Adv corrupts S, the matching publication data items which S is entitled to retrieve in the correctness requirement; (b) when Adv corrupts MS, the number of matching publication data items in each execution of subprotocol *PbMatch*. Given this intended leakage, a formal privacy definition can be derived using known approaches from the cryptography literature [5]. Note that such protocols, even when all communication is encrypted, can leak information to an eavesdropper, such as the number of matching publications, as it is intended to be leaked to S by the correctness requirement. We study how to limit this leakage in Sect. 4.

3 Enhanced Functionality for PS and DR Protocols

In this section we describe our privacy-preserving transformations of any DR protocol into a PS protocol. Our first result is the following

Theorem 1. Assuming the existence of pseudo-random functions, and of a secure 3-party DR protocol π_{dr} for equality-based queries, there exists (constructively) a secure 3-party pull-mode PS protocol π_{ps} for equality-based subscriptions, satisfying:

1. publication correctness;
2. privacy against any polynomial-time adversary Adv corrupting any one among S, P or MS (that is, other than intentionally revealed data, π_{ps} only leaks to MS the number of matching publication data items in any execution of $PbMatch$)
3. latency and round complexity of π_{dr} is the same as those of π_{ps};
4. if π_{dr} has communication complexity linear in number of matching records, then π_{ps} has communication complexity linear in the number of matching publications.

Among mentioned examples of equality-based query and subscription types, Theorem 1 is applicable to index subscriptions, keyword, range and conjunction subscriptions. Remarkably, even if π_{dr} leaks information like 'access pattern' to encrypted data to the help server HS, its application in constructing π_{ps} does not result in any leakage of this same type. This is due to the following: in PS protocols, encrypted publications are only processed once and are deleted afterwards, while in DR protocols, encrypted data records remain stored with HS until they are explicitly deleted.

Description of protocol π_{ps}. We now describe the four subprotocols (*Init* for initialization, *Subscribe* for subscription, *Publish* for publication, and *PbMatch* for pull-mode matching) of our PS protocol. The overall main idea consists of the following ingredients: P and MS create an encrypted database from a batch of publications issued by P; S defines a subscription as a database query, and finally an execution of the *PbMatch* subprotocol can be defined as an execution of the *Answer* subprotocol. We note that our publication, subscription and pull-based match models well mirror the database record, query and answer models, respectively. Thus, this main idea almost defines the entire construction, by preserving efficiency of the original DR protocol. Only two more refinements are needed to satisfy correctness and privacy requirements. With respect to correctness, we note a potential issue: *Subscribe* may be run before *Publish*, while Query needs to run after *DbSetup*. We circumvent this issue as follows: during *Init*, a first batch of publications is collected and used by MS with Db-Setup to create a first publication database; later, the next batches of publications for the next publication databases are collected by MS between any two consecutive executions of *PbMatch*. With respect to privacy, note that repeated use of the same key k during Subscribe and Publish may result in subscription leakage to MS (e.g., repeated occurrences of the same subscription). We avoid this issue using a fresh session key k_i at the i-th execution of *Subscribe*, for $i \geq 1$. Each session key is derived from the originally agreed upon key k using standard key derivation techniques. A high-level pictorial description of the protocol can be found in Fig. 3.

Our next result and protocol are somewhat dual and simpler than our first ones. Formally, we obtain the following

Theorem 2. Assuming the existence of pseudo-random functions, and of a secure 3-party pull-mode PS protocol π_{ps} for equality-based queries, there exists

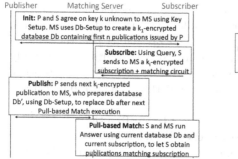

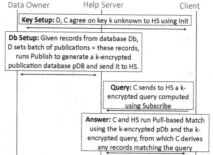

Fig. 3. Our construction of PS protocols   **Fig. 4.** Our construction of DR protocols

(constructively) a secure 3-party DR protocol π_{dr} for equality-based subscriptions, satisfying:

1. publication correctness;
2. privacy against any polynomial-time adversary Adv corrupting any one among C, D or HS (that is, other than intentionally revealed data, π_{dr} only leaks the number of matching records to HS for each execution of subprotocol $Answer$);
3. latency and round complexity of π_{ps} is the same as in π_{dr};
4. if π_{ps} has communication complexity linear in number of matching publications, then π_{dr} has communication complexity linear in the number of matching records.

Among the mentioned examples of equality-based query and subscription types, Theorem 2 is directly applicable to index, keyword, conjunction and range queries. A pictorial description of the protocol can be found in Fig. 4.

4   Enhanced Confidentiality for both Types of Protocols

In this section we describe our main results on enhanced confidentiality against eavesdroppers of DR and PS protocols. First, we define the problem of confidentiality against eavesdroppers in both protocol types. Then, we define a padding algorithm that reduces confidentiality loss while limiting communication increase. Using entropy, this loss can be shown to be optimal within the considered class of padding algorithms.

The eavesdropper confidentiality problem. As proved in [3], in any DR protocol in our model, including both those from the literature and the one obtained from Theorem 2, an eavesdropper can infer information about the number of matching database records. Note that this happens even when the communication is encrypted, since encryption, as is well known, does not hide the length of the plaintext. Padding is an often mentioned approach to reduce such leakage. We study a constrained version of the problem where we use an additive constraint on the amount of affordable padding, and ask the following questions: (1) what is the reduction in leakage to the adversary under any such padding strategies, and (2) is there an optimal padding strategy, where optimality is in the sense of minimizing leakage about m to an eavesdropper. (Note that although we study the problem for DR protocols, a similar study can be done for PS protocols, where an eavesdropper can infer information about the number of publications matching a given subscription.)

Let $X(i)$ denote the random variable that is $= 1$ (resp., 0) if the i-th database record matches (resp., does not match) the client's query, for $i = 1, \ldots, n$. We assume that all $X(i)$ are independently and uniformly distributed on $\{0, 1\}$. Also, let hwX denote the random variable that is equal to the Hamming weight (i.e., the number of 1's) in the vector $X = (X(1), \ldots, X(n))$.

Let pA be an efficient (possibly probabilistic) *padding algorithm* that takes as input $m \in \{1, \ldots, n\}$ and always returns a non-decreasing output $m' = pA(m)$; that is, for any $m \in \{1, \ldots, n\}$, with probability 1, it holds that $m' \geq m$. We say that pA is a *c-restricted* padding algorithm if for any $m \in \{1, \ldots, n\}$, with probability 1, it holds that $m' = pA(m) \leq c \cdot m$. Let $phwX$ denote the random variable returning the output of algorithm pA on input a value drawn from random variable hwX.

To analyze the information leaked about m, we use the well-known notion of entropy of a random variable, denoting as H the entropy function which maps a random variable to a real number ≥ 0. In what follows, we study the conditional entropy $H(X|phwX = m')$, modeling the uncertainty that an (even infinitely powerful) adversary has on matching bits $X(1), \ldots, X(n)$, after eavesdropping a communication consistent with m' matching records, for some m' returned by a c-restricted padding algorithm.

Entropy-based confidentiality analysis. First of all, we analyze the uncertainty on X from a value for the number of matching records hwX. Then, we define a c-restricted padding algorithm pA and show the implied uncertainty on X from the resulting value for $phwX_{pA}$. Finally, we show that algorithm pA is optimal, in that it maximizes the uncertainty among all c-restricted padding algorithms.

Uncertainty on X from a value for hwX. Let m be an integer in $\{1, \ldots, n\}$. We observe that $\mathrm{Prob}[X = x|hwX = m]$ is 0 when the Hamming weight of n-bit vector x, denoted as $hw(x)$, is $\neq m$. Otherwise, when $hw(x) = m$, we have that

$$\mathrm{Prob}[X = x|hwX = m] = \frac{\mathrm{Prob}[X = x] \cdot \mathrm{Prob}[hwX = m|X = x]}{\sum_x \mathrm{Prob}[X = x] \cdot \mathrm{Prob}[hwX = m|X = x]}$$

$$= \frac{2^{-n} \cdot 1}{\sum_{x:hw(x)=m} 2^{-n} \cdot 1} = \frac{2^{-n}}{\binom{n}{m} \cdot 2^{-n}} = \frac{1}{\binom{n}{m}},$$

where the first equality follows from Bayes' rule, and the second on the assumption of X's distribution. Denoting $p_{x,m} = \mathrm{Prob}[X = x|hwX = m]$, we obtain that

$$H(X|hwX = m) = -\sum_x p_{x,m} \log(p_{x,m}) = -\sum_{x:hw(x)=m} p_{x,m} \log(p_{x,m}) = \log\binom{n}{m}.$$

Defining an algorithm pA. Let m be an integer in $\{1, \ldots, n\}$. We define the c-restricted padding algorithm pA as the algorithm that maps m to the next larger integer m' that is an integer multiple of c. Formally, $m' = (q+1)c$, where (q, r) is the only pair of non-negative integers such that $m = qc + r$. Note that pA is a deterministic algorithm.

Uncertainty on X from a value for $phwX_{pA}$. We observe that $\text{Prob}[X = x|phwX = m]$ is 0 when $hw(x) \notin \{m - c + 1, \ldots, m\}$ or m is not an integer multiple of c. Otherwise, when $hw(x) \in \{m - c + 1, \ldots, m\}$ and $m = kc$, for some positive integer k, we have that

$$\text{Prob}[X = x\,|\,phwX_{pA} = m'] = \frac{\text{Prob}[X = x]\cdot\text{Prob}[phwX_{pA} = m'|X = x]}{\sum_x \text{Prob}[X = x]\cdot\text{Prob}[phwX_{pA} = m'|X = x]}$$

$$= \frac{2^{-n}\cdot 1}{\sum_{hw(x)\in[m'-c+1,m']} 2^{-n}\cdot 1} = \frac{2^{-n}}{\sum_{j=m'-c+1}^{m'}\binom{n}{j}\cdot 2^{-n}}$$

$$= \frac{1}{\sum_{j=m'-c+1}^{m'}\binom{n}{j}},$$

where the first equality follows from Bayes' rule. Denoting $p_{x,m'} = \text{Prob}[X = x|phwX_{pA} = m']$, we obtain that $H(X|phwX_{pA} = m')$ is equal to

$$-\sum_x p_{x,m'} \log(p_{x,m'}) = -\sum_{hw(x)\in[m'-c+1,m']} p_{x,m'} \log(p_{x,m'}) = \sum_{j=m'-c+1}^{m'}\binom{n}{j}.$$

Optimality of padding algorithm pA. Note that the described algorithm pA always increases the uncertainty on X since $H(X|phwX_{pA} = m')$ is strictly larger than $H(X|hwX = m)$. It turns out that pA is the best algorithm among all c-restricted padding algorithms. This can be proved into two parts, depending on whether we consider deterministic or probabilistic algorithms, and the proof is based on the above computed expressions and known properties of the entropy function.

Implications on DR and PS protocols. Consider a DR protocol, where a help server HS can augment its answer to C based on a c-restricted padding algorithm. Because of our analysis above, this increases the eavesdropper's uncertainty on the Hamming weight of vector X denoting how many database records were matched with C's query, and this increase is optimal among all c-restricted padding algorithms. Consider a PS protocol obtained from a DR protocol via Theorem 1, where additionally a matching server MS can augment its answer to S based on a c-restricted padding algorithm. Because of our analysis above, this increases the eavesdropper's uncertainty on the Hamming weight of vector X denoting the number of publications matching S' subscription, and this increase is optimal among all c-restricted padding algorithms.

Acknowledgements. Part of this work was supported by the Intelligence Advanced Research Projects Activity (IARPA) via Department of Interior National Business Center (DoI/NBC) contract number D12PC00520. The U.S. Government is authorized to reproduce and distribute reprints for Governmental purposes notwithstanding any copyright annotation hereon. Disclaimer: The views and conclusions contained herein are those of the authors and should not be interpreted as necessarily representing the official policies or endorsements, either expressed or implied, of IARPA, DoI/NBC, or the U.S. Government.

References

1. Chor, B., Kushilevitz, E., Goldreich, O., Sudan, M.: Private information retrieval. J. ACM **45**(6), 965–981 (1998)
2. Di Crescenzo, G., Burns, J., Coan, B., Schultz, J., Stanton, J., Tsang, S., Wright, R.N.: Efficient and private three-party publish/subscribe. In: Lopez, J., Huang, X., Sandhu, R. (eds.) NSS 2013. LNCS, vol. 7873, pp. 278–292. Springer, Heidelberg (2013)
3. Di Crescenzo, G., Cook, D., McIntosh, A., Panagos, E.: Practical private information retrieval from a time-varying, multi-attribute, and multiple-occurrence database. In: Atluri, V., Pernul, G. (eds.) DBSec 2014. LNCS, vol. 8566, pp. 339–355. Springer, Heidelberg (2014)
4. Feige, U., Kilian, J., Naor. M.: A minimal model for secure computation (extended abstract). In: Proceedings of ACM STOC, pp. 554–563 (1994)
5. Goldreich, O.: General cryptographic protocols: the very basics. In: Secure Multi-Party Computation, pp. 1–27 (2013)
6. Goldreich, O., Micali, S., Wigderson, A.: How to play any mental game or a completeness theorem for protocols with honest majority. In: Proceedings of ACM STOC, pp. 218–229 (1987)
7. Jarecki, S., Jutla, C.S., Krawczyk, H., Rosu, M., Steiner, M.: Outsourced symmetric private information retrieval. In: Proceedings of ACM CCS (2013)
8. Kushilevitz, E., Ostrovsky, R.: Replication is not needed: single database, computationally-private information retrieval. In: Proceedings of IEEE FOCS, pp. 364–373 (1997)
9. Pappas, V., Krell, F., Vo, B., Kolesnikov, V., Malkin, T., Choi, S.G., George, W., Keromytis, A.D., Bellovin, S.: Blind seer: a scalable private DBMS. In: Proceedings of IEEE SOSP (2014)
10. Yao, A.C.-C.: How to generate and exchange secrets (extended abstract). In: Proceedings of IEEE FOCS, pp. 162–167 (1986)

Privacy Preserving Probabilistic Record Linkage Using Locality Sensitive Hashes

Ibrahim Lazrig[1], Toan Ong[2], Indrajit Ray[1(✉)], Indrakshi Ray[1], and Michael Kahn[2]

[1] Department of Computer Science, Colorado State University, Fort Collins, USA
{lazrig,indrajit,iray}@cs.colostate.edu
[2] Anschutz Medical Campus, University of Colorado, Denver, USA
{Toan.Ong,Michael.Kahn}@ucdenver.edu

Abstract. As part of increased efforts to provide precision medicine to patients, large clinical research networks (CRNs) are building regional and national collections of electronic health records (EHRs) and patient-reported outcomes (PROs). To protect patient privacy, each data contributor to the CRN (for example, a health-care provider) uses anonymizing and encryption technology before publishing the data. An important problem in such CRNs involves linking records of the same patient across multiple source databases. Unfortunately, in practice, the records to be matched often contain typographic errors and inconsistencies arising out of formatting and pronunciation incompatibilities, as well as incomplete information. When encryption is applied on these records, similarity search for record linkage is rendered impossible. The central idea behind our work is to create characterizing signatures for the linkage of attributes of each record using minhashes and locality sensitive hash functions before encrypting those attributes. Then, using a privacy preserving record linkage protocol we perform probabilistic matching based on Jaccard similarity measure. We have developed a proof-of-concept for this protocol and we show some experimental results based on synthetic, but realistic, data.

1 Introduction

The problem of privacy preserving record linkage arises in many data sharing applications that limit the access to certain information on a need-to-know basis. A typical example of this problem is that of record linkage in large clinical research networks. As part of increased efforts to provide precision medicine to patients, large clinical research networks (CRNs) are building regional and national collections of electronic health records (EHRs) and patient-reported

This work was partially supported by a grant from Colorado State University, by NIST under contract 70NANB158264, and by NSF under grants IIP1540041 and CNS1619641. Any opinions, findings, recommendations, or conclusions reported in this work are those of the author(s) and do not necessarily reflect the views of the NIST or the NSF.

Published by Springer International Publishing Switzerland 2016. All Rights Reserved
S. Ranise and V. Swarup (Eds.): DBSec 2016, LNCS 9766, pp. 61–76, 2016.
DOI: 10.1007/978-3-319-41483-6_5

outcomes (PROs). To protect patient privacy, each data contributor to the CRN (for example, a health-care provider) uses anonymizing and encryption technology before publishing the data. A medical researcher (data subscriber) on the other hand requests medical data from different data contributors and needs to aggregate the records of different patients. The challenging scenario occurs when many competitor data publishers are willing to anonymously and securely share some information with a subscriber, but do not want to share the encryption keys in order to protect their clients' privacy. The researcher is interested in finding linked (matched) patient records across the datasets and to be able to retrieve updates on some previously queried patients as well. In addition, the subscriber is not only interested in finding deterministically matched records only, but also records that potentially matches with high probability.

If the data is encrypted with a shared (or same) key, the matching process could be performed deterministically [11]. However, in a typical real-world setting, where the data publishers operate independently of each other, there is no guarantee that the same datum is consistent across different publishers. This occurs owing to factors such as, different structures (FName versus First Name), semantics (whooping cough vs. pertussis), typographic and formatting errors (John vs. Jhon), or the way the data is captured, entered and maintained by each entity. As a result, deterministic matching becomes difficult or ineffective. If the data is encrypted with different keys (as would typically be done by independent data publishers that do not trust each other), finding matches between the records are even more challenging. For privacy preserving record matching to be effective under such circumstances, we need to consider as many of the discrepancies in the data as possible that can potentially occur during acquisition (input) such as spelling mistakes, formatting errors, abbreviations, punctuations, pronunciations, users background, or different underlying assumptions about the structure of the data, and attempt to determine how similar the encrypted data are.

In this work, we build upon our previous secure record matching protocol [11], that performs a deterministic record matching using the services of a *semi-trusted* broker, in order to construct a *probabilistic* record matching protocol. It takes into account the different types of discrepancies mentioned above. Probabilistic in the context of this work means that the matching is performed based on the likelihood of similarity with certain probability. We call the set of attributes used to perform the record matching, the *linkage attributes*. (Note that in the literature the term "quasi-identifier" is often used for the combination of attributes used for linkage. We do not use the term "quasi-identifier" because it explicitly excludes attributes that are themselves unique identifiers. In our case, the linkage attributes can be key attributes too.) In order to hide the identities of the matched entities from all of the parties, the matching process is performed on encrypted data under different keys. Any two records of different data sets are said to be matched if they belong to the same individual/entity. In our demonstration, we use personal identification information as the linkage attributes (e.g. names. SSN, email address, DOB, Driving License number, etc.) for finding candidates for record matching. However, our protocol is easily generalizable to any other attributes that are of interest.

1.1   Related Work

The record linkage problem is defined as the process of finding records belonging to the same entity, across two or more data sets [6]. It has been widely studied in the context of linking records stored on different databases so as to identify duplicate records that appear to be different. Approximate comparison of string values and distance measures allow researchers to deal with data discrepancies and errors that causes such apparent differences in duplicate records [2,12,13,15]. In this work, we rely on Jaccard similarity measure that is calculated based on the common sub-strings of bi-grams between the strings to be compared. The min-hash technique, which has been proven to be a good approximation to the Jaccard similarity [2,12], is used to construct a locality-sensitive hash function that speeds up the calculation of the Jaccard similarity [12].

Sharing individual data, such as medical or financial records, among multiple parties is a two edge sword that has its research benefits and privacy concerns for both the parties (who might be competitive) and the subjects (individuals) whose data is to be shared. Because privacy is a big concern, many research has been conducted to address privacy issues in the record linkage of shared data. The research resulted in the development of a number of privacy preserving record linkage protocols. Some of the protocols allow the parties to directly communicate and perform the matching process, and some utilize the service of a third party to accomplish the task of record matching. Our work belongs to the second category, where the third party blindly performs the matching process.

Some research developed protocols targeted at private set intersection [3,7,9] and secure multi-party computation (SMC) [1,4,5,8] to solve the record linkage problem. However these techniques do not fit directly in our scenario because either they require a shared key or the parties involved learns the result of the computation. Further more, some of these techniques do not scale very well with the number of parties and the size of the data sets, and incur large computation or communication overhead [19].

In [10], a framework for privacy-preserving approximate record linkage is proposed. The framework is based on a combination of secure blocking and secure matching. The secure blocking is based on phonetic algorithms statistically enhanced to improve security, and the secure matching is performed using a private approach of the Levenshtein Distance algorithm. The main advantage of blocking is that it results in a huge decrease of record comparisons.

A three-party protocol, proposed in [17], relies on identical encryption at the sources and uses Bloom filters to perform similarity search. The linkage center performs probabilistic record linkage with encrypted personally identifiable information and plain non-sensitive variables. To guarantee similar quality and format of variables and identical encryption procedure at each site, the linkage center generates semi-automated pre-processing and encryption templates based on information obtained via a new method called data masking that hides personal information.

Similarity preserving data transformation approaches like [14,16,18,20] have been also presented. In [16], a protocol that provides privacy at the levels of both data and schema matching was presented. In this protocol, records are mapped into an Euclidean space using a set of pre-defined reference values and distance function, while preserving the distances between record values. Then the semi-trusted (HBC) third party will compare the records in the metric space in order to decide their matching. The secure schema matching requires global schema, provided by the third party, on which the parties map their own local schemas. In [20], an approach based on the work in [16], that doesn't need a third party was presented. A complex plain is created then an adjustable width slab is moved within the complex plain to compute likely matched pairs. In [14], public reference tables are used to encode names as the distance to all reference points. Then a third party will estimate the distance between pairs based on their encoding.

In [18], a Bloom filters with a set of cryptographic hash functions are used to encode the attributes of the data records. The encoded records are then compared via a set-based similarity measure.

Most of these protocols where either theoretically or experimentally proven to be efficient. However most of these works do not fit directly into our scenario [1, 3, 7, 9, 19] Because The data source parties participate in the matching process will know the matching results, or they work for deterministic match [3, 7], require a shared key [17], or rely on expensive SMC operations that do not scale very well with the size of the data [1, 4, 5, 8].

2   Problem Formulation, Definitions and Background

We abstract the problem as that of a group of $n \geq 2$ publishers (data sources) $\{P_1, \cdots, P_n\}$, with n data bases $\{D_1, \cdots, D_n\}$ who would like to share information with another group of $m \geq 1$ subscribers (e.g. researchers) $\{S_1, \cdots, S_m\}$ while protecting the privacy of their clients. At the end of the linkage process, we require that 1) the subscriber(s) gets the linked records identified by some random non-real ids, 2) none of the publishers knows the result of the linkage process, or that a certain client's information exists at other party's records, 3) none of the parties, including the party conducting the linkage process, should know the real identity of any client that it did not know a priori.

Definition 1 - *Linkage Attributes:* *For a database D_i of publisher P_i with a schema $C = (A_1, \cdots, A_w)$ that has a set of w attributes, we define the set of linkage fields $L \subseteq C$ as a subset of $t \leq w$ attributes that uniquely define the personal identity of the database records. We denote the linkage fields set as $L = \{L_1, \cdots, L_t\}$ and the set of records of D_i as $R = \{R_1, \cdots, R_v\}$. We refer to the value of the linkage field L_j of the record R_k by $R_k \cdot L_j$.*

Definition 2 - *Linkage Parameters:* *We associate with the linkage fields L sets of linkage parameters K, St, W, such that for each linkage field $L_i \in L$, we define some linkage parameters, $K_i \in K$ that represents the number of hash functions used for similarity calculations of the values of that field, similarity threshold $0 \leq St_i \leq 1$ which defines the minimum similarity threshold to consider* the values of the linkage field as a match, and Linkage Field weight $w_i \in W$: $\sum_{1 \leq j \leq t} w_j = 1$ that represents the importance of that field in the matching decision.

Definition 3 - *Field Match Score:* Given two values $R_j \cdot L_i, R_k \cdot L_i$ of linkage field L_i of two records R_j, R_k, similarity function Sim, field similarity threshold St_i, and field weight w_i, a field match score FM_i is defined as:

$$FM_i(R_j \cdot L_i, R_k \cdot L_i) = \begin{cases} 0 & if\ Sim(R_j \cdot L_i, R_k \cdot L_i) < St_i \\ w_i \cdot Sim(R_j \cdot L_i, R_k \cdot L_i) & otherwise \end{cases}$$

Definition 4 - *Record Match Decision:* Given a similarity threshold TR and a set of Field Match scores $\{FM_i : 1 \leq i \leq t\}$ of two records R_j, R_k, the record match decision RM of R_j, R_k is defined as:

$$RM(R_j, R_k) = \begin{cases} Match & if\ \sum_{1 \leq i \leq t} FM_i \geq TR \\ Non-Match & otherwise \end{cases}$$

2.1   Adversary Model

This work derives from the deterministic matching protocol of our previous work [11] that relies on a *semi-trusted* broker. Data publishers are considered competitors who do not want to share data with each other. Each publisher tries to determine information about the clients of competitor publisher, or at a minimum, tries to determine if any one of its clients is also a client of its competitor. However, publishers are also honest in the execution of the protocol steps and are willing to share information with subscribers *privately*, that is, without revealing real identities, and *securely*, that is, without any leakage of information to other data publishers, and without revealing the publisher's identity to the subscribers.

A data subscriber, on the other hand, needs to determine if any information that came from different publishers belong to the same individual so they could be grouped together as such and treated accordingly. For example, if a researcher is looking for the side effects of a new drug used for skin treatment on patients who has kidney problems, then he has to match patients from the Dermatology and Nephrology departments to find patients under these conditions. We need to allow such grouping at the subscriber side.

Further more, the subscriber is allowed to issue *retrospective* queries regarding some individual client, for example, update queries regarding the progress of treatment of certain patients. Subscribers (researchers) are considered curious in the sense they will try to determine the real identities of the individuals. Some information about individual identities might be leaked from their non-identification information (i.e. eye color, age, weight, etc.) using statistical inference techniques. This is a separate problem that needs to be addressed with anonymization (i.e. k-anonymity) or other sanitization methods, and is not considered in this work.

The broker is honest in the sense that it will not collude with any of the parties, but is curious and not trusted to keep a secret, secret. The broker will work as a mediator between the data publishers and the subscribers by honestly performing the following tasks:

- Hide the source of information (publishers and clients' identities) from the subscribers.
- Blindly determine record linkages among the encrypted publishers' records and assign alternate random identifiers to the linked records before sharing them with the subscribers. The broker will just know the linkages between two encrypted records without knowing the real identifiers.

2.2 The Secure Deterministic Matching Protocol

The current work builds on our previous work [11] where we introduced the deterministic matching protocol using a semi-trusted broker. To facilitate understanding of the current protocol we briefly describe the previous work. Our previous protocol has three phases, the *setup phase*, the *encryption of query results* phase, and the *secure matching phase*:

- *Setup phase*: It is executed only once. In this phase the publishers collaboratively and securely create a set of *encryption key converters*, one for each publishers, using El-Gamal homomorphic encryption and the broker's public key pk. The inputs to this phase are each publisher's initial temporary encrypted key converter $t_{i \to i} = \mathsf{Enc}_{\mathsf{pk}}(r_i^{-1})$, and the publisher's secret key sk_i, where r_i is an initial random secret of this publisher d_i. At the end of this phase, each publisher has its initial key converter value $(t_{i \to final})$ securely processed (using homomorphic operations under the broker's public key) by all other publishers. Then publisher d_i sends its final encrypted key converter value to the broker, and saves a copy of it for future updates in case new publishers join the system or to refresh its secret key. Then, For each $t_{i \to final}$, the broker extracts the key conversion δ_i using its private key sk such that:

$$\delta_i = \mathsf{Dec}_{\mathsf{sk}}(t_{i \to final}) = r_i^{-1} \prod_{\substack{j=1 \\ j \neq i}}^{N} sk_j$$

- *Encryption of query results phase*:
  Each publisher has the publicly known ElGamal EC parameters, i.e., the curve parameters $E(\mathbb{F}_q)$ and the point on the curve P of prime order n. The public/private key pair will be $(r_i \cdot \mathsf{sk}_i \cdot P, r_i \cdot \mathsf{sk}_i)$ and both of the keys are kept secret. Each publisher encrypts the identification part of its data set id, which in our multiplicative scheme needs to be a scalar. We denote by $\mathsf{E}(.)$ the encryption of ElGamal based on EC.
  The publisher first hashes the identifying part of every record in its data set using a universal hash function H. Then uses its secret key multiplied by the corresponding random value, $(r_i \cdot \mathsf{sk}_i)$, to encrypt the resulting hash. That is, the encryption of any identifier id will be:

$$\mathsf{E}_{(r_i \cdot \mathsf{sk}_i)}(H(id)) = H(id) \cdot r_i \cdot \mathsf{sk}_i \cdot P$$

Finally, the publisher substitutes the real identifying part, *id*, by $E_{(r_i \cdot sk_i)}(H(id))$ for all records in its data set before being sent to the broker. Publishers can avoid having the broker store the key converter $(\delta_i)_{i \in [N]}$. For this purpose, each publisher encrypts the identifiers of the query results with a new random value r_i, updates the key converter $t_{i \rightarrow final}$, then sends these results to the broker accompanied with the new key converter. This solution adds negligible communication overhead, but ensures a zero-key stored on the broker side.

– *Secure matching phase*:

The broker receives the encrypted identifiers under different keys from different publishers. The broker's job is to merge similar clients' records from different publishers such that they will map to the same newly generated identifier. It uses the δ_i values to convert any identifier *id* encrypted by publisher d_i under its secret key $(r_i \cdot sk_i)$, to a value encrypted under a different unknown secret key Δ, i.e., $E_\Delta(H(id))$. The key $\Delta = \prod_{i=1}^{N} sk_i$ is resulting from the product of all the secret keys of all publishers, and cannot be computed by the broker who posses only the key converters of publishers. In order to perform the secure record matching, the broker re-encrypts the encrypted identifying parts of the records coming from the publisher d_i using the corresponding key converter δ_i as:

$$E_{\delta_i}\left(E_{(r_i \cdot sk_i)}(H(id))\right) = E_\Delta(H(id))$$

3 The Secure Probabilistic Matching Protocol

In order to allow the parties to perform secure similarity match based on Jaccard measure, we improve our previous deterministic protocol to perform the match probabilistically with a predefined threshold. We improve the string set representation of the matching (linkage) attributes, then create signatures based on Locality Sensitive Hash scheme explained below. To prevent any correlation analysis, the signatures are lexicographically sorted and encrypted using the publishers' secret keys.

3.1 Minhash Functions and Similarity

To calculate the similarity of two strings A and B, we use the Jaccard Similarity measure. First the two strings are converted to a set representation S_A, S_B respectively (e.g. using bi-grams). Then the Jaccard similarity, $Sim(A, B)$, is calculated on S_A and S_B as:

$$Sim(A, B) = \frac{|S_A \cap S_B|}{|S_A \cup S_B|}$$

If $Sim(A, B)$ is close to 1, then A and B are very similar. Let Ω be the set of all possible values of the set representation of the strings (e.g. all possible bi-grams of the alphabet), then MinHash (also called min-wise hash) is computed by applying a random permutation $\pi : \Omega \to \Omega$ on any given set S and selecting the minimum value.

$$MinHash_\pi(S) = min\{\pi(S)\}$$

It was proven by A. Broder [2] that the probability of the minhashes of any two sets S_A and S_B being the same is equal to the Jaccard similarity of the two sets; that is:

$$Pr(MinHash_\pi(S_A) = MinHash_\pi(S_B)) = \frac{|S_A \cap S_B|}{|S_A \cup S_B|} = Sim(A, B)$$

Thus, we can estimate the Jacard similarity of the two strings A and B by choosing a set of n (e.g. $n = 100$) independent random permutations, apply them to each string set representation to get a set of n minhashes (we also use the term signatures) of those strings, and compute how many corresponding minhashes of the two sets are equal. It is possible to simulate the n random permutations by n independent random hash functions (e.g. selecting a hash function and use n different random seeds).

3.2   Locality Sensitive Hashing – LSH

Locality sensitive hashing or LSH is a well known technique in the information retrieval community, that is used for determining similar items by hashing them in such a way that their hash values will collide with high probability. Let St_1, St_2 be a similarity metric (e.g. Jaccard similarity) and P_1, P_2 be two probabilities, then a family of functions $\mathcal{H}$ (e.g. minhashes) is called the (St_1, St_2, P_1, P_2)-sensitive LSH if for every $h \in \mathcal{H}$ and any x, y:

1. if $Sim(x, y) \geq St_1$, then the probability that $h(x) = h(y)$ is at least P_1.
2. if $Sim(x, y) \leq St_2$, then the probability that $h(x) = h(y)$ is at most P_2.

From above, a family of K minhash functions with a similarity threshold St_0 is a $(St_0, 1 - St_0, St_0, 1 - St_0)$-sensitive LSH for Jaccard similarity. For a better accuracy of the similarity estimation it is preferred to have St_1 and St_2 as close as possible and P_1 and P_2 as far as possible. We construct a $(St_0, 1 - St_0, \gamma, \beta)$-sensitive LSH family from a family of K minhash functions by grouping the minhashes (while keeping the order) into b groups of size r each, such that $K = b \cdot r$, and then hash each group to get b new signatures. Hence, $\gamma = 1 - (1 - St_0^r)^b$ and $\beta = (1 - St_0^r)^b$, where the probability that the new b signatures of x and y agree in at least one signature is γ.

We can further reduce the number of false positives by requiring that the b-signatures of x and y agree on at least m signatures (e.g. $m = 2$), then the probability of the b signatures to agree in at least m signatures will be:

$$\sum_{m \leq i \leq b} \binom{b}{i} St_0^{r \cdot i} (1 - St_0^r)^{b-i}$$

However, experiments show that $m = 1$ is sufficient.

3.3   Choosing LSH Parameters

For a similarity threshold St_0, and K minhash functions we set the values of b (number of groups/signatures) and r (number of minhash values in each group) such that for any two strings x,y that have $Sim(x,y) \geq St_0$, the probability of getting at least m out of b of their corresponding signatures to match is greater than 0.5. This is done as follows:

$m \simeq b \cdot St_0^r$ and $b = K/r$ so $r = K \cdot St_0^r/m$ or $r = ln(r \cdot m/K)/ln(St_0)$, solve for r then use $b = \lfloor K/r \rfloor$ to calculate b. All the values K,b, and r must be integers. The similarity threshold could also be approximated based on r and b as $St_0 \simeq (1/b)^{1/r}$.

3.4   String Set Representation

In order to apply the LSH technique to get the signatures of the strings, we first need to convert the strings to sets of Q-grams (e.g. Bi-grams, for Q=2). In our implementation we extend the bi-gram set representation of our strings in such a way that it accounts for missing and flipped character positions. We add bi-grams constructed from tri-grams with the middle character being deleted. For example, the *the extended set representation* of the string **abcde** is constructed as follows:

- create the set of bi-grams B as $B = \{\_a, ab, bc, cd, de, e\_\}$
- create the set of Tri-grams T as $T = \{\_ab, abc, bcd, cde, de\_\}$
- From T create the set of extensions X as $X = \{\_b, ac, bd, ce, d\_\}$
- The Extended set E will be $E = B \cup X$

With this extension the possibility of matching strings with flipped character increases; for example the two strings **John** and **Jhon** will be considered a match with .75 Jaccard similarity using this technique. While the same strings without this extension will have .25 Jaccard similarity. We represent dates as strings and append some characters before and after the month, day and year components to make the bi-grams generated form those components look different in case they have the same digits.

3.5   Creation of LSH Signatures

During the setup phase, all data sources (publishers) agree on the set of size t linkage fields $L = \{L_1, \cdots, L_t\}$ and their corresponding similarity computation parameters, which are K_i hash functions (or, it could be one hash function with K_i different seeds), and similarity threshold St_i for each linkage field $L_i \in L$. We would like to emphasize here that those linkage fields not necessarily a single database attribute, they might be concatenations of certain attributes, as it is the case in many record matching works. Then each party calculates b_i (number of groups/signatures) and r_i (number of minhash values in each group) for each record linkage field L_i as discussed in Sect. 3.3 above. The steps for signature creation are as follows: We denote by $Sig_j^{(i)}$ the set of signatures of the column

i of record j, and $ESig_j^{(i)}$ is its corresponding encrypted signatures. Each party A with records set $R_A = \{R_1, \cdots, R_n\}$ having linkage fields $L = \{L_1, \cdots, L_t\}$, creates the linkage field signatures for each record $R_j \in R_A$, $1 \le j \le n$ as follows:

- For each linkage field value $R_j.L_i \in R_j$ create its corresponding Encrypted signature $ESig_j^{(i)}$ as follows:
    1. Convert the value $R_j.L_i \in R_j$ to an extended bi-grams set E
    2. Apply K_i hash functions to the set E and get the K_i minhash values $minh = \{min(h_f(E)) : 1 \le f \le K_i\}$
    3. Group the set $minh$ into b_i groups of r_i items each, and without changing their order, i.e. $G_x = \{minh[(x-1)*r_i+1]\| \cdots \|minh[x*r_i]\}, 1 \le x \le b_i$. Then, using a universal hash function H, hash each group into one value getting the set of b_i signatures of the value $R_j.L_i$ as: $Sig_j^{(i)} = \{H(G_g) : 1 \le g \le b_i\}$
    4. The encrypted signatures of the value $R_j.L_i$ will be:
       $ESig_j^{(i)} = \{E_{sk_{A,L_i}}(Sig_j^{(i)}[g]\|g\|L_i) : 1 \le g \le b_i\}$, where sk_{A,L_i} is the secret key of party A for linkage attribute L_i. This secret key could be the same for all attributes.
- sort $ESig_j^{(i)}$ values in lexicographical order and append them as new field to the record.

3.6   Record Matching Phase

Each data source (publisher) will send the encrypted signatures of the linkage fields (columns) (as separate or combined) table(s) along with random record identifiers of its data set to the broker. To determine if record $A.R_k$ matches the record $B.R_j$, the broker executes the following steps:

- For each set of encrypted signatures of each linkage column ($L_i \in L$) of both records i.e. $A.R_k.ESig_k^{(i)}$, and $B.R_j.ESig_j^{(i)}$, apply the key-conversion as follows:
    Use the key converter of A (δ_A values) to convert the signatures of linkage fields $A.R_k.ESig_k^{(i)}$ of the record $A.R_k$ encrypted by publisher A under its secret key sk_A, to signatures encrypted under a different secret key Δ, i.e., $E_\Delta(Sig_k^{(i)})$ for every linkage field L_i. The key $\Delta = \prod_{p=1}^{N} sk_p$ is resulting from the product of all the secret keys of all parties (publishers). That is,

$$E_{\delta_A}\left(ESig_k^{(i)}\right) = E_{\delta_A}\left(E_{sk_A}(Sig_k^{(i)})\right) = E_\Delta(Sig_k^{(i)})$$

The same applies to B, that is,

$$E_{\delta_B}\left(ESig_j^{(i)}\right) = E_{\delta_B}\left(E_{sk_B}(Sig_j^{(i)})\right) = E_\Delta(Sig_j^{(i)})$$

- Compare the resulting signature sets encrypted under the same key Δ, $B.E_\Delta(Sig_j^{(i)})$ and $A.E_\Delta(Sig_k^{(i)})$ to find the number of equal signatures es_i and update the results table for this linkage field L_i. If the number of equal signatures is zero (0), then the similarity between these two values of this linkage field is less than the pre-set similarity threshold St_i, and hence the field match score $FM_i(R_j \cdot L_i, R_k \cdot L_i)$ will be zero. Otherwise, calculate the Estimated similarity of the two records for this linkage field L_i as $S_i \simeq (es_i/b_i)^{1/r_i}$, then calculate the field match score based on its weight w_i using the Eq. 3 shown in Sect. 2. $FM_i(R_j \cdot L_i, R_k \cdot L_i) = w_i \cdot S_i$

– To make a record match decision $RM(R_j, R_k)$ and declare the records R_j and R_k as a match or not, first compute the overall record match score using the field match scores computed in the previous step.

$$RecScore = \sum_{1 \leq i \leq t} FM_i$$

Then compare the record match score with the pre-set record match threshold TR as shown in Eq. 4 in Sect. 2. If a match is found, save the matched record identifiers as a matched pair in the results table.

At the end, the broker will have an association (mapping) between the record random identifiers of the publishers based on the scores computed from the matched signatures of the corresponding fields. For example, suppose we have two publishers A, and B that send the encrypted signatures of their records as tables with the following schema:

Publisher A: $A.col_1 SigTable(ARecId, Col_1 Sigs)$, $A.col_2 SigTable(ARecId, Col_2 Sigs)$, $\cdots$, $A.col_t SigTable(ARecId, Col_t Sigs)$
Publisher B: $B.col_1 SigTable(BRecId, Col_2 Sigs)$, $B.col_2 SigTable(BRecId, Col_2 Sigs), \cdots$, $B.col_t SigTable(BRecId, Col_t Sigs)$

Then the Broker will find the matched records and create the mappings between A's record Ids and B's record Ids and save them as new table with a schema similar to this: $matchingResultTable(ARecId, BRecid, Score)$.

4 Implementation and Results

To evaluate the performance and the accuracy of this protocol, we implemented it and tested it against some data sets of different sizes and using combinations of different linkage fields. We adopted the following two approaches, (1) using each single attribute as a linkage field, and (2) using concatenation of some attributes as a linkage field. We evaluated the accuracy and performance based on these two approaches.

We define accuracy in terms of *precision* and *recall* based on true positive (TP), false positive (FP), true negative (TN) and false negative(FN). **TP** (True Positive) is the number of originally-matching records that are correctly identified as match. **FP** (False Positive) is the number of originally-non-matching records that are falsely identified as match. **TN** (True Negative) is the number of originally-non-matched records correctly identified as a non-match. Finally, **FN**

(False Negative) is the number of originally-matched records falsely identified as a non-match. Based on these values, we compute the following:

1. **TPR** (True Positive Rate) Or Sensitivity/recall: Fraction of originally matched records that are correctly declared as match: $TPR = \frac{TP}{TP+FN}$
2. **TNR** (True Negative Rate) Or Specificity: Fraction of originally non-matched records that are correctly declared as non-match: $TNR = \frac{TN}{TN+FP}$
3. **PPV** (Positive Predictive Value) Or Precision: Fraction of correctly matched records from all records declared as a match: $PPV = \frac{TP}{TP+FP}$
4. **ACC** (Accuracy): Fraction of records correctly declared as a match and correctly declared as non-match: $ACC = \frac{TP+TN}{TP+TN+FP+FN}$
5. F_1 **score** (F-Measure) is the harmonic mean of precision (PPV) and recall (TPR), calculated as $F_1 score = 2 \times \frac{(PPV \times TPR)}{(PPV+TPR)}$.

4.1   Results of Using Realistic Synthetic Dataset

We use two datasets generated by the *Mocaroo* realistic data generator (http://www.Mocaroo.com) and consisting of 10 K records each, and 6 K of the records are true matches. The record attributes (fields) used in this data were (ID, SSN, FirstName, LastName, email, DOB, Gender, ZipCode). We used two versions of the datasets, one is more corrupted than the other. We opt to use realistic synthetic datasets for many reasons, like known linkage results, shareable dataset for reproducibility (i.e., synthetic data don't require IRB approval), and controlled error/missing values rate. The data contains randomly generated real names, SSNs, addresses, and so other attributes. The corruption percentage is based on the number of modified (removed/inserted/swapped) characters to simulate errors occurred when acquiring the data (input into the database). The greater the data corrupted the more errors it contains.

We ran an extensive set of experiments with different configurations on both versions of the datasets (less corrupted and highly corrupted), and for convenience we will discuss only some of them here. After some experiments using signatures for single attributes, we picked similarity threshold for each attribute (low threshold to allow more permissiveness, and high threshold for strictness in the matching criteria).

1. **Using the Less corrupted Vs. the highly corrupted Datasets:**
   The more corrupted the data the lower the similarity between the records will be. So the similarity threshold of each linkage field that effect the its signatures creation will effect the matching results as well. For more permissiveness the threshold should be low, and vice versa. However the lower threshold will effect the False positive rate, so it is better to keep false positive as low as possible. For example, the F1-score result of two experiments of low (ssn = 0.85, first = 0.65, last = 0.65, email = 0.75, DateOB = 0.85, zip = 0.85) and high (ssn = 0.85, first = 0.75, last = 0.75, email = 0.75, DateOB = 0.85, zip = 0.85) thresholds settings of seven different sets of combinations of the single attributes, and using the less corrupted data is shown in Fig. 1, where the sets used are:

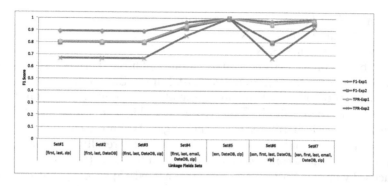

Fig. 1. F1 score using low (Exp1) and high (Exp2) Similarity thresholds for single attributes, and different combinations (Color figure online)

- Set#1: [first, last, zip]
- Set#2: [first, last, DateOB]
- Set#3: [first, last, DateOB, zip]
- Set#4: [first, last, email, DateOB, zip]
- Set#5: [ssn, DateOB, zip]
- Set#6: [ssn, first, last, DateOB, zip]
- Set#7: [ssn, first, last, email, DateOB, zip]

2. Using Single Attributes Vs. Concatenated Attributes as Linkage Attributes

Using logical expressions constructed from combinations of single attributes gives more flexibility to form matching criteria, and allows fine tuning of the matching threshold of each attribute separately. However it incurs more computation and storage overhead and make the signatures more susceptible to frequency attacks on some attributes. On the other hand, using the concatenated values of certain attributes before creating the signatures will limit the matching criteria to the combinations of these concatenations and reduce the flexibility of matching conditions. However such concatenated attributes, if properly constructed, will reduce the computations required in both signature creation and matching process, and limit the frequency attacks.

In our experiments we used the first technique to evaluate the accuracy of the protocol, and since the signatures are encrypted from the source with different keys, the frequency analysis is only possible if conducted by the broker. If the publishers use new random with each signature, update their key-converter δ and include it with the signatures, they can limit the broker frequency attack to those matched attributes, though will add communication overhead.

Table 1 shows the results of using four different combinations of the set of attributes. The top part of the table for the combinations using single attributes signatures, each has its similarity threshold, the bottom part of the table for the concatenated attributes and the similarity threshold is set for the whole concatenated attributes of each combination. The combinations are as follows:

- comb1: First Name, Last Name, Date of birth
- comb2: Date of birth, SSN
- comb3: Last name, SSN
- comb4: Three Letters First Name, Three Letters Last Name, Soundex(First Name), Soundex (Last Name), Date of birth, SSN

Any two records matched by any of the above combinations is considered a match. From the results in Table 1, we were able to fine tune the threshold similarity of each attribute, using the single attribute technique, to control the true positives and false positive and get better results. It is much harder to do that in the second technique. The combination (Comb4) where constructed by creating a new attribute (we named "Special1") that consists of the concatenations of the first four parts of comb4 above (i.e. "Three Letters First Name" + "Three Letters Last Name" + "Soundex (First Name)" + "Soundex (Last Name)"), then create the signatures for it.

Table 1. Matching quality results of using single and concatenated combinations of attributes with different similarity thresholds settings

Using signatures of single attributes						
Sim. Threshold for (SSN,First,Last,DOB,Special1)	TP	FP	PPV	ACC	F1	Time (ms)
(0.85, 0.85, 0.85, 0.85, 0.85)	5161	14	0.997	0.915	0.924	384589
(0.85, 0.85, 0.85, 0.95, 0.85)	4916	2	1	0.891	0.901	261302
(0.85, 0.75, 0.75, 0.98, 0.85)	5022	0	1	0.902	0.911	498038
Using signatures of concatenated attributes						
Sim. Threshold for (comb1, comb2, comb3, comb4)	TP	FP	PPV	ACC	F1	Time (ms)
(0.95, 0.95, 0.95, 0.95)	5140	9	0.998	0.913	0.922	3895
(0.98, 0.988, 0.99, 0.99)	4710	0	1	0.871	0.880	2009
(0.98, 0.98, 0.98, 0.95)	4848	0	1	0.885	0.894	2364

Finally, Table 1 also shows the time used in the matching process using both techniques. It is evident how the second technique out performed the first, for the reasons mentioned above. In conclusion, our system achieved good matching quality results with good performance.

5   Conclusion

In this paper, we addressed the problem of privacy preserving probabilistic record linkage across multiple encrypted datasets when the records to be matched contain typographic errors and inconsistencies arising out of formatting and pronunciation incompatibilities, as well as incomplete information. We create characterizing signatures for the linkage of attributes of each record using minhashes and locality sensitive hash functions before encrypting those attributes. Then, using a privacy preserving record linkage protocol we perform probabilistic matching based on Jaccard similarity measure. We show some experimental results based on synthetic, but realistic, data. The results show that our matching protocol is flexible and achieved good matching quality without too much computation or communication overhead. Our future work will focus on improving the matching quality results by incorporating automation methods for selecting the best matching criteria and properly adjusting the similarity thresholds and weights of the attributes. In terms of security we will work on making the secure matching protocol resilient to collusion by making the broker collude with at least k out of n parties in order to get the encryption key.

References

1. Atallah, M.J., Kerschbaum, F., Du, W.: Secure and private sequence comparisons. In: Proceedings of the 2003 ACM Workshop on Privacy in the Electronic Society, WPES 2003, pp. 39–44. ACM, Washington, DC (2003)
2. Broder, A.: Identifying and filtering near-duplicate documents. In: Giancarlo, R., Sankoff, D. (eds.) CPM 2000. LNCS, vol. 1848, pp. 1–10. Springer, Heidelberg (2000)
3. De Cristofaro, E., Tsudik, G.: Practical private set intersection protocols with linear complexity. In: Sion, R. (ed.) FC 2010. LNCS, vol. 6052, pp. 143–159. Springer, Heidelberg (2010)
4. Durham, E., Xue, Y., Kantarcioglu, M., Malin, B.: Quantifying the correctness, computational complexity, and security of privacy-preserving string comparators for record linkage. Inf. Fusion 13(4), 245–259 (2012)
5. Feigenbaum, J., Ishai, Y., Malkin, T., Nissim, K., Strauss, M.J., Wright, R.N.: Secure multiparty computation of approximations. ACM Trans. Algorithms 2(3), 435–472 (2006)
6. Fellegi, I.P., Sunter, A.B.: A theory for record linkage. J. Am. Stat. Assoc. 64(328), 1183–1210 (1969)
7. Freedman, M.J., Nissim, K., Pinkas, B.: Efficient private matching and set intersection. In: Cachin, C., Camenisch, J.L. (eds.) EUROCRYPT 2004. LNCS, vol. 3027, pp. 1–19. Springer, Heidelberg (2004)
8. Hazay, C., Lindell, Y.: Efficient protocols for set intersection and pattern matching with security against malicious and covert adversaries. In: Canetti, R. (ed.) TCC 2008. LNCS, vol. 4948, pp. 155–175. Springer, Heidelberg (2008)
9. Huang, Y., Evans, D., Katz, J.: Private set intersection: are garbled circuits better than custom protocols? In: Proceedings of the 19th Annual Network and Distributed System Security Symposium, San Diego, California, February 2012
10. Karakasidis, A., Verykios, V.S.: Secure blocking + secure matching = secure record linkage. J. Comput. Sci. Eng. 5(3), 223–235 (2011)
11. Lazrig, I., et al.: Privacy preserving record matching using automated semi-trusted broker. In: Samarati, P. (ed.) DBSec 2015. LNCS, vol. 9149, pp. 103–118. Springer, Heidelberg (2015)
12. Leskovec, J., Rajaraman, A., Ullman, J.: Mining of Massive Datasets. Cambridge University Press, Cambridge (2014)
13. Navarro, G.: A guided tour to approximate string matching. ACM Comput. Surv. 33(1), 31–88 (2001)
14. Pang, C., Gu, L., Hansen, D., Maeder, A.: Privacy-preserving fuzzy matching using a public reference table. In: McClean, S., Millard, P., El-Darzi, E., Nugent, C. (eds.) Intelligent Patient Management. SCI, vol. 189, pp. 71–89. Springer, Heidelberg (2009)

15. Porter, E.H., Winkler, W.E., Census, B.O.T., Census, B.O.T.: Approximate String Comparison and Its Effect on an Advanced Record Linkage System. U.S. Bureau of the Census, Research report (1997)
16. Scannapieco, M., Figotin, I., Bertino, E., Elmagarmid, A.K.: Privacy preserving schema and data matching. In: Proceedings of the 2007 ACM SIGMOD International Conference on Management of Data, SIGMOD 2007, pp. 653–664. ACM, Beijing, China (2007)
17. Schmidlin, K., Clough-Gorr, K.M., Spoerri, A.: Privacy preserving probabilistic record linkage (P3rl): a novel method for linking existing health-related data and maintaining participant confidentiality. BMC Med. Res. Methodol. 15(1), 1–10 (2015)
18. Schnell, R., Bachteler, T., Reiher, J.: Privacy-preserving record linkage using bloom filters. BMC Med. Inform. Decis. Mak. 9(1), 1–11 (2009)
19. Vatsalan, D., Christen, P., Verykios, V.S.: An efficient two-party protocol for approximate matching in private record linkage. In: Proceedings of the Ninth Australasian Data Mining Conference, AusDM 2011, vol. 121, pp. 125–136. Australian Computer Society, Darlinghurst, Australia (2011)
20. Yakout, M., Atallah, M.J., Elmagarmid, A.: Efficient private record linkage. In: Proceedings of the 25th IEEE International Conference on Data Engineering, ICDE 2009, pp. 1283–1286, March 2009

Access Control

Mining Hierarchical Temporal Roles
with Multiple Metrics

Scott D. Stoller[✉] and Thang Bui

Department of Computer Science, Stony Brook University, Stony Brook, USA
stoller@cs.stonybrook.edu

Abstract. Temporal role-based access control (TRBAC) extends role-based access control to limit the times at which roles are enabled. This paper presents a new algorithm for mining high-quality TRBAC policies from timed ACLs (i.e., ACLs with time limits in the entries) and optionally user attribute information. Such algorithms have potential to significantly reduce the cost of migration from timed ACLs to TRBAC. The algorithm is parameterized by the policy quality metric. We consider multiple quality metrics, including number of roles, weighted structural complexity (a generalization of policy size), and (when user attribute information is available) interpretability, i.e., how well role membership can be characterized in terms of user attributes. Ours is the first TRBAC policy mining algorithm that produces hierarchical policies, and the first that optimizes weighted structural complexity or interpretability. In experiments with datasets based on real-world ACL policies, our algorithm is more effective than previous algorithms at their goal of minimizing the number of roles.

1 Introduction

Role-based access control (RBAC) offers significant advantages over lower-level access control policy representations, such as access control lists (ACLs). RBAC policy mining algorithms have potential to significantly reduce the cost of migration to RBAC, by partially automating the development of an RBAC policy from an access control list (ACL) policy and possibly other information, such as user attributes [4]. The most widely studied versions of the RBAC policy mining problem involve finding a minimum-size RBAC policy consistent with (i.e., equivalent to) given ACLs. When user attribute information is available, it is also important to maximize interpretability (or "meaning") of roles—in other words, to find roles whose membership can be characterized well in terms of user attributes. Interpretability is critical in practice. Researchers at HP Labs report

This material is based on work supported in part by NSF under Grants CNS-1421893, CCF-1248184, and CCF-1414078, ONR under Grant N00014-15-1-2208, and AFOSR under Grant FA9550-14-1-0261. Any opinions, findings, and conclusions or recommendations expressed in this material are those of the authors and do not necessarily reflect the views of these agencies.

© IFIP International Federation for Information Processing 2016
Published by Springer International Publishing Switzerland 2016. All Rights Reserved
S. Ranise and V. Swarup (Eds.): DBSec 2016, LNCS 9766, pp. 79–95, 2016.
DOI: 10.1007/978-3-319-41483-6_6

"the biggest barrier we have encountered to getting the results of role mining to be used in practice" is that "customers are unwilling to deploy roles that they can't understand" [2]. Algorithms for mining meaningful roles are described in, e.g., [8,11].

Temporal RBAC (TRBAC) extends RBAC to limit the times at which roles are enabled [1]. TRBAC supports an expressive notation, called *periodic expressions*, for expressing sets of time intervals during which a role is enabled. A role's permissions are available to members only while the role is enabled. This allows tighter enforcement of the principle of least privilege.

This paper presents an algorithm for mining hierarchical TRBAC policies. It is parameterized by a policy quality metric. We consider multiple policy quality metrics: number of roles, *weighted structural complexity* (WSC) [8], a generalization of syntactic policy size, *interpretability* (INT) [8,11], described briefly above, and a compound quality metric, denoted WSC-INT, that combines WSC and INT. Our algorithm is the first TRBAC policy mining algorithm that produces hierarchical policies, and the first that optimizes WSC or interpretability.

Our algorithm is based on Xu and Stoller's elimination algorithm for RBAC mining [11] and some aspects of Mitra *et al.*'s pioneering algorithm for mining flat TRBAC policies (i.e., policies without role hierarchy) with minimal number of roles [6,7], which inspired our work. Our algorithm has four phases: (1) produce a set of candidate roles, (2) merge candidate roles where possible, (3) organize the candidate roles into a role hierarchy, and (4) remove low-quality candidate roles. The generated policy is not guaranteed to have optimal quality. Fundamentally, this is because the problem of finding an optimal policy is NP-complete (this follows from NP-completeness of the untimed version of the problem ([8]).

To evaluate the algorithm, we created datasets based on real-world ACL policies from HP, described in [2] and used in several evaluations of role mining algorithms, e.g., [7,8,11]. We could simply extend the ACLs with temporal information to create a temporal user-permission assignment (TUPA), and then mine a TRBAC policy from the TUPA and attribute data. However, it would be hard to evaluate the algorithm's effectiveness, because there is nothing with which to compare the quality of the mined policies. Therefore, we adopt a similar methodology as Mitra *et al.* [7]. For each ACL policy, we mine an RBAC policy from the ACLs and synthetic attribute data using Xu and Stoller's elimination algorithm [11], pseudorandomly extend the RBAC policy with temporal information numerous times to obtain TRBAC policies, expand the TRBAC policies into equivalent TUPAs, mine a TRBAC policy from each TUPA and fixed attribute data, and compare the average quality of the resulting TRBAC policies with the quality of the original TRBAC policy, with the goal that the former is at least as good as the latter.

We created two datasets, using different temporal information when extending RBAC policies to obtain TRBAC policies. For the first dataset, we use simple periodic expressions, each of which is a range of hours that implicitly repeats every day. For the second dataset, we use more complex periodic expressions based on a hospital staffing schedule.

In experiments using number of roles as the policy quality metric, Mitra *et al.*'s algorithm, designed to minimize number of roles, produces 34 % more roles than our algorithm, on average. In experiments using WSC-INT as the policy quality metric, our algorithm succeeds in finding the implicit structure in the TUPA, producing policies with comparable (for the first dataset) or moderately higher (for the second dataset) WSC and better interpretability, on average, compared with the original TRBAC policy.

We explored the effect of different inheritance types on the quality of the mined policy and found that weakly restricted inheritance leads to policies with significantly better WSC and slightly better interpretability, on average. We experimentally evaluated the benefits of some design decisions and quantified the cost-quality trade-off provided by a parameter to our algorithm that limits the number of candidate roles.

2   Background on TRBAC

An *RBAC policy* is a tuple $\langle User, Perm, Role, UA, PA, RH \rangle$, where *User* is a set of users, *Perm* is a set of permissions, *Role* is a set of roles, $UA \subseteq U \times Role$ is the user-role assignment, $PA \subseteq Role \times Perm$ is the permission-role assignment, and $RH \subseteq Role \times Role$ is the role inheritance relation (also called the role hierarchy). Specifically, $\langle r, r' \rangle \in RH$ means that r is senior to r', hence all permissions of r' are also permissions of r, and all members of r are also members of r'. A role r' is *junior to* role r if rRH^+r', where RH^+ is the transitive closure of RH.

A *periodic expression* (PE) is a symbolic representation for an infinite set of time intervals. The formal definition of periodic expressions in [1,7] is standard and somewhat complicated; instead of repeating it, we give a brief intuitive version. A *calendar* is an infinite set of consecutive time intervals of the same duration; informally, it corresponds to a time unit, e.g., a day or an hour. A sequence of calendars $C_1, \ldots, C_n, C_d$ defines the sequence of time units used in a periodic expression, from larger to smaller. A periodic expression has the form $\sum_{k=1}^{n} O_k \cdot C_k \; \triangleright \; d \cdot C_d$ where $O_1 = all$, O_k is a set of natural numbers or the special value *all* for $2 \le k \le n$, and d is a natural number. The first part of a PE (before $\triangleright$) identifies the set of starting points of the intervals represented by the PE. The second part of the PE (after $\triangleright$) specifies the duration of each interval.

For example, consider the sequence of calendars Quadweeks, Weeks, Days, hours, where a Quadweek is four consecutive weeks—similar to a month, but with a uniform duration. The periodic expression $[all \cdot$ Quadweeks $+ \{1,3\} \cdot$ Weeks $+ \{1,2,3,4,5\} \cdot$ Days $+ \{10\} \cdot$ Hours $\triangleright 8 \cdot$ Hours$]$ represents the set of time intervals starting at 9am (the time intervals in each calendar are indexed starting with 1, so for Hours, 1 denotes the hour starting at midnight, 2 denotes the hour starting at 1am, etc.) and ending at 5pm (since duration is 8 h) of every weekday (assuming days of the week are indexed with 1 = Monday) during the first and third weeks of every quadweek.

A *bounded periodic expression* (BPE) is a tuple $\langle [begin, end], pe \rangle$, where *begin* and *end* are date-times, and *pe* is a periodic expression. A BPE represents the set of time intervals represented by *pe* except limited to the interval $[begin, end]$.

A *role enabling base* (REB) is a set of BPEs, representing the union of the sets of time intervals represented by the BPEs.

A *temporal RBAC (TRBAC) policy* is a tuple $\langle User, Perm, Role, UA, PA, RH, IT, REBA \rangle$, where the first six components are the same as for an RBAC policy, IT is the inheritance type (described below), and $REBA$ is the role enabling base assignment (REBA), which is a mapping from roles in $Role$ to REBs [1]. A role r is enabled during the set of time intervals represented by $REBA(r)$.

We consider two types of inheritance [5]. In both cases, a senior role r inherits permissions from each of its junior roles r'. With *weakly restricted inheritance*, denoted by $IT = WR$, a permission inherited from r' is available to members of r during the time intervals specified by $REBA(r)$. With *strongly restricted inheritance*, denoted by $IT = SR$, a permission inherited from r' is available to members of r during the time intervals specified by $REBA(r')$.

A *temporal user-permission assignment (TUPA)* is a set of triples of the form $\langle u, p, reb \rangle$, where u is a user, p is a permission, and reb is a REB (even though reb is not associated with a role, we call it a REB, because it has the same type as a REB). We refer to such a triple as an *entitlement triple*. Such a triple means that u has permission p during the set of time intervals represented by reb. A TUPA should contain at most one entitlement triple for each user-permission pair. A TUPA can therefore be regarded as a mapping from user-permission pairs to REBs.

The meaning of a role r in a TRBAC policy π, denoted $[\![r]\!]_\pi$, is a TUPA that expresses the entitlements granted by r, taking inheritance into account. The meaning $[\![\pi]\!]$ of a TRBAC policy π is a TUPA that expresses the entitlements granted by π.

3   The Relaxed TRBAC Policy Mining Problem

A *policy quality metric* is a function from TRBAC policies to a totally-ordered set, such as the natural numbers. The ordering is chosen so that small values indicate high quality.

Number of roles is a simplistic but traditional policy quality metric.

Weighted Structural Complexity (WSC) is a generalization of policy size [8]. We adapt WSC to TRBAC. For a TRBAC policy π of the above form, the WSC of π is defined by $\mathrm{WSC}(\pi) = w_1|Role| + w_2|UA| + w_3|PA| + w_4|RH| + w_5\mathrm{WSC}(REBA)$, where the w_i are user-specified weights, $|s|$ is the size (cardinality) of set s, and $\mathrm{WSC}(REBA)$ is the sum of the sizes of the REBs in $REBA$. The size of an REB is the sum of the sizes of the BPEs in it. The size of a BPE is the size of the PE in it (the beginning and ending date-times are always the same size, so we ignore them). The size of a PE is the sum of the sizes of the sets in it plus 1 for the duration, with the special value *all* counted as a set of size 1.

Interpretability is a policy quality metric that measures how well role membership can be characterized in terms of user attributes. *User-attribute data* is a tuple $\langle A, f \rangle$, where A is a set of attributes, and f is a function such that $f(u, a)$ is the value of attribute a for user u. An *attribute expression* e is a function from the set A of attributes to sets of values. A user u *satisfies* an attribute expression e iff $(\forall a \in A.\ f(u,a) \in e(a))$. For example, if $A = \{dept, level\}$, the function e with $e(dept) = \{CS\}$ and $e(level) = \{2,3\}$ is an attribute expression, which can be written with syntactic sugar as $dept \in \{CS\} \wedge level \in \{2,3\}$. We refer to the set $e(a)$ as the conjunct for attribute a. Let $\llbracket e \rrbracket$ denote the set of users that satisfy e. For an attribute expression e and a set U of users, the *mismatch* of e and U is defined by $\mathrm{mismatch}(e, U) = |\ \llbracket e \rrbracket \ominus U|$, where the symmetric difference of sets s_1 and s_2 is $s_1 \ominus s_2 = (s_1 \setminus s_2) \cup (s_2 \setminus s_1)$. The *attribute mismatch* of a role r, denoted $\mathrm{AM}(r)$, is $\min_{e \in E} \mathrm{mismatch}(e, \mathrm{asgndU}(r))$, where E is the set of all attribute expressions, and $\mathrm{asgndU}(r) = \{u \mid \langle u, r \rangle \in UA\}$. We define policy interpretability INT as the sum over roles of attribute mismatch, i.e., $\mathrm{INT}(\pi) = \sum_{r \in Role} \mathrm{AM}(r)$.

Compound policy quality metrics take multiple aspects of policy quality into account. We combine metrics by Cartesian product, with lexicographic ordering on the tuples. Let $\mathrm{WSC\text{-}INT}(\pi) = \langle \mathrm{WSC}(\pi), \mathrm{INT}(\pi) \rangle$.

A TRBAC policy π is *consistent* with a TUPA T if they grant the same permissions to the same users for the same sets of time intervals. When the given TUPA contains noise, it is desirable to weaken this requirement. A TRBAC policy π is ϵ-*consistent* with a TUPA T, where ϵ is a natural number, if they grant the same permissions to the same users for the same sets of time intervals, except that, for at most ϵ entitlement triples $\langle u, p, reb \rangle$ in T, the policy π either does not grant p to u or grants p to u at fewer times than reb [7]. Note that consistency is a special case of ϵ-consistency, corresponding to $\epsilon = 0$.

The *relaxed TRBAC policy mining problem* is: given a TUPA T and a policy quality metric Q_{pol} and a consistency threshold ϵ, find a TRBAC policy π that is ϵ-consistent with T and has the best quality, according to Q_{pol}, among policies ϵ-consistent with T. Note that auxiliary information used by the policy quality metric, e.g., user-attribute data, is implicitly considered to be part of Q_{pol} in this definition. Note that the temporal part of T strongly influences π, even using WSC with $w_5 = 0$, because it determines how entitlements can be grouped in roles.

Suggested role assignments for new users. The system can compute and store a best-fit attribute expression e_r for each role r, i.e., an attribute expression that minimizes the attribute mismatch for r. When a new user u is added, the system can suggest that u be made a member of the roles for which u satisfies the best-fit attribute expression, and it presents these suggested roles in descending order of the attribute mismatch.

4 TRBAC Policy Mining Algorithm

Inputs to the algorithm are the TUPA T, the type of inheritance IT to use in the generated policy, the consistency threshold ϵ, and the policy quality metric Q_{pol}. User attribute data, if available, is used only indirectly, *via* the policy quality metric, if it considers interpretability.

R_{init} = new Set()
for u in U
  for $\langle P, reb \rangle$ in permREB(u, T)
        $\cup$ permREB$^+(u, T)$
    addRole$(R_{\text{init}}, \{u\}, P, reb)$
    for bpe in reb
      addRole$(R_{\text{init}}, \{u\}, P, \{bpe\})$
 	
permREB$(u, T) =$
$\{\langle P, reb \rangle \mid (\exists p.\langle u, p, reb \rangle \in T)$
        $\wedge P = \{p \mid \langle u, p, reb \rangle \in T\}\}$
 	
permREB$^+(u, T) =$
$\{\langle P, reb \rangle \mid (\exists p.\langle u, p, reb \rangle \in T)$
        $\wedge P = \{p \mid \langle u, p, reb' \rangle \in T$
            $\wedge reb \sqsubseteq reb'\}\}$
	function addRole(R, U, P, reb)
	// *if there is an existing role with*
	// *permissions P and REB reb,*
	// *add users in U to it, otherwise*
	// *create a new role with users U,*
	// *permissions P, and REB reb.*
	if U, P, or reb is empty
	  return
	if $\exists\ r$ in R s.t. asgndP$_0(r) = P$
	               $\wedge$ REBA$(r) = reb$
	  asgndU$_0(r)$.addAll(U)
	else
	  r = new Role()
	  asgndP$_0(r) = P$
	  asgndU$_0(r) = U$
	  REBA$(r) = reb$
	  R.add(r)

Fig. 1. Phase 1.1: Generate initial roles. "s.t." abbreviates "such that".

Phase 1: Generate roles. Phase 1 generates initial roles and then creates additional candidate roles by intersecting sets of initial roles.

Phase 1.1: Generate initial roles. Pseudocode for generating initial roles appears in Fig. 1. The set of permissions P that each user u has for exactly the same REB reb are grouped to form the permissions of an initial role; this is the effect of using permREB in Fig. 1. If there are any permissions that u has for a REB that semantically contains reb, then we also create another role that has those permissions in addition to permissions in P; this is the effect of using permREB$^+$. In addition, for each BPE bpe in reb, we create an initial role with permissions P and with REB $\{bpe\}$. The algorithm uses a semantic containment relation $\sqsubseteq$ on PEs, BPEs, and REBs: $x_1 \sqsubseteq x_2$ iff the set of time instants represented by x_1 is a subset of the set of time instants represented by x_2.

Phase 1.2: Intersect roles. Phase 1.2 starts to construct a set R_{cand} of candidate roles, by adding to R_{cand} all of the initial roles in R_{init} and all non-empty intersections of all subsets of the initial roles. In other words, for each subset of initial roles, if the intersection of their permission sets is a non-empty set P, and the intersection of their REBs is a non-empty REB reb, then create a candidate role with permissions P, REB reb, and the union of their user sets. REBs are intersected semantically, not syntactically; for example, if reb_1 represents 9am–5pm on Mondays and Wednesdays, and reb_2 represents 1pm–2pm on Mondays and Fridays, then their intersection is a REB that represents 1pm–2pm on Mondays. This phase is similar to role intersection in CompleteMiner [10] and the elimination algorithm [11].

This phase is expensive for large datasets. We use two techniques to reduce the cost when necessary; they provide a trade-off between cost and policy quality. (1) Compute intersections for all pairs (instead of all subsets) of initial roles, as in FastMiner [10]. This reduces the worst-case complexity of this step and the overall algorithm from exponential to quadratic. (2) Compute intersections involving only the largest roles, specifically, roles whose relative size is in the top RIC (mnemonic for "role intersection cutoff"), where $0 \leq RIC \leq 1$. For example, $RIC = 0.3$ means that intersections are computed among roles whose size is in the top 30 %. Role size is quantified as covEntit(r), defined below.

Phase 2: Merge roles. Phase 2 merges candidate roles to produce a revised set of candidate roles. We use three types of merges. (1) If candidate roles r and r' have the same set of users U and the same REB *reb*, then they are replaced with a new role with users U, permissions asgndP$_0$(r) $\cup$ asgndP$_0$(r'), and REB *reb*. (2) If candidate roles r and r' have the same users U and same permissions P, then they are replaced with a new role with users U, permissions P, and REB $reb(r) \sqcup reb(r')$. The function $\sqcup$ denotes semantic union of REBs; in other words, $reb_1 \sqcup reb_2$ is a REB that represents the set of time instants represented by reb_1 or reb_2. We distinguish two sub-cases. (2a) If reb_1 and reb_2 represent disjoint sets of time intervals, then $reb_1 \sqcup reb_2$ is simply $reb_1 \cup reb_2$. (2b) If reb_1 and reb_2 represent sets of overlapping or consecutive time intervals, then BPEs in them are merged, if possible, to simplify the result. For example, if reb_1 represents 9am-noon on weekdays, and reb_2 denotes noon-5pm on weekdays, then $reb_1 \sqcup reb_2$ contains a single BPE denoting 9am–5pm on weekdays.

Phase 3: Construct role hierarchy. Phase 3 organizes the candidate roles into a role hierarchy with full inheritance. A TRBAC policy has *full inheritance* if every two roles that can be related by the inheritance relation are related by it, i.e., $\forall r, r' \in R.\ [\![r]\!]_\pi \supseteq [\![r']\!]_\pi \Rightarrow \langle r, r' \rangle \in RH^*$. Guo *et al.* call this property *completeness* in the context of RBAC [3].

Phase 3.1: Compute inheritance. Phase 3.1 determines inheritance relationships between candidate roles, based on the requirement of full inheritance. Function isAncestorFullInher(r', r) tests whether r' is an ancestor of r with full inheritance; if $IT = WR$, the function avoids inheritance relationships that would lead to cycles in the role hierarchy.

isAncestorFullInher(r', r) =
  asgndP$_0$(r') $\subseteq$ asgndP$_0$(r) $\wedge$ asgndU$_0$(r) $\subseteq$ asgndU$_0$(r')
  $\wedge\ (IT = SR \Rightarrow REBA(r') \sqsubseteq REBA(r))$
  $\wedge\ (IT = WR \Rightarrow \neg(\text{asgndP}_0(r) \subset \text{asgndP}_0(r') \wedge \text{asgndU}_0(r') \subset \text{asgndU}_0(r)))$

This function is called for every pair of candidate roles. If isAncestorFullInher(r', r) is true, and there is no intervening role $\bar{r}$ such that isAncestorFullInher($r', \bar{r}$) isAncestorFullInher($\bar{r}, r$), then r' is a parent of r. This phase produces maps *parents* and *children*, such that *parents*(r) and *children*(r) are the sets of parents and children of r, respectively.

Phase 3.2: Compute assigned users and permissions. Phase 3.2 computes the directly assigned users asgndU(r) and directly assigned permissions asgndP(r) of each role r, by removing inherited users and permissions from the role's originally assigned users asgndU$_0(r)$ and originally assigned permissions asgndP$_0(r)$.

Phase 4: Remove roles. Phase 4 removes roles from the candidate role hierarchy if the removal preserves ϵ-consistency with the given ACL policy and improves policy quality. When a role r is removed, the role hierarchy is adjusted to preserve inheritance relations between parents and children of r, and the sets of directly assigned users and permissions of other roles are expanded to contain users and permissions that they previously inherited from r.

The order in which roles are considered for removal affects the final result. We control this ordering with a *role quality metric* Q_{role}, which maps roles to an ordered set, with the interpretation that large values denote high quality (note: this is opposite to the interpretation of the ordering for policy quality metrics). Low-quality roles are considered for removal first. We use a role quality metric that is a temporal variant of the role quality metric in [11] that gave the best results in their experiments. Specifically, $Q_{role}(r) = \langle \text{redun}(r), \text{clsSz}(r) \rangle$, where redun$(r)$ and clsSz(r) are defined next, and the ordering on these tuples is lexicographic order.

The *redundancy* of a role r measures how many other roles also cover the entitlement triples covered by r. We say that a role r *covers* an entitlement triple t if $t \in [\![r]\!]_\pi$. Removing a role with higher redundancy is less likely to prevent subsequent removal of other roles, so we eliminate roles with higher redundancy first. The redundancy of role r, denoted redun(r), is the negative of the minimum, over entitlement triples $\langle u, p, reb \rangle$ covered by r, of the number of removable roles that cover $\langle u, p, reb \rangle$ (we take the negative so that roles with more redundancy have lower quality). A role is *removable* in policy π, denoted removable(r) (the policy is an implicit argument), if the policy obtained by removing r is ϵ-consistent with T.

The *clustered size* of a role r measures how many entitlements are covered by r and how well they are clustered. A first attempt at formulating this metric (ignoring clustering) might be as the fraction of entitlement triples in T that are covered by r. As discussed in [11], it is better for the covered entitlement triples to be "clustered" on (i.e., associated with) fewer users rather than being spread across many users. The clustered size of r is defined to equal the fraction of the entitlements of r's members that are covered by r. In the temporal case, each entitlement triple $\langle u, p, reb \rangle$ is weighted by the fraction of the time represented reb that is covered by $REBA(r)$.

$$\text{covEntit}(r) = \sum_{\substack{u \in \text{asgndU}(r) \\ p \in \text{asgndP}(r)}} \frac{\text{dur}(REBA(r))}{\text{dur}(T(u,p))} \qquad \text{clsSz}(r) = \frac{\text{covEntit}(r)}{|\text{entitlements}(\text{asgndU}(r), T)|}$$

where $T(u, p)$ is the REB reb such that $\langle u, p, reb \rangle \in T$, dur$(reb)$ is the fraction of one time unit in calendar C_1 that is covered by reb, and entitlements(U, T) is the set of entitlement triples in T for a user in U. For example, if the sequence of calendars is $C_1 = \text{Year}, \ldots, C_n = \text{Hour}, C_d = \text{Hour}$, and reb is 9am–5pm every day, then $\text{dur}(reb) = 1/3$, since reb covers $1/3$ of the time in a year.

Our algorithm may remove a role even if the removal worsens policy quality slightly. Specifically, we introduce a *quality change tolerance* δ, with $\delta \geq 1$, and we remove a role if the quality Q' of the RBAC policy resulting from the removal is related to the quality Q of the current RBAC policy by $Q' < \delta Q$ (recall that, for policy quality metrics, smaller values are better). Choosing $\delta > 1$ partially compensates for the fact that a purely greedy approach to policy quality improvement is not an optimal strategy.

Pseudocode for removing roles appears in Fig. 2. It repeatedly tries to remove all removable roles, until none of the attempted removals succeeds in improving the policy quality. The policy π is an implicit argument to auxiliary functions such as removeRole and addRole. Function addRole(r) adds role r to the candidate role hierarchy: inheritance relations involving r are added, and the assigned users and assigned permissions of r's newly acquired ancestors and descendants are adjusted by removing inherited users and permissions. Removing a role r and then restoring r using addRole leaves the policy unchanged.

The following auxiliary functions are used in removeRole. isDescendant(r,r') holds if r is a descendant of r', as determined by following the parent-child relations in the *children* map. The set of authorized users of r, denoted authU(r), is the set of users in asgndU(r) or asgndU(r') for some r' senior to r; this is the same as in RBAC. The notion of authorized permissions must be defined differently in TRBAC than RBAC, because, with strongly-restricted inheritance, the inherited permissions of a role r may be associated with REBs different than $REBA(r)$. With strongly-restricted inheritance, the set of authorized permissions of r, denoted authP(r), is the set of permission-REB pairs $\langle p, reb \rangle$ such that (1) each directly assigned permission of r is paired with $REBA(r)$ and (2) each permission p inherited by r is paired with the semantic union of the REBs of the junior roles from which it is inherited. With weakly-restricted inheritance, authP(r) is the set of permission-REB pairs $\langle p, REBA(r) \rangle$ such that p is in asgndP(r) or asgndP(r') for some r' junior to r; we use a set of pairs for uniformity with the case of strongly-restricted inheritance.

5 Datasets

Our datasets are based on real-world ACL policies from HP, described in [2], and the high-fit synthetic attribute data for these ACL policies described in [11]; see those references for general information about the policies. As outlined in Sect. 1, for each ACL policy, we mine an RBAC policy from the ACLs and the attribute data using Xu and Stoller's elimination algorithm [11], and pseudo-randomly extend the RBAC policy with temporal information several times to obtain TRBAC policies. For each ACL policy except americas_small, we create 30 TRBAC policies. For americas_small, which is larger, we create only 10 TRBAC policies, to reduce the running time of the experiments. We extend the RBAC policies in two ways, using different temporal information.

π = policy from Phase 3
$q = Q_{pol}(\pi)$
$workL$ = list of removable roles in π
$changed$ = true
while $\neg$empty($workL$) $\wedge$ $changed$
  sort $workL$ in ascending order by Q_{role}
  $changed$ = false
  for r in $workL$
   removeRole(r)
   // if ϵ-consistency is violated,
   // restore r.
   if $|T \setminus [\![\pi]\!]| > \epsilon$
    addRole(r)
    $workL$.remove(r)
   else
    // if policy quality improved,
    // keep the change.
    if $Q_{pol}(\pi) < \delta q$
     $changed$ = true
     $q = Q_{pol}(\pi)$
     $workL$.remove(r)
    else
     // undo the change, i.e., restore r
     addRole(r)
	function removeRole(r)
	for *parent* in *parents*(r)
	  // remove r from its parents
	  children(*parent*).remove(r)
	  for *child* in *children*(r)
	   // if child is not a descendant of parent
	   // after removing r, add an inheritance
	   // edge between child and parent.
	   if $\neg$ isDescendant(*child*,*parent*)
	    children(*parent*).add(*child*)
	    parents(*child*).add(parent)
	  for u in asgndU(r)
	   // if u is not authorized to parent after
	   // removing r, add u to assigned users
	   // of parent.
	  if $u \notin$ authU(*parent*)
	    asgndU(*parent*).add(u)
	  for *child* in *children*(r)
	   parents(*child*).remove(r)
	   for p in asgndP(r)
	    // if p is not fully authorized to child
	    // after removing r, add p to assigned
	    // permissions of child.
	    if $\langle r, REBA(child) \rangle \neg \in$ authP(*child*)
	     asgndP(*child*).add(p)
	R_{cand}.remove(r)

Fig. 2. Phase 4: Remove roles.

Dataset with simple PEs. A *simple PE* is a range of hours (e.g., 9am–5pm) that implicitly repeats every day. This dataset uses the same simple PEs as in [7], namely, [6, 11], [7, 10], [8, 9], [8, 11], [9, 11], [10, 11], [10, 12], [11, 13], [14, 15], [16, 17]. These PEs are designed to cover various relationships between intervals, such as overlapping, consecutive, disjoint, and nested. We choose the number of PEs in each REB pseudorandomly using a similar probability distribution as in [7], namely, $pr(1) = 0.78, pr(2) = 0.2, pr(3) = 0.02$. We choose the specific PEs in each REB pseudorandomly using a uniform distribution.

Dataset with complex PEs. For this dataset, we use periodic expressions based on a hospital staffing schedule, based on discussions with the Director of Timekeeping at Stony Brook University Hospital. The periodic expressions are not taken directly from the hospital's staffing schedule, but they reflect its general nature. The schedule does not repeat every week, but rather every few weeks, because weekend duty rotates. Clinicians may work 3 days/week for 12 hours/day starting at 7am or 7pm, or 5 days/week for 8.5 hours/day starting at 7am, 3pm, or 11pm. We create two instances of each of these five types of work schedules, by pseudorandomly choosing the appropriate number of days of the week in each of

the four weeks of a Quadweek. Each REB is based on exactly one of the resulting 10 work schedules. Multiple PEs are needed to represent work schedules
that wrap around calendar units; for example, a 7pm–7am shift is represented
using two PEs, with time intervals 7pm-midnight and midnight-7am. The PEs
are based on the following sequence of calendars: C_1=Quadweeks, C_2=Days,
C_3=Hours, C_d=Hours. The days in a Quadweek are numbered 1..28. Including
Week in the sequence of calendars is not helpful, because most workers' schedules
do not repeat on a weekly basis.

6   Evaluation

The experimental methodology is outlined in Sect. 1. All experiments use quality
change tolerance $\delta = 1.001$ (this value gave the best results for the experiments
in [11]), $\epsilon = 0$, All and $w_i = 1$ for all weights in WSC. The policy quality metric is
WSC-INT, and the inheritance type is weakly restricted, except where specified
otherwise.

Our Java code, datasets, and an extended version of the paper are available
at www.cs.stonybrook.edu/stoller/policy-mining/. Periodic expressions are an
abstract data type with two implementations: (1) simple PEs, as defined in
Sect. 5, and implemented as pairs of integers, and (2) (general) PEs, as defined in
Sect. 2, and implemented as arrays of arrays of integers. These implementations
are used in the experiments in Sects. 6.1 and 6.2, respectively. Running times
include the cost of an end-to-end correctness check that checks equivalence of
the input TUPA and the meaning of the mined TRBAC policy; the average
cost is about 7 % of the running time. The experiments were run on a Lenovo
IdeaCentre K430 with a 3.4 GHz Intel Core i7-3770 CPU.

6.1   Experiments Using Dataset with Simple PEs

In experiments on this dataset, role intersection is configured to use FastMiner
for emea and americas_small, CompleteMiner for the other policies, and RIC = 1
for all policies.

Comparison of original and mined policies. Fig. 3 shows detailed results from
experiments on this dataset. In the column headings, μ is mean, σ is standard deviation, CI is half-width of 95 % confidence interval using Student's t-
distribution, and time is the average running time in minutes:seconds. There is
no standard deviation column for INT, because interpretability is unaffected by
the REBA and is the same for all TRBAC policies generated by extending the
same RBAC policy. Ignore the last 2 columns for now. The averages and standard deviations are computed over the TRBAC policies created by extending
each RBAC policy. The WSC of the mined TRBAC policy ranges from about
1 % lower (for apj) to about 11 % higher (for domino) than the WSC of the original TRBAC policy. The interpretability of the mined policy ranges from about
35 % lower (for firewall-2) to about 1 % higher (for apj) than the interpretability

Dataset	Original Policy			Mined Policy						Time	Avg $|R|$	
	WSC		INT	WSC			INT				OurAlg	Mitra+
	μ	σ		μ	σ	CI	μ	σ	CI	μ		
americas_small	6975	7.5	189	7100	78	29	140	7	2.5	58:56	297	
apj	4879	10.0	385	4826	22	8.1	388	3.5	1.2	1:04	468	527
domino	449	2.5	23	499	70	26	20	1.5	0.57	0:02	30	40
emea	3929	4.4	32	4038	68	25	32	0.2	0.07	0:49	100	115
firewall1	1533	4.1	48	1653	58	22	44	3.7	1.4	1:45	97	130
firewall2	960	1.4	7	966	9.2	3.4	5	1.0	0.38	0:02	12	17
healthcare	168	1.4	14	168	3.9	1.5	14	0.42	0.16	0:01	15	25

Fig. 3. Results of experiments with simple PEs.

of the original TRBAC policy. On average over the seven policies, the WSC is 3 % higher, and the interpretability is 12 % lower. Thus, our algorithm succeeds in finding the implicit structure in the TUPA and producing a policy with comparable WSC and better interpretability, on average, than the original TRBAC policy.

Comparison of inheritance types. We ran our algorithm again on the same dataset, specifying strongly restricted inheritance for the mined policies. This caused a significant increase in the WSC of the mined policies. The percentage increase averages 67 % and ranges from 15 % for apj to 140 % for firewall-1. Intuitively, the reason for the increase is that, with strongly restricted inheritance, the temporal information associated with directly assigned and inherited permissions may be different, and this may prevent removing inherited permissions from a role's directly assigned permissions. Inheritance type has less effect on the average INT, increasing (worsening) it by about 9 % on average, excluding the outlier firewall-2, for which the average INT decreases from 4 to 1.

Evaluation of choice of initial roles. We evaluated two ways of reducing the cost of the algorithm by creating fewer initial roles. (1) We modified Phase 1.1 to create fewer initial roles by removing the use of permREB+ in Fig. 1. Note that Mitra et al.'s algorithm does not use an analogue of permREB+. This change increased the average WSC by 36 % on average over the policies used in this experiment (all except emea and americas_small, which were omitted because of their longer running time), ranging from 13 % for apj to 69 % for healthcare. It increased (worsened) the average INT by 37 % on average over those policies, ranging from 9 % for apj to 67 % for domino. (2) We modified Phase 1.1 to create fewer initial roles by removing the first call to addRole. Note that Mitra et al.'s algorithm does not include an analogue of this call. This change increased the average WSC by 8 % on average over the policies used in this experiment (all except emea and americas_small), ranging from 7 % for domino and firewall-2 to 9 % for apj. It increased (worsened) the average INT by 7 % on average over those policies, ranging from 0 % for firewall-2 to 11 % for domino.

Comparison with Mitra et al.'s algorithm. We ran Mitra *et al.*'s algorithm [7], and our algorithm with number of roles as policy quality metric (because Mitra *et al.* use this metric), on our dataset with simple PEs. Their code supports only simple PEs, so we used only the simple PE dataset in the comparison. Their code, implemented in C, gave an error ("malloc: ...: pointer being freed was not allocated") on some TRBAC policies generated for emea and firewall-1; we ignored those results. Their code did not run correctly on americas_small, so we omitted it from this comparison.

The last two columns of Fig. 3 show the numbers of roles generated by the two algorithms. Standard deviations are omitted to save space but are small: on average, 3 % of the mean, for both algorithms. Mitra *et al.*'s algorithm produces 34 % more roles than ours, on average. Our algorithm produces hierarchical policies, and their algorithm produces flat policies, but this does not affect the number of roles. There are many other differences between the algorithms, discussed in Sect. 7, which contribute to the difference in results. The above paragraph on evaluation of choice of initial roles describes two experiments that explore differences between our algorithm and Mitra *et al.*'s and quantify the benefit of those differences. The effects of some other differences between our algorithms, such as the use of elimination *vs.* selection in Phase 4, were investigated in the untimed case in [11] and likely have a similar impact here.

6.2   Experiments Using Dataset with Complex PEs

In experiments on this dataset, role intersection is configured to use CompleteMiner for firewall2 and FastMiner for the other policies.

Comparison of original and mined policies. Fig. 4 shows detailed results from experiments on this dataset. The original TRBAC policies here have higher WSC than the ones in Sect. 6.1, because complex PEs have higher WSC than simple PEs. For apj, emea, and firewall1, we created 5 TRBAC policies (instead of 30) from each, to reduce the running time of the experiments. The WSC of the mined TRBAC policy ranges from about 2 % higher (for firewall2) to about 57 % higher (for firewall1) than the WSC of the original TRBAC policy. The interpretability of the mined TRBAC policy ranges from about 34 % lower (for healthcare) to about 2 % higher (for apj) than the interpretability of the original TRBAC policy. On average over the six policies, the WSC is 20 % higher, and the interpretability is 16 % lower. Thus, our algorithm finds most of the implicit structure in the TUPA and produces a policy with moderately higher WSC and better interpretability, on average, than the original TRBAC policy. The results can be improved by using larger RIC, at the expense of higher running time.

The higher running times, compared to the dataset with simple PEs, are due primarily to the larger number of candidate roles created by role intersection (there are more overlaps between REBs in this dataset), and secondarily to the larger overhead of manipulating more complex PEs.

Dataset	Original Policy			Mined Policy						RIC	Time
	WSC		INT	WSC			INT				
	μ	σ		μ	σ	CI	μ	σ	CI		μ
apj	16836	159	385	17434	337	419	391	1.9	2.3	0.7	50:43
domino	1156	49	23	1278	80	30	16	1.8	0.7	1	0:35
emea	5975	99	32	8683	284	353	32	0	0	0.7	201:10
firewall1	3712	97	48	5832	199	247	46	2.2	2.8	0.7	165:30
firewall2	1269	37	7	1291	52	19	5.3	0.68	0.3	1	1:00
healthcare	560	35	14	582	40	15	9.3	1.7	0.6	1	8:57

Fig. 4. Results of experiments with complex PEs.

Benefit of general PEs. PEs can be translated into sets of simple PEs. For example, the REB $\{[all \cdot \text{Weeks} + \{1,2,7\} \cdot \text{Days} + \{1\} \cdot \text{Hours} \rhd 8 \cdot \text{Hours}]\}$ can be translated to the REB $\{[1,9], [25,33], [145,153]\}$. However, PEs are generally more compact and efficient. In experiments with the healthcare policy, using this translation and simple PEs was about 19x slower than using general PEs.

Effect of role-intersection cutoff. We investigated the cost-benefit trade-off when varying the role-intersection cutoff RIC. Figure 5 shows running time and WSC as functions of RIC, averaged over three of the smaller policies (domino, firewall2, healthcare). The trade-off is favorable: as RIC decreases, running time decreases more rapidly than WSC increases. For example, at RIC = 0.8, running time is 40 % lower than with RIC = 1, and WSC is only 13 % higher.

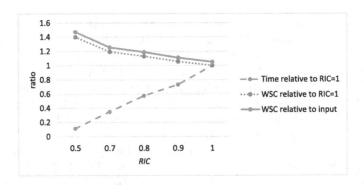

Fig. 5. Relative running time and relative WSC as functions of RIC. (Color figure online)

7 Related Work

We discuss related work on TRBAC policy mining and then related work on RBAC mining. Role mining (for RBAC or TRBAC) is also reminiscent of some other data mining problems, but algorithms for those other problems are not well suited to role mining. For example, association rule mining algorithms are designed to find rules that are probabilistic in nature. They are not designed to produce a set of rules strictly consistent with the input that completely covers the input and is minimum-sized among such sets of rules.

7.1 Related Work on TRBAC Policy Mining

Mitra *et al.* define a version of the TRBAC policy mining problem and present an algorithm for mining a TRBAC policy from a TUPA [7]. It is an improved version of their earlier work [6].

Our algorithm is more flexible, because it can optimize a variety of metrics, including WSC and interpretability. Their algorithm is designed to optimize only the number of roles. The importance of interpretability is discussed in Sect. 1. WSC is a more general measure of policy size than number of roles and can more accurately reflect expected administrative cost. For example, the average number of role assignments per user is a measure of expected administrative effort for adding a new user [9], and this can be reflected in WSC by giving appropriate weight to the size of the user-role assignment.

Our algorithm produces hierarchical TRBAC policies. Their algorithm produces flat TRBAC policies. Role hierarchy is a well-known feature of RBAC that can significantly reduce policy size and administrative effort by avoiding redundancy in the policy.

Some other differences are: (1) Our algorithm determines which candidate roles to include in the final policy by elimination of low-quality roles, instead of selection of high-quality roles. We showed that elimination gives better results in the untimed case [11]. (2) Our algorithm creates more initial roles than theirs. The benefit of creating these additional initial roles is shown in Sect. 6.1 in the paragraph on evaluation of choice of initial roles. Their algorithm creates unit roles, which are similar to initial roles but have only one permission; our algorithm does not create unit roles. (3) Our algorithm performs fewer types of role intersections than theirs. Specifically, it omits types of role intersections that create PEs with time intervals that do not appear in the input, since these PEs are probably not natural (intuitive) ones in the application domain.

Our implementation supports periodic expressions for specifying temporal information, while theirs supports only ranges of hours that implicitly repeat every day. Design and implementation of operations on sets of PEs is non-trivial.

7.2 Related Work on RBAC Mining

A survey of work on RBAC mining appears in [4]. The most closely related work is Xu and Stoller's elimination algorithm [11]. We chose it as the starting point for design of our algorithm, because in the experiments in [11], it optimizes WSC more effectively than Hierarchical Miner [8], while simultaneously achieving good interpretability, and it optimizes WSCA, an interpretability metric defined in [8], more effectively than Attribute Miner [8].

Our algorithm retains the overall structure of the elimination algorithm but differs in several ways, due to the complexities created by considering time. Our algorithm introduces more kinds of candidate roles than the elimination algorithm, because it needs to consider grouping permissions that are enabled for the same time or a subset of the time of other permissions. Our algorithm attempts to merge candidate roles; the elimination algorithm does not. Construction of the role hierarchy is significantly more complicated than in the elimination algorithm; for example, with strongly restricted inheritance, a permission p can be inherited by a role r from multiple junior roles with different REBs, which may together cover all or only part of the time that p is available in r. This also complicates adjustment of the role hierarchy when removing candidate roles. The role quality metric used to select roles for removal is more complicated, to give preference to roles that cover permissions for more times.

Acknowledgements. We thank the authors of [7]—Barsha Mitra, Shamik Sural, Vijayalakshmi Atluri, and Jaideep Vaidya—for sharing their code and datasets with us and helping us understand their work.

References

1. Bertino, E., Bonatti, P.A., Ferrari, E.: TRBAC: A temporal role-based access control model. ACM Trans. Inf. Syst. Secur. **4**(3), 191–233 (2001)
2. Ene, A., Horne, W.G., Milosavljevic, N., Rao, P., Schreiber, R., Tarjan, R.E.: Fast exact and heuristic methods for role minimization problems. In: Proceedings of the 13th ACM Symposium on Access Control Models and Technologies (SACMAT), pp. 1–10. ACM (2008)
3. Guo, Q., Vaidya, J., Atluri, V.: The role hierarchy mining problem: discovery of optimal role hierarchies. In: Proceedings of the 2008 Annual Computer Security Applications Conference (ACSAC), pp. 237–246. IEEE Computer Society (2008)
4. Hachana, S., Cuppens-Boulahia, N., Cuppens, F.: Role mining to assist authorization governance: how far have we gone? Int. J. Secure Softw. Eng. **3**(4), 45–64 (2012)
5. Joshi, J.B.D., Bertino, E., Ghafoor, A.: Temporal hierarchies and inheritance semantics for GTRBAC. In: Proceedings of the Seventh ACM Symposium on Access Control Models and Technologies, pp. 74–83. ACM (2002)
6. Mitra, B., Sural, S., Atluri, V., Vaidya, J.: Toward mining of temporal roles. In: Wang, L., Shafiq, B. (eds.) DBSec 2013. LNCS, vol. 7964, pp. 65–80. Springer, Heidelberg (2013)
7. Mitra, B., Sural, S., Atluri, V., Vaidya, J.: The generalized temporal role mining problem. J. Comput. Secur. **23**(1), 31–58 (2015)
8. Molloy, I., Chen, H., Li, T., Wang, Q., Li, N., Bertino, E., Calo, S.B., Lobo, J.: Mining roles with multiple objectives. ACM Trans. Inf. Syst. Secur. **13**(4), 36:1–36:35 (2010)
9. Uzun, E., Lorenzi, D., Atluri, V., Vaidya, J., Sural, S.: Migrating from DAC to RBAC. In: Samarati, P. (ed.) DBSec 2015. LNCS, vol. 9149, pp. 69–84. Springer, Heidelberg (2015)

10. Vaidya, J., Atluri, V., Warner, J.: RoleMiner: mining roles using subset enumeration. In: Proceedings of the 13th ACM Conference on Computer and Communications Security (CCS), pp. 144–153. ACM (2006)
11. Xu, Z., Stoller, S.D.: Algorithms for mining meaningful roles. In: Proceedings of the 17th ACM Symposium on Access Control Models and Technologies (SACMAT), pp. 57–66. ACM (2012)

Inter-ReBAC: Inter-operation of Relationship-Based Access Control Model Instances

Jason Crampton and James Sellwood[✉]

Royal Holloway University of London, Egham, UK
jason.crampton@rhul.ac.uk, james.sellwood.2010@live.rhul.ac.uk

Abstract. Relationship-based access control (ReBAC) models define authorization policies and make authorization decisions on the basis of relationships between the entities in a system. We present a framework through which multiple ReBAC model instances can interoperate so that requests initiated in one system may target resources in a second system. Further, our framework is able to support requests passing through a chain of inter-connected systems, thus enabling many systems to be connected together or a single large system to be decomposed into numerous component subsystems. Whilst the underlying principles of this framework can be applied to any ReBAC model, we introduce its formal application to our RPPM model [3], the first, and most actively developing, general computing ReBAC model.

Keywords: Access control · Path condition · Relationship · Principal matching · Policy graph · Principal activation · Authorization · Secure inter-operation

1 Introduction

Access control is a fundamental security service, employed within a system to manage the interaction between (user) processes and (system-protected) resources. Historically, access control in general-purpose computing systems has used discretionary and role-based access control (RBAC) models. Recent work on *relationship-based access control* (ReBAC), inspired originally by social networks [1,2,6], has shown that alternatives are viable for both specialist and general computing applications [4,5,8]. In ReBAC, the specification and evaluation of authorization policies is based on the relationships which exist between entities of a system. The use of paths of relationships has several advantages over roles, not least because they can naturally reflect the more complex, context-specific nature of human interaction which otherwise requires the use of many, highly parameterized, roles [3].

Whilst the consideration of paths of relationships is key to request evaluation in any ReBAC model, different models support varying capabilities and

© IFIP International Federation for Information Processing 2016
Published by Springer International Publishing Switzerland 2016. All Rights Reserved
S. Ranise and V. Swarup (Eds.): DBSec 2016, LNCS 9766, pp. 96–105, 2016.
DOI: 10.1007/978-3-319-41483-6_7

constructs for representing and processing these relationships. However, the relationships between entities in the modelled system are, intuitively, always represented as an edge-labelled graph. Such system graphs indicate the scope of a model instance; the system's entities (vertices in the graph), relationships (labelled edges), and policies are bounded by the graph and the system's authorization requests are evaluated within it. Whilst a system is modelled by a single ReBAC model instance (and therefore by a single graph), there are several motivating situations in which multiple model instances may need to interact.

Firstly, systems are frequently connected together in order to support a wider range of services. In such cases, a subject in one system may request to perform an action on an object in a remote system. Currently such requests cannot be supported in ReBAC models unless a single "super-graph"[1] model captures every entity and relationship within the two, and all intermediary, systems. This requires global policies, outside of the "authority" of any one component system, putting at risk the autonomy of all. The inter-connection of discrete autonomous subgraphs is, therefore, desirable. Secondly, ReBAC models containing very large system graphs (stand-alone, or super-graph as just discussed) will be impacted by the fact that request evaluation in such models has a time complexity linked to the number of nodes in the graph, whether they are relevant to the request being evaluated or not. It is, therefore, desirable to decompose such very large system graphs into smaller discrete autonomous subgraphs. Whilst request evaluation complexity in each of these subgraphs will still be linked to the number of nodes, the practical complexity is expected to be greatly reduced as many requests will only involve a subset of subgraphs (assuming appropriate routing is available).

We, therefore, develop a framework by which two ReBAC system graphs may be connected and requests initiated in one may be authorized in the other. We introduce a formal application of this framework in RPPM, as we believe RPPM is naturally suited to this task. It supports the modelling of general computing environments, to which inter-operation is highly relevant. Further, its two step request evaluation process and use of security principals provide a natural "break point" at which a request may be transferred from one system to another (particularly when employing graph-based policies). RPPM provides a convenient basis for combining paths from multiple graphs without searching end-to-end across the, potentially numerous, inter-connected system graphs.

Due to space limitations we do not provide a review of the operation of stand-alone RPPM instances; this background can be found in [3,4]. Section 2 introduces the Inter-RPPM framework as a specific example of our ReBAC inter-operation approach. Section 3 describes its request evaluation process. In Sect. 4 we discuss related work and in Sect. 5 we draw conclusions. The Appendix contains pseudocode for three algorithms required to support Sect. 3.

---

[1] We use the term super-graph to identify a large system graph which models multiple systems which might otherwise be modelled by distinct stand-alone system graphs.

2   Inter-RPPM

The goal of our inter-operation framework is to connect distinct and autonomous system graphs in such a way that we are not required to define and evaluate relationship paths traversing a single super-graph. We, therefore, introduce an inter-operation framework which maintains the autonomy of individual system graphs by preserving their individual request evaluation scopes, system models and policies. In order to provide connectivity between system graphs, a construct external to the system graphs is required. We, therefore, introduce the concept of a *bridged system group* and employ bridging relationships[2], called *bridges*, between *hub* entities within distinct component system graphs. A request to access a remote resource will need to be evaluated by a sequence of RPPM systems. Bridges provide the link through which we propagate information about the outcome of each system's "local" request evaluation to the next system in the sequence; where it subsequently informs another local evaluation.

We employ a hierarchical dot notation to label elements: that is $G.v$ and $G'.v$ represent different nodes (with the same label v) when G and G' are distinct system graphs.[3] When all of the elements of a tuple, such as (v, v', r), belong to the same system graph G, we will write $G.(v, v', r)$ to simplify notation.

Definition 1. *Let* $\mathcal{G} = \{G_1 = (V_1, E_1), \ldots, G_n = (V_n, E_n)\}$ *be a set of system graphs. A* bridge *is an edge of the form* $(G_i.v, G_j.v, \textsf{bridge-to})$ *such that* $G_i \neq G_j$. *A* bridged system group *is a pair* $(\mathcal{G}, \beta)$, *where* β *is a set of bridges.*

Informally, a bridged system group comprises two or more RPPM model instances whose system graphs are connected by one or more bridges. Each bridge connects two hub entities; one each from two distinct component system graphs. We illustrate this framework with a simple example which we construct from two, initially disconnected, model instances, identified by their system graphs $G_1 = (V_1, E_1)$ and $G_2 = (V_2, E_2)$, shown schematically in Fig. 1a.

In Fig. 1b we illustrate the inter-connection of G_1 and G_2 through the bridge $(G_1.h, G_2.h', \textsf{bridge-to})$ and develop the example further in Fig. 1c to incorporate three system graphs inter-connected via six bridges.[4] Bridges are directed – $(G_1.h', G_3.h', \textsf{bridge-to})$ connects $G_1.h'$ to $G_3.h'$, but not vice versa – and are represented by an arrow. However, there may also exist a bridge $(G_3.h', G_1.h', \textsf{bridge-to})$ in which case we will use a double-headed arrow to represent the pair of bridges between $G_1.h'$ and $G_3.h'$.

Any bridged system group defines inter-system paths, obtained by traversing the bridges. A *system graph sequence* defines the sequence of system graphs along

---

[2] We require an extra-model administrator to be responsible for the management of these bridging relationships.

[3] Where there is no ambiguity through context or element naming we continue to leave out the prefix for convenience and clarity. So we do not prefix V_1 and E_1 in $G_1 = (V_1, E_1)$, for example.

[4] Note that the example of Fig. 1c could equally represent three distinct system graphs which have been connected together, or a large stand-alone system graph which has been decomposed into three subsystems.

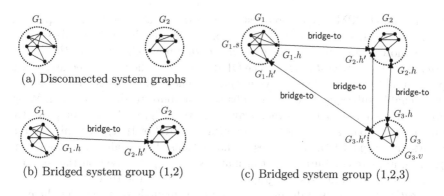

Fig. 1. Bridged system group examples

such a path, where no system graph may be repeated and the directionality of the bridging relationships constrain the sequence. System graph sequences are a key component of the request evaluation process as they identify a path from the system originating a request to the system graph containing the target object. Multiple such paths may exist; we require that the access control policy decision point (PDP) within a system be able to determine the single, least cost path.

To achieve this we require that an extra-model administrator assign costs to bridges, and that hub entities maintain and exchange system path information using a modified path-vector routing protocol. Each hub communicates with adjacent hubs to which it directs a bridging relationship, retrieving the cost of their total (least) cost path to every other hub, and therefore every other system graph, in the bridged system group (where an infinite cost indicates an unreachable hub).[5] Upon receiving these path costs the hub adds to each the cost of the bridge connecting it to that neighbour; it will then update its local system path table to reflect the least cost path (if it didn't already know it) to every remote hub, along with which adjacent hub each least cost path passes via. A system's PDP can collate this information from each of its local hub entities in order to determine the single, least cost path to a target system graph, or to determine that no such path exists. Henceforth, when identifying a system graph sequence between two system graphs we assume the least cost such sequence.

3   Request Evaluation in Inter-RPPM

The basic RPPM model evaluates local requests within a stand-alone system graph using two steps: *compute principals* (where principal-matching rules are evaluated to determine whether security principals match to the request) and *compute authorizations* (where authorization rules are evaluated to determine if the matched security principals are authorized to perform the requested action).

---

[5] The directionality of bridges is enforced by hub entities not exchanging system path information against the direction of an incident bridge.

Within Inter-RPPM, remote requests are made by a subject $G.s$ to perform a remote action $G'.a$ (where $G \neq G'$) on a remote object $G'.v$. To support these remote actions we introduce an *originating remote request (ORR)* and an *incoming remote request (IRR)*.[6] The ORR represents the remote request as it is specified within the originating system graph. The IRR contains additional data which enable subsequent system graphs to contribute to the evaluation. When processing remote requests, every traversed system graphs' PDP employs the compute principals step (whether evaluating an ORR or IRR), but only the target system graph's PDP computes authorizations. Essentially, non-originating system graphs re-compute the set of matched principals based on the set computed by the preceding system graph and identified in the IRR.

A *policy graph* is used during the compute principals step to order the evaluation of principal-matching rules and to enable principals to be "activated" when specific other principals are matched to a request.

Definition 2. *Given a system graph $G = (V, E)$ and a set of principals P, a policy graph G_ρ is a directed acyclic graph with a unique root (of in-degree 0) such that each vertex is a principal-matching rule (ϕ, ψ, p). The set of principals includes a special principal called the* null *principal and the principal-matching rule for the root is defined to be* (all, none, null).

The edges of the policy graph determine which rules trigger other rules. The concept of the principal-matching rule's target is extended to support rules in which the targets (positive, ϕ, and negative, ψ) may identify sets of principals which must exist (or not) in the current set of matched principals or, as previously, paths of relationships which must exist (or not) in the system graph. More formally, we evaluate a policy graph with respect to a request, in order to compute a set of matched principals, as per Algorithm 1 (see Appendix).[7]

A remote request is initiated in the originating system graph as an originating remote request (ORR), which is evaluated as per Algorithm 2 (see Appendix).[8]

Definition 3. *Given two distinct system graphs $G = (V, E)$ and $G' = (V', E')$ in a bridged system group $(\mathcal{G}, \beta)$, an originating remote request takes the form $G.q = (G.s, G'.v, G'.a)$,[9] where $G.s \in V$, $G'.v \in V'$ and $G'.a \in G'.A$.*

---

[6] Recall that a system graph sequence will document the chain of system graphs between the originating system graph and the target system graph.

[7] Note that we do not add the null principal to the set of matched principals (line 4 of Algorithm 1) so that it does not interfere with authorization decisions, no matter the conflict resolution strategy employed; and that the algorithm is passed a set of matched principals to which any it matches are added.

[8] In Algorithms 2 and 3 calls to EvaluatePolicyGraph have been simplified, removing the system graph and policy graph arguments so as to highlight the start entity, target entity, and set of matched principals arguments.

[9] Note that the originating remote request $G.q = (G.s, G'.v, G'.a)$ retains the same underlying *structure* as a local request made within the same system graph $G.q = G.(s, v, a)$.

When processing the ORR, the originating system's PDP must take into account that the target object is located in a distinct system graph from the subject. Therefore, the ORR is processed by performing compute principals between the subject and the hub entity which links the originating system graph to the next graph in the system graph sequence (lines 1, 3 and 4).[10] Note that line 4 passes an empty set to the EvaluatePolicyGraph algorithm (defined in Algorithm 1) as no principals have yet been matched to this remote request. The result of processing the policy graph is a set of matched principals for traversing the originating system graph. This is then passed, along with the details of the request, across the bridging relationship to the next system in the system graph sequence (lines 5 and 6).[11]

In non-originating system graphs, the remote request takes the form of an incoming remote request (IRR), evaluated as per Algorithm 3 (see Appendix); its processing differs in intermediate and target system graphs. Within an IRR, the subject component of the ORR is replaced with a tuple identifying the originating subject, the hub entity through which the request was received by the current system and the set of matching principals which resulted from the preceding system's processing of the request.

Definition 4. *Given a bridged system group* $(\mathcal{G}, \beta)$ *and a system graph sequence* $(G_1, \ldots, G_{i-1}, G_i, \ldots, G_\ell)$, *an* incoming remote request *processed by system graph* $G_i = (V_i, E_i)$ *takes the form* $G_i.q = ((G_1.s, G_i.h, G_{i-1}.[\![\rho]\!]), G_\ell.v, G_\ell.a)$, *where* $G_i.h \in V_i$ *is the hub through which the request entered* G_i *and* $G_{i-1}.[\![\rho]\!]$ *is the set of matched principals computed by the preceding system graph.*

When processing an IRR in an **intermediate system graph**, the system's PDP must take into account that neither the subject nor target object are located in the current system graph. Therefore, the IRR is processed by performing compute principals between two hub entities: the hub entity $G_i.h$ through which the request entered the system and the hub entity which links the intermediate system graph to the next graph in the system graph sequence (lines 4 and 5). The set of matched principals from the preceding system graphs is input into the graph policy evaluation (line 5) and may result in additional principals being activated (and added to it), as discussed in Sect. 2. As with processing an ORR, the cumulative set of matched principals that results is then passed, along with the details of the request, across the bridging relationship to the next system in the system graph sequence (lines 6 and 7). This process continues until it reaches the target system.

When processing an IRR in the **target system graph**, the policy graph evaluation is performed between the hub entity through which the request entered the system and the object of the request, note $G_i = G_\ell$ (line 10). Once again this makes use of the preceding system graph's set of matched principals. However,

---

[10] The function DetermineLeastCostPathToSystemGraph requires the PDP to interrogate its local hubs and to collate their responses, as described in Sect. 2.

[11] An appropriate mechanism (e.g. digital signatures) must be in place to enable the receiving system to ensure the authenticity and freshness of such details.

once a local set of matched principals is determined the compute authorizations step is performed. This allows a set of authorization decisions to be determined (line 11). A definitive decision is then determined, with RPPM's default decision process and conflict resolution process employed as with local requests (line 12).

4   Related Work

Whilst our work in respect of ReBAC inter-operation is novel, the inter-operation of other access control model instances has been considered in previous literature. In particular, research into the use of RBAC in multi-domain scenarios has led to several approaches to inter-operation based principally upon role mapping.

Shehab *et al.* define a distributed secure interoperability protocol in which users are assigned roles in remote domains based upon cross domain access agreements [10]. The order in which roles are acquired within each domain they access is referred to as the user's access path. These paths are checked to ensure the principles of autonomy and security [7] are both satisfied. In Inter-RPPM remote requests, by construction, are unable to target local resources and the outcome of local request evaluation is unchanged by the additions discussed in this paper. Therefore, both of these principles are satisfied trivially.

Shafiq *et al.* take this further by introducing a policy composition framework that integrates the RBAC policies of initially distinct domains [9]. They, additionally, implement a conflict resolution technique to deal with conflicts which may arise from the differences in how each domain models or references its access control policies. Within Inter-RPPM we have intentionally avoided integrating the policies of component model instances, and instead have provided a framework through which those policies may be applied to remote requests.[12] This places a greater requirement upon the manual definition of appropriate policies within each component model instance; however, it ensures a consistent policy language.

5   Conclusion

We have defined an inter-operation framework through which multiple RPPM system graphs may be connected and remote authorization requests may be evaluated. The connecting of systems is commonplace; however, the ability to decompose large systems into inter-connected smaller systems is a significant contribution of this paper and of particular importance in the application of ReBAC models. Decomposition enables a trade-off to be made between the computational complexity of a ReBAC model against the number of model instances which are employed to control authorizations within a large system.

The inter-connection of ReBAC (system) graphs through directed bridging relationships, and the use of system graph sequences and the path-vector routing

---

[12] That being said we support the use of remote principals where desired to provide for more robust policies.

protocol to identify paths between those graphs is applicable to remote request evaluation, no matter the model. This paper introduces its formal application in RPPM, although it is equally applicable to our more recent model, ARPPM [5] (something we leave for future work).[13] In cases where principal abstraction is not available, however, an alternative means of allowing each component graph's evaluation to contribute must be developed. We leave the development of such mechanisms to future work, only noting that an end-to-end path approach will produce a super-graph and thus, potentially, be limited by the increase in computational complexity associated with an increase in the number of nodes.

Appendix: Algorithms

The pseudocode for the algorithms used to support inter-connection of RPPM instances is shown below.

Algorithm 1. EvaluatePolicyGraph (ordered compute principals)

Require: System graph $G = (V, E)$, start node $u \in V$, target node $v \in V$, policy graph $G_\rho = (V_\rho, E_\rho)$, and set of matched principals $[\![\rho]\!]$
Ensure: Returns set of matched principals $[\![\rho]\!]$
1: **while** Perform breadth-first search of G_ρ starting at root vertex **do**
2:     Evaluate current vertex, $(\phi, \psi, p) \in V_\rho$
3:     **if** $G, u, v \models \phi$ **and** $G, u, v \not\models \psi$ **then**
4:         **if** $p \neq$ null **then**
5:             $[\![\rho]\!] \leftarrow [\![\rho]\!] \cup p$
6:         **end if**
7:     **else**
8:         Prune child vertices from evaluation
9:     **end if**
10: **end while**

Algorithm 2. ProcessORR

Require: System graph $G = (V, E)$, ORR $G.q = (G.s, G'.v, G'.a)$, policy graph $G.G_\rho = G.(V_\rho, E_\rho)$
Ensure: Malformed ORR rejected **or** set of matched principals $G.[\![\rho]\!]$ sent to next system graph in system graph sequence
1: $LCP_{G,G'} \leftarrow$ DetermineLeastCostPathToSystemGraph(G')
2: **if** G' reachable **then**
3:     $G.h \leftarrow$ IdentifyLocalHubForLCP$(LCP_{G,G'})$
4:     $G.[\![\rho]\!] \leftarrow$ EvaluatePolicyGraph$(G.s, G.h, \emptyset)$
5:     $G''.h \leftarrow$ IdentifyNeighbourHubForLCP$(LCP_{G,G'})$
6:     Securely send $G.q$ and $G.[\![\rho]\!]$ to $G''.h$ via $G.h$
7: **else**
8:     Reject malformed ORR
9: **end if**

---

[13] We believe that administrative requests will always be local to a model instance (maintaining system autonomy) and so only operational requests (equivalent to the requests discussed in this paper) may be conducted remotely.

Algorithm 3. ProcessIRR

Require: System graph $G_i = (V_i, E_i)$, IRR $G_i.q = ((G_1.s, G_i.h, G_{i-1}.[\![\rho]\!]), G_\ell.v, G_\ell.a)$, policy
    graph $G_i.G_\rho = G_i.(V_\rho, E_\rho)$
Ensure: Set of matched principals $G_i.[\![\rho]\!]$ sent to next graph in system graph sequence (intermediate
    system graph) **or** authorization decision made (target system graph)
1: **if** $G_i \neq G_\ell$ **then**
2:    // intermediate system graph
3:    $LCP_{G_i, G_\ell} \leftarrow$ DetermineLeastCostPathToSystemGraph(G_ℓ)
4:    $G_i.h' \leftarrow$ IdentifyLocalHubForLCP(LCP_{G_i, G_ℓ})
5:    $G_i.[\![\rho]\!] \leftarrow$ EvaluatePolicyGraph$(G_i.h, G_i.h', G_{i-1}.[\![\rho]\!])$
6:    $G_{i+1}.h \leftarrow$ IdentifyNeighbourHubForLCP(LCP_{G_i, G_ℓ})
7:    Securely send $G_i.q$ and $G_i.[\![\rho]\!]$ to $G_{i+1}.h$ via $G_i.h'$
8: **else**
9:    // target system graph
10:    $G_i.[\![\rho]\!] \leftarrow$ EvaluatePolicyGraph$(G_i.h, G_\ell.v, G_{i-1}.[\![\rho]\!])$
11:    $G_i.[\![\varrho]\!] \leftarrow$ ComputeAuthorizations$(G_i.[\![\rho]\!])$
12:    DecideAuthorizationResult$(G_i.[\![\rho]\!], G_i.[\![\varrho]\!])$
13: **end if**

References

1. Carminati, B., Ferrari, E., Perego, A.: Enforcing access control in web-based social networks. ACM Trans. Inf. Syst. Secur. **13**(1), 191–233 (2009)
2. Cheng, Y., Park, J., Sandhu, R.: A user-to-user relationship-based access control model for online social networks. In: Cuppens-Boulahia, N., Cuppens, F., Garcia-Alfaro, J. (eds.) DBSec 2012. LNCS, vol. 7371, pp. 8–24. Springer, Heidelberg (2012)
3. Crampton, J., Sellwood, J.: Path conditions and principal matching: a new approach to access control. In: Osborn, S.L., Tripunitara, M.V., Molloy, I. (eds.) 19th ACM Symposium on Access Control Models and Technologies, SACMAT 2014, London, ON, Canada, June 25–27, 2014, pp. 187–198. ACM (2014). http://doi.acm.org/10.1145/2613087.2613094
4. Crampton, J., Sellwood, J.: Relationships, paths and principal matching: a new approach to access control. CoRR abs/1505.07945 (2015)
5. Crampton, J., Sellwood, J.: ARPPM: administration in the RPPM model. In: Bertino, E., Sandhu, R., Pretschner, A. (eds.) Proceedings of the Sixth ACM on Conference on Data and Application Security and Privacy, CODASPY 2016, New Orleans, LA, USA, March 9–11, 2016, pp. 219–230. ACM (2016). http://doi.acm.org/10.1145/2857705.2857711
6. Fong, P.W.L.: Relationship-based access control: protection model and policy language. In: Sandhu, R.S., Bertino, E. (eds.) CODASPY, pp. 191–202. ACM (2011)
7. Gong, L., Qian, X.: Computational issues in secure interoperation. IEEE Trans. Softw. Eng. **22**(1), 43–52 (1996). http://dx.doi.org/10.1109/32.481533
8. Rizvi, S.Z.R., Fong, P.W.L., Crampton, J., Sellwood, J.: Relationship-based access control for an open-source medical records system. In: Weippl, E.R., Kerschbaum, F., Lee, A.J. (eds.) Proceedings of the 20th ACM Symposium on Access Control Models and Technologies, Vienna, Austria, June 1–3, 2015, pp. 113–124. ACM (2015). http://doi.acm.org/10.1145/2752952.2752962

9. Shafiq, B., Joshi, J., Bertino, E., Ghafoor, A.: Secure interoperation in a multidomain environment employing RBAC policies. IEEE Trans. Knowl. Data Eng. **17**(11), 1557–1577 (2005). http://dx.doi.org/10.1109/TKDE.2005.185

10. Shehab, M., Bertino, E., Ghafoor, A.: SERAT: secure role mapping technique for decentralized secure interoperability. In: Ferrari, E., Ahn, G. (eds.) SACMAT 2005, 10th ACM Symposium on Access Control Models and Technologies, Stockholm, Sweden, June 1–3, 2005, Proceedings, pp. 159–167. ACM (2005). http://doi.acm.org/10.1145/1063979.1064007

Role-Centric Circle-of-Trust in Multi-tenant Cloud IaaS

Navid Pustchi[⊠] and Ravi Sandhu

Institute for Cyber Security and Department of Computer Science,
University of Texas at San Antonio, San Antonio, TX, USA
tam498@my.utsa.edu, ravi.sandhu@utsa.edu

Abstract. Currently, collaboration is a major challenge in adopting cloud Infrastructure-as-a-Service (IaaS). Enterprise work-flow intrinsically mandates collaboration across its tenant boundaries as well as with associated organizations' tenants in the cloud. In this paper, we investigate a Circle-of-Trust approach where tenants establish trust within a circle of tenants for the purpose of collaboration. We present a novel extension of role-centric access control models to provide collaboration in the context of homogeneous and heterogeneous circles. In a homogeneous circle, our approach allows tenants to equally assert cross-tenant user assignments to enable access to shared resources. In a circle with non-uniform tenants, attributes are added to distinguish user-assignments where tenants are differentiated by type in the heterogeneous circle. Particularly, tenant-trust relation is established within a group of tenants authorizing user-role assignments across tenants.

Keywords: Circle-of-Trust · Federation · Attribute-based access control · Collaboration · Multi-tenant · Authorization · Security

1 Introduction

Cloud IaaS is firmly accepted by enterprises for its cost benefits, reliability, and dynamicity at scale [12]. Its benefits are well documented and well practiced in the industry, but still organizations resist to fully migrate to cloud IaaS which arises from security, performance, and vendor lock-in concerns. Enabling collaboration mitigates such concerns regarding vendor lock-in and different security levels required, and improves performance by utilizing distinct cloud providers.

In multi-tenant platforms which utilize shared physical infrastructure, users' data are isolated into tenants to protect privacy and integrity. A tenant could be an organization, a department of an organization, or an individual cloud consumer, which is represented by an account in AWS [1] or a domain in OpenStack [2]. Furthermore, current cloud service providers offer federation APIs to enable collaboration between tenants such as AWS and OpenStack platforms. Besides federation between two tenants, collaboration can also be established

© IFIP International Federation for Information Processing 2016
Published by Springer International Publishing Switzerland 2016. All Rights Reserved
S. Ranise and V. Swarup (Eds.): DBSec 2016, LNCS 9766, pp. 106–121, 2016.
DOI: 10.1007/978-3-319-41483-6_8

between a set of organizations where tenants adhere to a common set of policies, trust relations and collaboration interfaces within a circle. We denote this collaboration model as a *Circle-of-Trust*. Scenarios such as a large enterprise with multiple tenants collaborating in a public cloud, an organization with tenants across public and private clouds, or tenants from multiple organizations performing collaborative tasks are motivating use cases for Circle-of-Trust.

In this paper we present novel role-based and role-centric attribute-based access control models to enable federation in a multi-tenant cloud IaaS Circle-of-Trust. Our scope of contribution is homogeneous and heterogeneous multi-tenant circles in cloud IaaS.

To better clarify the concept, consider the example in Fig. 1 where ACME, a multinational technology corporation, aims to implement its enterprise requirements with cloud services. ACME migrates its IT infrastructure to a public cloud service provider where each tenant represents a department. ACME utilizes multiple tenants to satisfy distinct security levels required for each department. For example, Finance Dept. resources should not co-locate in the same tenant with Research & Development Dept., as Finance Dept. retains sensitive data. Furthermore, ACME organizational structure demands collaboration between its departments which is thereby required in its cloud adoption. To

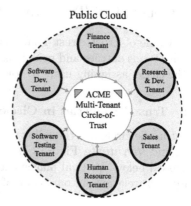

Fig. 1. ACME corporation Multi-Tenant Circle-of-Trust.

this end, ACME establishes a Circle-of-Trust among its tenants in the cloud and starts adding its tenants to the circle. For instance a new tenant created as Sales tenant in ACME, requests to join the circle. Adding additional tenants requires all ACME circle members to agree on trusting the new Sales tenant. When Sales tenant joins the circle, it trusts members assertions and its assertions are likewise trusted by other ACME circle members. In particular, Circle-of-Trust offers an association of ACME principals to collaborate in the circle.

Role-based access control (RBAC) [5,16] and its variations has been successfully applied to cloud IaaS providing collaboration within single-cloud [17,18] and multi-cloud systems [13]. In RBAC access permissions are assigned to roles and roles are assigned to users. Roles are central to RBAC for formulating policy and its commercial success, where it abstracts permissions into roles and role relations. With its dominance for the past two decades, RBAC limitations have been recognized leading to a push towards using attributes [6,7,15] with roles [9]. One method, is to add attributes to roles as role-centric attributes which takes advantage of roles' simplicity and attributes flexibility [8]. Attributes are defined as name:value pairs representing entities' properties. We anticipate cloud service providers will incorporate ABAC features to their current RBAC models such as role-centric to adopt convenience of RBAC with flexibility of ABAC models.

Our contribution in this paper is to design multi-tenant role-centric models with cross-tenant user-assignments. To our knowledge this is the first work considering role-centric models in Circle-of-Trust context.

The remainder of this paper is organized as follows. Section 2 overviews trust properties applicable in Circle-of-Trust and corresponding trust relations between tenants. In Sect. 3, our multi-tenant role-based access control in circle denoted MT-RBAC$_c$ is proposed and specified. Section 4 introduces our multi-tenant role-centric attribute-based model in circle denoted MT-RABAC$_c$. Related work and conclusion is presented in Sects. 5 and 6 respectively.

2   Concept of Trust in Circle

In a Circle-of-Trust, trust relationships are defined between all circle entities. We use terms entities and principals interchangeably. Principals make assertions in the circle, assigning users to roles.

2.1   Trust Properties in Circle

Trust in the circle has the following properties, *entity coupling, initiation, direction,* and *transitivity.* Figure 2 gives a logical hierarchy of these trust properties discussed below. Vertical placement of characteristics is selected to better illustrate trust relations in our scope of contribution.

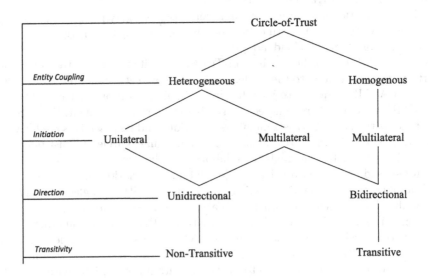

Fig. 2. Circle-of-Trust characterization.

Entity Coupling (Homogeneous vs. Heterogeneous). In a circle-of trust, type of entities engaging in interactions determines homogeneity or heterogeneity of the circle, shaping its authorized interactions between tenants. Moreover, with each circle type a set of trust properties are applicable. By *homogeneous circle* we denote the case where entities are uniform. For instance a circle of universities forms a homogeneous circle. In a homogeneous circle, collaborating principals are equally authorized to make cross-tenant authorization assertions. A *heterogeneous circle*, is an association of non-uniform entities where each type of entity is authorized specifically to make certain assertions. For instance, a circle consisting of universities, insurance companies, and banks establishes a heterogeneous circle. In this scenario, universities can assign users to discounted insurance plans in insurance companies while insurance companies cannot assign their users to resources in the universities. In this paper, we use type and domain interchangeably denoting the type of entities in a heterogeneous circle.

Initiation (Multilateral vs. Unilateral). If trust initiation to join a circle is required to be confirmed by all circle members, trust is considered *multilateral*. In special situations when joining members are not authorized to make assertions (in heterogeneous circles) trust initiation is not required to be confirmed by all circle members denoted as *unilateral* trust. For instance a domain of insurance companies joins a heterogeneous, unilateral circle of institutions. Insurance entities in the circle are not authorized to make assertions whilst institution entities are authorized to assert their users to discounted plans available to universities.

Direction (Bidirectional vs. Unidirectional). In a circle, direction of trust determines whether both participating circle members have equal authorizations or only one side is authorized to make assertions. If partners are authorized equally to make assertions, trust relation is *bidirectional*, otherwise it is *unidirectional* trust. Homogeneous circles' relations are bidirectional while heterogeneous circles support both trust directions. Unilateral heterogeneous circles such as given example above are only unidirectional in trust relations. Circle of universities is an example of bidirectional trust in a homogeneous circle. Sharing files in Dropbox is an example of a unidirectional trust where a user can share files with a group of users unidirectionally.

Transitivity (Transitive vs. Non-transitive). In a trust relation when principal "A trusts B" and "B trusts C" result in implication that "A trusts C", trust relation is denoted as transitive. In a homogeneous circle, bidirectional trusts are essentially transitive where all members trust and likewise trusted by other circle members. In heterogeneous unidirectional circles, trust relations cannot be transitive. For example, in the heterogeneous unidirectional circle of institutions, banks, and insurance companies, an institution can assign students to bank specific account types in banks whilst banks can assign employees to health insurances in insurance companies. Considering heterogeneous domains in the circle, a university trusting a bank and a bank trusting an insurance entity does not necessarily imply that the university can assign students to insurance resources.

In this paper, we consider multilateral, bidirectional, and transitive trust relationships for homogeneous circles. Trust relations between tenants in heterogeneous circles are considered multilateral, unidirectional, and non-transitive.

In the following we identify how trust relations authorize cross-tenant assignments in a Circle-of-Trust federation model.

2.2   Tenant-Trust in Circle

In a circle, trust is defined between tenants as *tenant-trust* relationship. In a unidirectional trust relationship, common in peer-to-peer, trust is initiated and established between two tenants denoted as trustor and trustee. In a trust relation, trustor tenant is willing to trust another tenant denoted as trustee tenant. In our scope, trust is initiated multilaterally between principals in a circle. In the context of circle, trustor and trustee are not distinguished in trust relations between tenants. We identify tenants involve in a cross-tenant assignment as user-owner and resource-owner tenants. User-owner tenant owns the users in the cross-tenant assignment and resource-owner tenant owns the roles to which users are assigned. Central to tenant-trust defined in this paper, is authorizing user-owner or resource-owner tenants to assert cross-tenant user-role assignments.

We use "$\lhd$" to represent tenant-trust where $T_A \lhd T_B$ signifies that tenant A trusts tenant B. In this relation, T_A is user-owner tenant and T_B is resource-owner tenant. Regardless of circle entity coupling, we define two types of tenant trust relations denoted as type-ϵ and type-ζ. Each tenant-trust relation type is applied to all tenants in the circle. In type-ϵ circle, user-owner tenants are authorized to assign users to roles in the circle. The following defines type-ϵ tenant-trust illustrated in Fig. 3a.

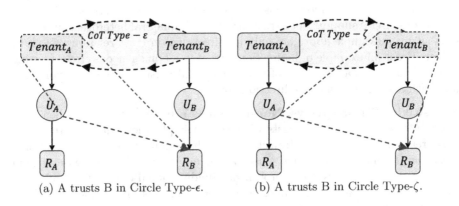

(a) A trusts B in Circle Type-ϵ.   (b) A trusts B in Circle Type-ζ.

Fig. 3. User-Role assignment in Circle-of-Trust Tenant-Trust.

Definition 1. *If $T_A \lhd_\epsilon T_B$, then tenant T_A is authorized to assign its users to T_B's roles. Tenant T_A controls user assignments.*

In type-ζ circle, resource-owner tenants are authorized to assign users in the circle to their roles. Type-ζ is defined as follows and is depicted in Fig. 3b.

Definition 2. *If* $T_A \triangleleft_\zeta T_B$*, then tenant* T_B *is authorized to assign* T_A*'s users to its roles. Tenant* T_B *controls user assignments.*

In homogeneous circles, all peers trust each other and trust is transitive, therefore $T_A \triangleleft T_B$ if and only if $T_B \triangleleft T_A$. However, in heterogeneous circles trust relations are unidirectional and non-transitive as a result $T_A \triangleleft T_B$ may not imply $T_B \triangleleft T_A$ or vise versa. Each tenant-trust type caters to a different security concern and objective in the Circle-of-Trust collaboration. Type-ϵ enable tenants in the circle to assign their users to roles of other tenants in the circle. The advantage is its simplicity to administer and implement as long as tenants' resources shared are not sensitive within the circle and tenants are willing to delegate user-role assignments to trusted tenants in the circle. For instance, an academic Circle-of-Trust is a motivation of this type of circle where academic tenants establish a Circle-of-Trust to share computing resources. Any academic tenant can assign its users to resources across tenants in the circle.

Type-ζ on the other hand, follows a different purpose to protect shared resources where user-role assignments are administered by resource-owner tenants. Tenants do not want to delegate trusted tenants permission to make assertions to their shared resources. A circle of financial institutions is a motivating example of type-ζ tenant-trust. Financial institutes do not want to expose their resources for collaboration in the circle since their resources are highly sensitive even with respect to trusted tenants in the circle. In this scenario, a resource-owner tenant administrator assigns users in the circle to its roles, authorizing access to its shared resources.

3   Homogeneous Role-Based Circle-of-Trust

This section introduces a multi-tenant role-based access control model to enable federation in a homogeneous Circle-of-Trust which we refer to as MT-RBAC$_c$. In a homogeneous circle, tenants are equally authorized to make assertions. Collaboration in MT-RBAC$_c$ is issued through cross-tenant user-role assignments with respect to circle types ϵ and ζ. MT-RBAC$_c$ model component sets and relations are depicted in Fig. 4. We use a circle of institutions called Cyber Security Research (CSR) shown in Fig. 5 as a running example to exemplify the concepts throughout this section. The formal definition of MT-RBAC$_c$ is given in Table 1. We discuss MT-RBAC$_c$ in parts through the following subsections, in context of these figures and table.

3.1   MT-RBAC$_c$ Basic Sets and Functions

The basic sets of MT-RBAC$_c$ are as follows: tenants (T), users (U), private roles (R_{prv}), public roles (R_{pub}), roles (R), operations (OPS), objects (OBS), and permissions ($PRMS$). Many of these are familiar from the traditional RBAC models [5,16] and will not be further discussed here. The new sets in MT-RBAC$_c$ are tenants (T) and private and public roles (R_{prv} and R_{pub} respectively).

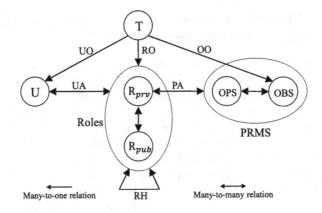

Fig. 4. Multi-Tenant RBAC Circle-of-Trust.

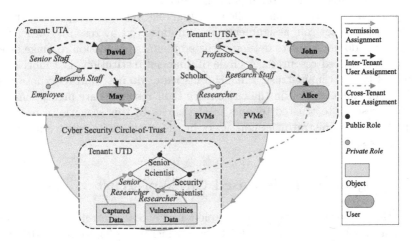

Fig. 5. Example of a Multi-Tenant RBAC$_c$ homogeneous Circle-of-Trust. (Color figure online)

A *tenant* is considered as a virtual container with tenant-specific environment for cloud services leased to cloud consumers. Practically, a tenant hosts a project, a department, or an organization. Each tenant is represented as $t \in T$ where T is the global set of tenants in the cloud. In Fig. 5, each tenant represents an institution, UTSA, UTA, and UTD respectively. Each user, role, and object is identified with a single owner tenant, shown within the dashed tenant boundary in Fig. 5. UTSA and UTD have similar Researcher roles, however in the cloud they are distinguished as Researcher#UTSA and Researcher#UTA. Similarly for objects and users.

Within each tenant the roles are partitioned into disjoint sets of public roles and private roles, R_{pub} and R_{prv} respectively, as depicted in Fig. 4 and expressed in Table 1 by the *owner* functions. In Fig. 5 private roles are shown as blue circles named in italics while public roles are shown as red circles named in regular script, e.g., the UTSA tenant has private roles Professor, Researcher and Research Staff and a public role Scholar.

A central principle of MT-RBAC$_c$ is that permission to role assignment can only occur within a tenant boundary, and only to private roles. This is formalized in the definition of the permission assignment (PA) relation in Table 1. It is our first departure from traditional RBAC which in general allows any permission to be assigned to any role.

3.2 MT-RBAC$_c$ Tenant-Trust and User-Role Assignment

A Circle-of-Trust (CoT) is a subset of tenants T who mutually trust each other within the scope of MT-RBAC$_c$. In Fig. 5, UTSA, UTA, and UTD form a homogeneous CoT of institutes. In general, multiple and possibly overlapping CoTs can be established among different subsets of tenants. For our purpose in this paper it suffices to focus on a single CoT. Tenant-trust between two members of a circle is indicated by the $\lhd$ symbol, which is a reflexive, transitive and symmetric relation.

MT-RBAC$_c$ distinguishes two kinds of trust, named type-ϵ and type-ζ and distinguished by a subscript applied to the symbols CoT and $\lhd$. In type-ϵ trust each tenant in the CoT_ϵ can assign users from another tenant in the circle to its own public roles. In type-ζ trust each tenant in the CoT_ζ can assign it own users to public roles belonging to another tenant in the circle. In Fig. 5, if CSR is a type-ϵ circle then the tenant administrator of UTA can assign its users, e.g., David and May, to roles in UTSA and UTD. If CSR is a type-ζ circle then the tenant administrator of UTA can assign users from UTSA, e.g., Alice and John, as well as users from UTD to roles in UTA. In both types of circles such cross-tenant user-role assignments is limited to public roles. These concepts are formalized in Table 1. These restrictions on user-role assignment constitute a second major departure from traditional RBAC.

3.3 Limited Role Hierarchy

A third significant departure from traditional RBAC is to limit the role hierarchy with respect to public and private roles. We use the symbol $\succeq$ to represent the role hierarchy where $r_1 \succeq r_2$ means that the permissions assigned to role r_2 are also available to users assigned to role r_1. MT-RBAC$_c$ imposes the following requirements on the role hierarchy.

- Private roles can inherit private roles only if both are owned by the same tenant, e.g., Senior Researcher $\succeq$ Researcher in the UTD tenant in Fig. 5.
- Private roles cannot inherit public roles. The Researcher role in UTD tenant cannot be senior to the Scholar role in UTSA.
- Public roles can inherit private roles only if both owned by the same tenant. In the UTD tenant, Security Scientist role inherits the Researcher role.

Table 1. MT-RBAC$_c$ component sets and functions.

Basic Sets and Functions

- T, U, R, OPS, and OBS (tenants, users, roles, operations, and objects, respectively). $t \in T$, $u \in U$, $r \in R$, $op \in OPS$, and $ob \in OBS$.
- R_{pub} is a set of public roles and R_{prv} is a set of private roles where $R_{pub} \subseteq R$, $R_{prv} \subseteq R$, $R_{pub} \cap R_{prv} = \emptyset$, and $R_{pub} \cup R_{prv} = R$.
- $PRMS = OPS \times OBS$, the set of permissions.
- $UO \subseteq U \times T$, a many-to-one user-to-tenant owner relation. Also written as $owner\_user : (u : U) \to T$, the mapping of user u into its owner tenant. Formally: $owner\_user(u) = t$ where $(u, t) \in UO$.
- $RO \subseteq R \times T$, a many-to-one role-to-tenant owner relation. Also written as $owner\_role : (r : R) \to T$, the mapping of role r into its owner tenant. Formally: $owner\_role(r) = t$ where $(r, t) \in RO$.
- $OO \subseteq OBS \times T$, a many-to-one object-to-tenant owner relation. Also written as $owner\_object : (ob : OBS) \to T$, the mapping of object ob into its owner tenant. Formally: $owner\_object(ob) = t$ where $(ob, t) \in OO$.
- $PA \subseteq PRMS \times R$, a many-to-many mapping permission-to-role assignment relation requiring that $((op, ob), r) \in PA \Rightarrow (owner\_object(ob) = owner\_role(r) \wedge r \in R_{prv})$. Also written as $assigned\_permissions : (r : R) \to 2^{PRMS}$, the mapping of role r into a set of permissions. Formally: $assigned\_permissions(r) = \{p \in PRMS \mid (p, r) \in PA\}$.

Tenant-Trust

- $CoT \subseteq T$, is a subset of T called Circle-of-Trust. For every two tenants that are member of CoT ($t_1, t_2 \in CoT$) trust relationship is written as $t_1 \lhd t_2$, which is symmetric so $t_1 \lhd t_2$ iff $t_2 \lhd t_1$, reflexive so $t_1 \lhd t_1$, and transitive.
- $HomogeneousCoT_\epsilon$, for all tenants t_1 where $t_1 \lhd_\epsilon t_2$, tenant t_1 is authorized to assign its users to public roles in t_2. Tenant t_1 controls t_1's users to t_2's roles assignments.
- $HomogeneousCoT_\varsigma$, for all tenants t_1 where $t_1 \lhd_\varsigma t_2$, tenant t_2 is authorized to assign users from t_1 to its public roles. Tenant t_2 controls t_1's users to t_2's roles assignments.

User Role Assignment

- $UA \subseteq U \times R$, a many-to-many mapping user-to-role assignment relation requiring that $(u, r) \in UA \Rightarrow (owner\_user(u) = owner\_role(r) \wedge r \in R_{prv}) \vee ((owner\_user(u) \lhd_\epsilon owner\_role(r) \vee owner\_role(r) \lhd_\varsigma owner\_user(u)) \wedge r \in R_{pub})$. Also written as $assigned\_user\_roles : (u : U) \to 2^R$, the mapping of user u into a set of roles. Formally: $assigned\_user\_roles(u) = \{r \in R \mid (u, r) \in UA\}$.

Limited Role Hierarchy

- $RH \subseteq R \times R$, is a partial order on R called hierarchy relation, written as $\succeq$, requiring that $(r_1, r_2) \in RH \Rightarrow ((owner\_role(r_1) = owner\_role(r_2)) \wedge \neg(r_1 \in R_{prv} \wedge r_2 \in R_{pub})) \vee ((owner\_role(r_1) \lhd_\epsilon owner\_role(r_2) \vee owner\_role(r_2) \lhd_\varsigma owner\_role(r_1)) \wedge (r_1, r_2 \in R_{pub}))$.

Authorized User Permissions Derived Function

- $authorized\_user\_permissions : (u : U) \to 2^{PRMS}$, the mapping of user u into a set of permissions. Formally: $authorized\_user\_permissions(u) =$

$$\bigcup_{r \in assigned\_user\_roles(u)} \bigcup_{r' \preceq r} assigned\_permissions(r').$$

– Public roles can inherit public roles from trusted tenants in the circle. In UTD tenant, Senior Scientist $\succeq$ Security Scientist where both are UTD's public roles. It is also possible for a public role of one tenant to be senior to a public role in another tenant. We include this possibility for generality, although role to role assignment is outside the scope of MT-RBAC$_c$.

3.4 MT-RBAC$_c$ Trust Properties

In terms of the circle trust properties of Sect. 2.1 MT-RBAC$_c$ is homogeneous in entity coupling since all tenants in the circle are treated equivalently. In term of initiation in joining or leaving a circle of trust, MT-RBAC$_c$ does not explicitly formalize this aspect. As such MT-RBAC$_c$ is neutral on this issue. Different models of initiation such a multilateral or unilateral are compatible with MT-RBAC$_c$. Regarding direction and transitivity, a circle in MT-RBAC$_c$ is explicitly defined to be bidirectional and transitive.

4 Heterogeneous Role-and-Attribute Based Circle-of-Trust

This section, introduces a multi-tenant role-centric attribute-based access control model (MT-RABAC$_c$) enabling federation in a heterogeneous Circle-of-Trust. Our model is motivated by a previously defined role-centric model [8] for combining roles and attributes. In a heterogeneous circle, entities are from non-uniform types. In MT-RABAC$_c$, tenants are not equally authorized and cross-tenant user-role assignments are limited with respect to tenant's domain type attribute.

MT-RABAC$_c$ adds attributes to enforce cross-tenant user-role assignment separation. Attributes are used to denote tenant types where tenants are only authorized to assert cross-tenant user assignments on certains type of tenants. Figure 6 depicts elements in MT-RABAC$_c$, where *tenant attributes (TATT)*, *user attributes (UATT)*, and *object attributes (OATT)* are added to the tenant, user, and object components of Fig. 4 respectively. We use a heterogeneous circle of institutions (UTA and UTSA) and a bank (BoA) in Fig. 7 as a running example to exemplify the concepts throughout this section. The extensions and modifications to the MT-RBAC$_c$ model to obtain MT-RABAC$_c$ are formally given in Table 2. Similar to the description of MT-RBAC$_c$ in the previous section, we will describe MT-RABAC$_c$ systematically in the following subsections, in context of the afore-mentioned figures and table.

4.1 MT-RABAC$_c$ User and Object Attributes and Meta-Attributes

An *attribute* is considered as a function which takes a tenant, user or object as input and return a value from the attribute's range. For example, an atomic-valued user attribute function such as *employeeType* returns employee status of a user *john* where $employeeType \in UATT$, $john \in U$ and $employeeType(john) = full\_time$. Range or scope of an attribute is a finite set of atomic values specifying

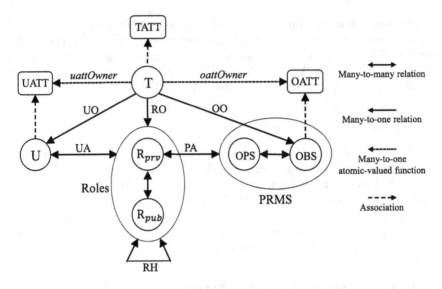

Fig. 6. Multi-Tenant Role-Centric ABAC Circle-of-Trust.

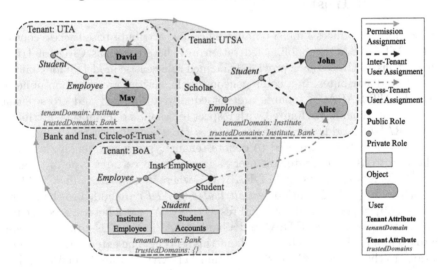

Fig. 7. Example of a Multi-Tenant RABAC$_c$ heterogeneous Circle-of-Trust. (Color figure online)

the valid range of attribute functions. Attribute functions either return a single value or set of values, which are respectively called *atomic-valued* and *set-valued* attribute types. In MT-RABAC$_c$, users and objects are respectively associated with attributes in the sets $UATT$ and $OATT$. Each user attribute $uatt \in UATT$ is a partial function since not every attribute is defined for every user. Similarly, each object attribute $oatt \in OATT$ is a partial function.

Each user and object attribute is owned by a single tenant. This is realized by means of meta-attributes *uattOwner* and *oattOwner*. Users and objects can only be assigned attribute values for attributes owned by the same tenant as the user or object. User and object attributes do not impact user-role assignment and are included in the model for generality and uniformity.

4.2   MT-RABAC$_c$ Tenant Attributes

Tenant attributes are fundamental to MT-RABAC$_c$ to enforce constraints on cross-tenant user-role assignments. Each tenant administrator can only assign values to its set of tenant attributes. In a heterogeneous circle, tenants are from different types which needs to be recognized in cross-tenant user-role assignments. To that end, we define a *domain* as a set of tenants grouped together with respect to their type in the system. Each domain is a subset of T defined in Table 2. For instance in Fig. 7, circle includes two types of tenants, Institute and Bank domains. Particularly, a tenant is related to a domain with an atomic-valued required attribute function, *tenantDomain*. It is defined as an atomic attribute to signify that each tenant only belongs to one domain. In Fig. 7, UTSA and UTA have Institute and BoA has Bank tenantDomain attribute values. Moreover, to separate user-role assignments in MT-RABAC$_c$, *trustedDomains* is defined as a required set-valued tenant attribute. In MT-RABAC$_c$, each tenant administrator specifies the group of domains it trusts with their assertions, including its own domain. For instance in Fig. 7, UTSA trusts assertions from Institute and Bank domain while UTA only trusts Bank domain assertions meaning UTA does not trust assertions from its own domain. In the heterogeneous circle in Fig. 7, BoA does not allow any assertions from tenants in the circle.

4.3   MT-RABAC$_c$ Tenant-Trust

In MT-RABAC$_c$, tenant-trust is limited with trustedDomains attributes. In type-ϵ circle, user-owner tenant can assign its users to roles from tenants which it is a member of their trustedDomains attribute set. In type-ζ, user assignment is modified to satisfy the condition where role-owner tenant can assign users from tenants in the circle, if it is a member of their trustedDomains attribute set. Type ϵ and ζ is defined in Table 2. In Fig. 7, if circle is a type-ϵ, then the tenant administrator of UTA can assign its users, e.g., David and May, to roles in UTSA since UTSA trusts assertions from its domain. If circle is a type-ζ, then the tenant administrator of BoA can assign users from UTSA, e.g., Alice and John, as well as users from UTA to roles in BoA since both UTSA an UTA trust assertions from Bank domain tenants.

   In this context, user-assignment is modified with respect to trustedDomains attributes. A user is assigned to a role only if

$$(owner\_user(u) = owner\_role(r) \land r \in R) \lor$$
$$(owner\_user(u) \vartriangleleft_\epsilon owner\_role(r) \land r \in R_{pub} \land$$
$$tenantDomain(owner\_user(u)) \in trustedDomains(owner\_role(r))) \lor$$
$$(owner\_user(u) \vartriangleleft_\zeta owner\_role(r) \land r \in R_{pub} \land$$
$$tenantDomain(owner\_role(r)) \in trustedDomains(owner\_user(u)))$$

Table 2. MT-RABAC$_c$ component sets and functions.

Basic Sets and Functions

- $TATT$, $UATT$, and $OATT$ represent finite set of tenant, user, and object attribute functions respectively.
- For each att in $TATT \cup UATT \cup OATT$, $Scope(att)$ represents the attribute's scope, a finite set of atomic values.
- $attType : TATT \cup UATT \cup OATT \to \{set, atomic\}$, specifies attributes as set or atomic valued.

Meta Attributes of User and Object Attributes

- $MATT = \{uattOwner, oattOwner\}$, required meta-attribute functions.
$uattOwner : (uatt : UATT) \to T$, required atomic user meta-attribute function, mapping user attribute $uatt$ to attribute owner tenant t.
$oattOwner : (oatt : OATT) \to T$, required atomic object meta-attribute function, mapping object attribute $oatt$ to attribute owner tenant t.

User Attribute

- Each user attribute function $uatt \in UATT$ is defined as a partial function mapping elements in U to atomic or set values.

$$\forall uatt \in UATT.uatt : U \hookrightarrow \begin{cases} Scope(uatt) & if\ attType(uatt) = atomic \\ 2^{Scope(uatt)} & if\ attType(uatt) = set \end{cases}$$

$uatt(u : U)$ is defined only if $uattOwner(uatt) = owner\_user(u)$.

Object Attribute

- Each object attribute function $oatt \in OATT$ is defined a partial function mapping elements in O to atomic or set values.

$$\forall oatt \in OATT.oatt : O \hookrightarrow \begin{cases} Scope(oatt) & if\ attType(oatt) = atomic \\ 2^{Scope(oatt)} & if\ attType(oatt) = set \end{cases}$$

$oatt(o : O)$ is defined only if $oattOwner(oatt) = owner\_object(o)$.

Tenant Attribute

- Each tenant attribute function $tatt \in TATT$ maps elements in T to atomic or set values.

$$\forall tatt \in TATT.tatt : T \to \begin{cases} Scope(tatt) & if\ attType(tatt) = atomic \\ 2^{Scope(tatt)} & if\ attType(tatt) = set \end{cases}$$

- D is a finite set of domains.
- $tenantDomain : (t : T) \to D$, required tenant atomic attribute function mapping tenant t to tenant domain d where $tenantDomain \in TATT$.
- $trustedDomains : (t : T) \to 2^D$, required tenant set attribute function mapping tenant t to the powerset of trusted domains D where $trustedDomains \in TATT$.

Tenant Trust

- $HeterogeneousCoT_\epsilon$, for all tenants t_1 where $t_1 \vartriangleleft_\epsilon t_2$, if $tenantDomain(t_1) \in trustedDomain(t_2)$, then tenant t_1 is authorized to assign its users to public roles in t_2. Tenant t_1 controls t_1's users to t_2's roles assignments.
- $HeterogeneousCoT_\zeta$, for all tenants t_1 where $t_1 \vartriangleleft_\zeta t_2$, if $tenantDomain(t_2) \in trustedDomain(t_1)$, then tenant t_2 is authorized to assign users from t_1 to its public roles. Tenant t_2 controls t_1's users to t_2's roles assignments.

User Role Assignment

- $UA \subseteq U \times R$, a many-to-many mapping user-to-role assignment relation requiring that $(u, r) \in UA \Rightarrow (owner\_user(u) = owner\_role(r) \wedge r \in R_{Prv}) \vee$
$(owner\_user(u) \vartriangleleft_\epsilon owner\_role(r) \wedge r \in R_{pub} \wedge$
$tenantDomain(owner\_user(u)) \in trustedDomains(owner\_role(r))) \vee$
$(owner\_user(u) \vartriangleleft_\zeta owner\_role(r) \wedge r \in R_{pub} \wedge$
$tenantDomain(owner\_role(r)) \in trustedDomains(owner\_user(u)))$.

In a Circle-of-Trust we allow only one trust type in the circle. We don't allow both type ϵ and ζ at once in a circle due to assignment conflict. Permission-assignment remains unchanged where a permission is assigned to a role only if

$$(owner\_role(r) = owner\_object(o) \land r \in R_{prv})$$

Authorized_user_permisisons denotes the set of permissions available to a user with respect to tenant types in the circle which is not changed from Table 1.

4.4 MT-RABAC$_c$ Trust Properties

In terms of the circle trust properties of Sect. 2.1 MT-RABAC$_c$ is heterogeneous in entity coupling since tenants in the circle are distinguished by their domain, and thereby not treated equivalently. In term of initiation in joining or leaving a circle of trust, MT-RABAC$_c$ does not explicitly formalize this aspect. As such MT-RABAC$_c$ is neutral on this issue. Different models of initiation such a multilateral or unilateral are compatible with MT-RBAC$_c$. Regarding direction and transitivity, a circle in MT-RBAC$_c$ is explicitly defined to be unidirectional and non-transitive.

5   Related Work

The Liberty Alliance Project [20] identified the conceptual framework and guidelines in a Circle-of-Trust as part of their federated identity vision. Considerable research on Circle-of-Trust has been devoted to identity federation such as [10] where trust requirements and patterns in a Circle-of-Trust identity federation are identified. In [3], Circle-of-Trust collaboration trust considerations in identity federation for assessment of entities' trust outside the circle are considered. Our work is focussed on authorization federation in a collaboration group of entities considered as tenants.

Sharing resources among organizations has been investigated in multiple aspects. ROBAC [21] extended RBAC to consider authorization in multiple organizations, but collaboration within organizations is not considered. GB-RBAC [11] extends RBAC with groups to support collaboration. In GB-RBAC, administrator cannot manage users in the groups. In our model, each tenant administers its collaboration policy by controlling users or roles in user-role assignments across the tenants in the circle. In [19], a dynamic coalition-based access control (DCBAC) model is proposed that allows automatic access to resources of one coalition entity by users from another coalition entity. O2O [4] defined an approach to deal with access control in interoperability context based on virtual private organizations (VPO) and role single-sign on (RSSO). Our contribution is differentiated based on the collaboration framework to enable collaboration between tenants. In O2O, each organization is responsible to define its security policy for roles whereas in our federation framework, each tenant defines its collaboration policy through public roles for a group of tenants in the circle.

Further in cloud IaaS, models such as CTTM [17] extended RBAC to enable collaboration in multi-tenant cloud systems. In [13], cross-tenant collaboration models discussed enabling federation in multi-cloud environments. In this paper, we focus on Circle-of-Trust federation compared to [17] and [13] where collaboration is enabled in a Peer-to-Peer federation. In ABAC collaboration in cloud, MT-ABAC [14] proposed collaboration between tenants by cross-tenant attribute assignment in cloud IaaS. Such attribute-based federation provides Peer-to-Peer collaboration, however our role-centric model provides federation in a circle.

6   Conclusion

This paper elaborated a fine-grained collaboration model in a Circle-of-Trust. We introduced the MT-RBAC$_c$ model in a homogeneous circle, in which collaboration is enabled through user to public role assignments. We identified, private and public roles with limited role hierarchy to control access on tenants' resources. Trust is defined on tenants with circle types ϵ and ζ authorizing user-owner and resource-owner tenants' assertions respectively. Moreover, tenant attributes in MT-RABAC$_c$ classifies tenants into domains in heterogeneous circles, where tenant-trust is defined conditionally with *trustedDomain* attributes. Using roles and attributes to enable cross-tenant user-role assignments is general and dynamic enough to address current issues while it is applicable to current platforms. For future work, we plan to extend this work with attribute-based models into further generalization in multi-cloud environments and implement proposed models in the current cloud platforms such as OpenStack.

Acknowledgement. This research is partially supported by NSF Grant CNS-1111925 and CNS-1423481.

References

1. Amazon AWS. https://aws.amazon.com/
2. OpenStack. http://www.openstack.org/
3. Boursas, L., Danciu, V.A.: Dynamic inter-organizational cooperation setup in circle-of-trust environments. In: Network Operations and Management Symposium, NOMS 2008, pp. 113–120. IEEE (2008)
4. Cuppens, F., Cuppens-Boulahia, N., Coma, C.: O2O: virtual private organizations to manage security policy interoperability. In: Bagchi, A., Atluri, V. (eds.) ICISS 2006. LNCS, vol. 4332, pp. 101–115. Springer, Heidelberg (2006)
5. Ferraiolo, D.F., Sandhu, R., Gavrila, S., Kuhn, D.R., Chandramouli, R.: Proposed NIST standard for role-based access control. TISSEC **4**(3), 224–274 (2001)
6. Hu, V.C., Ferraiolo, D., et al.: Guide to attribute based access control (ABAC) definition and considerations. NIST Special Publication, 800:162 (2014)
7. Hu, V.C., Kuhn, D.R., Ferraiolo, D.F.: Attribute-based access control. Computer **2**, 85–88 (2015)
8. Jin, X., Sandhu, R., Krishnan, R.: RABAC: role-centric attribute-based access control. In: Kotenko, I., Skormin, V. (eds.) MMM-ACNS 2012. LNCS, vol. 7531, pp. 84–96. Springer, Heidelberg (2012)

9. Kuhn, D.R., Coyne, E.J., Weil, T.R.: Adding attributes to role-based access control. Computer **6**, 79–81 (2010)
10. Kylau, U., Thomas, I., Menzel, M., Meinel, C.: Trust requirements in identity federation topologies. In: International Conference on Advanced Information Networking and Applications, AINA 2009, pp. 137–145. IEEE (2009)
11. Li, Q., Zhang, X., Xu, M., Wu, J.: Towards secure dynamic collaborations with group-based RBAC model. Comput. Secur. **28**(5), 260–275 (2009)
12. Mell, P., Grance, T.: The NIST definition of cloud computing (2011)
13. Pustchi, N., Krishnan, R., Sandhu, R.: Authorization federation in IaaS multi cloud. In: Proceedings of Security in Cloud Computing, pp. 63–71. ACM (2015)
14. Pustchi, N., Sandhu, R.: MT-ABAC: a multi-tenant attribute-based access control model with tenant trust. In: Qiu, M., Xu, S., Yung, M., Zhang, H. (eds.) NSS 2015. LNCS, vol. 9408, pp. 206–220. Springer, Heidelberg (2015). doi:10.1007/978-3-319-25645-0_14
15. Sandhu, R.: The authorization leap from rights to attributes: maturation or chaos? In: Proceedings of SACMAT, pp. 69–70. ACM (2012)
16. Sandhu, R.S., Coyne, E.J., Feinstein, H.L., Youman, C.E.: Role-based access control models. Computer **29**(2), 38–47 (1996)
17. Tang, B., Sandhu, R.: Cross-tenant trust models in cloud computing. In: Proceedings of International Conference on IRI, pp. 129–136. IEEE (2013)
18. Tang, B., Sandhu, R., Li, Q.: Multi-tenancy authorization models for collaborative cloud services. In: Proceedings of CTS, pp. 132–138. IEEE (2013)
19. Warner, J., Atluri, V., Mukkamala, R.: A credential-based approach for facilitating automatic resource sharing among ad-hoc dynamic coalitions. In: Jajodia, S., Wijesekera, D. (eds.) Data and Applications Security 2005. LNCS, vol. 3654, pp. 252–266. Springer, Heidelberg (2005)
20. Wason, T., Cantor, S., Hodges, J., Kemp, J., Thompson, P.: Liberty ID-FF Architecture Overview. Liberty Alliance, Piscataway (2004)
21. Zhang, Z., Zhang, X., Sandhu, R.: ROBAC: scalable role and organization based access control models. In: Proceedings of CollaborateCom, pp. 1–9. IEEE (2006)

A Comparison of Logical-Formula and Enumerated Authorization Policy ABAC Models

Prosunjit Biswas[(✉)], Ravi Sandhu, and Ram Krishnan

Institute for Cyber Security, University of Texas at San Antonio, San Antonio, USA
prosun.csedu@gmail.com, {ravi.sandhu,ram.krishnan}@utsa.edu

Abstract. Logical formulas and enumeration are the two major ways for specifying authorization policies in Attribute Based Access Control (ABAC). While considerable research has been done for specifying logical-formula authorization policy ABAC, there has been less attention to enumerated authorization policy ABAC. This paper presents a finite attribute, finite domain ABAC model for enumerated authorization policies and investigates its relationship with logical-formula authorization policy ABAC models in the finite domain. We show that these models are equivalent in their theoretical expressive power. We also show that single and multi-attribute ABAC models are equally expressive.

1 Introduction

Attribute Based Access Control (ABAC) has gained considerable attention from businesses, academia and standard bodies, such as NIST [6], in recent years. ABAC uses attributes on users, objects and possibly other entities (e.g. context or environment) and specifies rules using these attributes to assert who can have which access permissions (e.g. read or write) on which objects. Although ABAC concepts have been around for over two decades there remains a lack of well-accepted ABAC models. Recently there has been a resurgence of interest in ABAC due to continued dissatisfaction with the three traditional models (DAC [14], MAC [12], RBAC [13]), and particularly with the limitations of RBAC.

To demonstrate expressive power and flexibility, several ABAC models including [7,15,16,18] have been proposed in past few years. These models adopt the conventional approach of designing attribute based authorization policies as logical formulas. Logical-formula authorization policies (LAPs) are powerful and convenient to specify even complicated business requirements in a concise way.

An alternate to specify authorization policies is by enumeration, called enumerated authorization policies (EAPs). Examples in this category include *Policy Machine (PM)* [5] and *LaBAC* [2]. These models demonstrate expressiveness by their ability to configure traditional models.

Thus, LAPs and EAPs are two viable approaches to express authorization policies in an ABAC model. While ABAC models with LAPs (denoted *LAP-ABAC*) have received considerable attention, design and development of ABAC

© IFIP International Federation for Information Processing 2016
Published by Springer International Publishing Switzerland 2016. All Rights Reserved
S. Ranise and V. Swarup (Eds.): DBSec 2016, LNCS 9766, pp. 122–129, 2016.
DOI: 10.1007/978-3-319-41483-6_9

with EAPs (denoted *EAP-ABAC*) are relatively neglected. As a result, there is scant literature on development of *EAP-ABAC*. Nonetheless, a comparison between these two approaches is required to further fundamental understanding of ABAC.

This paper presents a finite attribute, finite domain model for *EAP-ABAC* and investigates its relationship with *LAP-ABAC* in the finite domain. We show that *LAP-ABAC* and *EAP-ABAC* are equivalent in theoretical expressive power. We also show that single and multi-attribute models are equally expressive.

Rest of this paper is organized as follows. Section 2 discusses different styles and scopes for ABAC. Section 3 presents multi-attribute *EAP-ABAC* and *LAP-ABAC* models. We show that these models are equivalent in theoretical expressive power in Sect. 4. Related work is presented in Sect. 5. Finally, Sect. 6 concludes the paper.

2   Authorization Policy Representation

In this section, we discuss two types of authorization policies—logical-formula and enumeration with respect to finite domain ABAC models.

Finite Domain ABAC Models. Most of the ABAC models (for example, [7,15,16,18]) assume a finite set of user and object attributes and that values of these attributes come from a finite set. This assumption is useful in many practical cases. For example, values of *roles*, *clearance* or *age* are bounded and mostly static. But attribute values can be unbounded as well. For example, if values of an attribute include users or objects in a system (e.g. the attribute *owner* for an object) and these values may grow indefinitely, they are unbounded. This paper focuses on finite-domain ABAC models that have a finite set of attributes with finite ranges for attribute values.

Logical-Formula Authorization Policy. A logical-formula authorization policy is defined as a boolean expression consisting of subexpressions connected with logical operators (for example, $\wedge, \vee, \neg$). These subexpressions compare attribute values with other attribute or constant values. LAPs are usually expressed in propositional logic and support a large set of logical and relational operators. A LAP grants an authorization request if the applicable formula evaluate true for attribute values of the requesting user and requested object. $Auth_{read} \equiv clearance(u) \succeq classification(o)$ is an example of LAP which allows a user to read an object if the user's clearance dominates classification of the object.

Enumerated Authorization Policy. An enumerated authorization policy consists of a set of tuples. Each tuple, represented as *(user-attr-values, obj-attr-values)*, grants privileges to a set of users to exercise an action on a set of objects identified by the user and object attribute values mentioned in the tuple. In an EAP, each tuple is distinct and grants privileges independently. User and object attribute values used in the tuple can be atomic or set valued. For example, *(mng, TS)* and *({mng, dir}, {TS,H})* are atomic and set valued tuples respectively.

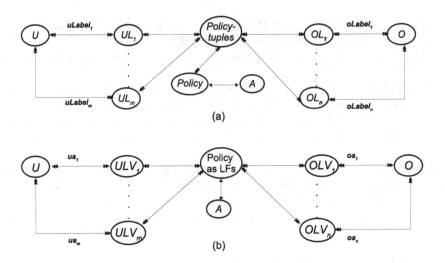

Fig. 1. Components of (a) $EAP\text{-}ABAC_{m,n}$ (b) $LAP\text{-}ABAC_{m,n}$

3 Finite Domain ABAC Models

In this section, we define a multi-attribute enumerated authorization policy ABAC model named $EAP\text{-}ABAC_{m,n}$ (shown in Fig. 1(a)). To the best of our knowledge, $EAP\text{-}ABAC_{m,n}$ is the first such model. *PM* [5] also defines a multi-attribute *EAP-ABAC* model, but its interpretation of attributes is different than the traditional interpretation of attributes as *(attr. name, value)* pairs. We also define a multi-attribute *LAP-ABAC* model named $LAP\text{-}ABAC_{m,n}$ (shown in Fig. 1(b)) by abstracting its policy language and potentially accepting any computational logic as policy language.

Multi-attribute *EAP-ABAC* ($EAP\text{-}ABAC_{m,n}$)**:** $EAP\text{-}ABAC_{m,n}$ has m user attributes and n object attributes. Components of $EAP\text{-}ABAC_{m,n}$ are shown in Fig. 1(a). The unbounded set of users and objects, and finite set of actions are represented by U, O and A respectively. The values denoted by UL_1, UL_2 through UL_m (UL_1 and UL_m are shown in the figure) represent range of m user attribute functions named $uLabel_1, uLabel_2$ through $uLabel_m$ respectively. Similarly, OL_1 OL_2 through OL_n specify values of n object attributes. For simplicity, we do not consider subjects or sessions, distinct from users, here. They do not materially affect the discussion.

The set of policies is represented by *Policy*. We define one policy per action. A policy is defined a set of policy-tuples. A policy-tuple includes subset of values for each user and object attribute.

The formal definition of the model and semantics of the authorization function are given in Table 1. Segment I of the table defines basic sets and relations discussed above. In Segment II, shows notation of policy tuples and defines a policy as subset of tuples. Finally, the authorization function $is\_authorized(s, a, o)$ is presented in Segment III. It allows a user u to perform an action a on an

Table 1. $EAP\text{-}ABAC_{m,n}$ model

I. Sets and relations
- U, O, and A (users, objects and actions respectively)
- $UL_1, UL_2, ...UL_m$ (values for $uLabel_1, uLabel_2, ... , uLabel_m$)
- $OL_1, OL_2, ...OL_n$ (values for $oLabel_1, oLabel_2, ... , oLabel_n$)
- $uLabel_i : U \to 2^{UL_i}$, for $1 \le i \le m$;
- $oLabel_i : O \to 2^{OL_i}$, for $1 \le i \le n$
II. Policy components
- $Policy\text{-}tuples = (2^{UL_1} \times 2^{UL_2} \times ... \times 2^{UL_m}) \times (2^{OL_1} \times 2^{OL_2} \times ... \times 2^{OL_n})$
- $Policy_a \subseteq Policy\text{-}tuples$ and $Policy = \{Policy_a | a \in A\}$
III. Authorization function
- $is\_authorized(u : U, a : A, o : O) = (\exists (ULS_1, ULS_2, ..., ULS_m, OLS_1, OLS_2, ...OLS_n)$ $\in Policy_a)[ULS_i \subseteq uLabel_i(u), \text{for } 1 \le i \le m \wedge OLS_i \subseteq oLabel_i(o), \text{for } 1 \le i \le n]$

Table 2. $LAP\text{-}ABAC_{m,n}$ model

I. Sets and relations
- U, O and A (set of users, objects and actions respectively)
- $UAV_1, UAV_2, ..., UAV_m$ (range of user attribute functions)
- $OAV_1, OAV_2, ..., OAV_n$ (range of object attribute functions)
- $UA = \{ua_1, ua_2, ..., ua_m\}$ (set of user attributes); $ua_i : U \to 2^{UAV_i}$, for $1 \le i \le m$
- $OA = \{oa_1, oa_2, ..., oa_n\}$ (set of object attributes); $oa_i : O \to 2^{OAV_i}$, for $1 \le i \le n$
II. Policy components
- $f_a : (2^{UAV_1}, ..., 2^{UAV_m}, 2^{OAV_1}, ..., 2^{OAV_n}) \to \{true, false\}$ (policy for $a \in A$).
- $LFs = \{f_a | a \in A\}$ (set of all policies)
III. Authorization function
- $is\_authorized(u:U, a:A, o:O) = \exists f_a \in LFs[f_a(ua_1(u), ua_2(u), ..., ua_m(u), oa_1(o),$ $oa_2(o), ...oa_n(o)) = true]$

object o if in the policy $Policy_a$ for action a, there exists a tuple that satisfies following conditions—(i) u possesses attribute values used in the tuple, and (ii) o is assigned attribute values mentioned in the tuple.

Multi-attribute $LAP\text{-}ABAC$ ($LAP\text{-}ABAC_{m,n}$): $LAP\text{-}ABAC_{m,n}$ is specified in Fig. 1(b). This model is based on LAPs. Other than authorization policies, this model is similar to $EAP\text{-}ABAC_{m,n}$. It defines a LAP as a boolean function f_a that takes values of m user and n object attributes as arguments. An authorization request for action a is granted if $f_a()$ is evaluated true for attribute values of requesting user and requested object. The formal definition is given in Table 2, similar to Table 1.

Table 3. Mappings

Equivalence of $EAP\text{-}ABAC_{m,n}$ ***and*** $EAP\text{-}ABAC_{1,1}$
I. From $EAP\text{-}ABAC_{m,n}$ *to* $EAP\text{-}ABAC_{1,1}$

- $U = U, O = O, A = A$
- $UL = 2^{UL_1} \times 2^{UL_2} \times ... \times 2^{UL_m};\ OL = 2^{OL_1} \times 2^{OL_2} \times ... \times 2^{OL_m}$
- $uLabel(u) = 2^{uLabel_1(u)} \times 2^{uLabel_2(u)} \times ... \times 2^{uLabel_m(u)}$
- $oLabel(u) = 2^{oLabel_1(o)} \times 2^{oLabel_2(o)} \times ... \times 2^{oLabel_n(o)}$
- $Policy_{a_{1,1}} = \{((ULS_1, ULS_2, ..., ULS_m), (OLS_1, OLS_2, ..., OLS_n)) |$
  $(\exists(ULS_1, ULS_2, ..., ULS_m, OLS_1, OLS_2, ..., OLS_n) \in Policy_a)\ [Policy_a \in Policy_{m,n}]\}$

II. From $EAP\text{-}ABAC_{1,1}$ *to* $EAP\text{-}ABAC_{m,n}$

- $EAP\text{-}ABAC_{1,1}$ is a special case of $EAP\text{-}ABAC_{m,n}$.

Equivalence of $EAP\text{-}ABAC_{m,n}$ ***and*** $LAP\text{-}ABAC_{m,n}$
III. From $EAP\text{-}ABAC_{m,n}$ *to* $LAP\text{-}ABAC_{m,n}$

- $UAV_i = UL_i$, for $1 \le i \le m$; $OAV_i = OL_i$, for $1 \le i \le n$
- $ua_i(u) = uLabel_i(u)$; $oa_i(o) = oLabel_i(o)$
- $f_a =$
$$\bigvee_{(ULS_1, ULS_2, ...ULS_m, OLS_1, OLS_2, ..., OLS_n) \in Policy_a} (\bigwedge_{1 \le i \le m} ULS_i \subseteq ua_i(u)) \wedge (\bigwedge_{1 \le i \le n} OLS_i \subseteq oa_i(u)$$

IV. From $LAP\text{-}ABAC_{m,n}$ *to* $EAP\text{-}ABAC_{m,n}$

- $UL_i = UAV_i$, for $1 \le i \le m$; $OL_i = OAV_i$, for $1 \le i \le n$
- $uLabel_i(u) = ua_i(u)$, for $1 \le i \le m$; $oLabel_i(o) = oa_i(o)$, for $1 \le i \le n$
- $Policy_a = \{(ULS_1, ULS_2, ..., ULS_m, OLS_1, OLS_2, ..., OLS_n) |$
  $f_a(ULS_1, ULS_2, ..., ULS_m, OLS_1, OLS_2, ..., OLS_n) = true\}$

Equivalence of $LAP\text{-}ABAC_{m,n}$ ***and*** $LAP\text{-}ABAC_{1,1}$
V. From $LAP\text{-}ABAC_{m,n}$ *to* $LAP\text{-}ABAC_{1,1}$

- $U = U_{m,n}; O = O_{m,n}; A = A_{m,n}; UAV = UAV_1 \times UAV_2 \times ... \times UAV_m$
- $OAV = OAV_1 \times OAV_2 \times ... \times OAV_m; ua(u) = ua_1(u) \times ua_2(u) \times ... \times ua_m(u)$
- $oa(u) = oa_1(u) \times ... \times oa_m(u)$
- $f_a =$
$$\bigvee_{f_{a_{m,n}}(ULS_1, ULS_2, ...ULS_m, OLS_1, OLS_2, ..., OLS_n) = true} (ULS_1(u) \times ... \times ULS_m(u) \subseteq ua(u)) \wedge$$
  $(OLS_1(o) \times ... \times OLS_n(o) \subseteq oa(o))$, for $ULS_i \subseteq UAV_i$ and $OLS_i \subseteq OAV_i$

VI. From $LAP\text{-}ABAC_{1,1}$ *to* $LAP\text{-}ABAC_{m,n}$

- $LAP\text{-}ABAC_{1,1}$ is a special case of $LAP\text{-}ABAC_{m,n}$.

Equivalence of $EAP\text{-}ABAC_{1,1}$ ***and*** $LAP\text{-}ABAC_{1,1}$
VII & VIII. From $EAP\text{-}ABAC_{1,1}$ *to* $LAP\text{-}ABAC_{1,1}$ *and vice versa*

- Special case of equivalence of $EAP\text{-}ABAC_{m,n}$ and $EAP\text{-}ABAC_{1,1}$.

---

4   Theoretical Expressive Power of EAP and LAP Models

This section establishes equivalence between different *EAP-ABAC* and *LAP-ABAC* models with respect to their theoretical expressive power. We consider single and multi-attribute *EAP-ABAC* and *LAP-ABAC* models. The relationship among the models we consider is schematically presented in Fig. 2. Single attribute and multi-attribute models are presented on left and right side of

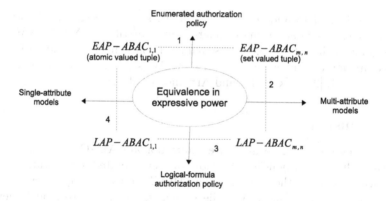

Fig. 2. Equivalence of EAP and LAP ABAC models

the Y-axis respectively. Enumerated and logical-formula policy models are presented above and below the X-axis respectively. These models all have set valued attributes. Policy tuples are represented differently in $EAP\text{-}ABAC_{1,1}$ and $EAP\text{-}ABAC_{m,n}$ models. The former uses atomic valued tuples (e.g. $(manager, TS)$) and the later uses set valued tuples (e.g. $(\{manager\}\{TS\})$).

Four different equivalences are discussed here labeled one to four in Fig. 2. They are equivalence of (i) single and multi-attribute EAP models, (ii) multi-attribute EAP and LAP models, (iii) single and multi-attribute LAP models, and (iv) single attribute LAP and EAP models.

The equivalence of single and multi-attribute EAP models are demonstrated in Segment I and II in Table 3. In Segment I, we show that multiple attributes can be represented as a single attribute comprising of cross product of values of multiple attributes. Segment II is trivial as $EAP\text{-}ABAC_{1,1}$ is a special case of $EAP\text{-}ABAC_{m,n}$. Segment III shows how to construct a LAP formula using m user and n object attributes from a enumerated policy of same set of attributes. Segment IV shows the converse. Similar to Segment I, Segment V shows how a logical formula of multiple user and object attributes can be represented as a logical formula of single user and object attributes. Segment VI is trivial as $LAP\text{-}ABAC_{1,1}$ is a special case of $LAP\text{-}ABAC_{m,n}$. The equivalence of single attribute EAP and LAP models presented in Segment VII and VIII is a special case of the equivalence of multi-attribute EAP and LAP models presented in Segment III and IV.

5   Related Work

Several ABAC models have been proposed in the literature. Most of them are based on LAPs. For example, $ABAC_\alpha$ [7] is among the first few models to formally define a $LAP\text{-}ABAC$. HGABAC [15] is a more general purpose $LAP\text{-}ABAC$ model. Other works include [8,11,16–18].

Damiani et al. [4] describe an informal framework for attribute based access control in open environments. Bonatti et al. [3] present a uniform structure to logically formulate and reason about both service access and information disclosure constraints according to related entity attributes. NIST ABAC guide [6] is significant in defining concepts, required components, considerations and architecture for designing an enterprise ABAC system. Other notable works include XACML [9], UCON [10] and Armando et al. [1].

6   Conclusion

We have presented a finite attribute, finite domain ABAC model using enumerated authorization policies. We show that enumerated authorization policy and logical-formula authorization policy ABAC models are equivalent in their theoretical expressive power. We believe, analysis of these two models beyond expressive power is required to better understand these models and ABAC in general.

Acknowledgement. This research is partially supported by NSF Grants CNS-1111925 and CNS-1423481.

References

1. Armando, A., et al.: SMT-based enforcement and analysis of NATO content-based protection and release policies. In: ABAC 2016, pp. 35–46. ACM (2016)
2. Biswas, P., Sandhu, R., Krishnan, R.: Label-based access control: an ABAC model with enumerated authorization policy. In: ABAC 2016. ACM (2016)
3. Bonatti, P., Samarati, P.: Regulating service access and information release on the web. In: Proceedings of CCS, pp. 134–143. ACM (2000)
4. Damiani, E., di Vimercati, S.D.C., Samarati, P.: New paradigms for access control in open environments. In: Signal Processing and Information Technology (2005)
5. Ferraiolo, D., et al.: The policy machine: a novel architecture and framework for access control policy specification and enforcement. JSA **57**(4), 412–424 (2011)
6. Hu, V.C., et al.: Guide to attribute based access control (ABAC) definition and considerations. NIST Spec. Publ. **800**, 162 (2014)
7. Jin, X., Krishnan, R., Sandhu, R.: A unified attribute-based access control model covering DAC, MAC and RBAC. In: Cuppens-Boulahia, N., Cuppens, F., Garcia-Alfaro, J. (eds.) DBSec 2012. LNCS, vol. 7371, pp. 41–55. Springer, Heidelberg (2012)
8. Lang, B., et al.: A flexible attribute based access control method for grid computing. J. Grid Comput. **7**(2), 169–180 (2009)
9. Moses, T., et al.: Extensible access control markup language (XACML) version 2.0. Oasis Standard (2005)
10. Park, J., Sandhu, R.: The UCON ABC usage control model. TISSEC **7**(1), 128–174 (2004)
11. Priebe, T., Dobmeier, W., Kamprath, N.: Supporting attribute-based access control with ontologies. In: ARES 2006, p. 8. IEEE (2006)
12. Sandhu, R.S.: Lattice-based access control models. Computer **26**(11), 9–19 (1993)
13. Sandhu, R.S., Coyne, E.J., Feinstein, H.L., Youman, C.E.: Role-based access control models. Computer **2**, 38–47 (1996)

14. Sandhu, R.S., Samarati, P.: Access control: principle and practice. IEEE Commun. Mag. **32**(9), 40–48 (1994)
15. Servos, D., Osborn, S.L.: HGABAC: towards a formal model of hierarchical attribute-based access control. In: Cuppens, F., Garcia-Alfaro, J., Zincir Heywood, N., Fong, P.W.L. (eds.) FPS 2014. LNCS, vol. 8930, pp. 187–204. Springer, Heidelberg (2015)
16. Shen, H.-B., Hong, F.: An attribute-based access control model for web services. In: PDCAT 2006, pp. 74–79. IEEE (2006)
17. Wang, L., Wijesekera, D., Jajodia, S.: A logic-based framework for attribute based access control. In: Proceedings of FMSE 2004, pp. 45–55. ACM (2004)
18. Yuan, E., Tong, J.: Attributed based access control (ABAC) for web services. In: Proceedings of the 2005 IEEE International Conference on Web Service. IEEE (2005)

Access Control for the Shuffle Index

Sabrina De Capitani di Vimercati[1], Sara Foresti[1], Stefano Paraboschi[2],
Gerardo Pelosi[3], and Pierangela Samarati[1(✉)]

[1] Università degli Studi di Milano, Crema, CR, Italy
{sabrina.decapitani,sara.foresti,pierangela.samarati}@unimi.it
[2] Università degli Studi di Bergamo, Dalmine, BG, Italy
parabosc@unibg.it
[3] Politecnico di Milano, Milano, Italy
gerardo.pelosi@polimi.it

Abstract. The shuffle index provides confidentiality guarantees for accesses to externally outsourced data. In this paper, we extend the shuffle index with support for access control, that is, for enforcing authorizations on data. Our approach bases on the use of selective encryption and on the organization of data and authorizations in two shuffle indexes. Our proposal enables owners to regulate access to their data supporting authorizations allowing different users access to different portions of the data, while at the same time guaranteeing confidentiality of access.

1 Introduction

The rapid advancement in ICT and the increasing adoption of cloud computing paradigms have produced an ever increasing reliance on external parties for storing and processing data. Together with the clear benefits in term of low cost and high availability (e.g., [11]), the involvement of external providers for storing data and providing services raises also issues of ensuring proper protection of information against the providers themselves (e.g., [12,15]). The research and industrial community have recognized these issues and investigated different aspects of the problem, with considerable attention paid to the need to maintain information confidential to the providers themselves that, even if trustworthy to provide the service, should not be allowed visibility over the stored data. In addition to the need to protect confidentiality of the stored data (*content confidentiality*), recent proposals have been devoting attention to the need to protect confidentiality of the accesses executed on the data (*access confidentiality*), that is, protecting confidentiality on the fact that an access aims at a specific piece of information or that two accesses aim at the same target (this latter also referred to as pattern confidentiality). There are several reasons for which access confidentiality should be protected, including the simple fact that breaches to access confidentiality may leak information on access profiles, and, in the end, even on the data themselves, therefore breaking data confidentiality itself. Among the recent proposals specifically considering the access confidentiality problem

S. Ranise and V. Swarup (Eds.): DBSec 2016, LNCS 9766, pp. 130–147, 2016.
DOI: 10.1007/978-3-319-41483-6_10

in database management scenarios (and therefore with attention to efficiency and functionality guarantees that should be provided) is the *shuffle index* [5]. The shuffle index provides an index-based hierarchical organization of the data supporting efficient and effective access execution and provides access confidentiality with limited (compared to classical solutions) performance overhead. The key idea to provide access confidentiality is a dynamic re-allocation of data at every access so to breach the otherwise static correspondence between data and physical blocks in which they are stored.

The shuffle index, while supporting accesses by multiple users [6], assumes all users to be entitled to access the complete data structure: data are encrypted with a key shared between the data owner and all users, and all users can retrieve and decrypt these data, hence accessing the plaintext content. Encryption is applied only to provide confidentiality (of content and access) with respect to the storing server. However, in many situations access privileges may need to be granted selectively, that is, different users should be authorized to view only a portion of the stored data. While existing solutions for enforcing authorizations in data outsourcing context in presence of honest-but-curious providers (e.g., *selective encryption* [2,3]) have emerged, they cannot be simply applied in conjunction with the shuffle index, given the specific characteristics of the index and its access execution, as well as the need to ensure access confidentiality guarantees.

In this paper, we provide an approach to support access control over the shuffle index (Sect. 2) to ensure that access to the data be granted only in respect of authorizations specified by the data owner. Our approach leverages the availability of selective encryption to provide a self-enforcing layer of protection over the data themselves. To allow for authorizations enforcement while maintaining access confidentiality guarantees, our approach makes use of two shuffle indexes: a primary index, storing and providing access to selectively encrypted data, and a secondary index, enabling enforcement of access control (Sects. 3 and 4). We show that our proposal correctly enforces the access control policy established by the data owner and has limited performance overhead (Sect. 5).

2   Shuffle Index

The *shuffle index* [5] is a dynamically allocated data structure offering access and pattern confidentiality while supporting efficient key-based data organization and retrieval. A data collection organized in a shuffle index is a set of pairs ⟨*index_value, resource*⟩ with *index_value* a candidate key for the collection (i.e., no two resources share the same value for *index_value*) used for index definition, and *resource* the corresponding resource associated with the index value. For simplicity, we assume the data collection to be a relational table $\mathcal{R}$ defined over a simplified schema $\mathcal{R}(I, Resource)$, with I the indexed attribute and *Resource* the resource content. At the *abstract* level, a shuffle index for $\mathcal{R}$ over I is an *unchained B+-tree* (i.e., there are no links between the leaves) with fan-out F defined over attribute I, storing the tuples in $\mathcal{R}$ in its leaves. Each node stores up to $F-1$ ordered values $v_1, v_2, \ldots, v_q$, and has as many children as the number of values stored plus one. The first child of a node is the root of the subtree including all values $v < v_1$; its last child is the root of the subtree including all values $v \geq v_q$; its i-the child ($i = 2, \ldots, q$) is the root of the subtree including all values $v_{i-1} \leq v < v_i$. Actual resources are stored in the leaves of the tree in association with their index value. At the *logical* level, each node is associated with a logical identifier. Logical identifiers are used in internal nodes as pointers to their children and do not reflect the order relationship among the values stored in the nodes. At the *physical* level, each node is stored in *encrypted form* in a physical block and logical identifiers are translated into physical addresses at the storing server. For the sake of simplicity, we assume that the physical address of a block storing a node corresponds to the logical identifier of the node itself. The encrypted node is obtained by encrypting the concatenation of the node identifier, its content (values and pointers to children or resources), and a randomly generated nonce (*salt*). Formally, block b storing node n is defined as $E(k, salt\|id\|n)$, where E is a symmetric encryption function with key k and id is the identifier of node n. Encryption protects the confidentiality of nodes content and the structure of the tree, as well as the integrity of each node and of the structure overall. Figure 1(c–e) illustrates an example the abstract (c), logical (d), and physical (e) level, respectively, of a shuffle index storing the 19 tuples in Fig. 1(a), indexed according to the values of attribute I. Actual tuples are stored in the leaves of the index structure, where, for simplicity, we however report only the index values.

To retrieve the tuple with a given index value in the shuffle index, the tree is traversed from the root following the pointers to the children until a leaf is reached. Since the shuffle index is stored at the server in encrypted form, such a process is iterative, with the client retrieving from the server (and decrypting) one node at a time to determine the child node to be read at the next level. To protect access and pattern confidentiality, in addition to storing nodes in encrypted form at the server, the shuffle index uses the following three techniques in access execution.

- *Cover searches*: in addition to the target value, additional values, called *covers*, are requested. Covers, chosen in such a way to be indistinguishable from the target and to operate on disjoint paths in the tree (also disjoint from the path of the target), provide uncertainty to the server on the actual target. If *num_cover* searches are used, the server will observe access to *num_cover*+1 distinct paths and corresponding leaf blocks, any of which could be the actual target.
- *Repeated access*: to avoid the server learning when two accesses refer to the same target since they would have a path in common, the shuffle index always produces such an observable by choosing, as one of the covers for an access, one of the values of the access just before it (if the current access is for the same target as the previous access, a new cover is used). In this way, the server always observes a repeated access, regardless of whether the two accesses refer to the same or to a different target.

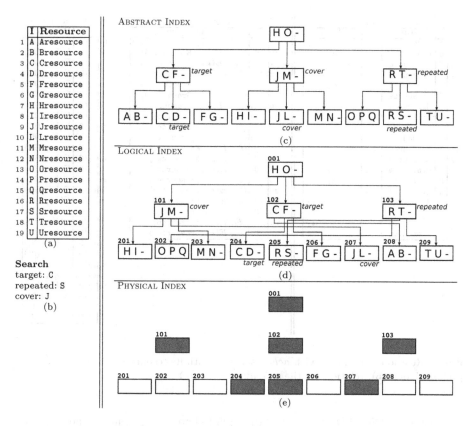

Fig. 1. An example of a relation (a), an access over it (b), and of abstract (c), logical (d) and physical (e) shuffle index

– *Shuffling*: at every access, the nodes involved in the access are shuffled (i.e., allocated to different logical identifiers and corresponding physical blocks), re-encrypted (with a different random salt and including the new identifier of the block) and re-stored at the server. Shuffling provides dynamic reallocation of all the accessed nodes, thus destroying the otherwise static correspondence between physical blocks and their content. This prevents the server from accumulating knowledge on the data allocation as at any access such an allocation is refreshed.

To illustrate, consider the shuffle index in Fig. 1(c–e) and the search in Fig. 1(b) for the tuple with index value C, assuming S as repeated access and J as fresh cover. The access entails reading (i.e., retrieving from the server) the nodes annotated in the figure, with the server only observing downloads of the corresponding encrypted blocks in Fig. 1(e) but not able to learn anything on the block content or on the roles (target, repeated, cover) of the blocks. Shuffling could produce, after the access, a re-allocation of the accessed nodes.

ORIGINAL RELATION

I	Resource	ACL		
1	A	Aresource	...	u_1	u_2	u_3
2	B	Bresource	...	u_1	u_2	
3	C	Cresource	...	u_1	u_2	
4	D	Dresource	...		u_2	u_3
5	F	Fresource	...		u_2	u_3
6	G	Gresource	...	u_1		u_3
7	H	Hresource	...	u_1		u_3
8	I	Iresource	...	u_1		
9	J	Jresource	...	u_1		
10	L	Lresource	...	u_1		
11	M	Mresource	...	u_1		
12	N	Nresource	...		u_2	
13	O	Oresource	...		u_2	
14	P	Presource	...		u_2	
15	Q	Qresource	...		u_2	
16	R	Rresource	...			u_3
17	S	Sresource	...			u_3
18	T	Tresource	...			u_3
19	U	Uresource	...			u_3

(a)

PRIMARY INDEX

I	Resource
12	$\iota(A)$	$\langle \ell_{123}, E(k_{123}, \text{Aresource})\rangle$
17	$\iota(B)$	$\langle \ell_{12}, E(k_{12}, \text{Bresource})\rangle$
4	$\iota(C)$	$\langle \ell_{12}, E(k_{12}, \text{Cresource})\rangle$
3	$\iota(D)$	$\langle \ell_{23}, E(k_{23}, \text{Dresource})\rangle$
7	$\iota(F)$	$\langle \ell_{23}, E(k_{23}, \text{Fresource})\rangle$
9	$\iota(G)$	$\langle \ell_{13}, E(k_{13}, \text{Gresource})\rangle$
10	$\iota(H)$	$\langle \ell_{13}, E(k_{13}, \text{Hresource})\rangle$
8	$\iota(I)$	$\langle \ell_1, E(k_1, \text{Iresource})\rangle$
6	$\iota(J)$	$\langle \ell_1, E(k_1, \text{Jresource})\rangle$
11	$\iota(L)$	$\langle \ell_1, E(k_1, \text{Lresource})\rangle$
2	$\iota(M)$	$\langle \ell_1, E(k_1, \text{Mresource})\rangle$
14	$\iota(N)$	$\langle \ell_2, E(k_2, \text{Nresource})\rangle$
5	$\iota(O)$	$\langle \ell_2, E(k_2, \text{Oresource})\rangle$
18	$\iota(P)$	$\langle \ell_2, E(k_2, \text{Presource})\rangle$
16	$\iota(Q)$	$\langle \ell_2, E(k_2, \text{Qresource})\rangle$
15	$\iota(R)$	$\langle \ell_3, E(k_3, \text{Rresource})\rangle$
19	$\iota(S)$	$\langle \ell_3, E(k_3, \text{Sresource})\rangle$
1	$\iota(T)$	$\langle \ell_3, E(k_3, \text{Tresource})\rangle$
13	$\iota(U)$	$\langle \ell_3, E(k_3, \text{Uresource})\rangle$

(b)

SECONDARY INDEX

I	Resource
10	$\iota_1(A)$	$E(k_1, \iota(A))$
18	$\iota_2(A)$	$E(k_2, \iota(A))$
22	$\iota_3(A)$	$E(k_3, \iota(A))$
5	$\iota_1(B)$	$E(k_1, \iota(B))$
6	$\iota_2(B)$	$E(k_2, \iota(B))$
9	$\iota_1(C)$	$E(k_1, \iota(C))$
25	$\iota_2(C)$	$E(k_2, \iota(C))$
27	$\iota_2(D)$	$E(k_2, \iota(D))$
4	$\iota_3(D)$	$E(k_3, \iota(D))$
19	$\iota_2(F)$	$E(k_2, \iota(F))$
3	$\iota_3(F)$	$E(k_3, \iota(F))$
11	$\iota_1(G)$	$E(k_1, \iota(G))$
7	$\iota_3(G)$	$E(k_3, \iota(G))$
20	$\iota_1(H)$	$E(k_1, \iota(H))$
24	$\iota_3(H)$	$E(k_3, \iota(H))$
15	$\iota_1(I)$	$E(k_1, \iota(I))$
12	$\iota_1(J)$	$E(k_1, \iota(J))$
8	$\iota_1(L)$	$E(k_1, \iota(L))$
1	$\iota_1(M)$	$E(k_1, \iota(M))$
14	$\iota_2(N)$	$E(k_2, \iota(N))$
23	$\iota_2(O)$	$E(k_2, \iota(O))$
26	$\iota_2(P)$	$E(k_2, \iota(P))$
2	$\iota_2(Q)$	$E(k_2, \iota(Q))$
13	$\iota_3(R)$	$E(k_3, \iota(R))$
16	$\iota_3(S)$	$E(k_3, \iota(S))$
21	$\iota_3(T)$	$E(k_3, \iota(T))$
17	$\iota_3(U)$	$E(k_3, \iota(U))$

(c)

Fig. 2. Relation of Fig. 1(a) with *acls* associated with its resources (a), relation for the primary index (b), relation for the secondary index (c)

For instance, 205→204, 204→207, 207→205 (where X→Y denotes the fact that the content of node X is moved to Y).

3 Primary and Secondary Indexes for Access Control

Providing access control means enabling data owners to regulate access to their data and selectively authorize different users with different views over the data. Figure 2(a) illustrates possible authorizations on the data of Fig. 1(a), considering three users (u_1, u_2, u_3). The figure reports, for each tuple r in the dataset, the corresponding $acl(r)$, that is the set of users authorized to access it. (Note that authorizations do not explicitly report the access privileges, which is considered to be 'read', since we assume access by users to be read-only, with write operations reserved to the owner.) When clear from the context, with a slight abuse of notation, in the following we will denote the access control list of a tuple r as either $acl(r)$ or $acl(r[I])$, with $r[I]$ its index value. For instance, $acl(A) = \{u_1, u_2, u_3\}$, while $acl(B) = \{u_1, u_2\}$.

Before diving into our solution, we note that there could be two natural and straightforward approaches to enforce authorizations in the shuffle index, each of which would have however limitations and drawbacks. A first natural approach would be to simply associate a key k_i with each user u_i and produce different replicas of the data. Each tuple would be replicated as many times as the number of users authorized to access it. Each copy would be encrypted with the key of the user for which it is produced. For instance, with reference to Fig. 2(a) three copies would be created for index value A and the corresponding resource Aresource, encrypted with keys k_1, k_2, and k_3, respectively. Different shuffle indexes would then be defined, one for each user, organizing and supporting accesses to the tuples that the user is authorized to access. Such an approach, besides bearing obvious data management problems (as replicas would need to be maintained consistent) would affect the protection offered by the shuffle index. In fact, it would organize each shuffle index only on a limited portion of the data (for each user, only those tuples that she can access, that is, less than half of the original tuples for each user in our example) with consequent limitations in the choice of covers. An alternative solution could then be to maintain the shuffle index as a single structure (so to build it on the complete dataset), and avoid replicas by producing only one encrypted copy for each tuple. Replicas can be avoided by considering different encryption keys not only for individual users but also for user sets (i.e., *acls*), with a user u_i knowing her encryption key k_i as well as those of the *acls* in which she is included. Each resource would then be encrypted only once and the encryption key with which it is encrypted known only to its authorized users. For instance, with reference to Fig. 2(a), Aresource would be encrypted with key k_{123} known to all users while Bresource would be encrypted with key k_{12} known to u_1 and u_2 only. While such selective encryption correctly enforces access to the encrypted resources, it leaves the problem of ensuring protection (and controlling the possible exposure) of the index values with which the shuffle index is organized. As a matter of fact, on one hand, leaving such index values accessible to all users for traversing the tree would disclose to every user the complete set of index values, even those of the tuples she is not authorized to access. On the other hand, such index values cannot be encrypted with the same encryption key used for the corresponding resources, as otherwise the ability to traverse the tree by users would be affected.

Starting from these observations, we build our approach essentially providing selective encryption while protecting index values themselves against unauthorized users without affecting their ability to retrieve those tuples they are authorized to access. Our approach is based on the definition of two different indexes. A *primary index*, defined over an encoded version of the original index values, and a *secondary index*, providing a mapping enabling users to retrieve the value to look for in the primary index. Both indexes make use of an encoding of the values to be indexed to make them intelligible only to authorized users. We then start by defining an encoding function as follows.

Definition 1 (Encoding Function). *Let $\mathcal{R}(I,Resource)$ be a relation with I defined over domain $\mathcal{D}$. A function $\iota : \mathcal{D} \to \mathcal{E}$ is an encoding function for I iff ι is:* (i) *non-invertible;* (ii) *non order-preserving;* (iii) *injective.*

Intuitively, an encoding function maps the domain of index values I onto another domain of values $\mathcal{E}$, avoiding collisions (i.e., $\forall v_x, v_y \in I$ with $v_x \neq v_y$,

$\iota(v_x) \neq \iota(v_y))$, and in such a way that the original ordering among values is destroyed. Also, non-invertibility ensures the impossibility of deriving the inverse function (from encoded to original values). For instance, an encoding function can be realized as a keyed cryptographic hash function operating on the domain of attribute I.

The second building block of our solution is the application of selective encryption, namely encryption of each resource with a key known only to authorized users. To apply selective encryption, we then define a key set for the encryption policy as follows.

Definition 2 (Encryption Policy Keys). *Let $\mathcal{R}(I,Resource)$ be a relation, $\mathcal{U}$ be a set of users, and, $\forall r \in \mathcal{R}$, $acl(r) \subseteq \mathcal{U}$ be the acl of r. The set $\mathcal{K}$ of encryption policy keys for $\mathcal{R}$ is a set $\mathcal{K} = \{k_i \mid u_i \in \mathcal{U}\} \cup \{k_{i_1,\dots,i_n} \mid \exists r \in \mathcal{R}, \{u_{i_1},\dots,u_{i_n}\} = acl(r)\}$ of encryption keys. Each key $k_X \in \mathcal{K}$ has a public label ℓ_X. Each user $u_i \in \mathcal{U}$ knows the set $\mathcal{K}_i = \{k_i\} \cup \{k_X \mid k_X \in \mathcal{K} \wedge i \in X\}$ of keys.*

Definition 2 defines all the keys needed (and the knowledge of users on them) to apply selective encryption, meaning to encrypt the data selectively so that only authorized users can access them while optimizing key management and avoiding data replication. The public label associated with a key allows referring to the key without disclosing its value. Note that knowledge by a user of all the keys of the access control lists to which she belongs does not require direct distribution of the keys to the user, since hierarchical organization of keys and use of publicly available tokens enabling key derivation can provide such a knowledge to the user [3].

We are now ready to define the first index used by our approach. This first index, called *primary*, is the one storing the actual data on which accesses should operate (i.e., tuples in $\mathcal{R}$). To provide selective access as well as enable all users to traverse the index without leaking to them information (index values and resources) they are not authorized to access, the index combines value encoding and selective encryption. Formally, the primary index is defined as follows.

Definition 3 (Primary Index – Data). *Let $\mathcal{R}(I,Resource)$ be a relation, I be the indexing attribute, ι be an encoding function for I computable only by the data owner, and $\mathcal{K}$ be the set of encryption policy keys for $\mathcal{R}$. A primary index for $\mathcal{R}$ over I is a shuffle index over relation $\mathcal{P}(I,Resource)$ having a tuple p for each tuple $r \in \mathcal{R}$ such that $p[I] = \iota(r[I])$ and $p[Resource] = \langle \ell_{i_1,\dots,i_n}, E(k_{i_1,\dots,i_n}, r[Resource]) \rangle$, with E a symmetric encryption function, $acl(r) = \{u_{i_1},\dots,u_{i_n}\}$, and $k_{i_1,\dots,i_n} \in \mathcal{K}$*

The primary index stores original data in encrypted form, encrypting each tuple with the key corresponding to its *acl* (i.e., known only to the users authorized to read the tuple). The inclusion in $r[Resource]$ of the label enables authorized users to know the key to be used for the decryption of the resource. The primary index is built on encoded values computable only by the data owner. For instance, the encoding function can be implemented through a cryptographic hash function, using a key k_o known only to the data owner (i.e., the encoded

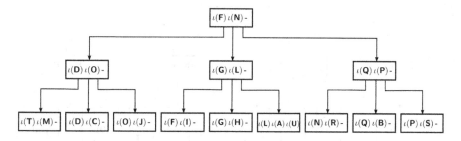

Fig. 3. Primary shuffle index for the relation in Fig. 2(b)

value $\iota(v)$ for a tuple r with index value v can be computed as $hash(v,k_o)$). Note that, although each resource singularly taken appears encrypted in the leaves of the primary index, all the nodes are (also) encrypted with a key k known to every user in the system. This second encryption layer is necessary to enable shuffling (Sect. 2).

Building the index on the encoded values provides protection of the original index values, and their order relationship, against users and storing server that observe the index on the encoded values. In fact, the encoding is non-invertible (hence the encoded values do not leak any information on the original values), and destroys the original ordering (hence the order relationship between encoded value does not leak anything on the order relationship among the original values).

Figure 2(b) illustrates a primary index $\mathcal{P}$ for our running example. The ordering among the encoded values is reported with numbers on the left of the table. Figure 3 illustrates the tree structure for such primary index. Note how the different order among the values to be indexed causes a different content within the leaves and a different ordering among them, with respect to the shuffle index in Fig. 1(a) built over the original (non-encoded) index values.

While the index on the encoded values provides the ability to traverse the tree to look for the resource associated with an encoded value, to retrieve a given resource (i.e., the resource corresponding to an original value for the indexing attribute) one would need to know the encoding of such value. For instance, resource Aresource would be stored in association with index value $\iota(A)$. The encoding (i.e., the fact that $\iota(A)$ corresponds to A) is however known only to the data owner.

The second index of our approach allows the data owner to selectively disclose to users the mapping of encoding ι, releasing to every user the mapping for (*all and only*) those values she is authorized to access. Such knowledge is provided to each user u_i encrypted with the user key k_i (so to make it non intelligible to other users and to the server) and is indexed with a user-based encoding, so to provide a distinct mapping for every user u_i, which can be computed only by u_i. The second index of our approach is therefore a *secondary* index providing user-based mapping as follows.

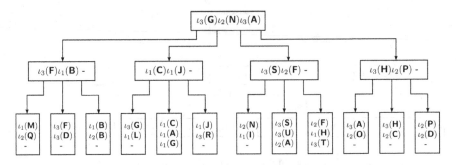

Fig. 4. Secondary shuffle index for the relation in Fig. 2(c)

Definition 4 (Secondary Index – User-based Mapping). *Let $\mathcal{R}(I,$ Resource) be a relation, I be the indexing attribute, $\mathcal{P}$ be a primary index for $\mathcal{R}$ over I with encoding function ι, $\mathcal{U}$ be a set of users, $\{\iota_i \mid u_i \in \mathcal{U}\}$ be a set of encoding functions for I such that ι_i is computable only by user u_i and by the data owner, and $\mathcal{K}$ be the set of encryption policy keys for $\mathcal{R}$. A secondary index for $\mathcal{R}$ and $\mathcal{P}$ is a shuffle index over relation $\mathcal{S}(I,Resource)$ having a tuple s for each pair $\langle r, u_i \rangle$, $r \in \mathcal{R}$ and $u_i \in acl(r)$, such that $s[I] = \iota_i(r[I])$ and $s[Resource] = E(k_i, \iota(r[I]))$, with E a symmetric encryption function and $k_i \in \mathcal{K}$.*

For instance, the encoding function of each user u_i can be implemented as a cryptographic hash function, using a key k_i known to user u_i only (i.e., $\iota_i(v) = hash(v,k_i)$). Figure 2(c) illustrates a secondary index for our running example. Again, the number on the left of the table is the ordering among the index values of the secondary index. Notice how, once again, the encoding does not convey any information on the ordering of the original index values. Note that the secondary index has a larger number of tuples than the original index, since the encoding of an original index value is encrypted as many times as the number of users who can access it. For instance, in our example, there are three instances of $\iota(A)$. Figure 4 illustrates the tree structure for the index in Fig. 2(c). We note however that the secondary index is very slim as the resources are simply the encryption, with the key of a user, of the owner encoding. While in our examples, for simplicity, we maintain the same topology, the structure of the secondary index is independent from the structure of the primary index, meaning that they may have different fan-out and height.

Note that the property of the encoding function of destroying the ordering among original index values is particularly important to guarantee protection. In fact, users will know all encoded values computed by the data owner (i.e., the co-domain of function ι), but will know the actual mapping (i.e., the actual value v corresponding to $\iota(v)$) only for the values they are allowed to access. Figure 5(a–b) illustrates a possible logical organization for the primary and secondary index of our example, where for simplicity of illustration we assume the logical organization to reflect (at this initial time) the abstract organization of the tree. We distinguish blocks of the primary and secondary index by adding prefix P and S, respectively, to their identifiers. The coloring represents the visibility of users u_1. Encoded values with grey background are those which remain non intelligible to u_1 as they are encoded with the mapping of other users (for the secondary index) or their owner encoding is not disclosed to u_1 (for the primary index).

Since encoding does not preserve ordering, encoded values non intelligible to a user will remain protected, as no inference can be drawn on them from their presence or order relationships with respect to other encoded values which are intelligible to her. For instance, consider the primary index in Fig. 5(b). User u_1, being authorized for B will know that $\iota(B)$ is the corresponding encoding. At the same time, however, $\iota(Q)$, stored in the same node, remains non intelligible to her. User u_1 simply observes the presence of another encoded value but will be able to infer neither its corresponding original value nor its order relationship with respect to B.

4   Access Execution

We now illustrate how the two indexes described in the previous section are jointly used for accessing a tuple of interest. To retrieve a tuple in $\mathcal{R}$ with value v for I, a user u_i would need to perform the following steps:

1. compute the user-based mapping $\iota_i(v) = hash(v, k_i)$;
2. search $\iota_i(v)$ in the secondary index $\mathcal{S}$, retrieving the corresponding encoded value $\iota(v)$;
3. search $\iota(v)$ in the primary index $\mathcal{P}$, retrieving the corresponding target tuple.

As an example, consider the indexes in Fig. 5(a–b) and suppose that user u_1 searches index value C. User u_1 computes $\iota_1(C) = hash(C, k_1)$ and then searches it in the secondary index in Fig. 5(a). The search returns block S205, from which $\iota(C)$ is retrieved. Hence, u_1 searches $\iota(C)$ in the primary index in Fig. 5(b). The search returns block P202, from which u_1 can retrieve resource Cresource.

Note that the steps above assume the searched value to be present in the index. If the value is not present in the secondary index, its user-based mapping does not appear in the block returned by step 2. In such a case, the process will continue providing a random value for the search in step 3, so to provide to the server the same observation as a successful search. Note also that the search for a value that is present in the dataset but for which the searching user is not authorized, present to the searching user the same observable as the search for a missing value (hence not disclosing anything to the user about values she is not authorized to access).

The steps above simply illustrate how to retrieve a target value. However, both the primary and the secondary index are shuffle indexes and accesses should not simply aim at the target value but should also be protected with the techniques (cover, repeated searches, and shuffling) devoted to protect access confidentiality. The application of these techniques on the two indexes is completely independent, meaning that the choice of covers, repeated searches, and shuffling

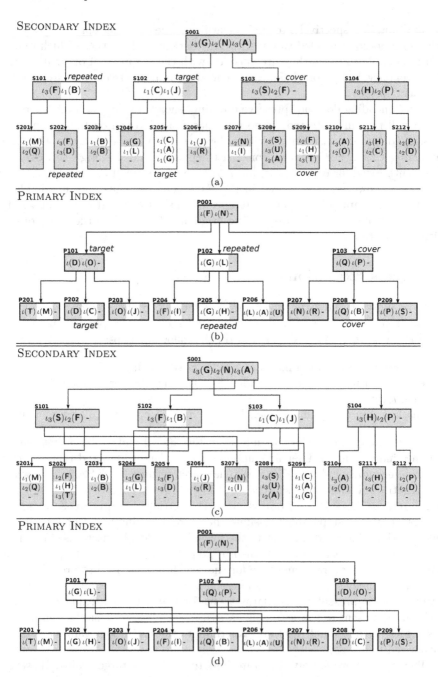

Fig. 5. Secondary and primary index before (a–b) and after (c–d) the access by u_1 over C. Secondary index: (i) cover: $\iota_2(\mathsf{F})$, (ii) repeated access: [S001,S101,S202], (iii) shuffling: S101→S102, S102→S103, S103→S101, S202→S205, S205→S209, S209→S202. Primary index: (i) cover: $\iota(\mathsf{Q})$, (ii) repeated access: [P001,P102,P205], (iii) shuffling: P101→P103, P102→P101, P103→P102, P202→P208, P205→P202, P208→P205. The gray background denotes encoded values non intelligible to u_1

can be completely independent in the two indexes. The only dependency among the two indexes is the fact that - clearly - the target to be searched in the primary index is the tuple retrieved by the search on the secondary index.

Covers, repeated searches, and shuffling on the primary and secondary index work essentially in the same way as they work in the shuffle index in absence of authorizations (Sect. 2). However, the nature of these indexes requires minor adjustments in their application, as follows.

– *Cover searches*. For both the secondary and the primary indexes, cover searches should be chosen from the set of *encoded values*, in contrast to the set of original values. The reason for this is that every user has limited knowledge on the set of original index values while she can have complete knowledge of the encoded values in the indexes (i.e., of the complete co-domains of all the encodings of all the users and the complete co-domain of the encoding of the owner). Since the encoding is non-invertible, this knowledge does not leak any information and allows the widest possible choice to the user.
– *Repeated accesses*. Repeated accesses for the primary and secondary indexes should refer to blocks, instead of specific values. The reason for this is that two subsequent accesses can be performed by two different users and therefore considering repeated searches referred to values would leak to the second user the target of the search of the previous user. Although such a leakage would be only on encoded values, we avoid it simply by assuming repeated accesses to be referred to blocks (and not to values) and to consider all accessed blocks, not only the target. At every access we then store at the server the identifiers of the blocks (target, covers, or repeated accesses) accessed during the last search. The knowledge of such identifiers is sufficient for a user to repeat an access to one of the paths visited by the search just before hers without revealing to the user the target of the previous search (which might have been performed by others).
– *Shuffling*. Shuffling works just like in the original proposal. We note that when shuffling, a user may move also content which is not intelligible to her. However, she will not be able to change the content for which she is not authorized (since she would not know the encryption key and tampering would be detected). Note that since all physical blocks stored at the server are encrypted (with a key shared between all users and the data owner) and encryption of the block as a whole is refreshed at every shuffle, the server cannot detect whether the content of a block (or part of it) has changed or not. Hence, the fact that a user can operate only on a portion of the block does not prevent correct execution of the shuffling operation.

The pseudocode of the algorithm accessing and managing the primary and the secondary index is reported in Appendix.

Figure 5(a–b) illustrates an example of access execution for search of value C by user u_1, assuming $\iota_2(F)$ as cover and path [S001,S101,S202] as repeated access for the secondary index, and $\iota(Q)$ as cover and path [P001,P102,P205] as a repeated access for the primary index. Accessed nodes are, besides the root, those annotated (as target, cover, or repeated) in the figure. Figure 5(c–d) illustrates the new structure of the indexes that would result assuming shuffling: for the secondary index as S101→S102, S102→S103, S103→S101, S202→S205, S205→S209, and S209→S202; for the primary index as P101→P103, P102→P101, P103→P102, P202→P208, P205→P202, P208→P205.

5   Analysis

We discuss the protection guarantees (i.e., the correct enforcement of authorizations and the protection of access and pattern confidentiality) and the performance of our approach.

Access control enforcement. To demonstrate that the primary and secondary indexes described in Sect. 3 guarantee the correct enforcement of the access control policy, we need to prove that each user u_i can access all and only the resources and index values in $\mathcal{R}$ she is authorized to access. Formally, $\forall u_i \in \mathcal{U}$: (i) u_i can access resource $r[Resource]$ iff $u_i \in acl(r)$; (ii) u_i can see an index value v iff $\exists r \in \mathcal{R}$ s.t. $r[I] = v$ and $u_i \in acl(r)$.

Consider a user u_i s.t. $acl(r) = \{u_{i_1}, \ldots, u_{i_n}\}$ and $u_i \in \{u_{i_1}, \ldots, u_{i_n}\}$. We need to show that u_i can retrieve the plaintext content of tuple r. A user u_i can retrieve and decrypt r iff: (i) u_i can compute $\iota_i(r[I])$; (ii) $\exists!s \in \mathcal{S}$ s.t. $s[I] = \iota_i(r[I])$ and $s[Resource] = E(k_i, \iota(r[I]))$; (iii) $\exists!p \in \mathcal{P}$ s.t. $p[I] = \iota(r[I])$ and $p[Resource] = \langle \ell_{i_1,\ldots,i_n}, E(k_{i_1,\ldots,i_n}, r[Resource]) \rangle$; and (iv) u_i can visit $\mathcal{S}$ and $\mathcal{P}$.

User u_i can compute $\iota_i(r[I])$ since it is defined as $hash(r[I], k_i)$ and u_i knows key k_i, by Definition 2. Tuple s exists and belongs to $\mathcal{S}$ by Definition 4. Tuple p exists and belongs to $\mathcal{P}$ by Definition 3. User u_i can decrypt the content of $s[Resource]$ as she knows $k_i \in \mathcal{K}_i$, and the content of $p[Resource]$ as she knows $k_{i_1,\ldots,i_n} \in \mathcal{K}_i$ because $u_i \in acl(r)$, by Definition 2. Any authorized user, including u_i, can visit both $\mathcal{S}$ and $\mathcal{P}$ since she knows both the encryption key k used by the data owner to encrypt nodes content to enable shuffling, and the co-domain of the encoding functions.

Consider now a user u_i s.t. $acl(r) = \{u_{i_1}, \ldots, u_{i_n}\}$ and $u_i \notin \{u_{i_1}, \ldots, u_{i_n}\}$. We need to show that u_i can access neither the plaintext content of $r[Resources]$, nor index value $r[I]$. It is immediate to see that u_i cannot access the plaintext content of the tuple since it is encrypted with a key k_X (Definition 3) that u_i does not know. In fact, by Definition 3, since u_i does not belong to $acl(r)$, she does not know the corresponding encryption key. User u_i cannot compute or guess index value $r[I]$ because $r[I]$ is never represented in internal or leaf nodes of the primary and secondary indexes; it is instead represented via its encoded value (i.e., $\iota(r[I])$ in the primary index and $\iota_j(r[I])$, $\forall u_j \in acl(r)$, in the secondary index). Since the encoding function is, by Definition 1, non-invertible, u_i cannot exploit her knowledge of encoded values to retrieve the corresponding original index values. Also, the traversal of the primary (and secondary) index does not reveal u_i anything about the original index values. In fact, by Definition 1, the encoding function does not preserve the order relationship among values. Hence, similar encoded values (e.g., represented in the same leaf) may not correspond to similar original values (and vice versa).

Access confidentiality. We first consider the storing server as our observer and analyze the protection offered by our proposal for the novel aspects introduced with respect to the shuffle index proposal in [7]. Like in the original proposal, we focus the analysis on the leaves of the shuffle index. In fact, nodes at a higher level are subject to a greater number of accesses, due to the multiple paths that pass through them, and are then involved in a larger number of shuffling operations, which increase their protection. A search operation on the primary and secondary index operates as in the original proposal. Hence, it enjoys the protection guarantees given by the combined adoption of covers, repeated searches, and shuffling. In the considered scenario, however, we operate with two indexes and each search for a value entails an access to the secondary index followed by an access to the primary index. The targets of the two accesses are related as they are the encoding of the same original index value. However, both indexes protect the target of accesses (as well as patterns thereof) and the covers and repeated searches adopted for the two indexes are different. This practice prevents the server from identifying any correspondence between the values in the leaves of the two indexes.

We now consider a user as our observer. A user can observe the blocks accessed by another user in a previous access (for repeated accesses), but she cannot identify the target of the access. In fact, this set of blocks includes the target, covers, and repeated accesses. Furthermore, each leaf stores multiple encoded values, which correspond to index values that are not close to each other since the encoding function is not order-preserving. A user can also possibly trace shuffling operations, but this would require her to download the whole index at each access.

Performance evaluation. The performance of the system is assessed as the average response time experienced by an authorized client when submitting an access request. System configurations providing a primary index and a secondary index with fixed heights and different fan-outs exhibit similar average response times for the client request. Moreover, varying the number of authorized users and the size of the access control lists do not significantly influence the performance of the system as long as the fan-out of the secondary index is chosen to be reasonably large. Our experiments show that the latency of the network is the factor with the greatest impact in a large-bandwidth LAN/WAN scenario. To assess the performance of our algorithm, we configured the primary index and the secondary index as 3-layer unchained $B+$-trees with fan-out 512, both of them built on a numerical candidate key of fixed-length to allow the indexing of more than 200K different values. The size of the blocks (nodes) of each index was 8KiB. The hardware used in the experiments included a client machine with an Intel Core i5-2520M CPU at 2.5GHz, L33MiB, 8GiB RAM DDR3 1066, running an Arch Linux OS. The server machine run an Intel Core i7-920 CPU at 2.6GHz, L38MiB, 12GiB, RAM DDR3 1066, 120GiB SSD disk running an Ubuntu OS. The network environment was configured through the NetEm suite for Linux operating systems to emulate a typical WAN interactive traffic with a round-trip time modeled as a normal distribution with mean of 100ms and standard deviation of 2.5ms. The performance figures obtained for accessing the secondary and the primary index exhibit an average value equal to 750ms, which compares favorably with the response time of 630ms experienced by the client when accessing two plain encrypted indexes (i.e., without shuffling).

6   Related Work

Classical works on data outsourcing protect data (content) confidentiality by wrapping a layer of encryption around them, and support query evaluation through indexes (i.e., metadata complementing the outsourced encrypted dataset) or through specific cryptographic techniques that support keyword-based searches (e.g., [10,18]). Solutions for protecting access and pattern confidentiality are based on Private Information Retrieval (PIR) techniques or on dynamically allocated data structures, which change the physical location where data are stored at each access (e.g., [1,5–8,13,14,16,17,19]). PIR solutions are computationally expensive and do not protect content confidentiality (e.g., [1,14]). The Oblivious RAM (ORAM) dynamic structure, which has been extensively studied, guarantees content, access, and pattern confidentiality (e.g., [19]). While preliminary proposals suffer from high computational and communication overheads, recent attempt to make ORAM more practical in real-world scenarios (e.g., ObliviStore [16] and Path ORAM [17]). Besides ORAM structure, also tree-based dynamically allocated structures have been studied that provide a good trade-off between privacy and performance (e.g., [5–8,13]). In particular, the shuffle index has first been proposed in [5] and then extended to support concurrent accesses by different users [6], to operate in a distributed scenario characterized by the presence of multiple (three) storage servers [8], and to support insertion and removal of tuples in the outsourced relation [7]. All these solutions, however, are based on the implicit assumption that a user can access either all the tuples in the leaves of the shuffle index or none of them.

A related line of work addresses the problem of enforcing access control restrictions over outsourced data. These solutions are based on the idea that the data themselves should enforce the access control policy. Current approaches follow two different strategies: selective encryption (e.g., [3]), and attribute-based encryption (e.g., [9]). Our work extends selective encryption proposals since we combine the shuffle index with selective encryption to enable efficient access to the data through a tree-based index, while not revealing to users index values they are not authorized to access [4].

7   Conclusions

We have presented an approach to enrich the shuffle index with access control. The enriched shuffle index provides guarantees of access confidentiality while enabling data owners to regulate access to their data selectively granting visibility to users. Also, like the original proposal, it has limited performance overhead.

Acknowledgements. This work was supported in part by the EC within the 7FP under grant agreement 312797 (ABC4EU) and within the H2020 under grant agreement 644579 (ESCUDO-CLOUD).

A   Access Execution Algorithm

Figure 6 illustrates the algorithm, executed at the client side, searching for a value in the primary and secondary index. The algorithm operates as discussed in Sect. 4 and relies on function **Search** to access the primary and secondary index structures.

Function **Search** receives as input the shuffle index $\mathcal{T}$ on which it should operate, the index value $target\_value$ target of the access, and the number num_cover of covers to be adopted. It returns the tuple r with index value $target\_value$ (if any). The function randomly chooses $num\_cover+1$ values in the domain of the (primary or secondary) index and it downloads from the server the identifiers of the blocks visited by the previous search (lines 1–3). It then visits the shuffle index level by level, starting from the root. At each level $level$, the function determines the identifiers of the nodes along the path to the target, covers, and repeated access (lines 5–8). If the block along the path to the target has been accessed by the previous search, it is repeated (an additional cover is used). The function downloads from the server and decrypts the blocks of interest (line 13) and shuffles their content (line 16). To guarantee the correctness of the search and of the index structure, the function updates the references to children of the nodes accessed at level $level$-1 (which are the parents of the nodes shuffled at level $level$), variables $target$, $repeated$, and $cover[1, \ldots, num\_cover]$ (lines 17–21). The nodes at level $level$-1 are then encrypted and written at the server. The identifiers of the nodes accessed at level $level$ are then used to update $repeated\_search[level]$ (line 23). Once the leaf node where $target\_value$ is possibly stored has been reached, the function extracts and returns the tuple with index value equal to $target\_value$ (lines 25–27).

Given the request by user u_i to search for value $target\_value$, the algorithm computes the user-based mapping $\iota_i(target\_value)$ and invokes function **Search** to search for such a value in the secondary index (lines 1–4). It decrypts the tuple retrieved by function **Search**, obtaining the encoded value $\iota(target\_value)$ for $target\_value$ (line 5). If such a value is not NULL (meaning that there is a tuple that u_i can access with index value equal to $target\_value$), the algorithm invokes function **Search** over the primary index, looking for $\iota(target\_value)$. It then computes/retrieves the encryption key necessary to decrypt the retrieved resource and decrypts it. It returns the plaintext resource to the user (lines 7–11). If the result of function **Search** over the secondary index is NULL, the algorithm runs a fake search over the primary index (not to disclose any information to other users and to the server about u_i's privileges) and returns an empty resource to the user (lines 12–14).

```
/* P, S : primary and secondary index */
/* num_cover : number of cover searches */
/* u_i,k_i : user performing the access and her key */
/* hash : non-invertible cryptographic hash function */
INPUT      target_value : value to be searched in the shuffle index
OUTPUT    resource with index value target_value

MAIN
1:  /* Phase 1: compute the user-based mapping ι_i(target_value) */
2:  target_idx := hash(target_value, k_i)
3:  /* Phase 2: search ι_i(target_value) in the secondary index */
4:  s := Search(S,target_idx,num_cover)
5:  target_idx := decrypt s[Resource] with k_i /* encoded value ι(target_value) */
6:  /* Phase 3: search ι(target_value) in the primary index */
7:  if  target_idx ≠ NULL then
8:      p := Search(P,target_idx,num_cover)
9:      k := retrieve key k with label ℓ, where p[Resource]=⟨ℓ,content⟩
10:     result := decrypt content with k
11:     return(result)
12: else target_idx := randomly choose a value for ι(target_value)
13:     Search(P,target_idx,num_cover)
14:     return(NULL)

SEARCH(T,target_value,num_cover)
1: repeated_search[0,...,T.height] := download and decrypt the blocks of accesses for T
2: randomly choose cover_value[1...num_cover+1] for target_value in the co-domain of hash
3: repeated := repeated_search[0] /* identifier of the root block */
4: for level:=1...T.height do
5:      /* identify the blocks to read from the server */
6:      target := identifier of the node at level level along the path to target_value
7:      cover[i] := id of the node at level level along the path to cover_value[i], i=1...num_cover+1
8:      repeated := block identifier in repeated_search[level] that is a descendant of repeated
9:      if target is the identifier of a node in repeated_search[level] then
10:         repeated := target, num_cover := num_cover−1
11:     ToGet := {target,repeated} ∪ cover[1...num_cover] /* ids of the blocks to be downloaded */
12:     /* read blocks */
13:     Nodes := download and decrypt the blocks with identifier in ToGet
14:     /* shuffle nodes */
15:     let π be a permutation of the identifiers of nodes in Nodes
16:     shuffle nodes in Nodes according to π
17:     update pointers to children of the parents of nodes in Nodes according to π
18:     encrypt and write at the server nodes accessed at iteration level − 1
19:     target := π(target)
20:     cover[i] := π(cover[i]), i=1...num_cover+1
21:     repeated := π(repeated)
22:     /* update the repeated search at level level */
23:     repeated_search[level] := ToGet
24: encrypt and write at the server nodes accessed at iteration T.height and repeated_search
25: let n∈Nodes the node with n.id_=target
26: let r∈n be the tuple such that r[I]=target_value
27: return(r)
```

Fig. 6. Shuffle index access algorithm

References

1. Cachin, C., Micali, S., Stadler, M.A.: Computationally private information retrieval with polylogarithmic communication. In: Stern, J. (ed.) EUROCRYPT 1999. LNCS, vol. 1592, pp. 402–414. Springer, Heidelberg (1999)
2. De Capitani di Vimercati, S., Foresti, S., Jajodia, S., Paraboschi, S., Samarati, P.: Over-encryption: management of access control evolution on outsourced data. In: Proceedings of VLDB, Vienna, Austria, September 2007

3. De Capitani di Vimercati, S., Foresti, S., Jajodia, S., Paraboschi, S., Samarati, P.: Encryption policies for regulating access to outsourced data. ACM TODS **35**(2), 12:1–12:46 (2010)

4. De Capitani di Vimercati, S., Foresti, S., Jajodia, S., Paraboschi, S., Samarati, P.: Private data indexes for selective access to outsourced data. In: Proceedings of WPES 2011, Chicago, IL, October 2011

5. De Capitani di Vimercati, S., Foresti, S., Paraboschi, S., Pelosi, G., Samarati, P.: Efficient and private access to outsourced data. In: Proceedings of ICDCS, Minneapolis, MN, June 2011

6. De Capitani di Vimercati, S., Foresti, S., Paraboschi, S., Pelosi, G., Samarati, P.: Supporting concurrency and multiple indexes in private access to outsourced data. JCS **21**(3), 425–461 (2013)

7. De Capitani di Vimercati, S., Foresti, S., Paraboschi, S., Pelosi, G., Samarati, P.: Shuffle index: efficient and private access to outsourced data. ACM TOS **11**(4), 19:1–19:55 (2015)

8. De Capitani di Vimercati, S., Foresti, S., Paraboschi, S., Pelosi, G., Samarati, P.: Three-server swapping for access confidentiality. IEEE TCC (2016). pre-print

9. Goyal, V., Pandey, O., Sahai, A., Waters, B.: Attribute-based encryption for fine-grained access control of encrypted data. In: Proceedings of CCS, Alexandria, VA, October–November 2006

10. Hacigümüs, H., Iyer, B., Mehrotra, S., Li, C.: Executing SQL over encrypted data in the database-service-provider model. In: Proceedings of SIGMOD, Madison, WI, June 2002

11. Jhawar, R., Piuri, V.: Fault tolerance management in IaaS clouds. In: Proceedings of ESTEL. Rome, Italy, October 2012

12. Jhawar, R., Piuri, V., Samarati, P.: Supporting security requirements for resource management in cloud computing. In: Proceedings of CSE. Paphos, Cyprus, December 2012

13. Lin, P., Candan, K.: Hiding traversal of tree structured data from untrusted data stores. In: Proceedings of WOSIS, Porto, Portugal, April 2004

14. Ostrovsky, R., Skeith III, W.E.: A survey of single-database private information retrieval: techniques and applications. In: Okamoto, T., Wang, X. (eds.) PKC 2007. LNCS, vol. 4450, pp. 393–411. Springer, Heidelberg (2007)

15. Samarati, P., De Capitani di Vimercati, S.: Cloud security: issues and concerns. In: Murugesan, S., Bojanova, I. (eds.) Encyclopedia on Cloud Computing. Wiley (2016)

16. Stefanov, E., Shi, E.: ObliviStore: high performance oblivious cloud storage. In: Proceedings of IEEE S&P, San Francisco, CA, May 2013

17. Stefanov, E., van Dijk, M., Shi, E., Fletcher, C., Ren, L., Yu, X., Devadas, S.: Path ORAM: an extremely simple oblivious RAM protocol. In: Proceedings of CCS, Berlin, Germany, November 2013

18. Wang, C., Cao, N., Ren, K., Lou, W.: Enabling secure and efficient ranked keyword search over outsourced cloud data. IEEE TPDS **23**(8), 1467–1479 (2012)

19. Williams, P., Sion, R., Carbunar, B.: Building castles out of mud: practical access pattern privacy and correctness on untrusted storage. In: Proceedings of CCS, Alexandria, VA, October 2008

Protection and Privacy of Data
and Big Data

Private and Secure Secret Shared MapReduce
(Extended Abstract)

Shlomi Dolev[1], Yin Li[2], and Shantanu Sharma[1(✉)]

[1] Ben-Gurion University, Beersheba, Israel
sharmas@cs.bgu.ac.il
[2] Xinyang Normal University, Xinyang, China

Abstract. Data outsourcing allows data owners to keep their data in
public clouds, which do not ensure the privacy of data and computations.
One fundamental and useful framework for processing data in a distributed fashion is MapReduce. In this paper, we investigate and present
techniques for executing MapReduce computations in the public cloud
while preserving privacy. Specifically, we propose a technique to out-
source a database using Shamir secret-sharing scheme to public clouds,
and then, provide privacy-preserving algorithms for performing search
and fetch, equijoin, and range queries using MapReduce. Consequently,
in our proposed algorithms, the public cloud cannot learn the database
or computations. All the proposed algorithms eliminate the role of the
database owner, which only creates and distributes secret-shares once,
and minimize the role of the user, which only needs to perform a simple operation for result reconstructing. We evaluate the efficiency by
(i) the number of communication rounds (between a user and a cloud),
(ii) the total amount of bit flow (between a user and a cloud), and
(iii) the computational load at the user-side and the cloud-side.

1 Introduction

Data and computation outsourcing move databases and computations from a private cloud to a public cloud, which is not under the control of a single user. Thus,
the outsourcing results in less burden on a private cloud in terms of the main-
tenance of databases, infrastructures, and executions of queries. Unfortunately,
the ease in storing data and executing computations in the public clouds implies
a risk of violating security and privacy of the databases and the computations.

Details appear as a technical report in [7]. We thank Jeffrey Ullman for valuable
comments. This work is supported by the Rita Altura Trust Chair in Computer
Sciences, Lynne and William Frankel Center for Computer Sciences, Israel Science
Foundation (grant 428/11), the Israeli Internet Association, and the Ministry of Science and Technology, Infrastructure Research in the Field of Advanced Computing
and Cyber Security.

S. Ranise and V. Swarup (Eds.): DBSec 2016, LNCS 9766, pp. 151–160, 2016.
DOI: 10.1007/978-3-319-41483-6_11

MapReduce [4] provides efficient and fault tolerant parallel processing of large-scale data without dealing with security and privacy of data and computations. The main obstacle for providing privacy-preserving framework for MapReduce in the adversarial (public) clouds is computational and storage efficiency. An adversarial cloud may breach the privacy of data and computations. In this paper, we present techniques for executing MapReduce computations in public cloud while preserving privacy.

Motivating examples. We present an example of equijoin to show the need for security and privacy of data and query execution using MapReduce in the public cloud.

Secure and privacy-preserving equijoin of two relations $X(A, B)$ and $Y(B, C)$. *Problem statement*: The join of relations $X(A, B)$ and $Y(B, C)$, where the joining attribute is B, provides output tuples $\langle a, b, c \rangle$, where (a, b) is in X and (b, c) is in Y. In the equijoin of $X(A, B)$ and $Y(B, C)$, all tuples of both the relations with an identical value of the attribute B should appear together for providing the final output tuples.

Consider that the relations X and Y belong to two organizations, *e.g.*, a company and a hospital, while a third user wants to perform the equijoin. However, both the two organizations want to provide results while maintaining the privacy of their databases, *i.e.*, without revealing the whole database to the other organization or the user. Hence, it is required to perform the equijoin in a secure and privacy-preserving manner.

Our contributions. We are interested in making a secure and privacy-preserving computation execution and storage-efficient technique for MapReduce computations in the public clouds. Hence, our focus is on *information-theoretically secure data and computation outsourcing technique* and query execution using MapReduce. Specifically, we use Shamir secret-sharing (SSS) [14] for making secret-shares of each tuple of a relation and send them to the clouds. A user can execute her queries using accumulating-automata (AA) [5] on these secret-shares without revealing queries/data to the cloud. We can perform `count` (Sect. 4.1), `search` and `fetch` operations (Sect. 4.2) in a privacy-preserving manner. *Due to the space limitation, we omit details of privacy-preserving range selection and equijoin, which may be found in* [7].

Related work. PRISM [2], PIRMAP [12], EPiC [1], MrCrypt [16], and Crypsis [15] provide privacy-preserving MapReduce execution in the cloud on encrypted data. However, all these protocols increase computation time due to dependency on encryption and decryption of data.

The authors [8] provide a privacy-preserving join operation using secret-sharing. However, the approach [8] requires that two different data owners share some information for constructing *an identical share for identical values* in their relations. The authors [9] provide a technique for data outsourcing using a variation of SSS. However, the approach [9] suffers from two major disadvantages, as follows: (*i*) in order to produce an answer to a query, the data owner has to work on all the shares, and hence, the data owner performs a lot of work instead of the cloud; and (ii) a third party cannot directly issue any query on secret-shares, and it has to contact with the data owner. In [9], the authors provide a way for constructing polynomials that can maintain the orders of the secrets. However, this kind of polynomial is based on an integer ring (no modular reduction) rather than a finite field; thus, it has potential security risk.

There are some other works [3,10,11] that provide searching operations on secret-shares. In [11], a data owner builds a Merkle hash tree [13] according to a query. In [10], a user knows the addresses of the desired tuples, so they can fetch all those tuples obliviously from the clouds without performing a search operation in the cloud.

Table 1. Comparison of different algorithms with our algorithms.

Algorithms	Communication cost	Computational cost		# rounds	Matching	Based on
		User	Cloud			
Count operation						
EPiC [1]	$\mathcal{O}(1)$	$\mathcal{O}(1)$	$\mathcal{O}(n)$	1	Online	E
Our solution 4.1	$\mathcal{O}(1)$	$\mathcal{O}(1)$	nw	1	Online	SS
Search and single tuple fetch operation						
Chor et al. [3]	$\mathcal{O}(nmw)$	$\mathcal{O}(1)$	$\mathcal{O}(nmw)$	$log_2 n$	Online	SS
PRISM [2]	$\mathcal{O}((nm)^{\frac{1}{2}}w)$	$\mathcal{O}((nm)^{\frac{1}{2}}w)$	$\mathcal{O}(nmw)$	q		E
Our solution 4.2	$\mathcal{O}(mw)$	$\mathcal{O}(mw)$	$\mathcal{O}(mw)$	1	Online	SS
Search and multi-tuples fetch operation						
rPIR [10]	$\mathcal{O}(nm)$	$\mathcal{O}(1)$	$\mathcal{O}(nmw)$	1	No	SS
PIRMAP [12]	$\mathcal{O}(nmw)$	$\mathcal{O}(mw)$	$\mathcal{O}(nmw)$	1	No	E
Goldberg [11]	$\mathcal{O}(n+m)$	$\mathcal{O}(m)$	$\mathcal{O}(nm)$	2	Offline	SS
Emekci et al. [9]	$\mathcal{O}(\ell m)$	$\mathcal{O}(\ell m)$	$\mathcal{O}(n)$	2	Offline	vSS
Our solution: knowing addresses 4.2	$\mathcal{O}((log_\ell n + log_2 \ell)\ell)$	$\mathcal{O}((log_\ell n + log_2 \ell)\ell)$	$\mathcal{O}((log_\ell n + log_2 \ell)\ell nw)$	$\lfloor log_\ell n \rfloor + \lfloor log_2 \ell \rfloor + 1$	Online	SS
Our solution: fetching tuples 4.2	$\mathcal{O}((n+m)\ell w)$	$\mathcal{O}((n+\ell m)w)$	$\mathcal{O}(\ell nmw)$	1	Online	SS
Equijoin						
Our solution (see in [7])	$2nwk + 2k\ell^2 mw$	$2nw + 2k\ell^2 mw$	$2\ell^2 kmw$	$2k$	Online	SS

Notations: Online: perform string matching in the cloud. Offline: perform string matching at the user-side. E: encryption-decryption based. SS: Secret-sharing based. vSS: a variant of SS. n: # tuples, m: # attributes, ℓ: # occurrences of a pattern ($\ell \leq n$), w: bit-length of a pattern.

To the best of our knowledge, there is no algorithm that (i) eliminates the need of a database owner except one time creation and distribution of secret-shares, (ii) minimizes the overhead at the user-side, and (ii) provides information-theoretically secure MapReduce computations in the cloud. In this paper, we build a technique for data and computation outsourcing based on SSS and AA [5]. In addition, our algorithms can *perform a string matching operation on secret-shares in the cloud, without downloading the whole database of the form of secret-shares.* However, most of the existing secret-sharing based privacy-preserving algorithms are unable to do string matching operations in the cloud; see Table 1.

The proposed technique overcomes all the disadvantages of the existing secret-sharing based data outsourcing techniques [3,8–11]. Thus, there is no need for (i) sharing information among different data owners, (ii) working at the database owners, except creation and distribution of secret-shares, (iii) having an identical share for multiple occurrences of a value, and (iv) a third party can directly execute her queries in the clouds without revealing her queries to the clouds.

2   System and Adversarial Settings

We consider, for the first time, data and computation outsourcing of the form of secret-shares to c *non-communicating* clouds that they do not exchange data with each other, only exchange data with the user or the database owner.

The system architecture. The architecture is simple but powerful and assumes the following:

STEP 1. A data owner outsources her databases of the form of secret-shares to c (non-communicating) clouds only once; see STEP 1 in Fig. 1. We use c clouds to provide privacy-preserving computations. Note that a single cloud cannot provide privacy-preserving computations using secret-sharing.

STEP 2. A preliminary step is carried out at the user-side who wants to perform a MapReduce computation. The user sends a query of the form of secret-shares to all c clouds to find the desired result of the form of secret-shares; see STEP 2 in Fig. 1. The query must be sent to at least $c' < c$ number of clouds, where c' is the threshold of SSS.

STEP 3. The clouds deploy a *master process* that executes the computation by assigning the *map tasks* and the *reduce tasks*; see STEP 3 in Fig. 1. The user interacts only with the master process in the cloud, and the master process provides the addresses of the outputs to the user. It must be noted that the communication between the user and the clouds is presumed to be the same as the communication between the user and the master process.

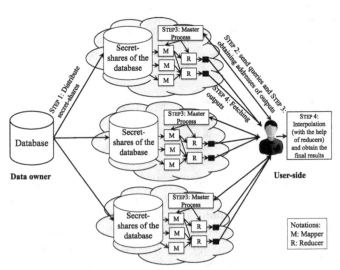

Fig. 1. The system architecture.

STEP 4. The user fetches the outputs from the clouds and performs interpolation (with the help of reducers) for obtaining the secret-values; see STEP 4 in Fig. 1.

Adversarial Settings. We assume, on one hand, that an adversary cannot launch any attack against the data owner. Also, the adversary cannot access the secret-sharing algorithm and machines at the database owner side. On the other hand, an adversary can access public clouds and data stored therein. A user who wants to perform a computation on the data stored in public clouds may also behave as an adversary. Moreover, the cloud itself can behave as an adversary, since it has complete privileges to all the machines and storage. Both the user and the cloud can launch any attack for compromising the privacy of data or computations. We consider an honest-but-curious adversary, which performs assigned computations correctly, but tries to breach the privacy of data or MapReduce computations. However, such an adversary does not modify or delete information from the data. We assume that an adversary can know less than $c' < c$ clouds locations that store databases and execute queries. In addition, the adversary cannot eavesdrop all the c' or c channels (between the database owner and the clouds, and between the user and the clouds). Hence, we do not impose private communication channels. Under such an adversarial setting, we provide a guaranteed solution so that an adversary cannot learn the data or computations. It is important to mention that an adversary can break our protocols by colluding c' clouds, which is the threshold for which the secret sharing scheme is designed for.

Parameters for analysis. We analyze our privacy-preserving algorithms on the following parameters: (i) *communication cost*: is the sum of all the bits that are required to transfer between a user and a cloud; (ii) *computational cost*: is the sum of all the bits over which a cloud or a user works; and (iii) *number of rounds*: shows how many times a user communicates with a cloud for obtaining the results.

3   Creation and Distribution of Secret-Shares of a Relation

Assume that a database only contains English words. Since the English alphabet consists of 26 letters, each letter can be represented as a unary vector with 26 bits. Hence, the letter 'A' is represented as $(1_1, 0_2, 0_3, \ldots, 0_{26})$, where the subscript represents the position of the letter; since 'A' is the first letter, the first value in the vector is one and others are zero. Similarly, 'B' is $(0_1, 1_2, 0_3, \ldots, 0_{26})$, and so on.

The reason of using unary representation here is that it is very easy for verifying two identical letters. The expression $S = \sum_{i=0}^{r} u_i \times v_i$, compares two letters, where $(u_0, u_1, \cdots u_r)$ and $(v_0, v_1, \cdots, v_r)$ are two unary representations. It is clear that whenever any two letters are identical, S is equal to one; otherwise, S is equal to zero. Binary representation can also be accepted, but the comparison function is different from that used in the unary representation [6].

A secure way for creating *secret-shares***.** When outsourcing a vector to the clouds, we use SSS and make secret-shares of every bit by selecting different polynomials of an identical degree. For example, we create secret-shares of the vector of 'A' $((1_1, 0_2, 0_3, \ldots, 0_{26}))$ by using 26 polynomials of an identical degree, since the length of the vector is 26. Following that, we can create secret-shares for all the other letters and distribute them to different clouds.

Since we use SSS, a cloud cannot infer a secret. Moreover, it is important to emphasize that we use *different* polynomials for creating secret shares of each letter; thereby multiple occurrences of a word in a database have different secret-shares. Therefore, a cloud is also unable to know the total number of occurrences of a word in the whole database.

Secret-shares of numeral values. We follow the similar approach for creating secret-shares of numeral values as used for alphabets. In particular, we create a unary vector of length 10 and put all the values 0 except only 1 according to the position of a number. For example, '1' becomes $(1_1, 0_2, \ldots, 0_{10})$. After that, use SSS to make secret-shares of every bit in each vector by selecting different polynomials of an identical degree for each number, and send them to multiple clouds.

4   Privacy-Preserving Query Processing on Secret-Shares Using MapReduce in the Clouds

4.1   Count Query

We present a privacy-preserving algorithm for counting the number of occurrences of a pattern, p, in the cloud; throughout this section, we denote a pattern by p. This algorithm is divided into two phases, as: PHASE 1: Privacy-preserving counting in the clouds and PHASE 2: Result reconstruction at the user-side.

In short, we apply a string matching algorithm, which is done using AA that compares each value of a relation with p. If a value and p match, it will result in 1; otherwise, we have 0. We apply the same algorithm on each value and accumulate all one that provide the number of occurrences of p. Note that all the values of a relation, a pattern, and the result, *i.e.*, 0 or 1, are of the form of secret-share.

Working at the user-side. A user creates unary vectors for each letter of p. In order to hide the vectors of p, the user creates secret-shares of each vector of p, as suggested in Sect. 3, sends them to c clouds. In addition, the user sends length (x) of p and the attribute of the relation (m') where to count p, to c clouds.

Working in the cloud. Now, a cloud has two things, as: (i) a relation of the form secret-shares, and (ii) a searching pattern of the form of secret-shares with its length, x. In order to count the number of occurrences of p, the mapper in the cloud performs $x + 1$ steps, see Table 2, for comparing the pattern with each value of the specified attribute of the relation.

At this time, the mapper is unable to know the value of the node N_{x+1} in each iteration and sends the final value of N_{x+1} to the user of form of a $\langle key, value \rangle$ pair, where a *key* is an identity of an input split over which the operation has performed, and the corresponding *value* is the final value of the node N_{x+1} of the form of secret-shares. The user collects $\langle key, value \rangle$ pairs from all the clouds or a sufficient number of clouds such that the secret can be generated using those shares.

Table 2. The steps executed by a mapper for a pattern of length x.

STEP 1: $N_1 = 1$, $N_x^0 = 0$
STEP 2: $N_2^{(i)} = N_1 \times v_1$
STEP 3: $N_3^{(i)} = N_2^{(i)} \times v_2$
$\vdots$
STEP $x+1$: $N_x^{(i)} = N_x^{(i-1)} + N_{x-1}^{(i)} \times v_{x-1}$

The notation $N_j^{(i)}$ shows that the node j is executing a step in iteration i. The final value of the node N_{x+1}, which is sent to the user, is the number of occurrences of the pattern

Result reconstruction at the user-side. We need to reconstruct the final value of the node N_{x+1}. The user has $\langle key, value \rangle$ pairs from all the clouds. All the values corresponding to a *key* are assigned to a reducer that performs Lagrange interpolation and provides the final value of the node N_{x+1}. If there are more than one reducer, then after the interpolation the sum of the final values shows the total occurrences of p.

Aside. If a user searches John in a database containing names like 'John' and 'Johnson,' then our algorithm will show two occurrences of John. However, it is a problem associated with string matching. In order to search a pattern precisely, we may use the terminating symbol for indicating the end of the pattern.

4.2   Search and Fetch Queries

In this section, we provide a privacy-preserving algorithm for fetching all the tuples containing p. The proposed algorithms first count the number of tuples containing p, and then, fetch all the tuples after obtaining their addresses. Specifically, we provide 2-phased algorithms, where: PHASE 1: Finding addresses of tuples containing p, and PHASE 2: Fetching all the tuples containing p.

Unary occurrence of a pattern. When only one tuple contains p, there is no need to obtain the address of the tuple, and hence, we fetch the whole tuple in a privacy-preserving manner. Here, we explain how to fetch a single tuple containing p.

Fetching the tuple. The user sends secret-shares of p. The cloud executes a map function on a specific attribute, and the map function matches p with i^{th} value of the attribute. Consequently, the map function results in either 0 or 1 of the form of secret-shares, if p matches the ith value of the attribute, then the result is 1. After that the map function multiplies the result (0 or 1) to all the m values of the ith tuple. In this manner, the map function creates a relation of n tuples and m attributes. When the map function finishes over all the n tuples, it adds and sends all the secret-shares of each attribute, as: $S_1||S_2||\ldots||S_m$ to the user, where S_i is the sum of the secret-shares of ith attribute. The user on receiving shares from all the clouds executes a reduce function that performs interpolation and provides the desired tuple containing p.

Aside. When we multiply the output of the string matching operation, which is of the form of secret-shares, to all the values in a tuple, it results in all the value of the tuple either 0 or 1 of the form of secret-shares. Thus, the sum of all the secret-shares of an attribute results in only the value of the attribute corresponding to the tuple containing p. By performing identical operations on each tuple and finally adding all the secret-shares of each attribute, the cloud is unable to know which tuple is fetched.

Multiple occurrences of a pattern. When multiple tuples contain p, we cannot fetch all those tuples obliviously without obtaining their addresses. Therefore, we first need to perform a pattern search algorithm to obtain the addresses of all the tuples containing p, and then, fetch the tuples in a privacy-preserving manner. Throughout this section, we consider that ℓ tuples contain p. This algorithms has 2-phases, as follow: PHASE 1: Finding the addresses of the desired ℓ tuples, and PHASE 2: Fetching all the ℓ tuples.

Tree-based algorithm. We propose a search-tree-based keyword search algorithm that consists of two phases, as: finding the address of the desired ℓ tuples in multiple rounds, and then, fetching all the ℓ tuples in one more round. We can also obtain the addresses (or line numbers) in a privacy-preserving manner, if there is only a tuple contains p. Thus, for the case of finding addresses of ℓ tuples containing p, we divide the whole relation into certain blocks such that each block belongs to one of the following cases:

1. A block contains no occurrence of p, and hence, no fetch operation is needed.
2. A block contains one/multiple tuples but only a single tuple contains p.
3. A block contains h tuples, and all the h tuples contain p.
4. A block contains multiple tuples but fewer tuples contain p.

Finding addresses. We follow an idea of partitioning the database and counting the occurrences of p in the partitions, until each partition satisfies one of the above mentioned cases. Specifically, we initiate a sequence of Query &Answer (Q&A) rounds. In the first round of Q&A, we count occurrences of p in the whole database (or in an assigned input split to a mapper) and then partition the database into ℓ blocks, since we assumed that ℓ tuples contain p. In the second round, we again count occurrences of p in each block and focus on the blocks satisfying Case 4. There is no need to consider the blocks satisfying Case 2 or 3, since we can apply the algorithm given for unary occurrence of a pattern, in both the cases. However, if the multiple tuples of a block in the second round contain p, *i.e.*, Case 4, we again partition such a block until it satisfies either Case 1, 2 or 3. After that, we can obtain the addresses of the related tuples using the method similar to the algorithm given for unary occurrence of a pattern.

Fetching tuples. We use the approach described in the naive algorithm for fetching multiple tuples after obtaining the addresses of the tuples.

5 Conclusion

MapReduce provides efficient large-scale data processing without dealing with the privacy and security of data and computations. In order to avoid overheads for maintaining and executing queries at the database owner side, a database is outsourced to untrusted public clouds that can reveal the database and computations. We proposed a new information-theoretically secure data and computation outsourcing technique. By the proposed techniques, users can execute their computations in the public cloud without any need of the database owner, and the cloud cannot learn the database or the computations. We provided MapReduce based privacy-preserving algorithms to execute `count`, `search`, and `fetch` quires in the public clouds. Due to the space limitation, privacy-preserving range queries and equijoin are presented in [7]. As compared to the existing algorithms, our algorithms provide perfect privacy protection without introducing computation and communication overhead.

References

1. Blass, E., et al.: EPiC: efficient privacy-preserving counting for MapReduce (2012)
2. Blass, E.-O., Di Pietro, R., Molva, R., Önen, M.: PRISM – privacy-preserving search in MapReduce. In: Fischer-Hübner, S., Wright, M. (eds.) PETS 2012. LNCS, vol. 7384, pp. 180–200. Springer, Heidelberg (2012)
3. Chor, B., Gilboa, N., Naor, M.: Private information retrieval by keywords. IACR Cryptol. ePrint Archive **1998**, 3 (1998)
4. Dean, J., Ghemawat, S.: MapReduce: Simplified data processing on large clusters. In: OSDI, pp. 137–150. USENIX Association (2004)
5. Dolev, S., Gilboa, N., Li, X.: Accumulating automata and cascaded equations automata for communicationless information theoretically secure multi-party computation (Extended abstract). In: SCC, pp. 21–29 (2015)
6. Dolev, S., Li, Y.: Secret shared random access machine. IACR Cryptol. ePrint Archive **2015**, 292 (2015)
7. Dolev, S., Li, Y., Sharma, S.: Private and secure secret shared MapReduce. Technical Report 16-01, Department of Computer Science, Ben-GurionUniversity of the Negev (2016). https://www.cs.bgu.ac.il/~frankel/reports.html
8. Emekçi, F., Agrawal, D., El Abbadi, A., Gulbeden, A.: Privacy preserving query processing using third parties. In: ICDE, p. 27 (2006)
9. Emekçi, F., Metwally, A., Agrawal, D., El Abbadi, A.: Dividing secrets to secure data outsourcing. Inf. Sci. **263**, 198–210 (2014)
10. Li, L., Militzer, M., Datta, A.: rPIR: Ramp secret sharing based communication efficient private information retrieval. IACR Cryptol. ePrint Archive **2014**, 44 (2014)
11. Lueks, W., Goldberg, I.: Sublinear scaling for multi-client private information retrieval. In: FC, pp. 168–186 (2015)
12. Mayberry, T., Blass, E., Chan, A.H.: PIRMAP: efficient private information retrieval for MapReduce. In: FC, pp. 371–385 (2013)
13. Merkle, R.C.: A digital signature based on a conventional encryption function. In: Pomerance, C. (ed.) CRYPTO 1987. LNCS, vol. 293, pp. 369–378. Springer, Heidelberg (1988)

14. Shamir, A.: How to share a secret. Commun. ACM **22**(11), 612–613 (1979)
15. Stephen, J.J., Savvides, S., Seidel, R., Eugster, P.: Practical confidentiality pre-serving big data analysis. In: HotCloud (2014)
16. Tetali, S.D., Lesani, M., Majumdar, R., Millstein, T.D.: MrCrypt: static analysis for secure cloud computations. In: OOPSLA, pp. 271–286 (2013)

Towards Creating Believable Decoy Project Folders for Detecting Data Theft

Stefan Thaler[1]([✉]), Jerry den Hartog[1], and Milan Petkovic[1,2]

[1] Technical University of Eindhoven,
Den Dolech 12, 5600 MB Eindhoven, Netherlands
{s.m.thaler,j.d.hartog}@tue.nl
[2] Philips Research Laboratories, High Tech Campus 34, Eindhoven, Netherlands
milan.petkovic@philips.com

Abstract. Digital data theft is difficult to detect and typically it also takes a long time to discover that data has been stolen. This paper introduces a data-driven approach based on Markov chains to create believable decoy project folders which can assist in detecting potentially ongoing attacks. This can be done by deploying these intrinsically valueless folders between real project folders and by monitoring interactions with them. We present our approach and results from a user study demonstrating the believability of the generated decoy folders.

Keywords: Data theft detection · Data theft · Intrusion detection · Decoy · Honey pot · Trap-based defense · Deception

1 Introduction

Digital data theft is becoming a huge problem in our ever more digitalized society. The total number of data breach incidents as well as the damage caused are rising an alarming rate. One strategy to detect ongoing digital attacks is baiting data thieves with digital decoys. These decoys are valueless, therefore any interaction with them is suspicious and will alert the responsible security offer.

One type of decoys is decoy documents. A decoy document is a file which contains seemingly sensitive information. These documents are usually stored with other sensitive documents and closely monitored. Interactions with them are reported and stored. However, while decoy documents are useful tools to obtain intelligence about an ongoing attack, most of a company's intellectual property comprises multiple files and folders, grouped together in a project folder. Yet, deceptive approaches as detection strategy are hardly used in this setting, since manually creating believable project decoys is a cumbersome, labor intensive task.

In this work we present a data-driven approach for dynamically creating new project folders from a set of existing folders based on multiple Markov models using maximum-likelihood parameter estimation. After the decoy model is learned, it can be used to sample believable project folders which resemble

S. Ranise and V. Swarup (Eds.): DBSec 2016, LNCS 9766, pp. 161–169, 2016.
DOI: 10.1007/978-3-319-41483-6_12

the original folders and can be used as deceptive bait. This deceptive bait can be placed between "real" projects. Assuming the decoys are properly monitored, they can aid in the detection of malicious activity around these real project files, since any interaction with a decoy is per definition suspicious. We have implemented a prototype and conducted a user study to evaluate whether the generated project decoys are perceived as being realistic.

We begin this paper with a brief review on related approaches in Sect. 2 to highlight gaps and motivate our approach. In Sect. 3 we describe our approach. We start by giving a high level intuition of our approach which is followed by a formal definition of our decoy model. In Sect. 4, we provide empirical evidence for the believability of the generated decoys. In Sect. 5 we discuss the results and limitations of our work. We conclude this paper by highlighting possible future improvements.

2   Related Work

Deception has been an element of warfare since a long time. In the context of IT security, Clifford Stoll reported one of the first uses of deception [9] to catch a hacker. Lance Spitzner coined the term honeypot and honeytoken [8], which are descriptive synonyms for computing resources that are created to deceive an attacker. Bringer et al.'s survey provides an overview over recent advances in the field [3].

In this paper we introduce a data-driven approach to create believable project folders that can be deployed to detect data theft attempts. Previous approaches focused on creating and placing single decoy documents([2, 10, 11, 13]) or file systems [6]. Conceptually we also create decoys to detect data theft. However, instead of creating single documents we focus on creating project folders with a believable structure, file names and properties.

3   Decoy Project Folder Generation

On a high level our approach can be divided into two phases, a *learning phase* and a *sampling phase*. Both phases are subdivided into two steps each.

The first step of the *learning phase* is to normalize the training data. In this step we replace properties of the source files and folders with placeholders. Examples of such properties are occurrences of the project name or access rights. We use this normalized training data to learn Markov chains representing the folders and property distributions, which is the second step of the learning phase. The decoy model is defined in Sect. 3.2.

In the *sampling phase* we use the previously learned model to generate decoy project folders. The first step of this phase is to generate the decoy directory structure. The second step is to instantiate the decoy project folder by assigning attributes to the nodes of the directory structure and replacing property placeholders with instantiation values.

3.1 Preliminaries and Assumptions

We assume the following concepts used in the paper are known: we will use first-order, finite-state, discrete-time, *Markov chains* (simply called Markov chains below) to model the co-occurrence of files and folders within one directory. We use the *maximizing likelihood estimator* [5] to learn the Markov chain parameters from observed sequences of files and folders.

In order to maximize the information of our learned decoy model, we will use a heuristic based on the *mutual information* [7] of files occurring together.

We will use a (finite) *forest* [4], i.e. a set of trees, to model our training file systems.

Learning requires multiple samples. To be able to effectively learn the content of folders we assume that two folders with the same name have similar contents.

Assumption 1. *If two folders within a context have the same name, they have similar contents.*

3.2 Definition of the Decoy Model

In this section we formally define our decoy model in a bottom-up manner.

To build the model we will use a training file system that contains a number of projects which structure objects such as files and directories in the form of a tree and assigns properties to these objects.

Definition 1. *We assume a fixed set of objects O, a set of attributes $\mathcal{A}$ and a (training) file system TT over these objects is given. Here an attribute $a \in \mathcal{A}$ is a function from objects to a domain Dom_a and file system TT is a forest over objects.*

Intuitively, Definition 1 states that we use a set of project folders as input for our decoy model. These project folders are organized within a directory tree, which is common in Windows- and Unix-based operating systems. An object represents a file or a folder within a project directory, and each file or folder has certain attributes such as a name, permissions or creation- and modification dates.

Some attributes are dependent on the project, for example filenames containing the project title or creation time of files that will be within the running time of the project. Therefore, to learn a common structure from different projects we 'normalize' the project to make them consistent. For example, we replace all occurrences of the project name by a 'placeholder'. We then refer to the normalized objects as nodes, and the normalized TT as NodeTree. For simplicity a file is represented as a node without children.

Definition 2. *We assume a fixed set $\mathcal{N}$, called Nodes, a node tree NT over nodes and normalization function $\mu : O \rightarrow \mathcal{N}$, mapping objects to nodes, are given.*

The only attribute that we assume is always there is 'name'. The other attributes may depend on the operating system, therefore we do not further specify them here. Instead, we simply assume they are available.

We aim to learn the content of folders. Assumption 1 states that similar names convey similar contents. Therefore, we group nodes (i.e. normalized files and folders) by their name. Next, we look at the content i.e. the children of these nodes.

Definition 3. *A **NameGroup** $NG(d)$ for a name $d \in Dom_{name}$ is the set nodes that have name d. A **NameGroupChildren** $NGC(d)$ for a name $d \in Dom_{name}$ is a set of sets, capturing the content of these folders.*

$$NG(d) = \{n \in N \mid name(n) = d\}$$

$$NGC(d) = \{ch(d') \cup \{s_s, s_e\} \mid d' \in NG(name(d))\}$$

Here, s_s represents an artificial node 'start state', i.e. the start of a directory and s_e represents the end of a directory.

From a NameGroupChildren we can find the frequencies of occurrence of nodes. However, simply taking their frequency may not be sufficient; some nodes will naturally occur together or will exclude each other. As such combination might allow an attacker to easily spot a fake project folders we need to take such dependencies into account. Thus we need to estimate the probability of certain nodes co-occurring in a folder. Yet, learning the complete joint probability of all nodes with any accuracy is not very realistic because the number of samples needed grows exponential with the number of (possible) children nodes of a node.

As a compromise we use Markov chains to model the probabilities. This allows taking into account pairwise dependencies between some nodes. In order to train our Markov chains we will treat the children of the nodes of a NameGroup as encountered observations. In this construction the order of the nodes matters; dependencies are only taking into account between the current and next node. After visiting an intermediate node this information is lost. As such nodes with a relevant dependency on each other should occur next to each other to ensure the dependency is expressed in the model.

Definition 4. *To help optimize the amount of information about dependencies that we can capture in our model we use a simple, greedy heuristic 'sorted' which starts with the start state s_s and then continuously selects follow-up nodes with maximum mutual information $max(I(n_i, n_{i+1}))$, where n_{i+1} has not been selected before. In case of a tie we prefer nodes that occur together often, i.e. $P(n_{i+1}|n_i)$ is higher. 'sorted' always ends with the end state s_e.*

Next, we want to learn a Markov chain with states S and a transition matrix P for a name group NG. That is, we want to learn a Markov chain that represents the distribution of files and folders of all directories with the same name (see Assumption 1). To do so, we treat the sets of nodes $c \in NGC(d)$ as sequence of 'observed events'.

Definition 5. *Let d be a name $d \in Dom_{name}$ and $NGC(d)$ the name group children of d. Then, we define the **states** S of the Markov Chain MC for a NGC with:*

$$S = (\bigcup_{c \in NGC(d)} c)$$

Furthermore, we will refer to a Markov chain MC that for the NameGroupChildren of a node $NGC(d)$ as MC_d. Next, we estimate transition probabilities of MC_d.

Definition 6. *Let us assume that each $c \in NGC(d)$ has been sorted by the heuristic which was introduced in Definition 4. Then the transition probabilities P for two successive nodes n_i, n_{i+1} of a Markov chain MC_d are estimated using a Maximum Likelihood Estimators, using each $c \in NGC(d)$ as an observed sequence of events.*

So far we have modeled single directories. A tree model captures a whole directory tree.

Definition 7. *The **tree model** TM is a function that maps a name $d \in Dom_{name}$ to a corresponding Markov chain MC_d.*

$$TM : d \rightarrow MC_d$$

In order to capture the probabilities of the node attributes, we learn the probability that certain nodes have. Here Assumption 1 is used to cluster the group of properties.

Definition 8. *The **attribute model** captures the frequency of occurrence of an attribute value within a name group. It is a function from $\mathcal{N}$ to probability measures $\mathcal{P}$ over the domain of a. $\mathcal{P}$ is defined as:*

$$\mathcal{P}_{a,NG(n)}(x) = \frac{\#\{n' \in NG(n) \mid a(n') = x\}}{\#NG(n)}$$

and the attribute model AM as:

$$AM(n, a) = \mathcal{P}_{a,NG(n)}$$

Finally, using the previous definitions we define our decoy model as follows:

Definition 9. *The **decoy model** DM comprises the tree model TM and attribute model AM. Intuitively, the tree model captures the learned, normalized directory structure, whereas the attribute model contains the learned, normalized file- and folder attributes.*

3.3   Sampling Decoys

A learned decoy model can be used to sample decoy project folders. First, the user chooses instantiation values for the placeholders, e.g. a project name for the decoy project. Then, the directory structure is created by a recursive random walk over the tree model. This recursive random walk starts with the Markov chain MC_p, where p is the placeholder for the project name. This random walk generates a set of nodes, which represents the content of this folder. The recursion step performs random walks over the Markov chains for each of these nodes.

Thereafter, we instantiate the generated directory structure, which outputs the decoy project folder. We randomly pick the attributes from the attribute model AM for each node of the directory structure. Finally, we replace all attribute placeholders with the chosen instantiation values and write the instantiated nodes as files or folders to the disk.

4   Validation

Decoys have several desirable properties ([2,12]), but the most important one is believability, i.e. capable of eliciting belief or trust [2]. Therefore, we have conducted a user study to validate whether human judges are able to distinguish between real projects and decoys. To conduct the experiments, we have implemented a prototype of our approach in Python 2.7.

Survey setup. In this study, we presented 30 software project folders to 27 human judges. Half of the presented software project folders were generated using our prototype, the other half were real project directories. The study participants were asked to decided which ones were real and which ones were decoys. The software project folders were shared on-line and the participants could click around freely within the projects.

We learned three different decoy models, one for Java projects, one for Python projects and one for Ruby on Rails projects. We chose three different project types to identify differences in the trained model and the effect of the believability of the decoy. In total we used 25 open source projects for each project type to learn the decoy models. The number 25 was determined using trial and error and based on believability and variability of the generated decoy projects. The "real" projects that we use for training were different from the "real" ones that we presented to the survey participants. We obtained the projects by searching GitHub for certain terms, e.g. "Java and Security" and chose popular projects to related topics. Since evaluating 30 projects would take a long time, the study was split into three parts, one for each project type. Each participant was free to chose which of the parts and the number of parts they wanted to complete. Each partial surveys contained a section with demographic questions.

We recorded the answers to the surveys as well as the clicks of the participants within the folders. We neither counted survey answers where we did not have any corresponding clicks nor clicks on folders that could not be correlated to participants of the study. The data was collected within the period from February 1st to February 8th in 2016.

In total, we had 27 unique participants and we have collected 23 complete surveys for Java, 19 for Python and 15 for Rails projects resulting in 570 answers. We rejected 27 answers where the monitoring showed that the corresponding project was not looked at by this user. Thus in total we collected 543 valid judgments.

The majority of our study participants (81.5 %) was highly educated, i.e. had a college or post graduate degree and also most of them (70.37 %) rated their own software development skills as average or better. Most of the participants (78.3 % / 68.3 %) who responded to the Java and Python part of survey stated that they have at least some knowledge of the Java programming language / Python programming language respectively, whereas only 20 percent of the participants had some knowledge of the Rails framework. On average participants rated their Java, Python and rails framework knowledge respectively as 2.87, 2.43 and 1.40 on a scale from 1 to 5 with 5 being the highest.

To avoid participants' bias towards project names, we replaced the project names that occurred in all files and folders of a project with a randomly numbered placeholder of the form Pxx, where xx was a randomly chosen number between 01 and 20. The study participants were informed about this measure. Apart from that, the participants knew that they were presented partially generated and partially real folder listings. To counter any bias originating from this knowledge, we phrased the evaluation question in a non-suggestive way, i.e.: *"The number of real/decoy projects does not necessarily have to be balanced. There may be 0 real projects, there may also be up to 10 real projects."*.

Survey results. In total, of the 543 valid answers 271 were on real projects and 272 were on decoy projects. 143 of the answers on real projects labeled them correctly as real and 128 declared them as decoys (52.7 %). 135 of the answers on decoys labeled them incorrectly as real and 137 were correctly identified as decoys (50.37 %). The average accuracy per project type was 52.19 % correct answers for Java projects, 53.63 % for Python projects and 46.32 % for Rails projects. In total 51.20 % of the 543 answers were correct.

The minimum recorded accuracy of the individual judges was 30 %, and about a quarter of the participant's accuracies were below 50 % total accuracy while the highest accuracy was 90 %. The total average individual performance was 53.3 %, which is slightly better than random guessing.

5 Discussion and Limitations

We have presented a data driven approach to create decoy project folder. These decoys may aid detecting potential data theft attacks by placing them closely monitored between real projects. A perfect decoy would be indistinguishable from the object it tries to mimic, therefore ideally the performance of the judges should be close to random guesses. In our believability study, the participants were able to identify real projects and decoys in 51.57 % of the answers, which suggests that they had difficulty distinguishing generated projects from real ones.

We have empirically shown that the generated decoys are perceived as believable, however, we did so in a limited way. We did not take into account some of the external factors that can influence the believability of the decoy, for example the context where a decoy is deployed, the choice of source projects that are used to train the decoy model as well as the choice of projects that decoys will be compared to during the study. In order to more properly interpret the results of our study, further investigations on a well-founded baseline are required. Finally, we have to validate whether the decoys can be effectively used to detect data-thefts.

Our proposed approach has some limitations. First of all, currently we need to specify instantiation parameters such as the name of the project decoy manually. We assume that these parameters contribute to the effectiveness of our approach, thus ideally they are also learned from the source projects as well as the target context. Next, our approach will not work if an attacker already knows which project they want to steal, because then they do not need to browse other projects to determine their value. Also, in other contexts simply refusing access to the data works better than deceiving an attacker [1]. Finally, potentially sensitive data could be leaked using our approach.

6   Conclusion and Future work

In this paper we presented a data driven approach based on first-order Markov chains that can be used to automate the generation of decoy project folders within a specific, topical context. We have implemented a prototype of this approach, generated decoy project folders and validated their perceived believability via a user study with 27 participants and 543 evaluated projects. The user study showed that the participants could only correctly identify 51.2 percent of the projects, which is only slightly better than random guessing.

To address the previously mentioned limitations and thereby improve our approach, we plan to include methods for learning and generating the patterns of existing file names so that we can create new ones. Furthermore, we believe that hybrid methods which are based on templates as well as on data could further improve the believability of the generated project folder structure. Additionally, we are investigating on methods to learn instantiation parameters such as the project name from existing sources.

While our approach has certain limitations, we envision decoy project folders being deployed as cheap, supportive measure to detect ongoing data thefts.

Acknowledgements. This work has been partially funded by the Dutch national program COMMIT under the THeCS project.

References

1. Biskup, J.: For unknown secrecies refusal is better than lying. In: Atluri, V., Hale, H. (eds.) Research Advances in Database and Information Systems Security. IFIP, vol. 43, pp. 127–141. Springer, New York (2000)
2. Bowen, B.M., Hershkop, S., Keromytis, A.D., Stolfo, S.J.: Baiting inside attackers using decoy documents. In: Chen, Y., Dimitriou, T.D., Zhou, J. (eds.) SecureComm 2009. LNICST, vol. 19, pp. 51–70. Springer, Heidelberg (2009)
3. Bringer, M.L., Chelmecki, C.A., Fujinoki, H.: A survey: recent advances and future trends in honeypot research. Int. J. 4, 63–75 (2012)
4. Diestel, R.: Graph Theory. GTM, vol. 173, 4th edn. Springer, Heidelberg (2010). ISBN 978-3-642-14278-9
5. Kemeny, J.G., Snell, J.L.: Finite Markov Chains, vol. 356. van Nostrand, Princeton (1960)
6. Rowe, N.C.: Automatic detection of fake file systems (2005)
7. Shannon, C.E., Weaver, W.: The Mathematical Theory of Communication. University of Illinois Press, Urbana (1949)
8. Spitzner, L.: Honeypots: catching the insider threat. In: Proceedings of the 19th Annual Computer Security Applications Conference 2003, pp. 170–179. IEEE (2003)
9. Stoll, C.P.: The cuckoos egg: tracing a spy through the maze of computer espionage (1989)
10. Voris, J., Boggs, N., Stolfo, S.J.: Lost in translation: improving decoy documents via automated translation. In: 2012 IEEE Symposium on Security and Privacy Workshops (SPW), pp. 129–133. IEEE (2012)
11. Whitham, B.: Canary files: generating fake files to detect critical data loss from complex computer networks. In: The Second International Conference on Cyber Security, Cyber Peacefare and Digital Forensic (CyberSec2013), pp. 170–179. The Society of Digital Information and Wireless Communication (2013)
12. Whitham, B.: Design requirements for generating deceptive content to protect document repositories (2014)
13. Yuill, J., Zappe, M., Denning, D., Feer, F.: Honeyfiles: deceptive files for intrusion detection. In: Proceedings from the Fifth Annual IEEE SMC Information Assurance Workshop, 2004, pp. 116–122. IEEE (2004). http://ieeexplore.ieee.org/xpls/abs_all.jsp?arnumber=1437806, http://www.dtic.mil/cgi-bin/GetTRDoc?AD=ADA484922

Practical Differentially Private Modeling of Human Movement Data

Harichandan Roy[1]([⊠]), Murat Kantarcioglu[1,2], and Latanya Sweeney[2]

[1] University of Texas at Dallas, Richardson, USA
{harichandan.roy,muratk}@utdallas.edu
[2] Harvard University, Cambridge, USA
{kantarcioglu,latanya}@fas.harvard.edu

Abstract. Exciting advances in big data analysis suggest that sharing personal information, such as health and location data, among multiple other parties could have significant societal benefits. However, privacy issues often hinder data sharing. Recently, differential privacy emerged as an important tool to preserve privacy while sharing privacy-sensitive data. The basic idea is simple. Differential privacy guarantees that results learned from shared data do not change much based on the inclusion or exclusion of any single person's data. Despite the promise, existing differential privacy techniques addresses specific utility goals and/or query types (e.g., count queries), so it is not clear whether they can preserve utility for arbitrary types of queries. To better understand possible utility and privacy tradeoffs using differential privacy, we examined uses of human mobility data in a real-world competition. Participants were asked to come up with insightful ideas that leveraged a minimally protected published dataset. An obvious question is whether contest submissions could yield the same results if performed on a dataset protected by differential privacy? To answer this question, we studied synthetic dataset generation models for human mobility data using differential privacy. We discuss utility evaluation and the generality of the models extensively. Finally, we analyzed whether the proposed differential privacy models could be used in practice by examining contest submissions. Our results indicate that most of the competition submissions could be replicated using differentially private data with nearly the same utility and with privacy guarantees. Statistical comparisons with the original dataset demonstrate that differentially private synthetic versions of human mobility data can be widely applicable for data analysis.

Keywords: Differential privacy · Human mobility · Utility · Hubway

1 Introduction

Sharing human related activity data can offer many important benefits to society. For example, mining human mobility data based on cell phone usage can reveal

© IFIP International Federation for Information Processing 2016
Published by Springer International Publishing Switzerland 2016. All Rights Reserved
S. Ranise and V. Swarup (Eds.): DBSec 2016, LNCS 9766, pp. 170–178, 2016.
DOI: 10.1007/978-3-319-41483-6_13

timely information about traffic conditions. "Smart cities" demonstrations show ways human activity data can improve city services. Often, these models require sharing beyond the person or even the government. A vision is that some of the best possible benefits result from sharing personal activity among organizations. However, the greater the sharing, the greater the risks may be of personal harms. So, privacy concerns may hinder widespread data sharing. Concerns are not unfounded. For example, by correlating location of the individual at a given time of the week, it may be possible to infer someone's religion. Similarly, privacy attacks ranging from stalking to sensitive information disclosure have been widely reported in practice against human mobility data [5,10].

Of course, personal data can be shared widely if it cannot be personally attributed to a specific person. The idea is that no one can be harmed if his information cannot be isolated in shared data. To address these kinds of privacy challenges, computer scientists have proposed mathematically rigorous techniques in the framework of differential privacy [7]. The main idea in differential privacy is that disclosed results do not change noticeably with the inclusion or exclusion of any given individual's data. Recently, differential privacy has been applied in many different settings ranging from answering basic count queries [2] to building support vector machines [8]. In almost all of these cases, the underlying differential privacy tools are designed for specific use cases and utility is defined and tested for that given use case (e.g., measuring utility for differential private count queries by comparing the euclidean distance between original count query results vs. differentially private results). Usually, it is not clear whether a given approach can support a wide range of uses to which an actual human data scientist may put the data. In this work, we try to understand whether we can provide differentially private synthetic data sets that can be shared instead of an original dataset with confidence that the resulting data will retain utility in different usage scenarios.

One challenge in understanding all the potential uses of a given dataset is that it is impossible to model human imagination. In other words, different data scientists may want to use the data in very different ways. To address this challenge, we look into an existing data set disclosed as a part of the *Hubway Data Visualization Challenge* [1]. *The Hubway* is a public bicycle sharing system with stations throughout Boston, Cambridge, Somerville and Brookline; and it is designed to provide a convenient form of active public transportation by providing access to bicycles. *The Hubway* system stores users' information and generates trip data every day. Hubway data contains users' bike rides history and some personal information, so if it is released publicly or shared with other stakeholders an adversary can take advantage of it and may potentially figure out private information of its target. In 2012, *Hubway* and *Metropolitan Area Planning Council (MAPC)* jointly hosted a challenge named *Hubway Data Visualization Challenge* asking participants to come up with some projects that involve visualizations, animations, artistic representations or interactive data analysis tools. After this challenge, there were reports that some of the disclosed data could be used to identify individuals using location information disclosed on

Twitter [9]. Still, submissions to the competition give us a good understanding of what data scientists may want to do with a given human mobility dataset.

To answer the question mentioned above, we propose a model built under differential privacy here. Our model generates differentially private synthetic human mobility dataset from an original dataset that preserves users' privacy. Furthermore, our synthetic dataset also shows a very good accuracy in most important statistical comparisons with the original dataset. Finally, we analyze whether the disclosed differentially private synthetic dataset can adequately provide what data scientists need by analyzing the utility of our disclosed data based on the Hubway challenge submissions. Main **contributions** of this paper are-

- We present a generic *Sanitization Model* built under differential privacy for *resource sharing based human mobility services* to generate differentially private synthetic dataset that preserves users' trip level privacy while sacrificing as little as possible data utility.
- To show the applicability of the generated synthetic data, we compute and compare the most compelling statistics from both synthetic and original datasets. We observe that synthetic data upholds a very impressive accuracy.
- Moreover, a thorough and extensive utility evaluation of synthetic distribution has been done with respect to four different utility metrics.

In Sect. 2, we talk about some preliminaries about differential privacy. Our sanitization model is described in Sect. 3. The experimental evaluation and possible application of it are discussed in Sects. 4 and 5. Section 6 talks about related works and the conclusion in Sect. 7.

2 Preliminaries

Definition 2.1. *Differential Privacy* [7]: A privacy mechanism $\mathcal{A}$ gives ϵ-differential privacy if for any database D and $\hat{D}$ differing on at most one record, and for any possible output $O \in Range(\mathcal{A})$,

$$Pr[\mathcal{A}(D) = O] \leq e^\epsilon \times Pr[\mathcal{A}(\hat{D}) = O] \tag{1}$$

where the probability is taken over the randomness of $\mathcal{A}$.

Definition 2.2. *Global Sensitivity* [7]: For any function $f : D \to \mathbb{R}^d$, the L1-sensitivity of f is,

$$\nabla f = \max_{D,\hat{D}} \| f(D) - f(\hat{D}) \|_1 \tag{2}$$

for all D, $\hat{D}$ differing on at most one record.

Theorem 2.3. *Laplace Mechanism* [7]: *For any function $f : D \to \mathbb{R}^d$, and $\epsilon > 0$, the following mechanism $\mathcal{A}$, called the Laplace Mechanism, is ϵ-differentially private:* $\mathcal{A}_f(D) = f(D) + \langle Lap(\nabla f / \epsilon) \rangle^d.$

3 Sanitization Model

In this section, we propose a *Sanitization Model*, shown in Algorithm 1, which is built under differential privacy. The model takes original dataset, D and privacy budget, ϵ as input and generates ϵ-differentially private synthetic data, $\hat{D}$ as output. *First*, it removes invalid entries and outliers from original dataset applying the statistical $3IQR$ [11] rule to attributes. *Second*, the attributes form some non-disjoint groups based on their associativity. The associativity among the attributes can be examined using well-known *Chi-square Test for Independence/Homogeneity* or *G-Test*. We would like to emphasize that, no statistics are disclosed as a part of this step here. We assume that the grouping of attributes is public information.[1] *Third*, the model builds desired synthetic distributions for each group which is described in Sect. 3.1. *Finally*, the synthetic dataset is generated by taking samples from these distributions and aggregating them together which is discussed in Sect. 3.2.

Algorithm 1. SanitizationModel(D, ϵ)

Input: Original Dataset D, Privacy budget ϵ
Output: Synthetic Dataset $\hat{D}$

1: remove invalid entries and outliers from D
2: $\mathbb{G} = \{<\mathcal{G}_1, \mathcal{G}_2, ..., \mathcal{G}_m>|(\mathcal{G}_i \cap \mathcal{G}_j) \neq \emptyset; 1 \leq i, j \leq m; \mathcal{G}_i, \mathcal{G}_j \subset \{\mathbb{X} = all\_attribute\_set\}\}$

3: $\hat{\varPhi} = \{<\hat{\phi}_1, \hat{\phi}_2, ..., \hat{\phi}_m>|\hat{\phi}_i = diff\_private\_dist\_of(\mathcal{G}_i, \epsilon); 1 \leq i \leq m\}$
4: $\hat{D} = \epsilon$-differentially private synthetic dataset sampling from $\hat{\varPhi}$

3.1 Constructing Synthetic Distributions

The first step of constructing a distribution is to create a contingency table (CT) for it. For any particular group $\mathcal{G}$, frequency distribution of all possible distinct combinations of values of all attributes belong to the group represents a CT of that group. Now using the equation mentioned in Theorem 2.3 if we add laplace noise to each frequency, it will become a synthetic CT. In case of negative values, we set them zero since frequency cannot be negative. The frequencies are then normalized to compute respective probability density function.

In our case, hubway dataset has nine attributes- (1) *id* (trip id), I, (2) *start_station_id*, S, (3) *end_station_id*, E, (4) *start_time*, ST, (5) *duration*, L, (6) *end_time*, ET, (7) *zip_code*, Z, (8) *subscription_type*, U and (9) *gender*, G. In step-2 of Algorithm 1, we divide the attributes into five groups: $\mathcal{G}_1$- $\{S, E\}$, $\mathcal{G}_2$- $\{S, ST\}$, $\mathcal{G}_3$- $\{S, E, L\}$, $\mathcal{G}_4$- $\{S, Z\}$, and $\mathcal{G}_5$- $\{Z, U, G\}$. Note that, we do not include ET in any group because it can be calculated from ST and L. For $\mathcal{G}_1$, we first make a CT and after adding laplace noise we convert the resulting synthetic CT finally to CDF which is represented as *Trip CDF*, $\hat{\varPhi}_T$. For $\mathcal{G}_2, \mathcal{G}_3, \mathcal{G}_4$ and $\mathcal{G}_5$,

---

[1] Since our main focus is slightly different, we skip the discussion about *Chi-square Test for Independence/Homogeneity* and *G-Test* here.

rather than making a single *CDF*, we make a number of *CDF*s for each group instead. More specifically for $\mathcal{G}_2$ and $\mathcal{G}_4$, we build a total of $|S|$ number of *CDF*s one corresponds to a specific station in S. Likewise, for $\mathcal{G}_5$ we build a total of $|Z|$ number of *CDF*s one for each zip code. $\mathcal{G}_2$ has an attribute ST which, in essence, is a combination of *year*, *month*, *date* and *hour* sub-attributes (we ignore *min* and *sec* here). Taking these four sub-attributes into account, we build a *CDF* for each start station in S. The *StartTime CDF* is denoted by $\hat{\Phi}_{ST}$. For $\mathcal{G}_4$, we build zip distribution for each start station and the *CDF* for this group is denoted by $\hat{\Phi}_{SZ}$. Similarly, for $\mathcal{G}_5$ we construct *Subscription-Gender* distribution for each zip and it is represented by $\hat{\Phi}_{ZUG}$. In case of $\mathcal{G}_3$, instead of fitting *duration* into an existing parametric distribution, we build total $||S| \times |S||$ empirical distributions for *Duration* where one corresponds to a particular combination of start and end stations. The reason for building empirical distributions is that they show better results than the fitted parametric *Exponential, Normal and Log-normal* distributions. And we build $||S| \times |S||$ duration distributions rather than only $|S|$ distributions like $\mathcal{G}_2$ and $\mathcal{G}_4$ because duration mainly depends on the distance between two stations. The number of bins is set to 7. These empirical distributions are indeed *CT*s for duration and their corresponding synthetic *CDF* is denoted by $\hat{\Phi}_{\mathcal{L}}$. Note that we add laplace noise to the degree that satisfies the equation stated in Theorem 2.3 to make synthetic distributions ϵ-differentially private. In all cases, global sensitivity ∇f is 2 since adding or removing or changing an entry can change the function value at most 2.

3.2 Differentially Private Synthetic Data Generation

In this section we will describe how to generate differentially private synthetic data for *The Hubway* from the distributions constructed in Sect. 3.1. Among nine attributes, *id I* is unique in the original dataset. Thus, we assign an unique id for each newly generated trip entry. The steps to generate other attributes of a particular trip, i, as follows: *First*, select a trip (s_i, e_i) by a random sampling from trip *CDF*, $\hat{\Phi}_T$ for i. *Second*, start time for trip i, st_i is randomly sampled from $\hat{\Phi}_{ST}(s_i)$. Here, $\hat{\Phi}_{ST}(s_i)$ returns sample from the start time *CDF* of station, s_i. Since it gives *year*, *month*, *date* and *hour* only, we add *min* and *sec* by taking samples from $Uniform(0, 59)$ distribution. *Third*, to get *duration* l_i for trip i, we need to take a random sample from duration distribution of trip (s_i, e_i), $\hat{\Phi}_{\mathcal{L}}(s_i, e_i)$. In this case, each sample taken from $\hat{\Phi}_{\mathcal{L}}(s_i, e_i)$ returns a bin with its start value, a and end value, b. To get the exact value of duration for trip, i, we take a random sample from $Uniform(a, b)$ distribution. By adding l_i to st_i, et_i is calculated accordingly. *Fourth*, we get z_i from a random sample taking from station-zip *CDF* of s_i, $\hat{\Phi}_{SZ}(s_i)$. *Finally*, a sample (z_i, u_i, g_i) is taken from $\hat{\Phi}_{ZUG}$ where z_i is restricted to the value computed in step *Fourth*.

4 Experimental Evaluation

In our experiment, we use hubway trip history data released in [1] in February 2014. It contains total of 1029739 entries. For simplicity and without loss of

Org.		Syn. (0.9)	
Pop. st.	Trips(%)	Avg. Trips(%)	σ
67	2.98	2.98	0.019
22	2.89	2.89	0.020
53	2.21	2.21	0.017
113	2.19	2.19	0.013
36	2.07	2.07	0.017

(a)

Org.		Syn. (0.9)	
Pop. st.	Trips(%)	Avg. Trips(%)	σ
67	3.04	3.04	0.015
22	2.89	2.89	0.020
74	2.22	2.22	0.020
36	2.14	2.14	0.014
113	2.11	2.11	0.012

(b)

Org.		Syn. (0.9)	
Pop. day	Trips(%)	Avg. Trips(%)	σ
2013-10-03	0.56	0.54	0.013
2013-10-02	0.55	0.52	0.011
2013-09-20	0.55	0.52	0.013
2013-09-17	0.54	0.53	0.012
2013-10-18	0.54	0.52	0.013

(c)

Org.		Syn. (0.9)	
Trip	Trips(%)	Avg. Trips(%)	σ
53 - 67	0.47	0.47	0.007
67 - 53	0.46	0.46	0.007
33 - 67	0.25	0.25	0.006
67 - 33	0.24	0.24	0.004
40 - 22	0.20	0.20	0.005

(d)

Fig. 1. Statistical Analysis: (a) Top 5 popular stations (outgoing trips), (b) Top 5 popular stations (incoming trips), (c) Top 5 popular days and (d) Popular Top 5 trip-routes in original and synthetic ($\epsilon = 0.9$) data [20 runs].

generality, we work on *nine* attributes among them. We will show some aspects of applicability and effective use of synthetic data in this section. Our experiments show that 0.9 is the lowest value of ϵ where we get maximum utility. We run the experiment 20 times and compute the following statistics in each run. In Fig. 1, we show the average and standard deviation σ of 20 runs.

For each station, there are two types of trips: *outgoing* and *incoming*. A trip is considered as *outgoing* to its starting station and as *incoming* to its destination. Both are statistics are important in practice and so we study both cases here. Figure 1(a) shows the *outgoing* trips percentage of top 5 popular stations in original data and their corresponding percentage in synthetic data with σ. As we observe, the percentages of trips shown in the table are identical in both datasets with very low deviation. Similar statistics considering *incoming* trips are shown in Fig. 1(b) and it holds similar observation. Besides popular stations, finding popular days is an another essential statistics needed for planning purposes. Figure 1(c) shows the top 5 popular days in original dataset with trips percentage and the corresponding percentage in synthetic data along with their standard deviation. As we see, the percentage of each of the popular days in original and synthetic data is almost same and the corresponding σ is very low as well. Finding popular trip routes is also another statistics that carries important information. In Fig. 1(d), we show the top 5 popular trip routes in original data and the corresponding statistics in synthetic datasets. Popularity is measured based on their percentages in entire dataset. The result shows that all top 5 popular trip routes in original data have same percentage of trips in synthetic data as well with very low σ.

We also compute some other statistics but due to space constraint the figures are not shown in the paper. We briefly discuss these statistics here. Comparing the trip percentages in different time periods between two datasets is another important measure for understanding utility. Results show that the noise impact is negligible and in all cases, *Morning*, *Afternoon* and *Night*, synthetic data preserves the original statistics almost precisely. For example, the difference in morning trip percentage is 0.15 with σ 0.103 only. Gender distribution for each station may be useful in some practical applications (e.g., targeting adds for given stations). We pick few stations randomly to see their gender distributions. According to the results, synthetic data shows promising results in this case as well. For example, station 67 has gender distribution: Male- 62.68 %, Female- 14.04 %, X- 23.28 % in original data and in synthetic data it is: 57.74 %, 19.00 %, 23.26 % with σ 0.25, 0.22 and 0.20 respectively. The subscription distribution per station seems another relevant statistics that has also a significant impact in resource optimizations (e.g., for *Smart City*). The subscription distribution of (*Registered, Casual*) for station 67 in original data is (76.72 %, 23.28 %) and in synthetic data it is (76.74 %, 23.26 %) with σ 0.20 which is to some extent identical with original statistics. Result is very much alike for other stations as well. However, the comparison between original and synthetic trip duration shows that synthetic data almost accurately measures overall average duration but failed to measure maximum and minimum durations precisely. The result is even worse if we use parametric distribution for duration. We notice in the empirical distribution that a significant number of cells have very low frequency. Due to this fact, a notable noise impact is reflected in the synthetic results.

Furthermore, we study four utility metrics (*Average Relative Error (Avg. RLE), Earth Mover's Distance (EMD), True Positive (TP)* and *Utility Loss (UL)*) to compare synthetic distributions with their original distributions. The results show that the range of *Avg. RLE* is $[0.06 - 0.30]$ with σ range $[0.003 - 0.015]$ for ϵ 0.1 to 1. *EMD*, *TP* and *UL* are $[0.06 - 0.99]$, $[95.25 - 97.5]$ and $[4.41 - 10.1]$ with σ range $[0.021 - 0.124]$, $[2.22 - 3.08]$ and $[2.22 - 3.03]$ respectively. Due to space constraints, figures are not shown here.

5 Discussion

In 2012, *Hubway* and *Metropolitan Area Planning Council (MAPC)* jointly hosted a challenge named *Hubway Data Visualization Challenge* [1] asking participants to come up with projects that involve visualizations, animations, artistic representations or interactive data analysis tool. It had received total 67 projects that used original data provided by the host. We went through short description and/or little demo provided with each of these projects to find out the statistics that were computed by most of the participants. The comparison of top 7 of these statistics are shown in Sect. 4 and it seems that releasing differentially private data preserves utility in each case.

Due to the way original data is released, we do not provide user level privacy, our synthetic data provides trip level instead (e.g., sensitivity is computed based on adding or removing one trip, not on adding or removing individual). The synthetic data is also provides more protection than original dataset w.r.t. *Intimate Stalker Threat* [10]. First, unlike the original data set, synthetic data does not release real time visit information. Moreover, it is ϵ-differentially private which means it hides a particular trip information with ϵ privacy. As a result, identity as well as location resolution would be more harder for an intimate stalker using the synthetic data compared to original data.

6   Related Work

Few works [2–4,6] have been done on publishing and characterizing human mobility based on cellular network and other spatio-temporal data. All these papers built their model under Differential privacy. Chen et al. [4] study the problem of publishing trajectory data of commuters in Montreal. In paper [3], authors make use of the variable-length n-gram model. Mir et al. [6] models the human mobility based on Call Detail Records from a cellular telephone network. Acs et al. [2] presents a new anonymization scheme to release the spatio-temporal density of Paris in France. All these papers addressed the specific utility goal. This inspires us to study the possible utility for arbitrary queries.

7   Conclusion

In this paper, we propose a sanitization model for hubway dataset built under differential privacy that preserves users' trip level privacy. To show the applicability and utility of the generated synthetic data for arbitrary range of queries, we compare the most essential and compelling statistics derived from both synthetic and original datasets. Based on the comparison results, we conclude that most of the information required by human analysts can be provided accurately by differentially private synthetic data. We also discuss that the synthetic data release could be used to reduce threats due attacks such as *Intimate Stalker* compared to original data release.

Acknowledgement. The research reported herein was supported in part by NIH awards 1R0-1LM009989 & 1R01HG006844, NSF CNS-1111529, CNS-1228198, CNS-1237235 & CICI-1547324.

References

1. Hubway data visualization challenge (2012). http://hubwaydatachallenge.org/
2. Acs, G., Castelluccia, C.: A case study: privacy preserving release of spatio-temporal density in paris. In: KDD, August 2014
3. Chen, R., Acs, G., Castelluccia, C.: Differentially private sequential data publication via variable-length n-grams. In: Proceedings of the 2012 ACM Conference on Computer and Communications Security, pp. 638–649. ACM (2012)

4. Chen, R., Fung, B., Desai, B.C., Sossou, N.M.: Differentially private transit data publication: a case study on the montreal transportation system. In: Proceedings of the 18th ACM SIGKDD International Conference on Knowledge Discovery and Data Mining, pp. 213–221. ACM (2012)

5. Chittaranjan, G., Blom, J., Gatica-Perez, D.: Mining large-scale smartphone data for personality studies. Pers. Ubiquit. Comput. **17**(3), 433–450 (2013)

6. Mir, D.J., Isaacman, S., R.C.M.M., Wright, R.N.: Dp-where: differentially private modeling of human mobility. In: BigData Conference, pp. 580–588 (2013)

7. Dwork, C., McSherry, F., Nissim, K., Smith, A.: Calibrating noise to sensitivity in private data analysis. In: Halevi, S., Rabin, T. (eds.) Theory of Cryptography. LNCS, vol. 3876, pp. 265–284. Springer, Heidelberg (2006)

8. Li, H., Xiong, L., Ohno-Machado, L., Jiang, X.: Privacy preserving RBF kernel support vector machine. BioMed Res. Int. **2014**, 10 (2014)

9. Mahmud, J., Nichols, J., Drews, C.: Where is this tweet from? inferring home locations of twitter users. ICWSM **12**, 511–514 (2012)

10. Sweeney, L.: Risk assessments of personal identification technologies for domestic violence homeless shelters (2005)

11. WIKIPEDIA: Interquartile range, interquartile range and outliers, 3IQR. http://en.wikipedia.org/wiki/Interquartile_range/

A Practical Framework for Executing Complex Queries over Encrypted Multimedia Data

Fahad Shaon[(✉)] and Murat Kantarcioglu

The University of Texas at Dallas, Richardson, TX 75080, USA
{fahad.shaon,muratk}@utdallas.edu

Abstract. Over the last few years, data storage in cloud based services has been very popular due to easy management and monetary advantages of cloud computing. Recent developments showed that such data could be leaked due to various attacks. To address some of these attacks, encrypting sensitive data before sending to cloud emerged as an important protection mechanism. If the data is encrypted with traditional techniques, selective retrieval of encrypted data becomes challenging. To address this challenge, efficient searchable encryption schemes have been developed over the years. Almost all of the existing searchable encryption schemes are developed for keyword searches and require running some code on the cloud servers. However, many of the existing cloud storage services (e.g., Dropbox (https://www.dropbox.com), Box (https://www.box.com/), Google Drive (http://drive.google.com/), etc.) only allow simple data object retrieval and do not provide computational support needed to realize most of the searchable encryption schemes.

In this paper, we address the problem of efficient execution of complex search queries over wide range of encrypted data types (e.g., image files) without requiring customized computational support from the cloud servers. To this end, we provide an extensible framework for supporting complex search queries over encrypted multimedia data. Before any data is uploaded to the cloud, important features are extracted to support different query types (e.g., extracting facial features to support face recognition queries) and complex queries are converted to series of object retrieval tasks for cloud service. Our results show that this framework may support wide range of image retrieval queries on encrypted data with little overhead and without any change to underlying data storage services.

1 Introduction

Cloud computing is being adopted by organizations and individuals to address various types of computation needs including file storage, archiving, etc. However, there have been several incidents of data leak in popular cloud storage service providers [1,25]. To ensure the security of the sensitive data and prevent any unauthorized access, users may need to encrypt data before uploading to cloud. If data uploaded to cloud is encrypted using traditional encryption techniques, executing search queries on the stored data become infeasible.

© IFIP International Federation for Information Processing 2016
Published by Springer International Publishing Switzerland 2016. All Rights Reserved
S. Ranise and V. Swarup (Eds.): DBSec 2016, LNCS 9766, pp. 179–195, 2016.
DOI: 10.1007/978-3-319-41483-6_14

To alleviate this situation many searchable encryption techniques have been proposed [4–6,9,11,13,16,19,20]. Among those approaches, searchable symmetric encryption (SSE) [4–6,9,13,16,19] emerges as an efficient alternative for cloud based storage systems due to minimal storage overhead, low performance overhead, and relatively good security.

However, almost all searchable encryption techniques require executing some code on the cloud servers to enable efficient processing. On the other hand, popular commercial personal cloud storage providers[1,2,3] only support basic file operations like read and write file that makes it infeasible to apply traditional SSE techniques. Furthermore, complex queries on multimedia data may require running different and expensive cryptographic operations. These limitations create a significant problem for wide adoption of SSE techniques. Therefore, developing SSE schemes that can run on the existing cloud storage systems without requiring the cloud service providers cooperation emerges as an important and urgent need. To our knowledge, only [19] considered a setup without computational support from the cloud storage but the proposed solution does not support efficient complex querying over encrypted data.

Even though, one can wish that an alternative SSE as a service could be offered in the near future by the cloud service providers, due to network effects, many of the existing users may not want to switch their cloud service providers. Therefore, any new "secure" cloud storage with SSE providers may have a hard time in getting significant traction. So supporting SSE on the existing cloud storage platforms without requiring any support from the cloud storage service providers is a critical need.

In addition, adoption of multimedia (e.g., image, music, video, etc.) data for social communication is increasing day by day. KPCB analyst Mary Meeker's 2014 annual Internet Trends report[4] states *1.8 billion* photos shared *each day*. However, indexing multimedia data is harder compared to text data. A significant pre-processing is required to convert raw multimedia data to a searchable format and queries made on multimedia data are complex as well. So building efficient cryptographic storage system that can easily handle multimedia content is a very important problem.

To address these challenges, in this paper, we propose an efficient searchable encryption scheme framework that can work on existing cloud storage services and can easily handle multimedia data. Our proposed framework only requires file storage and retrieval support from cloud storage services. Furthermore, by leveraging the extensible extract, transform and load operations provided by our framework, very complex queries can be executed on the encrypted data. As an example, we show how our framework could be used to run face recognition queries on encrypted images. To our knowledge, this is the first system that can support *complex queries* on encrypted multimedia data *without significant*

---

[1] https://www.dropbox.com.

[2] https://www.box.com/.

[3] http://drive.google.com/.

[4] http://www.kpcb.com/blog/2014-internet-trends.

computational support from the cloud service provider (i.e., without running customized code in the cloud). *Main contributions* of this work can be summarized as follows:

- We propose a generic outsourcing framework that enables secure and efficient querying on any data. Our framework supports complex querying on any encrypted data by allowing queries to be represented as series of simple equality queries using the features extracted from the data. Later on, these extracted features are transformed into encrypted indexes and these indexes are loaded to cloud and leveraged for efficient encrypted query processing.
- We prove that our system satisfies adaptive semantic security for dynamic SSE.
- We show the applicability of our framework by applying it to state-of-the-art image querying algorithms (e.g., face recognition) on encrypted data.
- We implement a prototype of our system and empirically evaluate the efficiency under various query types using real world cloud services. Our results show that our system introduces very little overhead, which makes it remarkably efficient and applicable to real-world problems.

The rest of the paper is organized as follows: Sect. 2 discusses previous related works, Sect. 3 provides the general setup and threat model of our system, Sect. 4 describes internal details of each phases, Sect. 5 extends our initial framework making it dynamic, in Sect. 6 we discuss the security of our system, Sect. 7 shows an application of our proposed framework, Sect. 8 shows the experimentations, and in Sect. 9 we conclude our work.

2   Related Work

Currently there are few ways to build encrypted cloud storage with content based search. Searchable symmetric encryption(SSE) is one of those, which allows users to encrypt data in a fashion that can be searched later on. Different aspects of SSE has been studied extensively as shown in an extensive survey of provably secure searchable encryption by Bösch et al. in [4]. Curtmola et al. [9] provided simple construction for SSE with practical security definitions, which was then adopted and extended by several others in subsequent work. Few works also looked into dynamic construction of SSE [5,13,14,16] so that new documents can be added after SSE construction.

Another branch of study related to SSE is supporting conjunctive boolean query. Cash et al. [6] proposed such a construction, where authors used multi-round protocol for doing boolean query with reasonable information leakage. In the process they also claimed to build the most efficient SSE in terms of time and storage. Kuzu et al. [15] proposed an efficient SSE construction for similarity search, where they used locality sensitive hashing to convert similarity search to equality search. There are also work towards supporting efficient range query, substring matching query, etc. [10], where a rich query is converted to an exact matching query. However, these constructions require specialized server. Importantly, we can easily adopt such a conversion technique in our framework.

Naveed et al. [19] proposed a dynamic searchable encryption schema with simple storage server similar to our setup. The system also hides certain level of access pattern. However, authors did not consider complex query problem in their work, which is one of the major challenges that we solved in this work.

Another way of querying encrypted database is oblivious RAM (ORAM) [11, 20] that also hides search access pattern and much secure. Despite recent developments [21], traditional ORAM remains inefficient for practical usage in cloud storage system as described in [3]. Furthermore, our proposed system converts complex operations into sequence of key value read and write operations, which can easily be combined with ORAM technique to hide the access pattern.

Qin et al. [22] proposed an efficient privacy preserving cloud based secure image feature extraction and comparison technique. Similar construction for ranked image retrieval is proposed by [17, 23, 29]. These systems depend on highly capable cloud server for preforming image similarity query.

Finally, there are few commercial secure cloud storage systems, e.g., SpiderOak[5], BoxCryptor[6],Wuala[7], etc. Even though these systems are easy to use and provide reliable security, these systems provide neither server based search nor complex query support. All these systems depend on either operating system or local indices to provide search functionalities. As a result, to provide search functionalities these systems need to download and decrypt all the data stored in cloud server, which might not be efficient solution in all circumstances.

3   Background and Threat Model

Searchable Symmetric Encryption (SSE) is one of the many mechanisms to enable search over encrypted data. In a SSE schema, we not only encrypt the input dataset, but also we create an encrypted inverted index. The index contains mapping of encrypted version of keywords (called trapdoors) to list of document ids that contains corresponding plain text keywords. Formally, a SSE schema is defined as collection of 5 algorithms $SSE = (Gen, Enc, Trpdr, Search, Dec)$ Given security parameter Gen generates a master symmetric key, Enc generates the encrypted inverted index and encrypted data sets from the input dataset. $Trpdr$ algorithm takes keywords as input and outputs the trapdoor, which is used by $Search$ algorithm to find list of documents associated with input keywords. Finally, the Dec algorithm decrypts the encrypted document given the id and proper key. We refer the reader to [9] for further discussion of SSE. Furthermore, in a typical SSE settings, Gen, Enc, $Trpdr$, and Dec are performed in a client device and the $Search$ algorithm is performed in a cloud server. For this reason, we need a server with custom computational support to run a SSE based system. Here, we focus on building a framework that enables us to build SSE alike schema

---

[5] https://spideroak.com/.

[6] https://www.boxcryptor.com/.

[7] https://www.wuala.com/.

with complex query processing capabilities using file storage servers that does not have custom computation support.

Threat Model. In this study, we consider a setup, where a user owns a set of documents, which includes multimedia documents. User wants to store these documents into a cloud storage server in encrypted form. User also wants to perform complex search queries over the encrypted data. Most importantly, user wants to utilize existing cloud storage service, which is not capable of executing any custom code provided by user. Formally cloud storage server $\mathcal{Z}$ can *only* preform *read* and *write* operations. This simple requirement of cloud storage server makes the system easily adoptable in several real world scenario. On the other hand, user have devices with sufficient computation power that can perform modern symmetric cryptography algorithms and are called clients.

In our system, the communication between server and client is done over encrypted channel, such as https. So eavesdroppers can not learn any meaning full information about the documents capturing the communication, apart form existence of such communication. We also assume that the cloud storage server $\mathcal{Z}$ is managed by Bob, who is semi-honest. As such, he follows the protocol as it is define but he may try to infer private information about the document he hosts. Furthermore, the system does not hide search access pattern, meaning Bob can observe the trapdoors in search query. Based on the encrypted file accesses after subsequent search queries Bob also can figure out trapdoor to document ids assignments. However, Bob can not observe the plain text keyword of trapdoors.

4   The Proposed System

Our main motivation is to build encrypted cloud storage that can support complex search query with support of simple file storage server. We generalize the required computations into a five phase *Extract, Transform, Load, Query, Post-Process (ETLQP)* framework. These five phases represent chronological order of operations required to create, store encrypted index, and perform complex operations. Figure 1(a) and (b) illustrates an overview of different phases in our system.

4.1   Extract

In this phase we extract necessary features from a dataset. Let, $\mathcal{D} = \{d_1, d_2, ..., d_n\}$ be a set of documents, $id(d_i)$ be the identifier of document d_i, $\Theta = \{\theta_1, \theta_2, ..., \theta_m\}$ be a set of m feature extractor functions. Functions in Θ can extract set of feature and value pairs (f, v) from documents. We build list U_i with all the feature value pairs extracted from d_i. For all the feature extractors $\theta_j \in \Theta$ we compute $(f, v) \leftarrow \theta_j(d_i)$ and store (f, v) in U_i. Finally we organize the result in $\mathcal{P}$, such that $\mathcal{P}[id(d_i)] \leftarrow U_i$. Such an example $\mathcal{P}$ is illustrated in Fig. 1(c). Here, we have four documents $\{D_1, ..D_4\}$. D_1 has feature value pairs $U_1 = \{(f_a, v_\alpha), (f_b, v_\beta), (f_b, v_\gamma)\}$, etc.

To clarify further, let us assume that, we want to build an encrypted image storage application that can preform location based query over the encrypted

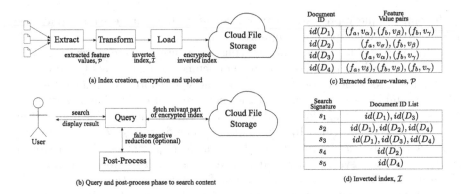

(a) Index creation, encryption and upload

(c) Extracted feature-values, $\mathcal{P}$

(b) Query and post-process phase to search content

(d) Inverted index, $\mathcal{I}$

Fig. 1. Overall workflow of our proposed system and important data structures. (a) Index creation consists of extract, transform and load phases. (b) Search consists of query and post-process phases. (c) $\mathcal{P}$, output of extract phase that maps document ids to feature value pairs, (d) Inverted index $\mathcal{I}$, that maps search signatures to document ids.

images. In other word, the system is capable of answering queries, such as, *find images taken in Italy*. To support such a query, we implement a feature extractor function θ_l, where θ_l extracts location information from image meta data. Output of θ_l is defined as a feature value pair (*"LOCATION"*, *"longitude and latitude of image"*). We define as many feature extractor necessary based on application need. However, all feature extractor functions returns values in similar format. In Sect. 7 we discuss in details how we defined more feature extractors and use those to answer much more complicated queries.

4.2   Transform

In this phase we transform the extracted feature values into much simpler form so that complex search operations can be expressed as series of equality searches. We compute search signatures s form feature-value pairs and associate corresponding documents with s. This association at query stage can be used to infer existence of a feature-value pair in a document. Essentially here we define sets of transform functions $\mathcal{T} = \{t_1, .., t_p\}$, where each transform function is designed to generate search signatures from a feature value pair (f, v) and $\mathcal{T}_f$ defines subset of transformation functions that can be applied to feature f.

With these transform functions $\mathcal{T}$, we generate an inverted index $\mathcal{I}$ that is indexed by search signatures and contains list of document ids. For all the feature value pairs in $\mathcal{P}$, we generate search signature $s_{f,v}^t \leftarrow t(f, v)$ where $t \in \mathcal{T}_f$. We build document id list V_s for all the unique search signature s that contains $id(D_i)$ if and only if there exists a feature value pair (f, v) that is in U_i and at least one transformation function t that generates search signature s. Finally we fill the inverted index $\mathcal{I}$ such that $\mathcal{I}[s] \leftarrow V_s$. In Fig. 1(d) we show such an example $\mathcal{I}$, which is created from $\mathcal{P}$ of Fig. 1(c). Here, search signature $s_1, s_2, s_3,$

s_4, s_5 are generated from feature value pairs (f_a, v_α), (f_b, v_β), (f_b, v_γ), (f_a, v_σ), (f_a, v_δ) accordingly.

Similarly, in our encrypted image storage application example, we define a transform function t_l that takes geographic location and document id as input, converts the location information to mailing address using reverse address lookup service, takes the country information and document id to construct a search signature using a collision resistant hash function.

Using such extract transform model has several benefits over adhoc model. The proposed model helps us to organize the necessary computation into modules, which intern increase development efficiency. The feature extractor functions can be reused in other project.

4.3   Load

In this phase we setup our encryption schema, encrypt the inverted index, and upload the encrypted version into a file storage server $\mathcal{Z}$. We initialize a master encryption key K, three random constants C_1, C_2, C_3, a secure pseudo random permutation function φ, and a keyed pseudo random function H. Given a key, φ encrypts data, φ^{-1} decrypts corresponding result, and H generates authentication code of messages. In addition, we define a small synchronized cache $\mathcal{C}$ and an encryption key K_C for encrypting the cache. $\mathcal{C}$ is always synchronized with storage server $\mathcal{Z}$. Synchronization is achieved by updating the server's version after any change in client's version and before updating the cache locally most recent version is downloaded from the server first. In $\mathcal{C}$, we store document id list size of all search signatures of $\mathcal{I}$, which is notated by $\mathcal{C}.freq$. Later, we also use this cache to store information related to individual files to make the query phase easier.

We divide all the document id lists in $\mathcal{I}$ into b length blocks and add padding to last block if needed. The value of b is determined by defining and minimizing a cost function (described in Subsect. 4.6). We generate trapdoors T_j^s and K_j^s for j^{th} block of document list of $\mathcal{I}[s]$. We use K_j^s to encrypt block contents and T_j^s as the key for encrypted inverted index $\mathcal{E}$. To query the inverted index later on, our system will regenerate these two trapdoors and perform inverse operations to build the original document id list. In addition, we store number of documents associated with a signature s in $\mathcal{C}.freq[s]$, then encrypt and upload the cache. Algorithm 1 describes the operations necessary for *load* phase.

4.4   Query

In previous phases we have created an encrypted inverted index and uploaded into file storage server $\mathcal{Z}$. Query and post-process phases are dedicated for querying the index and returning proper output to user. First, given a user query q, we extract and transform it to a set of search signatures $\mathcal{Q}$. We use number of document ids per block, stored in $\mathcal{C}.freq$, to compute block counts, which in turn used to compute trapdoors K_j^s and T_j^s for each block of search signatures.

Algorithm 1. Load encrypted index

1: **Require:** K = Master key, $\mathcal{I}$ = Inverted index of search signatures, $\mathcal{C}$ = Synchronized cache, K_C = encryption key for cache, $\mathcal{Z}$ = File storage server.
2: $b \leftarrow optimize(\mathcal{I})$
3: **for all** signature s in $\mathcal{I}$ **do**
4:     $blocks_s \leftarrow \lceil \frac{|\mathcal{I}[s]|}{b} \rceil$
5:     **for** $j = 1 \rightarrow blocks_s$ **do**
6:         $T_j^s \leftarrow H(K, s \mathbin\Vert j \mathbin\Vert C_1)$, $K_j^s \leftarrow H(K, s \mathbin\Vert j \mathbin\Vert C_2)$
7:         $sub \leftarrow \mathcal{I}[s].slice((j-1) \times b, j \times b)$
8:         $\mathcal{E}[T_j^s] \leftarrow \varphi(K_j^s, pad(sub))$
9:     **end for**
10:     $\mathcal{C}.freq[s] \leftarrow |\mathcal{I}[s]|$
11: **end for**
12: **for all** trapdoor t in $\mathcal{E}$ **do**
13:     $\mathcal{Z}.write(t, \mathcal{E}[t])$
14: **end for**
15: $C_{sig} \leftarrow H(K_C \mathbin\Vert C_3, 1)$
16: $\mathcal{Z}.write(C_{sig}, \varphi(K_C, \mathcal{C}))$

Using these trapdoors we retrieve and decrypt document ids. Finally, the result is organized into a hash table $\mathcal{R}$ such that $\mathcal{R}[s] = \mathcal{I}[s]$ for all $s \in \mathcal{Q}$. Algorithm 2 contains the detail operations of query phase.

Algorithm 2. Query

1: **Require:** K = Master key, q = Query, b = block size, $\mathcal{Z}$ = File storage server
2: $\mathcal{Q} \leftarrow$ Extract and Transform q
3: **for all** search signatures s in $\mathcal{Q}$ **do**
4:     $blocks_s \leftarrow \lceil \frac{\mathcal{C}.freq[s]}{b} \rceil$
5:     **for** $i = 1 \rightarrow blocks_s$ **do**
6:         $T_j^s \leftarrow H(K, s \mathbin\Vert j \mathbin\Vert C_1)$, $K_j^s \leftarrow H(K, s \mathbin\Vert j \mathbin\Vert C_2)$
7:         $L \leftarrow \mathcal{Z}.read(T_j^s)$
8:         add $\varphi^{-1}(K_j^s, L)$ in $\mathcal{R}[s]$
9:     **end for**
10: **end for**
11: **return** $\mathcal{R}$

4.5 Post-Process

In this step we further process the result of query phase to remove false positive entries. Given result set $\mathcal{R}$ from query phase for query q, we remove id of document that does not match the original query. Therefore, $\mathcal{R}.remove(id(d))$ if $q(d) \neq True$. Query that only contains exact search features, this phase is optional.

4.6   Optimal Block Size Analysis

Block size has a direct impact on performance of our proposed system. Larger block size implies waste of space for padding and smaller block size implies many blocks to process. So we need to find an optimal value of block size b that keeps the over all cost to minimal. In our construction for each block we have a fixed cost and a dynamic cost that is related to block length. We define fixed cost as α and co-efficient of dynamic cost β. Cost can be in terms of time and size. Both linearly depends on block size in our construction. So cost for a b length block is $(\alpha + \beta \times b)$. Let, $\mathcal{J}(s)$ is $|\mathcal{I}[s]|$ meaning document id list size for search signature s and total cost $\mathcal{G}(b)$ for blocking and encrypting given inverted index $\mathcal{I}$ for block length b then $\mathcal{G}(b) = \sum_{s \in \mathcal{I}} \left\lceil \frac{\mathcal{J}(s)}{b} \right\rceil (\alpha + \beta \times b)$. We want to minimize the above function for b. However, if contains a ceiling function, which can not be minimize by taking derivatives and equating to zero. So we approximate the probability distribution of $\mathcal{J}$, i.e., lengths of document id list in $\mathcal{I}$. We assumed that, distribution is Pareto distribution, which is defined by probability density function (PDF) $f(x|\gamma, x_m) = \frac{\gamma x_m^\gamma}{x^{(\gamma+1)}}$, where x is the random variable, γ is distribution parameter, and x_m is minimum value of x. After several algebraic simplification (explained in details in full version [24]), we find the first order derivative

$$\mathcal{G}'(b) = \beta - x_m^\gamma \beta b^{-\gamma} + (\alpha + \beta b) x_m^\gamma \gamma b^{-\gamma-1} - \gamma x_m^\gamma b^{-\gamma} (\frac{\alpha}{b} + \beta) - \frac{\gamma x_m^\gamma}{\gamma - 1} b^{-\gamma-1} \alpha$$

Now we minimize b by setting $\mathcal{G}'(b) = 0$ and solving the equation for b. In experimentation we observe that method of moments estimation for x_m and γ gives almost correct value.

5   Dynamic Document Addition

Here we are going to improve our algorithms to support dynamic addition of documents. Given a new document set for addition we first perform extract and transform to build an inverted index. Next we compute number of blocks and number of empty spaces in last block for each signature the cache $\mathcal{C}$. If there exists empty space we fill the empty spaces than create new blocks as needed. On the other hand, if a new signature is observed in new inverted index we perform exact same steps of load. Due to space limitation we deffer further discussion on dynamic document addition for full version of the paper [24].

6   Security

Over the years, many security definitions have been proposed for searchable encryption for semi-honest model. Among those simulation based adaptive semantic security definition by Curtmola et al. [9] is widely used in literature. Later it is customized to work under random oracle model in [14]. We adapt this definition to prove our security model. In short, we define, history $\mathcal{H}_\eta$, trace λ (the maximum amount of information that a data owner allows its leakage to an adversary) and view v (the information that is accessible to an adversary) of our system and show the existence of polynomial size simulator $\mathcal{S}$ such that the simulated view $v_S(\mathcal{H}_\eta)$ and the real view $v_R(\mathcal{H}_\eta)$ of history $\mathcal{H}_\eta$ are computationally indistinguishable. Due to space limitation we defer the formal security proof to our full version [24].

7   Application of ETLQP Framework

As an application of our ETLQP framework we built an image storage system that saves encrypted images in cloud storage and built an encrypted index to search later on. Before going into further detail of our ETLQP framework implementation we briefly describe Fuzzy Color and Texture Histogram (FCTH) [7], Eigenface [27], Locality Sensitive Hashing (LSH) [12], and range query to exact query conversion mechanism [10].

Fuzzy Color Texture Histogram (FCTH) [7] is an histogram of image that combines texture and color information. It is widely used in content based image retrieval systems (CBIR), e.g. [8,18]. FCTH of an image can be considered as a vector with 192 dimensions and distance between FCTH vector of images can be used to determine similarity among images.

Eigenface [27] is a very well studied, effective yet simple technique for face recognition using static 2D face image. In summary, face images are considered as a point in a high dimensional space. An eigenspace consisting few significant eigen vectors are computed for approximating faces in a training face dataset. Next, test face images are projected into the computed eigenspace. Distances of test face images and all training faces images are computed. If any distance is bellow a pre-determined threshold then those faces are considered a match for associated test face. A detail formal explanation of eigen-face schema is presented in full version [24].

Locality sensitive hashing is a technique widely used to reduce dimensions. Core concept of LSH is to define a family of hash functions such that similar items belong to same bucket with high probability. More specifically we utilized LSH in euclidean space and adopted widely accepted projection over random line technique described in [2]. Let, r be a random projection vectors, v be an input vector, o be a random number used as offset, and w be bucket length parameter fixed by user. The bucket id is computed by $Round(\frac{v.r+o}{w})$ function. Finally, several such projection vectors are used to generate several bucket ids for a single input vector. In this setting, nearby items will share at least a same bucket with very high probability.

Range query to exact query conversion. We adopt the range query mechanism described in [10]. Let, a be a discrete feature that has value ranging from 0 to 2^{t-1}, meaning it requires t bits to represent in binary. We first create binary tree of t depth representing the complete range. Each leaf node (at depth t) represent an element in the range and we level all left edge as 0 and right edge as 1. So, the path from the root to a leaf node essentially represent the binary encoding of that leaf. In transform phase, we convert an input value of the range to t feature-value tuples, where the feature is concatenation of field name, depth i and value is binary encoding of inner node at depth i. During the query phase given a range we first find the cover as described in [10], create the corresponding search signatures and perform the query.

7.1 ETLQP for Image Storage

To build an application using ETLQP framework described system section, programmer has to define proper extract and transformation functions. Load, Query and Post-Process phases remain the same. For our image storage software we consider four features *location* - where the picture was take, *time* - when the picture was taken, *texture and color* - for searching similar pictures, and *faces* - for face recognition. In our implemented system queries of first two features are equality search and later two are similarity search. Similarity searches are difficult to perform since result not only contains exact matches but also contains results that are similar. So, we need to have a similarity measure for the feature in question. To accomplish such a similarity queries we utilize LSH, which essentially helps us to convert the query to sequence of equality search. In addition, result of LSH can contain false positives. We need extra post processing to remove those.

Extract. Location and time data are extracted from Exif[8] meta-data. Exif is a very popular standard for attaching image meta-data into image used by all popular camera manufacturers. Camera with Global Positioning System (GPS) module can store longitude and latitude of a picture taken into Exif data, which can be extracted easily using available libraries[9]. We use FCTH for similarity analysis and used a open source implementation of FCTH analyzer [18]. Finally, for face recognition using Eigenface, we extract frontal faces from images using haar cascade [28] frontal face pattern classifier.

Transform. Now we define appropriate transformations for extracted features. Main idea behind the definition of transformation functions is to make the query easier later on. So definition of transformation functions is mainly guided by the query demand.

- **Location.** Location information in terms of longitude and latitude is difficult to use in practice. We use OpenStreetMap's reverse geolocation service[10] to determine address of latitude and longitude associated with the image. To make query easier later, we generate search signatures of six sub-features of the address - full address, city, county, country, state, and zip.
- **Time.** Similarly we break created date of an image into five sub-features - complete date, year, month, day of month, and day of week. We generate search signatures based on these sub-features. In addition, to support range

---

[8] http://www.cipa.jp/std/documents/e/DC-008-2012_E.pdf.

[9] https://drewnoakes.com/code/exif.

[10] http://wiki.openstreetmap.org/wiki/Nominatim.

query based on date we convert the time into unix time stamp that essentially represents seconds passed from 1 *January* 1970 without considering the leap second. Then we divide the time stamp by number of seconds in a day (86400), that gives us the number of days passed from epoch. Finally, we build the range query binary tree with depth 20, which essentially is capable of covering dates till year 4840. Then we create the feature value list as described earlier.

- **Texture and Color.** In the extract phase we extracted FCTH of provided image, which is a 192 dimensional vector. We can treat each dimension as different sub features but that will make it difficult to perform similarity search later on. Instead we define an euclidean LSH schema that put near elements into same bucket and use the bucket ids to generate search signatures.
- **Face.** We built an eigenface schema with extracted face images. Again to preserve similarity we built an euclidean LSH schema with weight vectors of faces and store the eigenspace related information into synchronized cache $\mathcal{C}$. In particular we store the average face, selected top eigenfaces, and weights of all faces. Storing such information is the major reason of defining the cache $\mathcal{C}$.

Query and Post-Process. With previously defined extract and transform functions client can perform *time queries*, such as find images that are taken on specific year, month, day of week, day of moth, or in a rang of dates, etc. Client can also perform *location queries*, such as find pictures taken in a country, state, city, etc. In both of these cases, we transform a query into encrypted search signatures and retrieve associated encrypted document ids from the cloud storage server. Finally we decrypt and display the result directly to the user. On the other hand, for face recognition and image-similarity query, we extract appropriate feature values from a query image and transform these values into LSH bucket ids of previously defined LSH schema. We generate encrypted search signature, retrieve encrypted document ids, and decrypt the result like date and time queries. However, before showing results to user we remove false positive results introduced by the LSH schema.

8 Experimental Evaluation

Setup. In our proposed design we have two components client and server. Client processes images, performs cryptographic operations, and produces encrypted inverted index that is stored in server. In query phase client retrieves partial index from the server based on user-query.

ETQLP client is written in Java using several other libraries for image feature extraction. Cryptographic operations are performed using Java Cryptographic Extension (JCE) implementation. During our experimentation, we execute the client program in a computer with *Intel(R) Core(TM) i7-4770 3.40 GHz* CPU, *16 GB* RAM running *Ubuntu 14.04.4 LTS*. Our implemented client can store encrypted inverted index into different types of servers.

- **File storage server in local network.** We developed a very simple web based storage service that has two end points file read and file write. Our server is written in Python (v2.7.6) using Flask (v0.10.1) microframework and files are stored in a MongoDB (v3.2.0). We deployed our local storage server in a machine with *Intel(R) Xeon(R) CPU E5420 2.50 GHz* CPU, *30 GB* of RAM running *CentOS 6.4*. In addition, our client computer is also in the same network.

- **Amazon S3**[11] is very popular commercial object and file storage system, which provides easy to use representational state transfer (REST) application program interface (API) for storing, retrieving and managing arbitrary binary data or file. Amazon also provides very extensive software development kit (SDK) for building applications to utilize it's services. In our implementation, search signatures of encrypted inverted index $\mathcal{E}$ are keys of S3 objects and content of the objects are associated encrypted document id list.

- **Personal file storage services.** In our implementation the client is capable to use popular commercial file storage services, for example - Dropbox[12], Box[13], and Google Drive[14]. *However, due to rate limitation of these services we could not perform extensive analysis.* Details are presented in full version [24].

Dataset. We randomly selected 20109 images from Yahoo Flickr Creative Commons 100 Million Dataset (YFCC100M) in [26], which contains basic information of 100 million media objects. Size of this random dataset is 42.3 GB, average file size is 2.15 MB, number of faces detected 7027, and 4102 images have latitude and longitude embedded in EXIF data.

Experiments. We measure performance of different phases of our framework for varying number of randomly selected images from above dataset. Horizontal axis of most of the reported graphs is number of randomly selected images used to build the index and vertical axis is the observation. We repeat each experiment for at least 3 times and report the average observation value. We extracted four features of the images as discussed in Sect. 7. Figure 2 illustrates size growth of unencrypted inverted index,

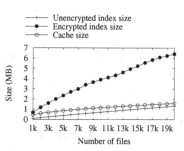

Fig. 2. Index and cache sizes

encrypted inverted index, and synchronized cache. The growth is linear, which implies index size increment is proportional to the number of files added. Moreover, in our experiment we observed that for 20000 images encrypted inverted index size is only 7.05 MB, which is about four average size images in our dataset. So size over head of our proposed system is very low.

We also observe that feature extraction is the most time consuming phase of our system. Figure 3(a) illustrates required time for extracting features. We observe that face detection and extraction time is the dominating factor in this phase. It requires 464.54 min to detect and extract faces from 20000 images in sequential manner, averaging about 1.39 s per image. In addition, other three

---

[11] https://aws.amazon.com/s3/.
[12] https://www.dropbox.com.
[13] https://www.box.com/.
[14] http://drive.google.com/.

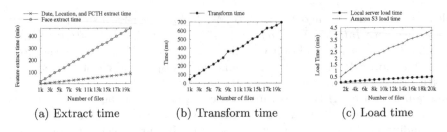

Fig. 3. Time required in different phases of building and uploading the index for different number of images.

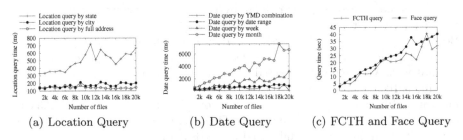

Fig. 4. Time required for different type of queries vs number of files.

features takes 85.87 min for 20000 images, averaging 0.26 s per images. Even though it looks like a long time for a lot of images but time required for individual image is very little. Furthermore, these experiments are done in sequential manner. A multi-threaded implementation will certainly reduce the over all time. In addition, in this prototype we implemented a separate program to call native OpenCV API to detect faces and communicate the results back to the main process, which added extra overhead. In contrast, transform phase is one of the fastest phase in our implementation. Here, extracted feature values are transformed into inverted index of search signatures and document ids. We observed that the growth is almost linear and for 20000 images it only requires 696 ms, shown in Fig. 3(b).

Next we encrypt and load the inverted index into a cloud storage server. In our experiments, we load the encrypted index into (1) Local server and (2) Amazon S3. Figure 3(c) shows the time required for encrypting and loading inverted index into local and Amazon S3 server. For 20000 images it requires 20.52 s to encrypt and load the entire inverted index split into 1 MB blocks into local storage server and 5.65 min to complete in Amazon S3 server. Furthermore, the time growth is linear due to the linear growth of index size.

Once encrypted inverted index are uploaded in storage server, we perform queries with different extracted features. In each of the cases we randomly select five value of the respected feature and perform the query and report the average. Figure 4 illustrates performance of the location, date, FCTH, and face queries. Among the location queries we observe that query by full address is fastest

Query by state takes longest to finish and query by city performs in between. This is because time require to finish a query is proportional to the number to blocks fetched and processed. Very few images are like to have same full address however more images likely to have common state or city. Among the date queries range query and query by year-month-date (YMD) combination is the fastest for similar reason. Finally, FCTH and face query requires longest time due to long extract, transform, and post-processing step. We had to keep our discussion short here because of space limitation. Detail analysis of these results and few more experiment results are presented in the full version [24].

9   Conclusion

In this study, we addressed the problem of searchable encryption with simple server that can support complex queries with multimedia data type. We made several contributions including an extensible general framework with security proof and its implementation. Our defined extract, transform, load, query and post-process (ETLQP) framework can build efficient searchable encryption scheme for complex data types (e.g., images). With this framework we can perform very sophisticated queries, such as face recognition, without needing cryptographic computational support from the server. Our implementation shows small overhead for building encrypted search index and performing such complex queries. In addition, we also show that overhead of general cryptographic operations is negligible compared to other necessary operations of a cloud based file storage system.

Acknowledgments. The research reported herein was supported in part by NIH awards 1R0-1LM009989 & 1R01HG006844, NSF CNS-1111529, CNS-1228198, & CICI-1547324.

References

1. Agarwal, A.: Web vulnerability affecting shared links. https://blogs.dropbox.com/dropbox/2014/05/web-vulnerability-affecting-shared-links/
2. Andoni, A., Indyk, P.: Near-optimal hashing algorithms for approximate nearest neighbor in high dimensions. Commun. ACM **51**(1), 117–122 (2008). http://doi.acm.org/10.1145/1327452.1327494
3. Bindschaedler, V., Naveed, M., Pan, X., Wang, X., Huang, Y.: Practicing oblivious access on cloud storage: the gap, the fallacy, and the new way forward. In: Proceedings of the 22nd ACM SIGSAC Conference on Computer and Communications Security, pp. 837–849. ACM (2015)
4. Bösch, C., Hartel, P., Jonker, W., Peter, A.: A survey of provably secure searchable encryption. ACM Comput. Surv. (CSUR) **47**(2), 18 (2015)
5. Cash, D., Jaeger, J., Jarecki, S., Jutla, C., Krawczyk, H., Rosu, M., Steiner, M.: Dynamic searchable encryption in very-large databases: data structures and implementation. In: Network and Distributed System Security Symposium, NDSS, vol. 14 (2014)

6. Cash, D., Jarecki, S., Jutla, C., Krawczyk, H., Rosu, M., Steiner, M.: Highly-scalable searchable symmetric encryption with support for boolean queries. Cryptology ePrint Archive, Report 2013/169 (2013). http://eprint.iacr.org/
7. Chatzichristofis, S., Boutalis, Y.: FCTH: fuzzy color and texture histogram - a low level feature for accurate image retrieval. In: Ninth International Workshop on Image Analysis for Multimedia Interactive Services, WIAMIS 2008, pp. 191–196, May 2008
8. Chatzichristofis, S., Boutalis, Y., Lux, M.: Img(rummager): an interactive content based image retrieval system. In: Second International Workshop on Similarity Search and Applications, SISAP 2009, pp. 151–153, August 2009
9. Curtmola, R., Garay, J., Kamara, S., Ostrovsky, R.: Searchable symmetric encryption: improved definitions and efficient constructions. In: Proceedings of the 13th ACM Conference on Computer and Communications Security, pp. 79–88. ACM (2006)
10. Faber, S., Jarecki, S., Krawczyk, H., Nguyen, Q., Rosu, M., Steiner, M.: Rich queries on encrypted data: beyond exact matches. In: Pernul, G., Ryan, P.Y.A., Weippl, E. (eds.) ESORICS 2015. LNCS, vol. 9327, pp. 123–145. Springer, Heidelberg (2015). doi:10.1007/978-3-319-24177-7_7
11. Goldreich, O., Ostrovsky, R.: Software protection and simulation on oblivious rams. J. ACM **43**(3), 431–473 (1996). http://doi.acm.org/10.1145/233551.233553
12. Indyk, P., Motwani, R.: Approximate nearest neighbors: towards removing the curse of dimensionality. In: Proceedings of the Thirtieth Annual ACM Symposium on Theory of Computing, STOC 1998, pp. 604–613. ACM, New York (1998). http://doi.acm.org/10.1145/276698.276876
13. Kamara, S., Papamanthou, C.: Parallel and dynamic searchable symmetric encryption. In: Sadeghi, A.-R. (ed.) FC 2013. LNCS, vol. 7859, pp. 258–274. Springer, Heidelberg (2013)
14. Kamara, S., Papamanthou, C., Roeder, T.: Dynamic searchable symmetric encryption. In: Proceedings of the 2012 ACM Conference on Computer and Communications Security, CCS 2012, pp. 965–976. ACM, New York (2012). http://doi.acm.org/10.1145/2382196.2382298
15. Kuzu, M., Islam, M.S., Kantarcioglu, M.: Efficient similarity search over encrypted data. In: 2012 IEEE 28th International Conference on Data Engineering (ICDE), pp. 1156–1167. IEEE (2012)
16. van Liesdonk, P., Sedghi, S., Doumen, J., Hartel, P., Jonker, W.: Computationally efficient searchable symmetric encryption. In: Jonker, W., Petković, M. (eds.) SDM 2010. LNCS, vol. 6358, pp. 87–100. Springer, Heidelberg (2010)
17. Lu, W., Swaminathan, A., Varna, A.L., Wu, M.: Enabling search over encrypted multimedia databases. In: IS&T/SPIE Electronic Imaging, p. 725418. International Society for Optics and Photonics (2009)
18. Lux, M., Chatzichristofis, S.A.: Lire: lucene image retrieval: an extensible Java CBIR library. In: Proceedings of the 16th ACM International Conference on Multimedia, MM 2008, pp. 1085–1088. ACM, New York (2008). http://doi.acm.org/10.1145/1459359.1459577
19. Naveed, M., Prabhakaran, M., Gunter, C.A.: Dynamic searchable encryption via blind storage. In: 2014 IEEE Symposium on Security and Privacy (SP), pp. 639–654. IEEE (2014)
20. Ostrovsky, R.: Efficient computation on oblivious RAMs. In: Proceedings of the Twenty-Second Annual ACM Symposium on Theory of Computing, STOC 1990, pp. 514–523. ACM, New York (1990). http://doi.acm.org/10.1145/100216.100289

21. Pinkas, B., Reinman, T.: Oblivious RAM Revisited. In: Rabin, T. (ed.) CRYPTO 2010. LNCS, vol. 6223, pp. 502–519. Springer, Heidelberg (2010)
22. Qin, Z., Yan, J., Ren, K., Chen, C.W., Wang, C.: Towards efficient privacy-preserving image feature extraction in cloud computing. In: Proceedings of the ACM International Conference on Multimedia, pp. 497–506. ACM (2014)
23. Raval, N., Pillutla, M.R., Bansal, P., Srinathan, K., Jawahar, C.: Efficient content similarity search on encrypted data using hierarchical index structures
24. Shaon, F., Kantarcioglu, M.: A Practical Framework for Executing Complex Queries over Encrypted Multimedia Data. https://eprint.iacr.org/2016/426
25. Stadmeyer, K.: Google drive update to protect to shared links (2014). https://security.googleblog.com/2014/06/google-drive-update-to-protect-to.html
26. Thomee, B., Shamma, D.A., Friedland, G., Elizalde, B., Ni, K., Poland, D., Borth, D., Li, L.J.: The new data and new challenges in multimedia research. arXiv preprint arXiv:1503.01817 (2015)
27. Turk, M., Pentland, A.: Eigenfaces for recognition. J. Cogn. Neurosci. 3(1), 71–86 (1991)
28. Viola, P., Jones, M.: Rapid object detection using a boosted cascade of simple features. In: Proceedings of the 2001 IEEE Computer Society Conference on Computer Vision and Pattern Recognition, CVPR 2001, vol. 1, p. I-511. IEEE (2001)
29. Xia, Z., Zhu, Y., Sun, X., Wang, J.: A similarity search scheme over encrypted cloud images based on secure transformation. Int. J. Future Gener. Commun. Network. 6(6), 71–80 (2013)

Security and Privacy in Social Networks and Collaborative Systems

Data Governance and Transparency
for Collaborative Systems

Rauf Mahmudlu, Jerry den Hartog, and Nicola Zannone[(⊠)]

Eindhoven University of Technology, Eindhoven, The Netherlands
r.m.o.mahmudlu@student.tue.nl, {j.d.hartog,n.zannone}@tue.nl

Abstract. As social networks, shared editing platforms and other collaborative systems are becoming increasingly popular, the demands for
proper protection of the data created and used within these systems
grows. Yet, existing access control mechanisms are not suited for the
challenges imposed by collaborative systems. Two main challenges should
be addressed: collaborative specification of permissions, while ensuring
an appropriate levels of control to the different parties involved, and
enabling transparency in decision making in cases where the access
requirements of these different parties are in conflict. In this paper we
propose a data governance model for collaborative systems, which allows
the integration of access requirements specified by different users based
on their relation with a data object. We also study the practical feasibility of enabling transparency by comparing different deployment options
for transparency in XACML.

1 Introduction

Collaborative systems such as social networking websites, document shar-
ing/editing platforms and audio/video conferencing tools, are gaining increasing
popularity over the years. These systems provide an environment wherein users
can collaborate and share information. This information, however, can be sensitive and, thus, needs to be protected from unauthorized access and accidental
loss or modification.

Access control is widely used to protect sensitive information. Access control
mechanisms rely on policies defining which actions users are allowed to perform
on data objects. However, existing authorization mechanisms are not able to
deal with the security demands of collaborative environments [21]. In particular,
we identify two main drawbacks that limit their application to collaborative
systems: the lack of *(i)* a data governance model for shared data objects and
(ii) transparency in decision making.

Most access control mechanisms assume that data objects are under the control of a single entity (e.g., the system or the owner). However, in collaborative
systems several users can contribute to the creation, governance and management of data [3,7]. For instance, data can be provided by one or more users,

© IFIP International Federation for Information Processing 2016
Published by Springer International Publishing Switzerland 2016. All Rights Reserved
S. Ranise and V. Swarup (Eds.): DBSec 2016, LNCS 9766, pp. 199–216, 2016.
DOI: 10.1007/978-3-319-41483-6_15

can be stored by some other user, and refer to yet other users where each of these users retains some level of authority on the data. In particular, each user can define its own authorization requirements for the protection of data. Therefore, we need a way to combine those requirements in order to define the policy ultimately regulating the access to data.

Several approaches for policy combination [8,11,12,14] and integration [13] have been proposed. These approaches provide strategies to combine policies specified by different entities and automatically resolve policy conflicts at evaluation time based on predefined priorities between decisions or based on the policy structure. However, they consider every user 'equally' and they do not account for the relation of users with the data to be protected in order to determine how user policies should be combined.

Although the use of these strategies is necessary to guarantee the proper functioning of the system as a conclusive decision has to be made (either allowing or denying the access to the data), it results in a decision making process that is non-transparent to users. Every user expects its policies to be enforced by the system. This, however, is often not possible, for instance when users specify conflicting authorization requirements for the same resource. To resolve policy conflicts, policy combination strategies sacrifice some policies to reach a conclusive decision. Authorization mechanisms make decisions in a blackbox manner [5] and, thus, users are often unaware whether their policies have actually been enforced. This lack of confidence may reduce the level of trust users have towards the system and thus users' willingness to engage in collaboration.

In a previous work [2] we have introduced the notions of *archetype* and *policy mismatch* to address these issues. Archetypes are used to represent the relation of users with a given data object. Policy mismatches are used to identify the difference between the authorization requirements of single users and the final decision enforced by authorization mechanisms. We have also shown how the notion of policy mismatch can be used as a baseline for the realization of transparent authorization mechanisms which increases user awareness about access decision making.

This paper extends our previous work in two directions. First, we propose a data governance model for collaborative systems, which allows the integration of authorization requirements specified by different users based on their relation with a data object. In particular, the governance model provides a general framework to reason on the level of authority that users have over shared data and allows the use of existing policy combination and integration strategies to resolve policy conflicts. Moreover, we investigate the feasibility of transparency in existing authorization mechanisms. In particular, we have developed a transparency service that has been deployed in SAFAX [10], an XACML-based framework offering authorization as a service. A main feature of SAFAX is that all the components of the XACML reference architecture are designed as loosely coupled services. We exploit the flexibility provided by this design to evaluate the impact of the transparency service with respect to different deployment models.

The remainder of the paper is organized as follows. The next section introduces preliminaries on XACML. Section 3 presents our approach to shared data control. Section 4 discusses the problem of decision mismatches, and Sect. 5 describes the design, implementation and deployment of the transparent service. Section 6 presents experimental results. Finally, Sect. 7 discusses related work, and Sect. 8 concludes the paper and provides directions for future work.

2   Preliminaries

This section provides preliminaries on XACML [14], the *de facto* standard for the specification and enforcement of access control policies. This work is based on XACML v2. However, it can be easily adapted to comply with XACML v3.

2.1   Policy Language

XACML provides an attribute-based language that allows the specification of composite policies by using three policy elements: *policy sets, policies* and *rules*. Policy sets comprise a list of policy sets and policies; policies comprise a list of rules. Rules specify an *effect*, i.e. whether an access request should be allowed (Permit) or denied (Deny). Each policy element has a (possibly empty) *target* which restricts the applicability of the policy element. The target is specified in terms of attributes characterizing the subject, resource, action and environment and denotes the access requests covered by the policy element. A rule may additionally have a *condition*, i.e. a predicate that must be satisfied for a rule to be applicable. Policy sets and policies can also be associated with *obligations*, i.e. mandatory requirements that have to be fulfilled.

The evaluation of an access request against a policy element results in an access decision. If the request matches both the target and condition of a rule, the rule is applicable to the request and yields the decision specified by its effect, either Permit or Deny. If the rule is not applicable, a NotApplicable decision is returned. If an error occurs during evaluation, an Indeterminate decision is returned. Each composite policy element (i.e., a policy set or a policy) specifies a *combining algorithm* that is used to combine the decisions of its comprising elements. XACML provides a number of combining algorithms: permit-overrides (pov), deny-overrides (dov), first-applicable (fa) and only-one-applicable (ooa). These algorithms evaluate composite policies based on the order of the policy elements and priorities between decisions. Hereafter, we use the following abstract notation to represent the policy evaluation process in XACML: $\mathcal{P}$ denotes the set of XACML policies, $\mathcal{Q}$ the set of access requests, and function $[\![p]\!] : \mathcal{Q} \to \{$Permit, Deny, NotApplicable, Indeterminate$\}$ denotes policy evaluation, i.e. $[\![p]\!](q)$ is the decision according to a policy $p \in \mathcal{P}$ for a request $q \in \mathcal{Q}$.

2.2   XACML Architecture

The XACML reference architecture is shown in Fig. 1. Access requests are intercepted by the *Policy Enforcement Point* (PEP). Upon receiving an access

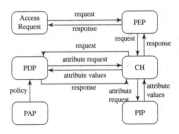

Fig. 1. XACML Architecture

request, the PEP forwards the request to the *Context Handler* (CH) which, after translating the request from the application's native format to XACML, sends it to the *Policy Decision Point* (PDP) for evaluation. The PDP fetches the policies from the *Policy Administration Point* (PAP). If additional attributes are required to evaluate the request, the PDP queries the CH for such attributes. The CH retrieves these attributes from the *Policy Information Point* (PIP) and sends them to the PDP. The PDP evaluates the request against the policies and returns a response specifying the access decision (and possibly a set of obligations to be fulfilled) to the CH. The CH sends the response to the PEP, which is responsible for the enforcement of the decision and the fulfillment of obligations.

3   Shared Data Control

In collaborative systems like social media and document sharing platforms, data objects can be under the control of multiple stakeholders. The level of authority that each stakeholder has on a shared data object depends on its relation with the object. In this section we discuss the problem of shared data control and propose an approach to regulate the access to data by taking into account both the authorization requirements of the stakeholders related to the data and their relationship with the shared data. We start by introducing a scenario in healthcare that is used as a running example throughout the paper.

Example 1. A University Medical Center (UMC) provides medical treatment for a variety of diseases. The UMC also has an advanced research program, and several researchers conduct clinical research studies within the UMC. Patient data are stored in a central database at the UMC. The UMC is responsible for guaranteeing the security of patient data and for determining the purposes and means of its processing. Different departments at the UMC can define policies to regulate the access to patient data. Here, we consider two such departments: the Security Department and the Data Center. The Data Center manages the UMC database and is mainly concerned that medical, research and administrative staff of the UMC have access to the data they need to perform their duties. On the other hand, the Security Department mainly focuses on the protection of patient data and on the compliance with regulations and laws that are in place.

Table 1. Access Requirements

Stakeholder	Access requirements
Alice	Her treating doctors and nurses can access her medical information
	Any other access to her information is denied
Caroline	Doctors and nurses can access her medical information
	Researchers can read her genetic information
	Any other access to her information is denied
UMC Data Center	Doctors and nurses can access patient information
	Researchers can access patient information
UMC Security Department	Medical staff can access patient data to provide medical treatment
	Technicians can access and modify patient data for maintenance purposes
Regulatory Body	Data subjects can access their medical information
	Personal data shall be collected and processed only if the data subject has given his explicit consent to their processing
	Access is allowed without data subject's consent to comply with a legal obligation imposed upon the controller
	Access is allowed without data subject's consent to protect the data subject's vital interests
National Privacy Authority	Unlawful and unfair data processing operations are forbidden
Ethical Medical Committee	Researchers can only access anonymized patient information

Our scenario focuses on Alice and Caroline, two monozygotic twins, who both rely on UMC's services for treatment. Caroline has also engaged in a clinical trial and shared her genetic information with the UMC for research purposes.

Privacy is a highly regulated subject, especially in healthcare. Most countries have regulations and laws in force, which impose stringent requirements on the collection and processing of personal data [6]. To explicitly model the access requirements defined by privacy regulations, we introduce a *Regulatory Body* as a stakeholder in our scenario.[1] This entity issues and revises regulations to protect the privacy of citizens. Privacy regulations like the EU Directive on data protection (Directive 1995/46/EC) require the creation of an independent authority to protect the fundamental rights of citizens. This authority, hereafter referred to as National Privacy Authority, has the task of overseeing the compliance of organizations with privacy regulations. Moreover, it can prohibit unlawful or unfair data processing operations. Next to the National Privacy Authority, we also consider an Ethical Medical Committee of the Ministry of Health. This entity defines requirements on the use of medical data, especially for research purposes.

Each aforementioned stakeholder can specify requirements to regulate the access and usage of data. These requirements are summarized in Table 1.

---

[1] Note that legal requirements can also define the relation between stakeholders. In the next section we will discuss how these requirements can be accommodated in the framework.

3.1   Data Governance Model

In collaborative systems, multiple stakeholders can contribute to the creation and management of data objects. Each stakeholder related to a data object should retain some authority on the object. However, not all these stakeholders might have the same level of authority. The degree of authority a user has depends on its role with respect to the data. Thus, the actual permissions on shared data should be defined by taking into account both stakeholders' access requirements and their relation with the data. In this section, we investigate a general framework to explicitly express the relations between stakeholders and data objects as well as to prioritize such relations.

To characterize the relation between stakeholders and shared data, we use the notion of archetype proposed in [2]. The archetypes for a shared data object capture the roles that stakeholders can have with respect to the object. The role determines the extent of control over the object. In this work we introduce the notion of archetype hierarchy to reflect the level of authority that users have on shared resources.

Definition 1. *Let A be the set of archetypes for a shared data object o. An archetype hierarchy H has the form:*

$$H = L \mid (L, pr, H)$$
$$L = (\sigma, [a_1, \ldots, a_n])$$
$$pr = t \mid + \mid -$$

A level L consists of a set of archetypes $a_1, \ldots, a_n \in A$, whose requirements are combined using an intra-level aggregator σ. An archetype hierarchy H is (recursively) built over levels by concatenating a level with a hierarchy according to a given priority pr that can be total (denoted by t), positive (denoted by $+$) or negative (denoted by $-$).

Intuitively, a level groups those archetypes that have the same level of authority on shared data. An intra-level aggregator specifies how the requirements of the stakeholders associated to the archetypes in a level should be evaluated. Our framework does not pose restrictions on the intra-level aggregator that can be used. In the next section we provide some examples of intra-level aggregators and discuss how they can be realized.

Example 2. Consider the genetic information provided by Caroline in the scenario of Example 1. We identify two main archetypes for this information: *Data Controller* and *Data Subject*. The Data Controller is the entity responsible for the security of the data and defines who can access a data element and how data can be processed. In our scenario, the UMC plays the role of Data Controller for Caroline's genetic information. In particular, the UMC Data Center and Security Department are two instances of the Data Controller. The Data Subject is the person to whom the information refers. In the scenario, Caroline is the Data Subject for her genetic information. In addition, given the twin relationship between Alice and Caroline, we also consider Alice as the Data Subject for the genetic information provided by Caroline. Next to these archetypes, we define an archetype for each of the other stakeholders in the scenario, namely Regulatory Body, National Privacy Authority and Ethical Medical Committee.

In an archetype hierarchy, levels are ordered according to the degree of authority that the archetypes forming a level have. We distinguish three types of priorities between levels: total, positive and negative. Total priority indicates that the access requirements associated to the higher level always override the ones associated to lower levels. However, in some cases only the positive access requirements (i.e., access requirements defining positive authorizations) associated to the higher level should take precedence; otherwise, the access requirements defined by stakeholders at the lower level should also be evaluated. This is achieved using the positive priority. Negative priority is the dual of positive priority where only negative requirements from the higher level take precedence.

Example 3. The archetypes for our running example, identified in Example 2, can be organized in a hierarchy. Figure 2a presents a graphical representation of this hierarchy. Regulatory Body has the highest priority. The next level comprises the Data Subject, followed by a level formed by the National Privacy Authority and the Ethical Medical Committee. The lowest level is formed by the Data Controller. In order to comply with data protection regulations and to satisfy the intrinsic characteristics of the roles, the following priorities are defined between levels:

- The Regulatory Body has the right to override the decisions of the Data Subjects to permit access to patients' medical records, e.g. to protect their vital interests or comply with legal obligations [6]. Therefore, a positive priority is used between the first and second level.
- Data Subjects have the right to determine who can (or cannot) access and process their information. However, even if they permit access to their information, the National Privacy Authority and the Ethical Medical Committee hold the right to deny it if the request is not in compliance with their requirements. Such a requirement is achieved through a negative priority between the Data Subject and the lower level.
- The National Privacy Authority and Ethical Medical Committee can influence how the Data Controller processes personal data. In particular, they can deny an unlawful or unfair access, or permit the access for research purposes regardless of the Data Controller's requirements. A total priority between the levels can be used to achieve this requirement.

3.2 Data Governance Instantiation

Access control policy languages like XACML allow stakeholders to express their access requirements as policies and provide means to combine these policies

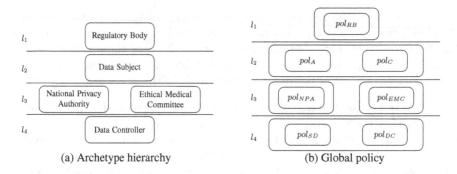

(a) Archetype hierarchy   (b) Global policy

Fig. 2. Data Governance Model and Instantiation for the scenario in Example 1

in a single policy (hereafter referred to as the *global policy*), which is used to determine the actual permissions on shared data. In this section, we present how the global policy can be created from user policies taking into account the archetype hierarchy. We first introduce a grammar for the specification of the global policy. This grammar is inspired by XACML, thus making the encoding into XACML policies straightforward.

Definition 2. *The global policy P_H is constructed upon the following grammar:*

$$P_H = P_L \mid (\mathsf{fa}, [P_L, P_H]) \mid (\mathsf{pov}, [P_L, P_H]) \mid (\mathsf{dov}, [P_L, P_H])$$
$$P_L = (ca, [P_a, \ldots, P_a])$$
$$P_a = (ca, [p_1, \ldots, p_n])$$

where $p_1, \ldots, p_n$ are user policies and ca represents a policy combining algorithm.

An archetype policy P_a combines the policies of those users who are associated to an archetype a. To this end, every archetype is associated with a policy combining algorithm that determines how the policies defined by the stakeholders having such an archetype are combined. A level policy P_L combines the policies associated to the archetypes in a level L. The combining algorithms used to construct archetype and level policies should reflect the security and privacy needs for the specific domain. In particular, the combining algorithm for level policies should reflect the constraints on the combination of archetypes in a level as given in the archetype hierarchy (Definition 1). Note that our policy language does not impose any restriction on the policy combining algorithms to be used to combine user policies and archetype policies.[2] For instance, archetype/level policies can make use of the standard XACML combining algorithms (see Sect. 2) or

---

[2] Although any combining algorithm can be used to combine user policies and archetype policies, the use of noncommutative algorithms can have undesired effects. In fact, these algorithms often represent a priority between policies based on their order (e.g., first-applicable in XACML), whereas there is no order within an archetype or a level.

more advanced combining algorithms such as the consensus and majority combining algorithms defined in [11]. The global policy is recursively built over level policies. This is necessary to account for the use of different priority between levels in the archetype hierarchy. Priorities are encoded in terms of combining algorithms. In particular, the total, positive and negative priorities are encoded using first-applicable (fa), permit-overrides (pov) and deny-overrides (dov), respectively.

Next we define how the global policy is constructed from the archetype hierarchy and user policies.

Definition 3. *Let A be the set of archetypes for an object o and U the set of users. Let $UA \subseteq U \times A$ be the user-archetype assignment, i.e. $(u, a) \in UA$ iff user u has archetype a. Let $\mathcal{P}$ be the set of user policies and let p_u denote the policy of user u. We denote by A2ca(a) the combining algorithm ca specified for archetype a. To combine user policies according to the archetype hierarchy, we first create archetype policies:*

$$\mathsf{A2P}(a) = (\mathsf{A2ca}(a), [p_{u_1}, \ldots, p_{u_m}])$$

where $u_1, \ldots, u_m$ are the users such that $(u_1, a), \ldots, (u_m, a)$ are in UA. Next, archetype policies are combined to form level policies:

$$\mathsf{L2P}((\sigma, [a_1, \ldots, a_n])) = (ca, [\mathsf{A2P}(a_1), \ldots, \mathsf{A2P}(a_n)])$$

where ca is the combining algorithm realizing the intra-level aggregator σ. The global policy is obtained by recursively combining level policies with respect to the priorities between levels:

$$\begin{cases} \mathsf{H2P}(L) = \mathsf{L2P}(L) \\ \mathsf{H2P}((L, pr, H)) = (\mathsf{pr2CA}(pr), [\mathsf{L2P}(L), \mathsf{H2P}(H)]) \end{cases}$$

where

$$\mathsf{pr2CA}(t) = \mathsf{fa} \qquad \mathsf{pr2CA}(+) = \mathsf{pov} \qquad \mathsf{pr2CA}(-) = \mathsf{dov}$$

In the next example we illustrate how to derive a global policy from the archetype hierarchy and user policies based on our running example.

Example 4. Figure 2b shows the structure of global policy G obtained by instantiating the archetype hierarchy in Fig. 2a based on the scenario given in Example 1. Formally, the global policy can be represented as follows:

$$G = \mathsf{pov}(pol_{RB}, \mathsf{dov}(\mathsf{pov}(pol_A, pol_C), \mathsf{fa}(\mathsf{wc}(pol_{NPA}, pol_{EMC}), \mathsf{dov}(pol_{SD}, pol_{DC}))))$$

Here we assume that the policies specified by the data subjects (i.e., Alice and Caroline) are combined using permit-overrides, i.e. access to the data is granted if at least one of the data subjects permits the access. The policies of the UMC Security Department and Data Center are combined using deny-overrides.

Finally, we combine the policies of the National Privacy Authority and the Ethical Medical Committee using the weak-consensus algorithm as defined in [11]. According to this algorithm, user policies should not conflict with each other: Permit a request if some user policies permit a request, and no user policy denies it; Deny a request if some user policies deny a request, and no user policy permits it; otherwise Indeterminate should be yielded.

4 Policy Mismatches

In the previous section, we have shown how the policies of different stakeholders can be combined by taking into account their relationship with the resource to be protected. Ideally, the authorization system should enforce the access requirements of all stakeholders. However, this is not always possible. In fact, users can have conflicting authorization requirements, which results in conflicting policies.

Many access control mechanisms like XACML use policy combining algorithms to automatically resolve policy conflicts. Although solving conflicts is necessary for an authorization mechanism to make a conclusive decision, it makes the decision making process non-transparent to users. Users expect their policies to be enforced by the authorization system; however, in practice, their policies can be overridden by the policies of other entities. The main problem is that, in most existing authorization systems, policy conflict resolution is embedded in the policy evaluation process and, thus, policy conflicts are not identified and/or recorded. This makes users unaware whether their policies have actually been enforced.

We argue that the lack of transparency can affect the collaboration among users and, in particular, their willingness of sharing sensitive information needed for the success of the collaboration. Below we exemplify this issue using our running example.

Example 5. As shown in Example 1, each stakeholder has certain authorization requirements over the genetic information provided by Caroline. Suppose that David, a researcher at the UMC, requests access to this information. Based on the global policy in Example 4 and access requirements in Table 1, the authorization system allows David to access the information. If we look at the requirements of the single users, we have that: the enforced decision is consistent with Caroline's and the UMC Data Center's policy; however, access should have been denied according to Alice's policies; finally, the Regulatory Body's policy returns a NotApplicable as it delegates the Data Subject the authority to decide whether its data can be used for research purposes and thus does not define a specific policy about researcher accessing genetic information. We can observe that Alice's access requirements are not enforced. This can reduce her trust towards the UMC and, thus, can make her reluctant to share information in the future.

We use the notion of *policy mismatch* introduced in [2] to capture policy conflicts.

Definition 4. *Let $p_1, \ldots, p_n$ be the policies of n users and p the global policy obtained by combining such policies. Given an access request q, a user i (with $i \in \{1, \ldots, n\}$) has a mismatch if $[\![p]\!](q) \neq [\![p_i]\!](q)$.*

A mismatch occurs when the decision enforced by the authorization system differs from the decision obtained evaluating the policy of a user. Likely, only mismatches where a user's policy is applicable (i.e., $[\![p_i]\!] \neq$ NotApplicable) are relevant for the user. However, we do not restrict the (type of) mismatches that can be reported to users. In particular, we allows each user to specify mismatches preferences, indicating the types of mismatches the user wants to be notified (see Sect. 5.1). In the next section, we show how the notion of mismatch can be used to augment the XACML reference architecture with a transparency service while being compliant with the XACML specification.

5 Transparency Service

The goal of this work is to enable collaborations between stakeholders in a trusted, secure and privacy-preserving way. Sharing resources and managing access to them are essential for such collaborations. However, as shown in the previous section, stakeholders may have conflicting authorization requirements. This section presents a *transparency service*, which aims to make the stakeholders engaged in a collaboration aware of these conflicts and how they are resolved by the authorization system.

The transparency service has been designed to be fully compliant with the XACML standard. This ensures that the service can be used within existing XACML implementations without these implementations being modified. In the remainder of the section, we discuss the design and implementation of the transparency service as well as possible deployment configurations within the XACML reference architecture.

5.1 Service Design

The transparency service aims to detect mismatches between the decision enforced by the authorization system and the access requirements of a certain stakeholder. Any mismatch found is then reported to the stakeholders whose decision was not enforced, provided they are interested in this type of discrepancy.

A naïve approach to identify decision mismatches would be to evaluate an access request against the global policy and against each user policy, and compare the obtained decisions. In particular, user policies could be stored separately in the PAP; then, the PDP can fetch one policy at the time for the evaluation of the access request. This naïve approach, however, has a number of drawbacks. First, the selective fetching of policies is not supported by most existing XACML implementations; they typically fetch all policies available in the PAP and then combine the decisions obtained evaluating the fetched policies using a root combining algorithm [14]. Therefore, this approach would requires a modification of existing XACML implementations. In addition, it requires instantiating the PDP for each user policy, affecting performance.

To address these drawbacks, we introduce *viewpoints* to distinguish user policies in the global policy. Every user u submits an XACML policy p_u implementing its authorization requirements. To reflect the viewpoint the target of p_u is extended with an environment attribute `ViewPoint`. Two values are assigned to this attribute: the identifier of u, representing the user viewpoint, and "*global*". The evaluation with respect the *global* perspective provides the access decision which is actually enforced by the authorization mechanism. It is worth noting that the target is applicable to a given access request (and thus a user policy is evaluated) only if at least one of these two attribute values for attribute `ViewPoint` is provided in the request. User policies are combined based on the role of the corresponding stakeholder with respect to the resource to be protected as described in Sect. 3. The resulting policy is stored in the PAP and is fetched by the PDP for the evaluation of access requests.

The architecture of the transparency service is presented in Fig. 3. The service comprises three main components: *Global Decision Handler*, *Mismatch Handler* and *Notification Handler*. The service allows users to specify their preferences about which mismatches they want to be notified (e.g., access is permitted whereas the user wants to deny it) along with their contact information. Upon receiving a request, the Global Decision Handler adds attribute `ViewPoint` with value "*global*" to the request and passes on the enriched request for evaluation. The response is passed on for enforcement; it is also sent to the Mismatch Handler. This component checks the mismatch preferences provided by every user to determine the users $u_1, \ldots u_n$ who are interested in mismatches corresponding to the decision reached. For each such user u, the Mismatch Handler creates a new access request which consists of the original request but now extended with attribute `ViewPoint` taking value u, the identifier of the user. As the policies specified by other users will not be applicable (due to a non-matching value for attribute `ViewPoint`) this request is only evaluated against the policy of the corresponding user. When a response to a viewpoint specific requests does not match the global decision and the user is interested in this specific type of mismatch, the Mismatch Handler calls the Notification Handler. This component retrieves the contact information of the users from the database and notifies them of the mismatches that occurred.

5.2   Service Implementation and Deployment

We have implemented the transparency service within the SAFAX framework [10]. SAFAX is an XACML-based architectural framework that offers authorization as a service. A main characteristic of SAFAX is that all components in the XACML reference architecture are designed as loosely coupled services. These services communicate with each other in JSON or XML via preregistered interfaces (defined in a service registry). SAFAX has been implemented in Java and runs on Apache Tomcat server using Jersey as a service framework. Back-end

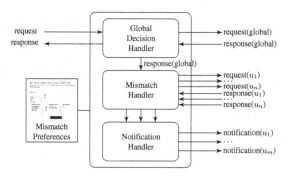

Fig. 3. Transparency Service Architecture

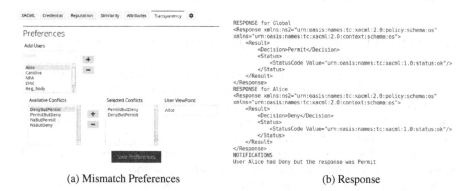

(a) Mismatch Preferences   (b) Response

Fig. 4. SAFAX GUI

persistent data are stored in a MySQL server. To manage the authorization service configuration and policies, SAFAX offers a User Interface (referred to as SAFAX GUI) that consumes SAFAX services.

The transparency service has been implemented as a SAFAX service and the SAFAX GUI has been extended to manage its configurations. Figure 4a shows a screenshot of the interface used to manage viewpoints and set stakeholders' mismatch preferences. These preferences are stored in a persistent database on the MySQL server and used by the Notification Handler to determine, for each stakeholder, which mismatches should be notified. For demonstration purposes, the evaluation outcome for every request and the notified mismatches are shown in the SAFAX GUI (Fig. 4b).

Thanks to the service-oriented nature of SAFAX, the transparency service can be deployed at two different locations within the XACML reference architecture. In particular, it can act as either PEP or PDP. Depending on its use, the transparency service and its interfaces have to be registered in the SAFAX service registry accordingly. As shown by the architectures in Figs. 5 and 6, the transparency service encapsulates rather than replacing the corresponding components. By creating a dependency between the transparency service and one

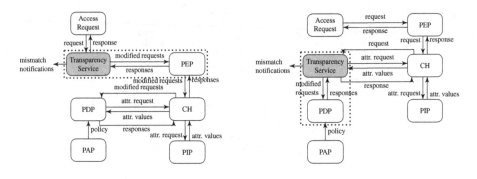

Fig. 5. Transparency Service as PEP   **Fig. 6.** Transparency Service as PDP

of the existing PEP and PDP services, the expected message flow for the corresponding configuration is achieved.

When the transparency service is used as PEP (Fig. 5), it can be seen as an external service offered to users by a (possibly) different provider. On the other hand, when the transparency service is used as PDP (Fig. 6), it can be seen as additional functionality offered by the authorization service itself. SAFAX is able to support both configurations without the need of modifying existing components due to its service-oriented nature. In contrast, other existing XACML implementations can only support the transparency service as an external service because they implement the XACML reference architecture as a monolithic component. Deployment of the transparency service as the PDP would require a modification of these XACML implementations.

6   Evaluation

As discussed in the previous section, the transparency service generates multiple requests to identify mismatches between the decision enforced by the system and user policies. Therefore, we need to evaluate the introduced overhead to ensure it does not affect user experience, thus hampering the adoption of the service in existing infrastructures. For the experiments we created a dataset consisting of policies of different size, where the size of a policy is characterized by the number of rules in the policy. Since the number of generated requests depends on the number of viewpoints, we added a varying number of viewpoints to these policies (i.e., 5, 10, 20, 30 and 40 viewpoints). The same policies were evaluated when the transparency service is deployed as PEP and PDP as well as when the transparency service is not used. We computed the average evaluation time over ten runs; a new policy dataset was created for each run.

The results of the experiments are shown in Fig. 7. These graphs show that the transparency service when deployed as PEP (Fig. 7b) introduces a larger overhead than when it is deployed as PDP (Fig. 7a). When the transparency service is deployed as PEP, every generated request has to be handled by the

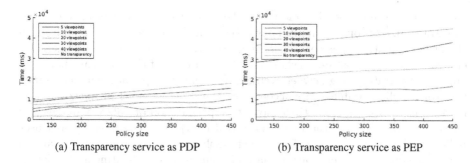

(a) Transparency service as PDP   (b) Transparency service as PEP

Fig. 7. Evaluation of the overhead introduced by the transparency service (Color figure online)

PEP, CH and PDP (see Fig. 5). On the other hand, when the service is deployed as PDP, requests are only handled by PDP (see Fig. 6), thus leading to a lower overhead. In addition to the deployment method, the results show that the evaluation time depends on the number of viewpoints and policy size. In particular, the number of viewpoints has an impact on the number of requests that are generated. The observed results imply that the delay introduced by the communication among the components of the system is more significant than the overhead due to the evaluation of the requests.

Although enabling transparency unavoidably comes at the cost of computation time, it should be noted that the decision enforced by the authorization mechanism is obtained from the evaluation of the request with the 'global' viewpoint. The other requests are only needed to detect policy mismatches and generate notifications. Therefore, they can be generated and evaluated offline to not affect the functioning of the system.

7   Related Work

With the growing popularity of collaborative systems, the risks of data breaches have increased due to the intrinsic difficulty of establishing a data government model for such systems. Several mechanisms have been proposed to balance the ease of collaboration and the level of security with collaborative systems (see [21] for a survey). For instance, solutions such as Role-Based Access Control [16], Task-Based Access Control [20] and Team-Based Access Control [19] use the roles within an organization, the purpose of the usage or group membership to regulate the access to sensitive data. While these solutions provide some basic features to enable access control in collaborative systems, they usually assume that data objects are under the control of a single entity and, thus, they lack support for policy administration of shared resources.

A few models have been proposed for collaborative authorization management of shared data. For instance, Squicciarini et al. [18] consider resources co-owned by multiple users who can separately specify their policies for the shared data, and use the Clarke-Tax model for the collective enforcement of these policies. Hu et al. [7] propose a multiparty access control model where, in addition to the owner of data, other controllers (e.g., contributor, dissiminator, stakeholders) can regulate the access to shared data. The owner of the data can choose an appropriate strategy (e.g., owner-overrides, full-consensus-permit, majority-permit) to resolve policy conflicts. To account for the different level of authority, the model uses a voting scheme that allows the specification of different weights for controllers. Similarly to the model proposed in [7], our governance model uses policy combination strategies for conflict resolution; however, our model allows a more fine-grained governance of shared resources by representing and ordering levels of authority through an archetype hierarchy that can be instantiated using an arbitrary combination of policy combining algorithms.

Policy combination strategies are often used by authorization mechanisms to define how policy conflicts should be resolved. Examples of conflict resolution strategies are: deny takes precedence [8], permit takes precedence [8], most-specific takes precedence [8,12] and explicit specification of priorities [17]. Similarly, Reeder et al. [15] propose specificity precedence, deny precedence, order precedence, recency precedence or the combination of these when a single strategy fails. The most prominent authorization mechanism that supports (most of) these strategies is XACML [14]. In particular, XACML encodes conflict resolution strategies as policy combining algorithms (see Sect. 2). Our solution, being based on XACML, natively supports these strategies as well. Moreover, given the extensible nature of XACML, accommodating other conflict resolution strategies as the ones proposed in [8,11,12] is straightforward.

Mazzoleni et al. [13] argue that policy combination algorithms provided by XACML, and in general conflict resolution strategies, are not enough to integrate policies specified by autonomous parties. To this end, they define a policy similarity process and a number of policy integration algorithms. The policy similarity process is used to analyze the behavior of policies with respect to access requests. The result of this analysis, along with policy integration preferences given by the users, is used to select the policy integration algorithms for building the global policy. Differently from [13], our framework integrates policies specified by multiple administration entities based on their relation with a data object, thus reflecting the level of authority that these entities have on the object. The policy similarity process and policy integration algorithms proposed in [13] can be employed in our framework to form archetype and level policies.

Although methods for integrating policies specified by autonomous entities (as well as conflict resolution strategies) are necessary to ensure the proper functioning of the system, their application makes access decision making non-transparent to users. Transparency has become a major demand for modern IT governance, social and medical systems [1,4,9]. However, very little research has been conducted towards its introduction into access control. To the best of our knowledge, CollAC [2] is the only work that proposes a transparent access control solution which detects conflicts during policy evaluation and notifies the users whose decisions have been overridden. This work extents [2] along two main directions. First, this work introduces archetype hierarchies to reason about the level of authority that users have over shared objects together with a method for obtaining the global policy from the archetype hierarchy and user policies. Moreover, we demonstrate how the notion of transparency can be accommodated in existing XACML-based access control mechanisms, thus showing its practical applicability.

8   Conclusion

This paper has introduced a governance model for collaborative systems, which enables the integration of the access requirements of all entities involved in the protection of a data object with respect to their relation with the object. This way, all entities are offered an appropriate level of control over shared resources. We have implemented the model in XACML, allowing each user to provide its requirements as a policy and using appropriate combining algorithms to achieve the right precedence between their policies.

Even if the use of combining algorithms is necessary to automatically resolve policy conflicts and thus guarantee the proper functioning of the system, it can result in a user's policy to be overruled without the user being aware. This may lower the user's trust in the system. To this end, we have introduced transparency in the decision making, allowing users to choose to be notified about conflicts between their access requirements and the decision enforced by the system. Our implementation within SAFAX shows that a transparency service can be deployed both as a PEP and a PDP. Our experiments show that deployment as a PDP has a lower overhead. While the solution is not optimized for performance, it can be applied to many scenarios, especially given the fact that the introduced overhead is not on the critical path for access to resources.

The proposed transparency service only notifies users about policy mismatches. To enhance user awareness, users should be also able to understand why a certain decision was taken [5]. An interesting direction for future work is to augment users' notification with information explaining why their policies were overridden.

Acknowledgments. This work has been partially funded by the ITEA2 projects FedSS (No. 11009) and M2MGrid (No. 13011), the EDA project IN4STARS2.0, and the Dutch national program COMMIT under the THeCS project.

References

1. Albrecht, U.V.: Transparency of health-apps for trust and decision making. J. Med. Internet Res. **15**(12), e277 (2013)
2. Damen, S., den Hartog, J., Zannone, N.: CollAC: Collaborative access control. In: Proceedings of CTS, pp. 142–149. IEEE (2014)
3. Damen, S., Zannone, N.: Privacy implications of privacy settings and tagging in facebook. In: Jonker, W., Petković, M. (eds.) SDM 2013. LNCS, vol. 8425, pp. 121–138. Springer, Heidelberg (2014)

4. de Fine Licht, J.: Transparency actually: how transparency affects public perceptions of political decision-making. Eur. Political Sci. Rev. **6**(02), 309–330 (2014)
5. Ghai, S.K., Nigam, P., Kumaraguru, P.: Cue: A framework for generating meaningful feedback in XACML. In: Proceedings of SafeConfig, pp. 9–16. ACM (2010)
6. Guarda, P., Zannone, N.: Towards the development of privacy-aware systems. Inf. Softw. Technol. **51**(2), 337–350 (2009)
7. Hu, H., Ahn, G.J., Jorgensen, J.: Multiparty access control for online social networks: model and mechanisms. TKDE **25**(7), 1614–1627 (2013)
8. Jajodia, S., Samarati, P., Sapino, M.L., Subrahmanian, V.S.: Flexible support for multiple access control policies. ACM Trans. Database Syst. **26**(2), 214–260 (2001)
9. Joshi, A., Bollen, L., Hassink, H.: An empirical assessment of it governance transparency: evidence from commercial banking. Inf. Sys. Manag. **30**(2), 116–136 (2013)
10. Kaluvuri, S.P., Egner, A.I., den Hartog, J., Zannone, N.: SAFAX – Anextensible authorization service for cloud environments. Front. ICT **2**(9) (2015)
11. Li, N., Wang, Q., Qardaji, W., Bertino, E., Rao, P., Lobo, J., Lin, D.: Access control policy combining: theory meets practice. In: Proceedings of SACMAT, pp. 135–144. ACM (2009)
12. Matteucci, I., Mori, P., Petrocchi, M.: Prioritized execution of privacy policies. In: Di Pietro, R., Herranz, J., Damiani, E., State, R. (eds.) DPM 2012 and SETOP 2012. LNCS, vol. 7731, pp. 133–145. Springer, Heidelberg (2013)
13. Mazzoleni, P., Crispo, B., Sivasubramanian, S., Bertino, E.: XACML policy integration algorithms. ACM Trans. Inf. Syst. Secur. **11**(1), 4:1–4:29 (2008)
14. OASIS XACML Technical Committee: eXtensible Access Control Markup Language (XACML) Version 2.0 (2005)
15. Reeder, R.W., Bauer, L., Cranor, L.F., Reiter, M.K., Vaniea, K.: Effects of access-control policy conflict-resolution methods on policy-authoring usability. CyLab, p. 12 (2009)
16. Sandhu, R.S., Coyne, E.J., Feinstein, H.L., Youman, C.E.: Role-based access control models. Computer **29**(2), 38–47 (1996)
17. Shen, H., Dewan, P.: Access control for collaborative environments. In: Proceedings of Conference on Computer-supported Cooperative Work, pp. 51–58. ACM (1992)
18. Squicciarini, A.C., Shehab, M., Paci, F.: Collective privacy management in social networks. In: Proceedings of WWW, pp. 521–530. ACM (2009)
19. Thomas, R.K.: Team-based access control (TMAC): a primitive for applying role-based access controls in collaborative environments. In: Proceedings of RBAC, pp. 13–19. ACM (1997)
20. Thomas, R.K., Sandhu, R.S.: Task-based authorization controls (TBAC): A family of models for active and enterprise-oriented authorization management. In: DBSec, pp. 166–181. Springer, Heidelberg (1997)
21. Tolone, W., Ahn, G.J., Pai, T., Hong, S.P.: Access control in collaborative systems. ACM Comput. Surv. **37**(1), 29–41 (2005)

Sharing-Habits Based Privacy Control in Social Networks

Silvie Levy[1(✉)], Ehud Gudes[1(✉)], and Nurit Gal-Oz[2(✉)]

[1] Department of Mathematics and Computer Science,
The Open University, Ra'anana, Israel
`silvie.levy@gmail.com, ehud@cs.bgu.ac.il`
[2] Department of Mathematics and Computer Science, Sapir College, Sederot, Israel
`galoz@cs.bgu.ac.il`

Abstract. We study users behavior in online social networks (OSN) as a means to preserve privacy. People widely use OSN for a variety of objectives and fields. Each OSN has different characteristics, requirements, and vulnerabilities of the private data shared. *Sharing-habits* refers to users' patterns of sharing information. These sharing-habits implied by the communication between users and their peers hides a lot of additional private information. Most users are not aware that the sensitive private information they share might leak to unauthorized users. We use several different well-known strategies from graph flows, and the sharing-habits of information flow among OSN users to define efficient and easy to implement algorithms for ensuring privacy preservation with a predefined privacy level.

1 Introduction

Online Social networks (OSN) are websites enabling users to build connections and relationships among each other. The OSN structure represents social interactions and relationships between entities which are the users of the OSN. Social networks are widely used by members for information sharing with the purpose of reaching as many friends as possible. The shared-information spread, is influenced by human decisions, and users are not fully aware of the possible consequences of their preferences when specifying access rules to their shared data. It is the responsibility of OSN administrators to effectively control the shared information, reduce the risk of information leakage, and constantly evaluate the potential risks of shared-information leakage. Most access rules are defined in terms of the degree of relationship required to access ones data. These rules are not refined enough to allow for dynamic denial of content from certain peers of the community.

We propose a model for access control that works with minimal user intervention. The model is based on users' patterns of sharing information denoted as *Sharing-habits*. Naturally some users are more likely to share information with others. To minimize the probability of information leakage, the social network is

© IFIP International Federation for Information Processing 2016
Published by Springer International Publishing Switzerland 2016. All Rights Reserved
S. Ranise and V. Swarup (Eds.): DBSec 2016, LNCS 9766, pp. 217–232, 2016.
DOI: 10.1007/978-3-319-41483-6_16

analyzed to determine based on these habits, the probability of information flow through network connections. In a graph representation of the network, where edges indicate relationship between users, the challenge is to select the set of edges that should be blocked to prevent leakage of the shared information to unwanted recipients. We review some methods for handling and preserving privacy in social networks, and present our new privacy preserving approach, based on sharing-habits data. Our model combines algorithms that use graph flow methods such as max-flow-min-cut, and contract. Experimental results show the effectiveness of these algorithms in controlling the flow of information sharing to allow sharing with friends while hiding from others. The paper is structured as follows: in the next section we review related work, in Sect. 3 we define the privacy assurance in OSN problem, and in Sect. 4 we present our method for dealing with this problem. We explain our evaluation method and primary results in Sect. 5 and conclude by summarizing our contribution and discussing directions for future work in Sect. 6.

2   Related Work

There are various types of Online Social Networks, each with different properties. Privacy preservation can be viewed and handled from various aspects. Carmagnola et al. [5] present a research about the factors that help users identification, and information leakage in social networks, based on entity resolution. They conducted a study on the possible factors that make users vulnerable to identification, and of personal information leakage, and the perception of users about privacy related to the spreading of their public data. To find the risk factors, they studied the relations between the user behavior (habits) on OSNs and the probability of users' identification. Kleinberg and Ligett [7] describe the social network as a graph where nodes represent users, and an edge between two nodes indicates that those two users are enemies that do not wish to share information. The problem of information sharing is described as the graph coloring problem, Kleinberg and Ligett [7] analyze the stability of solutions for this problem, and the incentive of users to change the set of partners with whom they are willing to share information. Tassa and Cohen [11], handle the information release problem, and present algorithms to compute an anonymization of the released data to a level of k-anonymity; the algorithm can be used in sequential and distributed environments, while maintaining high utility of the anonymized data. Vatsalan et al. [3] conducted a survey of privacy-preserving record linkage (PPRL) techniques, with an overview of techniques that allow the linking of databases between organizations while at the same time preserving the privacy of these data. In this paper Vatsalan et al. [3] present taxonomy of PPRL which characterize the known PPRL techniques along 15 dimensions, highlight shortcomings of current techniques avenues for future research. Jaehong and Ravi [6] present the ORIGIN CONTROL access control model where every piece of information is associated with its creator forever. Ranjbar and Maheswaran [1], describe the social network as a graph where nodes represent users, and an edge between two nodes indicates that those two users are friends that wish to share information. They present algorithms for defining communities among users, were the information is shared among users within the community, and algorithms for defining a set of users that should be blocked in order to prevent the shared information from reaching the adversaries, and leaking outside the community. In OSN, communities are subsets of users connected to each other; the community members have common interests and high levels of mutual trust, it can be described by a connected graph, where each user is a node in the graph, and an edge connecting two nodes indicates a relationship between two users. A community is defind by Ranjbar and Maheswaran [1] from the view point of an individual user. *myCommunity* is defined as the largest sub-graph of users who are likely to receive and hold the information without leaking. In other words, myCommunity is the subset of an individual users friends that have intense and frequent interactions and describes a grouping abstraction of a set of users that surrounds an individual based on the communication patterns used for information sharing. Our study is based on the ideas described in their paper; while they only share information within the defined community, and block users that might leak information to adversaries, we relax the limitation defined in their study, and block only edges on the path to the adversaries, instead of blocking all the information from the source user to the users that might leak the information.

3   The Privacy Assurance in OSN Problem

In this section we define the general problem of privacy assurance in OSN and our proposed method that uses information from users sharing-habits.

Let $G = (V, E)$ be a directed graph that describes a social network, where V is the set of network's users, and E is the set of directed and weighted edges representing the users' information flow relationships. An edge $(u_i, u_j) \in E$ exists only if u_i shares information with u_j. The distance between two vertices, $dist_G(u_i, u_j)$ is the length of the shortest path from u_i to u_j in G. *Ego* is an individual focal node, it is the specific user from which we consider the information flow. A network has as many egos as it has nodes, *ego-community* is the collection of ego and all nodes to whom ego has a connection at some path length. The δ-community of a user, represented by the ego vertex u_i is the sub-graph $G_\delta(u_i) = (V_\delta(u_i), E_\delta(i))$, where for each $v_i \in V_\delta(u_i)$, $v_i \neq u_i$, $dist_G(u_i, v_i) \leq \delta$.

The following definitions are as defined by Ranjbar et al. [1]: p_i is the probability that user u_i is willing to share the information with some of his friends.

$$p_i = \begin{cases} (outflow/inflow) & (outflow < inflow), \\ 1 & (outflow \geq inflow). \end{cases} \tag{1}$$

– Outflow is the number of sharing interactions from u_i to his friends.
– Inflow is the number of sharing interactions from $u_i's$ friends to u_i.

The likelihood of u_i sharing information with u_j along the edge (u_i, u_j) is represented by $w_{i,j}$, the weight on the edge (u_i, u_j); This weight is derived from the relationship between u_i and u_j, it is a fixed number indicating the willingness of u_i to share information with u_j, it does not change or change very infrequently, and may be set by the user. The probability of flow between two neighbor users, u_i and u_j is denoted as p_{ij}, and calculated by $p_{i,j} = p_i \times w_{i,j}$. Since the flow may change quite often this probability may also changes with it. We assume that the user behavior is consistent; user u_i shares all the data with user u_j with probability $p_{i,j}$. This probability can change with time, but it does not depend on the content of the shared information. The Probability of Information Flow (PIF), is the maximum probability of information flow throughout the entire paths between u_i and u_j. A path probability flow between u_i and u_j is the flow of the edge with the minimum $p_{i,j}$. It is denoted as $PATH_{i,j}$. The PIF is the maximum among of all paths between u_i and u_j of $PATH_{i,j}$. The function f which denotes flow, is computed by using the log of the edges' probabilities on a path between u_i and u_j. To prevent information flow from one user to another we search for the minimal set of edges that when removed from the community graph, or blocked, disables the flow. We denote this set of blocked edges as B. Note that after edges are removed, the PIF and therefore f should be recomputed.

3.1   Problem Goal

Our aim is to enable a user u_i to share information with as many friends and acquaintances as possible, while preventing information leakage to adversaries within the user's community. Ranjbar et al. [1] describe a method for sharing information within the source user u_i defined community, while blocking users (friends and acquaintances) that might leak information to adversaries. We relax the limitation due to blocking friends, and instead of blocking all the information from the source user u_i to the users that might leak the information, block only edges on the path from u_i to his adversaries. We use the following criteria to define and evaluate the resulting u_i ego-community graph:

1. Minimum Friends Information Flow: the minimum information flow from u_i to every user within his community must preserve a certain percentage of the original information flow to every user denoted by α.
   Let $G_\delta(u_i) = (V_\delta(u_i), E_\delta(u_i))$ be the δ-community of $u_i, v \in V(u_i)$

   $$f(u_i, v) \geq \alpha \cdot f_{original}(u_i, v) \tag{2}$$

2. Close Friends Distance: Close friends are defined by their distance from u_i. $G_\beta(u_i) = (V_\delta(u_i), E_\delta(u_i))$ is the β-community of $u_i, v \in V(u_i)$, $\beta < \delta$. This criteria reflects the requirement that all the users within $u_i's$ β-community must receive the entire information from u_i, and cannot be blocked.
   Let B be the set of blocked edges, than

   $$B \subset \{(u_s, u_t)|d_{G_\delta}(u_i, u_s) \geq \beta, u_s, u_t, u_i \in V_{G_\delta}(u_i)\} \tag{3}$$

We assume that there are no adversaries within $u_i's$ β-community, otherwise the above condition can never be fulfilled.

3. Maximum Adversaries Information Flow: the maximum information flow from u_i to each of his adversaries cannot be more than γ from the original information flow to each adversary.

$$f(u_i, u_{adv}) \leq \gamma \cdot f_{original}(u_i, u_{adv}) \qquad (4)$$

For example the threshold parameters can be: $\alpha = 0.9$, $\beta = 2$, and $\gamma = 0.1$. The problem goal is to remove the least number of edges such that the three Eqs. 2, 3, 4 will be satisfied.

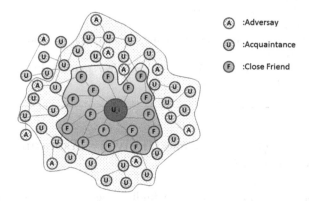

Fig. 1. $u_i's$ community graph (Color figure online)

Figure 1 describes a δ-community graph for u_i. The dotted area surrounds $u_i's$ δ-community graph with $\delta = 4$, i.e. all acquaintances within distance ≤ 4. The blue area surrounds $u_i's$ β-community, i.e. all friends within distance ≤ 2.
As shown by the figure the δ-community of friends is much larger than the β-community of close friends.

3.2   Cuts in Graphs

A cut in a graph is a set of edges between two subsets of a graph, one containing u_i, and the other containing $u_i's$ adversaries, such that when removed, prevents information flow from one subset to the other.
A naive algorithm for solving the problem would be an algorithm that finds any cut between the adversaries' set and $u_i's$ community, and defines this cut as the blocked edges list. Algorithm 1 is a naive algorithm for blocked users.

The naive algorithm is not suitable for our problem, since it doesn't comply with the (1) Minimum Friends Information Flow, (2) Close Friends Distance-criteria of our problem. Condition (1) requires minimum information flow from u_i to all members in $u_i's$ community, the naive algorithm doesn't handle this requirement. Condition (2) defines close friends by their distance from u_i, the naive algorithm doesn't handle this requirement. While the naive algorithm is not sufficient to our problem, it is important for understanding the theoretical problem defined here.

Algorithm 1. Naive algorithm for blocked users

Input: $G = (V, E)$ a directed graph that describes the social network.

    u_i the ego user.

    δ the community distance criteria.

    $AdversariesList$: the list of $u_i's$ adversaries.

Output: B:the set of blocked edges.

1: set $B = \emptyset$

2: **for all** $u_j \in V$ and $(u_j \notin AdversariesList)$ and $(dist_G(u_i, u_j) \leq \delta)$ **do**

3:    insert u_j to $V_\delta(u_i)$

4: **for all** $u_j \in AdversariesList$ **do**

5:    insert u_j to $V_\delta(adversaries)$

6: Choose any cut between the community graph, $V_\delta(u_i)$ and the adversaries $V_\delta(adversaries)$.

7: **for all** $e_{ij} \in \{$the cut between $V_\delta(u_i)$ and $V_\delta(adversaries)\}$ **do**

8:    insert e_{ij} to B

9: **return** B

---

4   The Sharing-Habits Based Privacy Assurance in OSN Solution

In our solution we propose a model for finding the set of edges that should be blocked in order to achieve maximum information sharing among the community of the information source with minimum information leak. Our model uses two methods for defining candidate sets for blocked edges, along with the evaluation method for choosing the best set to be blocked. Our method consists of two major steps, the first is the initialization step that creates a multi-graph with a super-vertex s_1 containing $u_i's$ β-community, this step is described in Subsect. 4.1. The second step described in Subsect. 4.2, uses two methods to find candidates-sets for blocked edges.

Algorithm 2 warps these steps to construct the set of edges to be blocked.

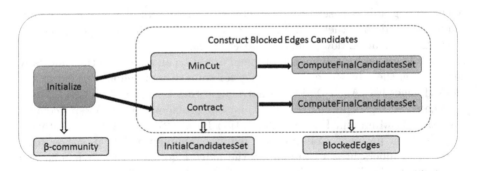

Fig. 2. Construct blocked edges main building blocks

Algorithm 2. Construct blocked edges
Input: u_i: the ego vertex.
      $G_\delta(u_i) = (V_\delta(u_i), E_\delta(u_i))$: $u_i's$ δ-community graph.
      α, γ: Flow thresholds.
      β: β-community distance.
      $AdversariesList$: the list of $u_i's$ adversaries.
Output: B:a set with edges to be blocked.

1: $MultiSet$ **function Initialize**$(u_i, G_\delta(u_i), \beta, AdversariesList)$
2: set $s_1 = \{u_i\}$
3: **for all** $(u_j \in G_\delta(u_i))$ and $(dist_{G_\delta}(u_i, u_j) \leq \beta)$ **do**
4:    **if** $(u_j \notin AdversariesList)$ **then**
5:       insert u_j to s_1
6:    **else**
7:       **return** $\emptyset$
8: **return** s_1
    {————Main————————}
9: $s_1 =$**Initialize**$(u_i, G_\delta(u_i), \beta, AdversariesList)$
10: **if** $(s_1 \neq \emptyset)$ **then**
11:    $InitialCandidatesSet=$**CondtructBlockedEdgesCandidates**$(u_i, G_\delta(u_i), s_1,$
     $AdversariesList, \alpha, \gamma)$
12: $B =$ **SelectBestBlockedEdges**$(InitialCandidatesSet)$
13: **return** B

Figure 2 describes the main building blocks of the algorithm for defining the edges to be removed from $u_i's$ δ-community in order to prevent information leakage to $u_i's$ adversaries.

Next we detail each one of these building blocks.

4.1 Initialization

The δ-community of $u_i's$ consists of all users u_j connected to u_i with a path with distance $\leq \delta$. The β parameter defines the size of the community of close friends. Therefore, a β-community of u_i would be a sub-graph contained in δ-community were $\beta \leq \delta$, as demonstrated in Fig. 1. The privacy criteria that is defined in Subsect. 3.1 requires that the entire information shared by u_i must be shared with $u_i's$ close friends (2). In order to comply with (2), the Initialization step creates a multi-graph with one super-vertex s_1 containing u_i and his close friends with distance $\leq \beta$. This step ensures that the algorithm won't define edges for blocking on paths between u_i and his close friends, since u_i and his close friends are in the same super-vertex, s_1, see Fig. 3.

Figure 3(a) describes a δ-community graph for u_0, with 10 members, $\delta=3$, 4 are close friends with distances=1 (blue vertices), 4 acquaintances (green vertices), and 2 adversaries (red vertices). Figure 3(b) describes the graph after initialization.

4.2   Construct Blocked Edges Candidates

We use two methods derived from flow problems, to find the initial candidates-set of edges to be blocked. This candidates-set is a cut between two sets of vertices, one set containing u_i, $u_i's$ β-community, and some vertices from of $u_i's$ δ-community. The other set containing the remaining part of $u_i's$ δ-community, and $u_i's$ adversaries.

This candidates-set is evaluated to filter out the final candidates-sets by selecting a set that complies with the required privacy criteria. This process is described in Sect. 4.3; the two methods we use for finding the initial candidates-sets of edges to be blocked are:

1. *Min-Cut*: based on Ford-Fulkerson [4], Max-flow-min-cut algorithm, to find the minimum cut between super-vertex s_1 that contains u_i and his close friends, and each of $u_i's$ adversaries. This process is described in Subsect. 4.2.1.
2. *Contract*: based on Karger et al. [9], contract algorithm, to find any cut between super-vertex s_1 that contains u_i and his close friends, and each of $u_i's$ adversaries. This process is described in Subsect. 4.2.2.

4.2.1   Block Edges by Min-Cut

Algorithm 3 implements the Sharing-habits privacy assurance based on the max-flow min-cut method by Ford and Fulkerson [4], and then checks for privacy criteria compliance:

1. Find a minimum cut between super-vertex s_1 and $u_i's$ adversaries [4].
2. Check if the cut complies with the required privacy criteria as defined in Subsect. 3.1, and select the final candidates-set. This process is described in Subsect. 4.3.

Algorithm 3. Block edges by Min-Cut

Input: u_i: the ego vertex.

    $G_\delta(u_i) = (V_\delta(u_i), E_\delta(u_i))$: $u_i's$ δ-community graph, after the initialization step.

    α, γ: Flow threshold.

    AdversariesList: the list of $u_i's$ adversaries.

Output: B:a set with edges to be blocked.

1: set $B = \emptyset$
2: $InitialBlockedEdges =$ FindMinCut(u_i,$G_\delta(u_i)$,$AdversariesList$)
3: **if** ($InitialBlockedEdges \neq \emptyset$) **then**
4:     B=ComputeFinalCandidatesSet(u_i,$G_\delta(u_i)$,$AdversariesList$,$InitialBlockedEdges$,α, γ)
5: **return** B

Algorithm 4. Block edges by Contract

Input: u_i : the source.

$G_\delta(u_i) = (V_\delta(u_i), E_\delta(u_i))$: $u_i's$ δ-community graph, after the initialization step.

α, γ: Flow thresholds.

$AdversariesList$: the list of $u_i's$ adversaries.

Output: B:the set with the blocked edges.

1: set $B = \emptyset$
2: $InitialBlockedEdges=$ ContractFindCut(u_i,$G_\delta(u_i)$, $AdversariesList$)
3: **if** ($InitialBlockedEdges \neq \emptyset$) **then**
4:     $B=$ComputeFinalCandidatesSet(u_i,$G_\delta(u_i)$,$AdversariesList$,$InitialBlockedEdges$,α, γ)
5: **return** B

Algorithm 5 is called by Algorithm 4 to find a cut between two vertices by randomly selecting an edge and contracting the two vertices connected by the selected edge into one super-vertex.

Algorithm 5. ContractFindCut

Find a cut in a graph by repeatedly contracting vertices into two super vertices
Input: $G_\delta(u_i) = (V_\delta(u_i), E_\delta(u_i))$: δ-community multi-graph, after the initialization step.

u_i: the source.

$AdversariesList$: the list of $u_i's$ adversaries.

Output: $CutSet$: the resulting cut.

1: set $CutSet = \emptyset$
2: **repeat**
3:    **if** (all edges (u,v) are tested) **then**
4:       **return** $CutSet$
5:    **else**
6:       choose an edge (u,v) uniformly at random from $E \setminus testededges$
7:       **if** (u and v don't contain each others' adversaries) **then**
8:          contract the vertices u and v to a super vertex w
9:          keep parallel edges, remove self loops
10: **until** (G has only two super-vertices)
11: set $CutSet =$ the edges between the two vertices
12: **return** $CutSet$

4.2.2 Block Edges by Contract

The minimum cut between $G_\beta(u_i)$, and $u_i's$ adversaries, found by BlockEdges-ByMinCut algorithm, might not be the optimal solution for our problem, since the edges in this cut may not satisfiy the privacy criteria. Thus, we use the contract algorithm, that finds a variety of other cuts possibly complying with the required privacy criteria.

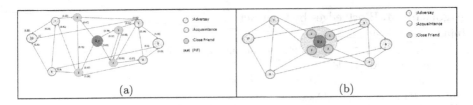

Fig. 3. $u'_0 s$ δ-community graph: (a) $u'_0 s$ community (b) after initialization (Color figure online)

Algorithm 4 implements the Sharing-habits privacy assurance based on the contract method by Karger and Stein [8,9].

In each iteration, the contract algorithm finds a different cut between the super-vertex containing $G_\beta(u_i)$ and the super-vertex containing $u'_i s$ adversaries. The contract algorithm repeatedly contract vertices to super-vertices until it gets two super-vertices connected by a set of edges that defines a cut between the two sets of vertices contained in each super-vertex.

Algorithm 4 is composed of the following main steps:

1. Find a cut between super-vertex $G_\beta(u_i)$ and $u'_i s$ adversaries; this step uses the contract algorithm presented [8,9]
2. Check if the cut complies with the required privacy criteria as defined in Subsect. 3.1, and select the final candidates-set. This process is described in Subsect. 4.3.

Figures 4 and 5 describe a simple community graph and some steps of one run of the contract algorithm.

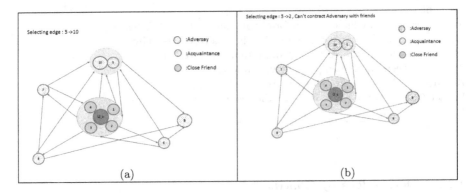

Fig. 4. Contract: (a) Edge (5,10) was randomly selected, (b) Edge (5, 2) cannot be selected, since the algorithm can't contract a super-vertex containing u_0 with a super-vertex containing $u'_0 s$ adversary. (Color figure online)

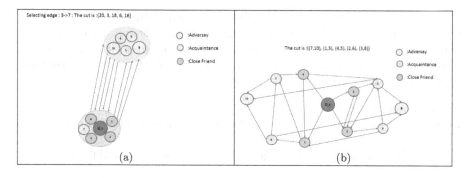

Fig. 5. Contract: (a) Edge (3, 7) is randomly selected (b) The obtained cut from one run of Contract algorithm (Color figure online)

4.3   Compute Final Candidates Set

After selecting the initial candidates-set of edges to be blocked, each method uses Algorithm 6 for selecting the final candidates-set of edges that should be removed from $u'_i s$ δ-community graph. In the first step of the algorithm, we check if by removing the initial-candidates-set of edges from $u'_i s$ δ-community graph, the remaining δ-community graph for user u_i complies with the required privacy criteria. If it doesn't comply with the required privacy criteria, we try to remove edges from the initial blocked candidates-set, and insert them back into

---

Algorithm 6. Compute final candidates-set

Input: u_i : the source.

G_{u_i}: $u'_i s$ δ-community multi-graph, after the initialization step.

$AdversariesList$: the list of $u'_i s$ adversaries.

$InitialBlockedEdges$: the list of edges to be blocked.

α, γ: Flow thresholds.

$EdgeMethod$: the method for selecting the next edge for unblocking.

Output: $BlockedEdges$: the final set of edges to be blocked.

1: **while** ((**ComputeCriteria**($u_i, G_{u_i}, AdversariesList, InitialBlockedEdges, \alpha, \gamma$)
   $\neq TRUE$) and ($InitialBlockedEdges \neq \emptyset$)) **do**
2:     **switch** ($EdgeMethod$)
3:     **case Random:**
4:         $e \leftarrow$ select random $(u, v) \in E_{u_i}$
5:     **case MaxPIF:**
6:         $e \leftarrow \arg\max_{(u,v) \in E_{u_i}} PIF$
7:     **case MinPIF:**
8:         $e \leftarrow \arg\min_{(u,v) \in E_{u_i}} PIF$
9:     **end switch**
10:     InitialBlockedEdges = InitialBlockedEdges $\setminus (u, v)$
11: $BlockedEdges = InitialBlockedEdges$
12: **return** $BlockedEdges$

$u_i's$ δ-community graph, until the remaining community graph complies with the required criteria, or until we tested the entire edges in the initial candidate-set, and couldn't find a set of edges to be blocked. We propose three methods for selecting and removing an edge from the initial candidates-set, and insert the selected edge back to δ-community graph:

1. Randomize: select an edge randomly.
2. Maximum PIF: select the edge with the maximum probability of information flow.
3. Minimum PIF: selecting the edge with the minimum probability of information flow.

Algorithm 6 implements the three methods and Algorithm 7 tests the criteria.

Algorithm 7. Compute the required criteria

Input: u_i : the source.

   G_{u_i}: $u_i's$ δ-community multi-graph, after the initialization step.

   AdversariesList: the list of $u_i's$ adversaries.

   BlockedEdges: the list of edges to be removed.

   α, γ: Flow thresholds.

Output: *ComplyCriteria*: indicator whether the community graph without the blocking-set complies with the required privacy criteria.

1: **for all** $v \in G_{u_i}$ **do**
2:    **if** $(f(u_i, v) < \alpha \cdot f_{original}(u_i, v))$ **then**
3:       **return** $FALSE$
4: **for all** $a_{adv} \in AdversariesList$ **do**
5:    **if** $(f(u_i, u_{adv}) > \gamma \cdot f_{original}(u_i, u_{adv}))$ **then**
6:       **return** $FALSE$
7: **return** $TRUE$

---

5   Evaluation

In this section we describe the evaluation method we use for the proposed algorithm, and the results we obtained using real data [10]. We first demonstrate our methods and the difference between them using a toy community.

5.1   Demonstration on a synthetic community

We demonstrate our algorithms on a small graph representing a synthetic community that we built from the example in [2], containing 11 vertices, and 23 edges. We selected community distance $\delta = 3$, close friends distance $\beta = 1$, and assigned 2 adversaries. The algorithms were tested with different probabilities of information flow from source user U_0 to the community members. In the following example, Fig. 6 describes the synthetic community graph with high

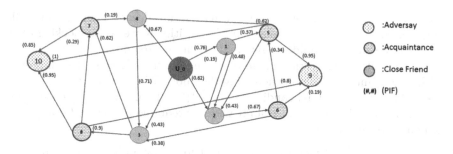

Fig. 6. Synthetic community graph with collision (Color figure online)

Table 1. PIF from U_0 to his community

User	1	2	3	4	5	6	7	8	9	10
MAX PIF	0.76	0.62	0.43	0.67	0.4332	0.4154	0.2949	0.4281	0.4115	0.4332

Table 2. Min-Cut candidates

Edge	PIF
(5,9)	0.95
(6,9)	0.19
(8,9)	0.8
(3,8)	0.9
(3,7)	0.62
(5,10)	1

Table 3. Contract candidates

Edge	PIF
(4,5)	0.62
(1,5)	0.57
(2,6)	0.67
(3,8)	0.9
(7,10)	0.85

probability of information flow on the edges to adversaries. This situation simulates a collision, and it is hard to select α and γ such that we get minimum leakage of information flow to $u_i's$ adversaries, and maximum information flow to $u_0's$ community.

In this community graph U_0 is the source, U_0 has four close friends: $1, 2, 3, 4$, four acquaintances: $5, 6, 7, 8$, and two adversaries: $9, 10$.
Each adversary has three incoming edges.
$\{(6,9), (5,9), (8,9)\}$ with probabilities $(0.19, 0.95, 0.8)$ respectively.
$\{(5,10), (7,10), (8,10)\}$ with probabilities $(1, 0.85, 0.95)$ respectively.

The maximum probability of information flow from U_0 to the members of his community graph is depicted in Table 1.

Next, using this example we show why the contract approach has better chance of finding a good set of edged that can be blocked while satisfying the privacy criteria.

Block edges by Min-Cut method. The Minimum cut found by Min-Cut method is depicted in Table 2. If we remove the initial candidates-set edges from

$u_0's$ community graph, the probability of information flow to 7 and 8 will be 0, meaning no flow at all. In the final step of Algorithm 6, we try unblocking each edge from the initial candidates-set, and reach the required privacy criteria, which is computed by Algorithm 7; in this example the only edge that improves the PIF to community without increasing the information leakage to $u_0's$ adversaries is $(3, 7)$, thus the final candidates-set is $\{(3, 7)\}$. In this example we can't define α, and γ with values that comply with the required privacy criteria, which is computed by Algorithm 7.

Block edges by Contract method. A Cut found by an iteration of contract method is depicted in Table 3.

If we remove the initial candidates-set edges, the probability of information flow to 5, 6, and 8 will be 0, meaning no flow at all. Algorithm 6 tries unblocking each edge from the initial candidtes-set, and reach the required privacy criteria, which is computed by Algorithm 7; the final candidates-set is empty, since each edge we unblock not only improves the information flow to $u_0's$ community, but also increases the information leakage to $u_0's$ adversaries.

It is obvious that when the edges to the adversaries have high probabilities, the max-flow-min-cut methods might not select those edges, and might not find a solution that comply with the required privacy criteria, while the contract method might find the trivial cut that contains only the edges to the adversaries, and thus comply with the required privacy criteria.

5.2   Test on SNAP Database

We evaluated our algorithms on the Facebook network data from Stanford Large Network Data-set Collection [10]. The SNAP library is being actively developed since 2004 and is organically growing as a result of Stanford research pursuits in analysis of large social and information networks. The website was launched in July 2009. The social network graph describes the Social circles from Facebook (anonymized) and consists 4,039 nodes (users), and 88,234 edges, it describes the Social circles from Facebook (anonymized). We took the structure and relationship from the SNAP database, and assigned random probabilities to the edges in the network graph in the following way. We defined four types of users, the type reflects the user's willing to share information: very high sharing users, medium, sometimes, and very low. For each user in the graph we randomly assigned a type. To conform the edges' probabilities to the users' types, we randomly assigned probabilities to the users' edges according to their types, from the following ranges: very high sharing users (probability 0.75-1), medium (0.5-0.75), sometimes (0.25-0.5), very low (0-0.25). The four types were generated uniformly among all the network users.

Preliminary Results. Tables 4, 5 summarize the results of four different evaluation runs, for different communities.

Table 4 presents four runs with the four different sub-communities. The community size is derived by the user selected as the sharing user. Friends column refers to the amount of first degree friends. Table 5 present the results obtained by

Table 4. Data size

Run	Vertices	Edges	Friends	Adversaries
1	334	968	15	2
2	1036	2428	26	3
3	1495	6886	40	10
4	206	3755	29	2

the four runs. Columns 2–3 and 4–5 present the initial set of edges to be blocked and the final set of edges found by min-cut and contract algorithm respectively. Columns 6–8 present the threshold parameters used for the run. The difference between the two algorithms is the method for finding the initial candidates set, min-cut versus contract. Both algorithms use the same method for computing the privacy criteria. For each community graph we performed the algorithms with extreme thresholds, $(\alpha = 0, \beta = 1, \gamma = 1,$ and $\alpha = 1, \beta = 1, \gamma = 0)$, and with random thresholds. The remark indicates which edges were found as candidates for blocking. We can see that in the simple case (e.g., run 1 and 2) the solution is trivial and the blocked edges were the edges to the adversaries. While both algorithm are complete, in the non trivial cases, min-cut finds the best solution with respect to blocking adversaries, while contract may return a compromised solution that is less efficient in blocking adversaries but allows more sharing with friend. However, the time performance of the contract is much better.

It is important to note that the contract algorithm if executed multiple times, is guaranteed to eventually find the optimal solution with respect to the threshold criteria. In the case where there is no solution, the contract algorithm will provide the best cut that satisfies the threshold.

Table 5. Evaluation runs results

Run	MinCut initial edges	MinCut final edges	Contract initial edges	Contract final edges	α	β	γ	Remark
1	2	2	7	7	0	0	1	All edges to adv
1	2	2	7	7	1	0	0	All edges to adv
1	2	2	7	7	0.783	1	0.5654	All edges to adv
2	2	2	2	2	0	0	1	contract = mincut = edges to adv
2	2	2	2	2	1	0	0	contract = mincut = edges to adv
2	2	2	2	2	0.056	1	0.4266	contract = mincut = edges to adv
3	29	29	5	5	0	0	1	mincut = adv, contract = mix
3	29	29	5	0	1	0	0	mincut = adv, contract = mix
3	29	29	12	0	0.8867	1	0.0376	mincut = adv, contract = mix
4	2	0	34	34	0	0	1	mincut = mix, contract = mix
4	2	0	51	19	1	0	0	mincut = mix, contract = mix
4	2	0	286	181	0.0846	1	0.6478	mincut = mix, contract = mix

6   Conclusion

The problem of uncontrolled information flow in social network is a true concern to ones privacy. In this paper we address the need to follow the social trend of information sharing while enabling the owner to prevent their information from flowing to undesired recipients. The goal of the suggested method is to find the minimal set of edges that should be excluded from ones community graph to allow sharing of information while blocking adversaries. To reduce side effect of limiting legitimate information flow, we minimize this impact according to the flow probability. Our algorithms can be used within the ORIGIN CONTROL access control model [6]. In this model every piece of information is associated with its creator forever. The set of cut edges found by our algorithms, is stored for each user and can be checked when the origin controlled information is accessed. This way the administrator can check whenever this information is access by a certain user, if the edge between them was cut for the originator user. In future work, we intend to expand the evaluation and test our algorithms on different types of social networks (e.g., twitter). We intend to further explore more approaches to identifying the edges to be blocked, such as genetic algorithm.

References

1. Maheswaran, M., Ranjbar, A.: Using community structure to control information sharing in online social networks. Comput. Commun. **41**, 11–21 (2014)
2. Rivest, R.L., Cormen, T.H., Leiserson, C.E.: Introduction to Algorithms, chap. 27, p. 581. MIT Press, Cambridge (1990). (2009)
3. Vassilios, V.S., Vatsalan, D., Christen, P.: A taxonomy of privacy-preserving record linkage techniques. Inf. Syst. **38**, 946–969 (2013)
4. Ford, L.R., Fulkerson, D.R.: Maximal flow through a network. Can. J. Math. **8**, 399–404 (1956)
5. Carmagnola, I.T.F., Osborne, F.: Escaping the big brother: an empirical study on factors influencing identification and information leakage on the web. J. Inf. Sci. **40**(2), 180–197 (2014)
6. Sandhu, R., Jaehong, P.: Originator control in usage control. In: Proceedings of the 3rd International Workshop on Policies for Distributed Systems and Networks, pp. 60–66. IEEE, Washington DC (2002)
7. Ligett, K., Kleinberg, J.: Information-sharing in social networks. Games Econ. Behav. **82**, 702–716 (2013)
8. Karger, D.R.: Global min-cuts in RNC, and other ramifications of a simple min-cut algorithm. In: Proceedings of the Fourth Annual ACM-SIAM Symposium on Discrete Algorithms, pp. 21–30. ACM, New York (1993)
9. Karger, D.R., Stein, C.: A new approach to the minimum cut problem. J. ACM **43**(4), 601–604 (1996)
10. Leskovec, J., Krevl, A.: SNAP Datasets: Stanford large network dataset collection, June 2014. http://snap.stanford.edu/data
11. Tassa, T., Cohen, D.J.: Anonymization of centralized and distributed social networks by sequential clustering. IEEE Trans. Knowl. Data Eng. **25**(2), 311–324 (2013)

Counteracting Active Attacks
in Social Network Graphs

Sjouke Mauw, Rolando Trujillo-Rasua$^{(\boxtimes)}$, and Bochuan Xuan

University of Luxembourg, CSC, SnT, Luxembourg City, Luxembourg
rolando.trujillo@uni.lu

Abstract. The growing popularity of social networks has generated interesting data analysis problems. At the same time, it has raised important privacy concerns, because social networks contain personal and sensitive information. Consequently, social graphs, which express the relations between the actors in a social network, ought to be sanitized or anonymized before being published. Most work on privacy-preserving publication of social graphs has focused on dealing with passive attackers while active attackers have been largely ignored. Active attackers can affect the structure of the social network graphs actively and use structural information, as a passive attacker does, to re-identify a user in a social graph. In this article we propose, to the best of our knowledge, the first anonymization method that resists to active attacks.

Keywords: Privacy · Social networks · Active attacks · Antidimension

1 Introduction

Human interaction and socialization has changed as communication and information technology evolves. Emotions, feelings, thoughts, can all be shared instantly by simply pressing a button in one's favorite social network application. This adds a degree of freedom to what we share and how we show it in comparison to, for example, face-to-face communication. While the latter is confined to a bounded physical space and builds upon the subtleties of human physical interaction, online social networks make it easier to disclose personal feelings as users are typically hidden behind a computer screen.

A social graph is a static representation of a social network; a sort of snapshot. Every vertex corresponds to a user who connects to other users through edges representing social links, e.g., friendship, co-authorship, and financial exchange. Researchers rely on graph theory and methods from modern sociology to extract useful knowledge by means of community detection, link prediction, identification of prominent actors, etc.

People tend to appreciate the discovery and revelation of new knowledge, but when it comes to personal information, one immediately perceives a privacy risk. Social graph analysis, although useful, may indeed jeopardize an individual's

© IFIP International Federation for Information Processing 2016
Published by Springer International Publishing Switzerland 2016. All Rights Reserved
S. Ranise and V. Swarup (Eds.): DBSec 2016, LNCS 9766, pp. 233–248, 2016.
DOI: 10.1007/978-3-319-41483-6_17

privacy. An adversary could identify a user in a published social graph and learn sensitive information such as political and religious preferences. Ergo, social graphs ought to be sanitized or anonymized before making them available for analysis.

A fundamental anonymization technique consists in removing identifying attributes from the social graph, such as name, email address, and social security number [8]. Other types of attributes, often called quasi-identifiers, which in combination may uniquely identify an individual, ought to be removed as well. This makes it harder to identify the user behind a node in a social graph, which is often call *re-identification*. The challenge is that even a simple graph without attributes attached to its vertices can be subject to re-identification attacks. For example, an adversary who knows the number of social links of a target victim can identify the victim as a *hub*[1] in the social network. The re-identification can be made more precise if the number of connections is unique in the network.

Re-identification attacks to social graphs are typically categorized as *passive* or *active*. In a passive attack the adversary attempts to re-identify the victim only after the social graph has been published. In an active attack, instead, the adversary proactively inserts sybil nodes in the network and tries to establish links with the targeted victims. The links are made in such a way that every victim connects to the set of sybil nodes in a unique and re-identifiable manner. Once the social graph is released, the adversary identifies his own set of sybil nodes, which are used to re-identify users by using their connections to the set of sybil nodes [1,13].

Active attacks are by definition stronger than passive attacks, yet little attention has been paid to counteract this type of privacy attack. The first privacy notion that accounts for such active privacy attacks has been proposed just recently in [10]. This notion, which is called (k, ℓ)-anonymity, expresses that a user cannot be re-identified with probability higher than $1/k$ by an active attacker able to introduce ℓ sybil nodes in the graph. It has been shown in [10] that real-life social graphs tend to be $(1,1)$-anonymous, which is the lowest privacy level possible. Indeed, in terms of offered privacy, (k, ℓ)-anonymity forms a lattice (a square grid) where $(1,1)$-anonymity is the minimum. This leads to the question whether it is possible to define privacy-preserving transformation techniques that defy active attacks by transforming a graph with low anonymity into a graph with higher anonymity that can be published without risking re-identification. In this paper, we take a first stab at defining such transformations. In particular, we will study the transformation of a graph into a graph with higher anonymity than $(1,1)$-anonymity, while only adding edges.

Contributions: In this article we propose, to the best of our knowledge, the first privacy-preserving anonymization approach that resists active attacks. We use the privacy measure (k, ℓ)-anonymity as proposed in [10] and provide an efficient method to transform a graph G into another graph G' such that G'

---
[1] A hub is a special node in a network with significant more connections than other nodes.

is not $(1,1)$-anonymous. That is to say, the obtained graph G' satisfies (k,ℓ)-anonymity with $k > 1$ or $\ell > 1$. Our anonymization method is based on edge addition operations only. As such, it preserves the original number of vertices in the graph. We provide a theoretical bound on the number of edges that our method needs to add in order to transform a graph into one that is not $(1,1)$-anonymous. Finally, we provide empirical results showing the impact of our transformational approach in terms of resistance to well-known active attacks such as the walk-based attack [1].

Structure of the Paper: Section 2 explains in detail passive and active privacy attacks in social graphs. Definitions and useful notions used throughout this article are provided in Sect. 3. Section 4 presents and proves properties of $(1,1)$-anonymous graphs, which form the theoretical foundation of the proposed anonymization approach (also introduced in Sect. 4). Section 5 consists of empirical evaluations of the proposed method on random graphs. Conclusions are drawn in Sect. 6.

2   Related Work

Most privacy notions for social graphs are based on k-anonymity [9], which was originally proposed as a privacy measure for microdata. We thus start this section by briefly depicting the role of k-anonymity in microdata, and how it has been adapted to social graphs in order to resist passive attacks. Related work on active attacks is provided at the end of this section.

k-anonymity in microdata. A pioneer study on re-identification attacks was published in 2002 by Sweeney [9]. Sweeney estimated that 87% of the population in United States can be uniquely identified by combining seemingly innocuous attributes such as gender, date of birth and zip code.

Background knowledge is what makes a privacy attacker stronger. Either through public sources (e.g., census data) or by malicious actions, an adversary harvests information about a target victim which is used later to re-identify the victim in other databases. Hence, the challenge is how to publish data in such a way that users cannot be re-identified, regardless of the adversary's background knowledge. A property known as *k-anonymity* gives a possible solution approach [8].

A dataset is said to satisfy k-anonymity if every record is indistinguishable from $k-1$ other records with respect to a given adversary's background knowledge. Consequently, k-anonymity ensures that the considered adversary cannot pinpoint the user behind a record with probability higher than $1/k$. Moreover, a k-anonymous dataset can still be considered useful for analysis; researchers are interested in aggregate data describing the general behavior of a population rather than in the characteristics of a single individual.

k-anonymity in social graphs. While Sweeney's revelation mainly concerns relational databases, later in 2009 Narayanan et al. showed that one third of social network users in Flickr and Twitter can be re-identified by a simple passive attack on the anonymized Twitter graph with only 12 % error rate [6]. Several notions of k-anonymity have been consequently proposed in order to mitigate the impact of passive attacks in social graphs.

Privacy notions based on k-anonymity rely on a proper definition of the adversary's background knowledge. In microdata this knowledge consists of a set of quasi-identifiers, while in social graphs it is normally defined as a structural property on the graph, e.g., vertex degree or distance. Two vertices are said to be indistinguishable if they are structurally equivalent with respect to the considered structural property. For example, Liu et al. [4] considered an adversary who knows the degree of the victim node. This simple structural property leads to the notion of k-degree anonymity, which is satisfied if for every vertex there exist $k - 1$ other vertices with the same degree.

A privacy notion strictly stronger than k-degree anonymity is k-neighbourhood anonymity [14]. This property requires that for every vertex v in the graph there exist at least $k - 1$ other nodes $v_1, ...v_{k-1}$ such that the subgraph induced by v's neighbours is isomorphic to the subgraph induced by v_i's neighbours, for every $i \in \{1, ..., k - 1\}$. This notion was soon generalized to k-automorphism [3, 15]. Two vertices u and v are equivalent if there exists an isomorphism from the graph to itself where u maps to v [3]. The problem, however, is that real-life social graphs can hardly satisfy k-anonymity with respect to automorphism [15].

Active attacks. The privacy notions described above do not account for an adversary with the ability to actively manipulate the structure of the social network. That would allow the adversary to influence the structural property of a victim node, which is actually stronger than just knowing structural information.

Backstrom et al. were the first to show the impact of active privacy attacks in social networks [1]. They propose an attack where the adversary plants a well-constructed and uniquely identifiable subgraph in the social network graph. The nodes in the adversary's subgraph are used to establish links with the victim nodes (e.g., by sending friendship requests), in such a way that every victim has a unique *fingerprint* of links to the adversary's subgraph. Once the social graph is released, the adversary retrieves the planted subgraph and re-identifies those nodes that preserve the expected fingerprint.

A recent improvement over the methods in [1] is the *Seed-and-Grow* attack proposed by Wei et al. [13]. They combine the creation of a uniquely identifiable subgraph with a progressive and self-reinforcing strategy, which starts with the initial fingerprint and extends to other new vertices by using the knowledge acquired during the re-identification procedure.

Preventing active attacks is challenging. Indeed, none of the privacy notions described above [3,4,14,15] is well-suited to counteract active attacks. To the best of our knowledge, the first privacy measure to evaluate the resistance of social graphs to active attacks was proposed just recently in [10]. Trujillo-Rasua and Yero model the adversary's background knowledge as the distance vector of a vertex with respect to the adversary's subgraph. This leads to the privacy notion (k, ℓ)-anonymity [10].

In this article we take a first step on defining graph transformations aimed at improving privacy in terms of (k, ℓ)-anonymity. Therefore, we provide in the next section a formal definition for this privacy concept and introduce various notations that we use throughout the article.

3 Preliminaries

We model a social graph $G = (V, E)$ as a simple graph where V represents individuals and E their relationships. The *distance* $d_G(v, u)$ between two vertices v and u in G is the number of edges in the shortest path connecting them. Often we simply write $d(v, u)$ if it does not lead to ambiguity. The *degree* of a vertex is the number of edges connected to it. An *end-vertex* is a vertex with degree one. The *eccentricity* $\epsilon_G(v)$ of a vertex v in a connected graph G is the greatest number of edges in a shortest path between v and any other vertex in G. We call a shortest path an *eccentricity path* for v if its length is equal to $\epsilon_G(v)$.

Definition 1 (Metric representation). *The* metric representation *of a vertex v with respect to an ordered subset of vertices $S = \{u_1, ..., u_t\}$ in a graph $G = (V, E)$ is the vector $r(v|S) = (d_G(v, u_1), \ldots, d_G(v, u_t))$.*

The metric representation is the structural property used in [10] to represent the adversary's background knowledge in active attacks.

Definition 2 (k-antiresolving set). *Let $G = (V, E)$ be a simple connected graph and let $S = \{u_1, \cdots, u_t\}$ be a subset of vertices of G. The set S is called a k-antiresolving set if k is the greatest positive integer such that for every vertex $v \in V - S$ there exist at least $k - 1$ different vertices $v_1, \cdots, v_{k-1} \in V - S$ with $r(v|S) = r(v_1|S) = \cdots = r(v_{k-1}|S)$.*

As an example, consider the star graph in Fig. 1. The distance from v_1 to any other vertex in the graph is 1, thus $\{v_1\}$ is a 4-antiresolving set. On the other hand, any set $\{v_i\}$ with $i \in \{2, 3, 4, 5\}$ is a 1-antiresolving set because $r(v_1|\{v_i\}) = (1)$ while $r(v_j|\{v_i\}) = (2)$ for every $j \in \{2, 3, 4, 5\}$ and $j \neq i$. Finally, we consider the subset $\{v_1, v_5\}$. We observe that $r(v_2|\{v_1, v_5\}) = r(v_3|\{v_1, v_5\}) = r(v_4|\{v_1, v_5\}) = (1, 2)$, implying that $\{v_1, v_5\}$ is a 3-antiresolving set.

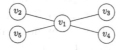

Fig. 1. A star graph.

Definition 3 (k-metric antidimension). *The k-metric antidimension of a simple connected graph $G = (V, E)$ is the minimum cardinality amongst the k-antiresolving sets in G.*

Considering again the star graph depicted in Fig. 1, we observe that $\{v_2\}$ is a 1-antiresolving set with cardinality 1. Ergo, the 1-metric antidimension of this graph is 1. Determining the 2-metric antidimension is a bit more troublesome. We should first notice that v_1 should be included in any 2-antiresolving set, while $\{v_1\}$ itself is a 4-antiresolving set. Therefore, the 2-metric antidimension of the star graph is greater than or equal to 2. However, the subset $\{v_1, v_i\}$ for every $i \in \{2, 3, 4, 5\}$ is a 3-antiresolving rather than a 2-antiresolving set. Consequently, the 2-metric antidimension of the graph in Fig. 1 is 3, given that $\{v_5, v_1, v_3\}$ is a 2-antiresolving set. We refer the interested reader to [2] and [11] for results on the metric dimension and the k-metric antidimension, respectively.

Definition 4 $((k, \ell)$-anonymity). *A graph G is said to meet (k, ℓ)-anonymity if k is the smallest positive integer such that the k-metric antidimension of G is lower or equal than ℓ.*

A graph G satisfying (k, ℓ)-anonymity ensures that every subset of vertices with cardinality at most ℓ is a k'-antiresolving set for some $k' \geq k$. Thus, every vertex in G is indistinguishable from at least $k - 1$ other vertices with respect to their metric representation to any subset of vertices of cardinality at most ℓ.

4   Protecting $(1, 1)$-anonymous Graphs

In this section we provide theoretical properties of $(1, 1)$-anonymous graphs, and use them to prove convergence of our anonymization method.

4.1   Properties of $(1, 1)$-anonymous Graphs

If G contains a 1-antiresolving set, say $\{v\}$, then there exists a vertex u such that $d(v, u) \neq d(v, w)$ for every $w \in V - \{v, u\}$. Following terminology from [10], we call such a vertex u a 1-*resolvable* vertex, in particular, we say that u is 1-*resolvable by* $\{v\}$. It follows that containing a 1-resolvable vertex is a sufficient and necessary condition for a graph G to be $(1, 1)$-anonymous.

Proposition 1. *A simple connected graph $G = (V, E)$ satisfies $(1, 1)$-anonymity if and only if it contains a 1-resolvable vertex.*

Proof. If G contains a 1-resolvable vertex v, then there exists a vertex u in G such that $\{u\}$ is a 1-antiresolving set. Ergo G is $(1, 1)$-anonymous.

Now, let us assume that G is $(1, 1)$-anonymous and that there does not exist a 1-resolvable vertex in G. This implies that there does not exist a 1-antiresolving set of cardinality 1 in G. Therefore, if a 1-antiresolving set in G exists then G is $(1, \ell)$-anonymous for some $\ell > 1$, otherwise G is (k, ℓ)-anonymous for some $k > 1$. In either case G is not $(1, 1)$-anonymous, which is a contradiction.   □

Because the presence of 1-resolvable vertices implies $(1, 1)$-anonymity, we are interested in finding those vertices in the graph which are 1-resolvable. A first trivial result in this direction is the following.

Lemma 1. *For every end-vertex v in a graph $G = (V, E)$ it holds that v's neighbour is 1-resolvable by $\{v\}$.*

Proof. We should first notice that if $|V| = 2$ then both v and v's neighbour are 1-resolvable. Thus, let us assume that $|V| > 2$ and let u be v's neighbour. Because any path to v passes through u, we obtain that $d(w, v) = d(w, u) + d(u, v) > d(u, v) = 1$ for every $w \in V - \{v, u\}$. Therefore, $\{v\}$ is a 1-antiresolving set and u is a vertex 1-resolvable by $\{v\}$.   □

A consequence of Lemma 1 is that every graph with end-vertices is $(1, 1)$-anonymous. Hereinafter we thus assume that social graphs do not contain end-vertices; they can be either removed from the social network or connected to other nodes. It is also worth remarking that, if v is an end-vertex, then v's neighbor lies in every eccentricity path of v. We prove next that, indeed, every vertex 1-resolvable by $\{v\}$ lies in an eccentricity path of v.

Lemma 2. *Let G be a simple connected graph, let $\{v\}$ be a 1-antiresolving set in G, and let $v_1 \cdots v_m$ be an eccentricity path of v, i.e., $v_1 = v$. For every vertex u that is 1-resolvable by $\{v\}$ there exists $i \in \{1, \ldots, m\}$ such that $u = v_i$.*

Proof. Let us assume that $u \neq v_i \ \forall i \in \{1, \ldots, m\}$. By definition, the eccentricity of v satisfies that $\epsilon(v) \geq d(v, w)$ for every $w \in V(G)$ and, in particular, $\epsilon(v) \geq d(v, u)$. Given that $d(v, v_m) = \epsilon(v) \geq d(v, u)$, there must exist $i \in \{1, \ldots, m\}$ such that $d(v, u) = d(v, v_i)$ (see Fig. 2 left). Consequently, either $u = v_i$ or u is not 1-resolvable by $\{v\}$, which both lead to a contradiction.   □

The next result is rather simple, yet it is the core of our anonymization approach. It provides a necessary condition for a vertex to be *not* 1-resolvable by vertices within a cycle of odd order.

Proposition 2. *A cycle graph C_n of odd order satisfies $(2, 1)$-anonymity.*

Proof. Every vertex v in C_n has two diametral vertices (see Fig. 2 right), ergo $\{v\}$ is a 2-antiresolving set.   □

Fig. 2. Left: An eccentricity path $v_1 - v_i - v_m$ and a vertex u located out of that path. Right: A cycle of odd order. A vertex (in Black) has the same distance to both diametral vertices (in Gray).

4.2   A Graph Transformation Approach

Our elimination approach of 1-resolvable vertices is based on Proposition 2 and Lemma 2. We aim at including all 1-resolvable vertices lying in a given eccentricity path into a cycle of odd order by adding a single edge. This transformation is defined as follows.

Definition 5 (v-transformation). *Let v be a vertex in a graph $G = (V, E)$ such that $\{v\}$ is a 1-antiresolving set, and let $v_1 \cdots v_m$ be an eccentricity path of v where $v_1 = v$. Let i and j be the lowest and largest positive integers, respectively, such that v_i and v_j are 1-resolvable by v in G. A v-transformation results in the graph $(V, E \cup \{(v_{i-1}, v_j)\})$ if $j - i$ is odd, otherwise in $(V, E \cup \{(v_{i-2}, v_j)\})$.*

The remaining results within this section are aimed at proving properties of a v-transformation in a graph.

Theorem 1. *Let $G = (V, E)$ be a simple connected graph, $\{v\}$ a 1-antiresolving set, and G' the graph resulting from a v-transformation in G. Let S be the set of vertices in G contained in an eccentricity path of v in G. Every $w \in S$ is not 1-resolvable by $\{v\}$ in G'.*

Proof. Let $v_1 \cdots v_m$ be an eccentricity path where $v_1 = v$. Let i and j be the lowest and largest positive integers, respectively, such that v_i and v_j are 1-resolvable by v in G. G_1 and G_2 denote the v-transformation of G when $j - i$ is odd and even, respectively. Next, we consider a vertex $w \in \{v_1, \ldots, v_m\}$ and analyze different cases regarding the position of w in the eccentricity path $v_1 \cdots v_m$. Figure 3 depicts the three scenarios.

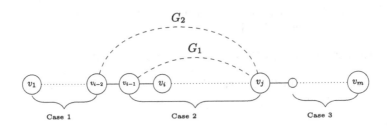

Fig. 3. An eccentricity path $v_1 - v_m$ within the graph G. The dashed edge G_1 (resp. G_2) represents the v_1-transformation if $j - i$ is odd (resp. even).

Case 1 ($w \in \{v_1, \ldots, v_{i-2}\}$). In this case w is not 1-resolvable by $\{v_1\}$ in G. Therefore, let $w' \in V - \{v_1, \ldots, v_m\}$ such that $d_G(v_1, w) = d_G(v_1, w')$. We choose $k \in \{1, \ldots, m\}$ to be the largest positive integer such that $d_G(v_1, w') = d_G(v_1, v_k) + d_G(v_k, w')$. On the one hand, it holds that $d_G(v_k, w') = d_{G_1}(v_k, w') = d_{G_2}(v_k, w')$. On the other hand, it is easy to note that $k < i - 1$, otherwise $d_G(v_1, w') \geq i - 1 > d_G(v_1, w)$. This implies that $d_G(v_1, v_k) = d_{G_1}(v_1, v_k) = d_{G_2}(v_1, v_k)$ and, thus, $d_G(v_1, w) = d_{G_1}(v_1, w) = d_{G_2}(v_1, w) = d_G(v_1, w') = d_{G_1}(v_1, w') = d_{G_2}(v_1, w')$. Ergo, w is not 1-resolvable by $\{v\}$ in G_1 and G_2.

Case 2 (w ∈ {v_{i-1}, ..., v_j}). Now consider that $w \in \{v_{i-1}, \ldots, v_j\}$, which means that w is contained in the cycles $v_{i-1} v_i \cdots v_j v_{i-1}$ and $v_{i-2} v_i \cdots v_j v_{i-2}$ from G_1 and G_2, respectively. Considering Proposition 2, we obtain that if $j - i$ is odd then w is not 1-resolvable by $\{v\}$ in G_1, otherwise w is not 1-resolvable by $\{v\}$ in G_2.

Case 3 (w ∈ {v_{j+1}, ..., v_m}). Finally, consider that $w \in \{v_{j+1}, \ldots, v_m\}$. In this case we obtain the following.

$$\begin{aligned} d_{G_1}(v_1, w) &= d_{G_1}(v_1, v_{i-1}) + d_{G_1}(v_{i-1}, v_j) + d_{G_1}(v_j, w) \\ &= d_G(v_1, w) - (j - i) \end{aligned} \tag{1}$$

Similarly we obtain:

$$d_{G_2}(v_1, w) = d_G(v_1, w) - (j - i + 1) \tag{2}$$

On the other hand, $d_{G_1}(v_1, w') = d_{G_1}(v_1, v_k) + d_{G_1}(v_k, w')$ and $d_{G_2}(v_1, w') = d_{G_1}(v_1, v_{k'}) + d_{G_1}(v_{k'}, w')$ for some $k, k' \in \{1, \ldots, m\}$. We notice that $d_{G_1}(v_k, w') = d_G(v_k, w')$ and $d_{G_1}(v_1, v_k) \geq d_G(v_1, v_k) - (j - i)$, which gives the following inequality.

$$d_{G_1}(v_1, w') \geq d_G(v_1, v_k) + d_G(v_k, w') - (j - i) \tag{3}$$

Analogously we obtain:

$$d_{G_2}(v_1, w') \geq d_G(v_1, v_{k'}) + d_G(v_{k'}, w') - (j - i + 1) \tag{4}$$

Moreover, $d_G(v_1, v_k) + d_G(v_k, w') \geq d_G(v_1, w') = d_G(v_1, w)$ and $d_G(v_1, v_{k'}) + d_G(v_{k'}, w') \geq d_G(v_1, w') = d_G(v_1, w)$, which applied to Eqs. 3 and 4 gives:

$$\begin{aligned} d_{G_1}(v_1, w') &\geq d_G(v_1, w) - (j - i) \\ d_{G_2}(v_1, w') &\geq d_G(v_1, w) - (j - i + 1). \end{aligned} \tag{5}$$

Finally, Eqs. 1 and 2 together with the inequalities in 5 give that $d_{G_1}(v_1, w') \geq d_{G_1}(v_1, w)$ and $d_{G_2}(v_1, w') \geq d_{G_2}(v_1, w)$. Therefore, there exists a vertex w'' in the $v_1 - w'$ path such that $d_{G_1}(v_1, w'') = d_{G_1}(v_1, w)$. We observe that $w'' \neq w$, given that $d_G(v_1, w') \geq d_{G_1}(v_1, w') \geq k$ implying that $d_G(v_1, w)$ must be greater or equal than k as well. We conclude that w is not 1-resolvable by $\{v\}$ in G_1. We draw the same conclusion for G_2 by following an analogous reasoning.

We conclude this proof by recalling Lemma 2, which states that every 1-resolvable vertex by $\{v\}$ lies in the path $v_1 \cdots v_m$. This means that i and j are unique amongst all eccentricity paths of v in G.   □

Theorem 1 states that a v-transformation G' satisfies that all vertices in G which are included in an eccentricity path of v are not 1-resolvable by $\{v\}$ in G'. Consider, for example, the vertex v_i in Fig. 3. While $d_G(v_1, v_i) \neq d_G(v_1, u)$ for every vertex u in G, it is easy to see that $d_{G_1}(v_1, v_i) = d_{G_1}(v_1, v_j)$ and $d_{G_2}(v_1, v_i) = d_{G_2}(v_1, v_{j-1})$. We next determine sufficient conditions by which a vertex not contained in an eccentricity path of v is not 1-resolvable by $\{v\}$ in a v-transformation.

Theorem 2. *Let $G = (V, E)$ be a simple connected graph, $\{v\}$ a 1-antiresolving set, and G' the graph resulting from a v-transformation in G. Let S be the set of vertices in G contained in an eccentricity path of v in G. Let $v_1 \cdots v_m$ an eccentricity path of v where $v_1 = v$. For a given vertex $w \in V - S$ let $k \in \{1, \ldots, m\}$ be the largest positive integer such that $d_G(v_1, w) = d_G(v_1, v_k) + d_G(v_k, w)$. Then $k < i$ or $k \geq j$ implies that w is not 1-resolvable by $\{v\}$ in G'.*

Proof. As above, we use G_1 and G_2 to denote the v-transformation of G when $j - i$ is odd and even, respectively, where i and j are the lowest and largest positive integers, respectively, such that v_i and v_j are 1-resolvable by v in G.

First, consider that $k < i$, in which case $d_G(v_1, w) < d_G(v_1, v_i)$, otherwise there exists $w' \in V - \{v_1, \ldots, v_m\}$ such that $d_G(v_1, w') = d_G(v_1, v_i)$, a contradiction. This means that $d_G(v_1, w) \leq i - 2$. Because G_1 and G_2 result from the addition of one edge to G, then $d_{G_1}(v_1, w) \leq d_G(v_1, w) \leq i - 2$ and $d_{G_2}(v_1, w) \leq d_G(v_1, w) \leq i - 2$. If $d_G(v_1, w) = i - 2$, then v_{i-1} and v_j satisfy that $d_{G_1}(v_1, w) = d_{G_1}(v_1, v_{i-1}) = i - 2$ and $d_{G_2}(v_1, w) = d_{G_2}(v_1, v_j) = i - 2$ in G_1 and G_2, respectively. If $d_G(v_1, w) < i - 2$, then $d_{G_1}(v_1, w) = d_{G_1}(v_1, v_l) = d_{G_2}(v_1, v_l)$ where $l = d_G(v_1, w) + 1$. We conclude that in both G_1 and G_2 the vertex w is not 1-resolvable by $\{v\}$.

Next, consider that $k \geq j$. Given that G_1 and G_2 result from the addition of the edge (v_{i-1}, v_j) and (v_{i-2}, v_j), respectively, to G, we obtain that $d_G(v_j, w) = d_{G_1}(v_j, w) = d_{G_1}(v_j, w)$. Therefore, we obtain the following equalities.

$$d_G(v_1, w) = d_G(v_1, v_j) + d_G(v_j, w)$$
$$d_{G_1}(v_1, w) = d_{G_1}(v_1, v_j) + d_G(v_j, w)$$
$$d_{G_2}(v_1, w) = d_{G_2}(v_1, v_j) + d_G(v_j, w)$$

Let v_l be the vertex in $v_1 \cdots v_m$ such that $d_G(v_1, v_l) = d_G(v_1, w)$. It should be noticed that $l > j$ and $d_G(v_1, v_l) = d_G(v_1, v_j) + d_G(v_j, v_l)$, hence $d_G(v_j, w) = d_G(v_j, v_l)$. As before, we obtain that $d_G(v_j, v_l) = d_{G_1}(v_j, v_l) = d_{G_1}(v_j, v_l)$. Because $d_G(v_j, w) = d_G(v_j, v_l)$, we can rewrite the equalities above as follows.

$$d_G(v_1, w) = d_G(v_1, v_j) + d_G(v_j, w)$$
$$d_{G_1}(v_1, w) = d_{G_1}(v_1, v_j) + d_{G_1}(v_j, v_l)$$
$$d_{G_2}(v_1, w) = d_{G_2}(v_1, v_j) + d_{G_2}(v_j, v_l)$$

Consequently, $d_{G_1}(v_1, w) = d_{G_1}(v_1, v_l)$ and $d_{G_2}(v_1, w) = d_{G_2}(v_1, v_l)$, implying that in both G_1 and G_2 the vertex w is not 1-resolvable by $\{v\}$. □

We observe that even if $i \leq k < j$ a vertex w can still remain not 1-resolvable by $\{v\}$ in a v-transformation. This is the case, for example, in the v_1-transformation shown by Fig. 4. We thus provide next a sufficient condition for a vertex w to be not 1-resolvable by $\{v\}$ in a v-transformation regardless of the position of k with respect to i and j.

Proposition 3. *Let $G = (V, E)$ be a simple connected graph, $\{v\}$ a 1-antiresolving set, G' the graph resulting from a v-transformation in G, and*

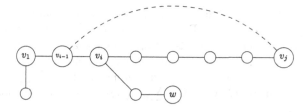

Fig. 4. An example showing that a v-transformation may create new 1-resolvable vertices.

$v_1 \cdots v_m$ *an eccentricity path of v where $v_1 = v$. For every $w \in V - \{v_1, \ldots, v_m\}$ it holds that $d_G(v_1, w) \leq m - j + i - 1$ implies that w is not 1-resolvable in G'.*

Proof. Let $v_1 \cdots v_m$ be an eccentricity path where $v_1 = v$. Let i and j be the lowest and largest positive integers, respectively, such that v_i and v_j are 1-resolvable by v in G. We call G_1 and G_2 to the v-transformation of G when $j - i$ is odd and even, respectively.

If $d_{G_1}(v_1, v_m) \geq d_{G_1}(v_1, w)$ then w is not 1-resolvable by $\{v_1\}$ in G_1. It is easy to note that $d_{G_1}(v_1, v_m) = d_{G_1}(v_1, v_{i-1}) + d_{G_1}(v_{i-1}, v_j) + d_{G_1}(v_j, v_m) = i - 1 + m - j$ and analogously $d_{G_2}(v_1, v_m) = i - 2 + m - j$. Given that $d_{G_1}(v_1, w) \leq d_G(v_1, w)$ and $d_{G_2}(v_1, w) \leq d_G(v_1, w)$ we conclude that if $d_G(v_1, w) \leq m - j + i - 1$ then w is not 1-resolvable by $\{v_1\}$ in G_1. Similarly, we can conclude that if $d_G(v_1, w) \leq m - j + i - 2$ then w is not 1-resolvable by $\{v_1\}$ in G_2.   □

Finally, we provide a convergence result for our approach.

Theorem 3. *Let G be a simple graph. We define a sequence of graphs G_i (for $i \geq 0$) inductively as follows:*

- *$G_0 = G$.*
- *If there exists a 1-antiresolving set $\{v\}$ in G_i then G_{i+1} is the result of applying a v-transformation to G_i.*
- *Otherwise, $G_{i+1} = G_i$.*

Let S_i be the set of vertices in G_i such that $v \in S_i$ implies that $\{v\}$ is a 1-antiresolving set in G_i. Then S_j is empty for $j \geq \sum_{\forall v \in V} \epsilon_{G_0}(v) - |V|$.

Proof. Consider $G_{i-1} = (V_{i-1}, E_{i-1})$ and $G_i = (V_i, E_i)$ where $G_{i-1} \neq G_i$. That is to say, G_i results from a v-transformation to G_{i-1} where $\{v\}$ is a 1-antiresolving set in G_{i-1}. Let $v_1 \cdots v_m$ be the eccentricity path of v in G_{i-1}, i.e., $v_1 = v$, such that $G_i = (V_{i-1}, E_{i-1} \cup \{(v_i, v_j)\})$ for some $i, j \in \{1, \ldots, m\}$.

On the one hand, $d_{G_i}(v_1, v_m) = d_{G_i}(v_1, v_i) + d_{G_i}(v_i, v_j) + d_{G_i}(v_j, v_m) = d_{G_{i-1}}(v_1, v_i) + 1 + d_{G_{i-1}}(v_j, v_m)$. On the other hand, by definition of a v-transformation the edge (v_i, v_j) satisfies that $j - i \geq 2$. Therefore, $d_{G_{i-1}}(v_i, v_j) \geq 2$, which implies that $d_{G_{i-1}}(v_1, v_m) > d_{G_i}(v_1, v_m)$. We conclude then that $\epsilon_{G_i}(v) < \epsilon_{G_{i-1}}(v)$.

The result above states that every v-transformation from G_{i-1} to G_i makes the eccentricity of v to decrease. Because an eccentricity path cannot be shorter than 1, the maximum number of v-transformations that can be applied to G_0 is bounded by $\epsilon_{G_0}(v) - 1$. Considering that every vertex could potentially form a 1-antiresolving set, we obtain the following upper bound: $\sum_{\forall u \in V} \epsilon_{G_0}(v) - |V|$. Consequently, the graph G_i with $i = \sum_{\forall v \in V} \epsilon_{G_0}(v) - |V|$ does not contain 1-resolvable vertices. $\qquad\square$

Our anonymization approach simply consists of the successive application of v-transformations until a graph without 1-resolvable vertices is found. The number of v-transformations depends on how fast these transformations converge to a graph without 1-resolvable vertices. According to Theorem 3, this number is upper bounded by $\sum_{\forall v \in V} \epsilon_G(v) - |V|$, which is higher than or equal to $|V|(\epsilon_G - 1)$ where ϵ_G is the eccentricity of G. Considering that finding the shortest path between every pair of vertices in a graph has computational complexity $\mathcal{O}(|V|^3)$, we obtain that the computational complexity of our method is $\mathcal{O}(|V|^4(\epsilon_G - 1))$.

We end this section by remarking that the upper bound provided in Theorem 3 is tight. That is, there exists a graph $G = (V, E)$ such that the number of edges added by our method is equal to $\sum_{\forall v \in V} \epsilon_G(v) - |V|$. Moreover, such an upper bound corresponds to the minimum number of edges required to transform G into G' through edge addition operations only and such that G' is not $(1,1)$-anonymous. The graph G we are referring to can be constructed as follows.

Consider the complete graph $C_n = (V, E)$ with n vertices $V = \{v_1, \ldots, v_n\}$. Given a vertex v_{n+1}, G is defined by $G = (V \cup \{v_{n+1}\}, E \cup \{(v_n, v_{n+1})\})$ (see Fig. 5). On the one hand, any edge added to G has the form (v_{n+1}, v_i) for some $i \in \{1, \ldots, n\}$, which makes the distance between v_{n+1} and v_i to become 1. On the other hand, if the edge (v_{n+1}, v_i) for some $i \in \{1, \ldots, n\}$ is not added to G, then the distance between v_{n+1} and v_i remains equal to 2, implying that v_{n+1} is 1-resolvable by $\{v_i\}$. Therefore, there exists only one transformation of G into a graph that is not $(1,1)$-anonymous, that is, the transformation to the complete graph C_{n+1}. This requires n additional edges, which is equal to $\sum_{\forall v \in V} \epsilon_G(v) - |V| = \epsilon_G(v_n) + \sum_{\forall v \in V - \{v_n\}} \epsilon_G(v) - |V| = 1 + 2n - (n+1) = n$.

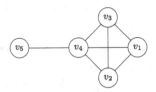

Fig. 5. An example graph.

5   Experiments

In this section we evaluate the proposed anonymization method in terms of privacy and utility loss[2]. Privacy is measured as the resistance of a graph to the *walk-based attack* introduced in [1], while utility loss is measured as the number of added edges.

5.1   The Walk-Based Attack

Given a social graph $G = (V, E)$, the walk-based attack consists of inserting new nodes $X = \{x_1, \ldots, x_n\}$ into G, resulting in the graph $G' = (V \cup X, E)$. The attacker chooses an arbitrary set $Y = \{y_1, \ldots, y_m\}$ of users in G as the target of the attack. For each vertex $y_i \in Y$, a subset $N_i \subseteq X$ is designated as the *fingerprint* of y_i, such that $i \neq j \implies N_i \neq N_j \ \forall i, j \in \{1, \ldots, m\}$. The fingerprint is created by connecting each vertex $y_i \in Y$ to all vertices in N_i. It is worth remarking that such a fingerprint is nothing but the metric representation of the vertex $y_i \in Y$ with respect to X, i.e., $r(y_i | X)$.

The goal of the attacker is to re-identify the set of vertices X in an anonymized version of G', which is used to re-identify the set of targeted vertices Y by considering their unique fingerprints with respect to X. To do so, the attacker creates random internal connections between the vertices in X by adding the edge (x_i, x_j) with probability $1/2$ for every $i \neq j \in \{1, \ldots, n\}$. We use $G(X)$ to denote the sub-graph in G' induced by the vertices in X. Once G' is released, the attacker computes the set $\mathcal{X}$ containing all sub-graphs in G' isomorphic to $G(X)$. Assuming that $G(X)$ does not have a trivial automorphism as advocated in [1], the adversary determines for each fingerprint N_i with $i \in \{1, \ldots, m\}$ the candidate set $V_i = \{v \in V | u \in N_i \iff d_{G'}(v, u) = 1\}$ containing all vertices in V whose fingerprint to $G(X)$ is determined by N_i. We consider that the adversary succeeds if all vertices in Y are correctly re-identified. Therefore, the probability of success of the attack is:

$$\frac{\sum_{G(X) \in \mathcal{X}} \prod_{1 \leq i \leq m} p_i}{|\mathcal{X}|} \quad \text{where} \quad p_i = \begin{cases} 1/|V_i| & \text{if} \quad y_i \in V_i \\ 0 & \text{otherwise.} \end{cases}$$

5.2   Empirical Evaluation on Random Graphs

In order to validate the performance of the proposed anonymization method we ran experiments on random graphs with different density values. We fix 50 as the number of vertices in each random graph, implying that every density value corresponds to a fixed number of edges. A random graph is thus created by adding random edges, i.e., connecting random pairs of vertices, until the desired number of edges is reached.

The density values range in $\{0.1, \ldots, 1\}$, while we considered attacks with 1 and 4 sybil nodes. For each density value and a given number of sybil nodes,

---

[2] Experiments were performed on the UL HPC platform [12].

we build a random graph G with the previously mentioned density. In order to simulate the walk-based attack, G is transformed into G' by adding the sybil nodes and their connections to the victim nodes. Two anonymized versions of G' are considered: G'_1 and G'_2 corresponding to our anonymization method and a random approach, respectively. The random approach consists in adding random edges to G'. The particularity is that the random approach adds as many edges as our approach, i.e., the number of edges in G'_1 is equal to the number of edges in G'_2. Doing so, both approaches perform equally in terms of utility loss. Their performance in terms of privacy are depicted in Fig. 6.

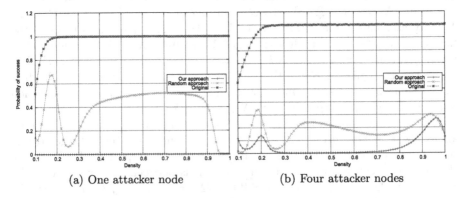

(a) One attacker node   (b) Four attacker nodes

Fig. 6. Two charts depicting the average probability of success of the walk-based attack in three types of graphs: random graphs ("Original"), random graphs anonymized by our method ("Our approach"), and random graphs anonymized by the random approach ("Random approach"). **Left:** the adversary can enrol a single node in the network. **Right:** the adversary can enrol four nodes. (Color figure online)

Figure 6 shows the average probability of success of the walk-based attack in $250,000$ random graphs, and their corresponding anonymization versions by our method and the random approach. Both anonymization approaches improve the resistance to the walk-based attack with respect to the original graph. Indeed, this attack succeeds with probability close to 1 on the original graphs for all density values above 0.2. Amongst the two anonymization approaches, ours performs significantly better for most density values. In particular, our method ensures that the probability of success of an adversary with the capability to insert a single attacker node into the network is 0.

The pronounced non-monotonic behaviour of the curves in Fig. 6 corresponds to the same type of behaviour of the curves in Fig. 7, which shows the average number of added edges by both our method and the random approach. It is indeed an open question what would be the trend of a curve depicting the minimum number of edges needed to transform a graph into another that is not $(1, 1)$-anonymous for different density values. We observe that, for example, 1 and 2 edges need to be added to a path graph of odd and even order, respectively. This means that such minimum number of edges does not depend on the graph density only.

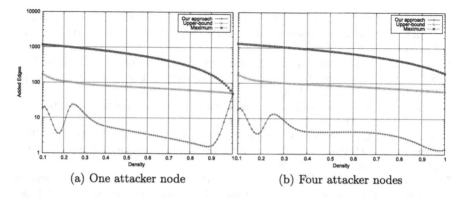

(a) One attacker node   (b) Four attacker nodes

Fig. 7. Two charts depicting the average number of edges added by our method, referred to as "Our approach". The charts also show the upper-bound as determined in Theorem 3 ("Upper-bound") and the maximum number of edges that can be added ("Maximum"). **Left:** the adversary can enrol a single node in the network. **Right:** the adversary can enrol four nodes. (Color figure online)

Figure 7 shows, as sketched in the previous section, that the minimum number of edges added by our method, the upper bound provided by Theorem 3, and the maximum number of edges that can be added, meet when the density of the random graph is 1 and the adversary adds a single node to the graph. This leads to the type of graph shown in Fig. 5. For other density values, the upper bound in Theorem 3 is clearly above the actual number of edges added by our technique.

6   Conclusions

In this article we have proposed, to the best of our knowledge, the first privacy-preserving transformation method for social graphs that counteracts active attacks. The proposed method is theoretically sound and outputs a graph that satisfies (k, ℓ)-anonymity with $k > 1$ or $\ell > 1$. We provide a theoretical upper-bound on the utility loss, in terms of number of added edges, of our approach. And we prove that such upper-bound is tight. Experiments on random graphs show that the proposed method effectively counteracts active attack even when the adversary is able to insert more than one sybil node in the network.

References

1. Backstrom, L., Dwork, C., Kleinberg, J.: Wherefore art thou r3579x?: Anonymized social networks, hidden patterns, and structural steganography. In: The 16th International Conference on World Wide Web, WWW 2007, pp. 181–190. ACM, New York (2007)
2. Harary, F., Melter, R.A.: On the metric dimension of a graph. Ars Combinatoria **2**, 191–1995 (1976)

3. Hay, M., Miklau, G., Jensen, D., Towsley, D., Weis, P.: Resisting structural re-identification in anonymized social networks. Proc. VLDB Endow. **1**(1), 102–114 (2008)

4. Liu, K., Terzi, E.: Towards identity anonymization on graphs. In: The 2008 ACM SIGMOD International Conference on Management of Data, SIGMOD 2008, pp. 93–106. ACM, New York (2008)

5. Mcauley, J., Leskovec, J.: Discovering social circles in ego networks. ACM Trans. Knowl. Discov. Data **8**(1), 4:1–4:28 (2014)

6. Narayanan, A., Shmatikov, V.: De-anonymizing social networks. In: The 30th IEEE Symposium on Security and Privacy, SP 2009, Washington, DC, USA, pp. 173–187. IEEE Computer Society (2009)

7. Panzarasa, P., Opsahl, T., Carley, K.M.: Patterns and dynamics of users' behavior and interaction: Network analysis of an online community. J. Am. Soc. Inf. Sci. Technol. **60**(5), 911–932 (2009)

8. Sweeney, L.: k-anonymity: A model for protecting privacy. Int. J. Uncertain. Fuzziness Knowl. Based Syst. **10**(5), 557–570 (2002)

9. Sweeney, L.: Uniqueness of simple demographics in the U.S. population. Technical Report, Carnegie Mellon University, Data Privacy Laboratory (2002)

10. Rolando Trujillo-Rasua and Ismael González Yero: k-metric antidimension: A privacy measure for social graphs. Inf. Sci. **328**, 403–417 (2016)

11. Trujillo-Rasua, R., Yero, I.G.: Characterizing 1-metric antidimensional trees and unicyclic graphs. Comput. J. (2016, in press). doi:10.1093/comjnl/bxw021

12. Varrette, S., Bouvry, P., Cartiaux, H., Georgatos, F.: Management of an academic HPC cluster: The UL experience. In: The International Conference on High Performance Computing & Simulation (HPCS 2014), Bologna, Italy, pp. 959–967. IEEE (2014)

13. Wei, P., Li, F., Zou, X., Jie, W.: A two-stage deanonymization attack against anonymized social networks. IEEE Trans. Comput. **63**(2), 290–303 (2014)

14. Zhou, B., Pei, J.: Preserving privacy in social networks against neighborhood attacks. In: The IEEE 24th International Conference on Data Engineering, ICDE 2008, Washington, DC, USA, pp. 506–515. IEEE Computer Society (2008)

15. Zou, L., Lei Chen, M., Özsu, T.: K-automorphism: A general framework for privacy preserving network publication. Proc. VLDB Endow. **2**(1), 946–957 (2009)

Reasoning about Security and its Cost

Formalizing Threat Models
for Virtualized Systems

Daniele Sgandurra$^{(\boxtimes)}$, Erisa Karafili, and Emil Lupu

Imperial College London, 180 Queen's Gate, London SW7 2AZ, UK
{d.sgandurra,e.karafili,e.c.lupu}@imperial.ac.uk

Abstract. We propose a framework, called *FATHoM* (FormAlizing THreat Models), to define threat models for virtualized systems. For each component of a virtualized system, we specify a set of security properties that defines its control responsibility, its vulnerability and protection states. Relations are used to represent how assumptions made about a component's security state restrict the assumptions that can be made on the other components. FATHoM includes a set of rules to compute the derived security states from the assumptions and the components' relations. A further set of relations and rules is used to define how to protect the derived vulnerable components. The resulting system is then analysed, among others, for consistency of the threat model. We have developed a tool that implements FATHoM, and have validated it with use-cases adapted from the literature.

1   Introduction

Addressing security concerns in computing systems requires careful consideration of the threats, usually described through *threat models*. But for virtualized systems, attacks, solutions and threat models have evolved considerably over the years [10]. Before presenting a security solution, research papers usually describe their *assumptions* on the environment where the solution is meant to be deployed. However, threat models are given in a *descriptive* rather than a formal syntax, which is also not standardized. As a consequence, many publications rely on implicit, and different, assumptions or lack clarity in their assumptions for which there is no commonly understood semantics. For example, different terms are used to refer to a component assumed to be insecure such as "malicious", "untrusted", "in control of the attacker", when the underlying assumption is whether the component is inside or outside the trusted computing base (TCB).

We believe that using a precise model for threat modelling in virtualized systems would help understanding: (i) the meaning of each assumption, by harmonizing the terminology; (ii) whether the threat model has included all the required assumptions at all architectural levels; and (iii) whether these assumptions are consistent. Currently, the *relations* among components, and how assumptions on one component impact (e.g., restrict) assumptions that can be made on other components, are usually not considered. We propose a model,

© IFIP International Federation for Information Processing 2016
Published by Springer International Publishing Switzerland 2016. All Rights Reserved
S. Ranise and V. Swarup (Eds.): DBSec 2016, LNCS 9766, pp. 251–267, 2016.
DOI: 10.1007/978-3-319-41483-6_18

FATHoM, that allows developers and system designers to precisely state the conditions under which a component can be assumed trusted (or untrusted) given that another component is assumed trusted (or untrusted). FATHoM allows designers to define and analyse a threat model to determine whether it is consistent and complete. The framework, which can be applied with fine granularity, can also be used to describe how components are protected. Furthermore, the framework is compositional.

The main contributions of this work are:

- a precise notation to define threat models (FATHoM), which considers the components' security states, the relations among them, and the rules to compute the derived security states based on the assumptions and the relations;
- a set of relations and rules used to define how to protect vulnerable components, derived by checking the threat model definition for consistency;
- a prototype tool that implements FATHoM that can be used to define and analyse threat models. FATHoM allows system designers to check the threat model for consistency, completeness, and equality among threat models given a subset of required states.

The paper is structured as follows. In Sect. 2 we list some existing threat models and discuss their limitations. In Sect. 3 we describe FATHoM, including the assumptions, relations and the composition rules. Section 4 describes how threat models are defined in the FATHoM prototype tool, and how they can be analysed. In Sect. 5 we show some instantiations of threat models using our approach. Section 6 discusses related works, while we conclude in Sect. 7.

2   Current Threat Models in Virtualized Systems

Virtualization is a technique used to emulate in software the physical properties of a computer, which is encapsulated in a *virtual machine* (VM) managed independently from other VMs. This allows physical resources such as processor, memory, storage and I/O channels, to be shared between concurrent VMs, while preserving isolation. This enables a more efficient use of the resources, e.g. on Cloud computing datacenters, as they can be allocated on-demand. A *virtual machine monitor* (VMM) is the software component that creates, manages and monitors VMs. In virtualized systems, the assumptions described in a *threat model* form the basis from which security control is enforced. For example, if in one threat model physical access is not considered possible, attacks trying to subvert the VMM from the lower levels may not be taken into account by the solution, but may still exist. Similarly, if the threat model assumes the VMM to be with no (exploitable) bugs, whereas the OS is vulnerable, then a proposed protection solution can be deployed directly inside the VMM while considering attacks against the kernel as possible. Threat models have considerably evolved over the years, in an attempt to cope with novel attacks. However, we lack a standard approach to define and analyse the threat models, which is used across the research community [10]. Some approaches, such as STRIDE [11], allow designers to draw trust boundaries across components, and check for a set of known (classes of) vulnerabilities. However, they are not used to check if the definition of threat model is consistent and, furthermore, it is not possible to perform custom analysis, e.g. to compare two threat models for equality. Note that inconsistencies in the description of a threat model can arise as the exact meaning of each assumption is not precise, and how assumptions on a component are related to assumptions on other components is not defined. It is therefore difficult to compare two threat models because, even if they appear similar, they could mean different things to their designers. Furthermore, if some component is not included in the model, the consequences to the trustworthiness of the model, when this component exists in the real world, are not determined. Concerning the nomenclature, the most common set of assumptions encountered in the literature is expressed using a terminology that includes terms such as *trusted*, *vulnerable* (or *exploitable*), *untrusted* or *malicious*. However, the words are not used consistently, or with a well understood semantics. Our goal is to provide a framework that enables the definition of the threat models more precisely and clearly. The properties and features of the model we want to provide are: (i) it should be easy to define a threat model based on this framework; (ii) it should be clear what the assumptions are; (iii) the threat model should be consistent and complete; (iv) it should be possible to compose several components together.

3   Language for the Threat Models

The system we represent is composed of different components that have different *security properties* (also called *security states*), and different *relations* between them. We denote by $\mathcal{A}$ the nonempty set of components of the system:

$$\mathcal{A} ::= \{A, B, C, \cdots\}.$$

Components can be added or removed from the system. We denote by *Insert* the function for adding a new component to the system, and by *Remove* the one that removes a component from the system:

$$Insert(\mathcal{A}, E) := \mathcal{A} \cup \{E\} \qquad\qquad Remove(\mathcal{A}, D) := \mathcal{A}\backslash\{D\}$$

where E is a new component inserted to $\mathcal{A}$, while D is removed from $\mathcal{A}$.

We denote by Φ the set of all formulas of our system. Given the set of components, $\mathcal{A}$, the formulas of our system $\phi \in \Phi$, are defined by the grammar:

$$\phi ::= true \mid false \mid \phi \wedge \phi \mid \phi \vee \phi \mid \phi \rightarrow \phi \mid (\phi) \mid \pi \mid \neg\pi \mid \rho$$
$$\pi ::= v(A), \text{ where } v \in \mathcal{V} \qquad\qquad \rho ::= \varrho(A, A), \text{ where } \varrho \in \mathcal{R}$$

where A is a component of our system ($A \in \mathcal{A}$), $\mathcal{V}$ is the set of all security properties of the components, and $\mathcal{R}$ the set of all relations between components. The connectors $\wedge$, $\vee$, $\rightarrow$, $(,)$, and $\neg$ are the standard ones. Through our language, we can define a set of *rules* which governs how the relations are used to compute the different properties of the components starting from other properties.

3.1   Security Properties of Components

The components of our system can have different *security properties*, for simplicity just *properties*, which are associated with their trustworthiness, reliability and restorability values. We divide the properties of our system in *basic, high-level, derived* and *accessory* properties, respectively divided in the following sets $\mathcal{V_B}$, $\mathcal{V_H}$, $\mathcal{V_D}$, $\mathcal{V_A}$, as represented in Table 1. These sets compose the set of properties of our system: $\mathcal{V} = \mathcal{V_B} \cup \mathcal{V_H} \cup \mathcal{V_D} \cup \mathcal{V_A}$.

Table 1. The Security Properties Sets for FATHoM

$\mathcal{V_B} = \{assContr, assSafe, assProt\}$

$\mathcal{V_H} = \{assTrust, assVuln, assUntrust, assMalic\}$

$\mathcal{V_D} = \{derContr, derSafe, derProt, derTrust, derVuln, derUntrust, derMalic\}$

$\mathcal{V_A} = \{derCanBeCompr, derCanBeExpl, derIsProt\}$

The designer has to specify only the assumptions of the basic properties, which are the most important ones. The rest of the properties are mostly syntactic sugar and can be derived from the basic properties and the relations. The high-level properties, $\mathcal{V_H}$, are constructed from the basic ones. As the high-level properties are commonly used, the designer sometimes specifies these properties instead of the basic ones. We distinguish between the derived and accessory properties ($\mathcal{V_D}$ and $\mathcal{V_A}$) of the system components and the assumed ones that are given by a designer. For sake of simplicity we will consider the high-level, derived, and accessory properties as properties of their own.

Basic Properties. The basic properties represent the main assumptions we can make about the properties of a component. These define whether the components are assumed to be under control of the defenders or the attackers, by using the *controlled* property (*trustworthiness*), assContr and ¬assContr respectively. When a component is controlled, we consider whether it is assumed to be *exploitable* or not by attackers (*reliability*), and thus can be compromised. We use the properties assSafe, and ¬assSafe, respectively for a reliable component and an exploitable (vulnerable) one. If the component is compromised (¬assContr), we consider whether it can be protected or not (*restorability*), and introduce *protectable* or *unprotectable*, respectively assProt and ¬assProt.

Derived Properties. The system also includes the derived version of the assumed properties: derContr, derSafe, and derProt, taken from $\mathcal{V_D}$. Note that the relations between these properties are the same as their assumed version. Thus, we omit the assumed/derived prefix for them in Fig. 1, which shows the security properties associated with system components. When a component is *Controlled* the relevant properties are *Safe* and *Vulnerable*, which specify whether a component A cannot be compromised ($Safe(A)$) or is vulnerable ($\neg Safe(A)$), because it has known vulnerabilities or is believed it can be maliciously exploited by an attacker. This property identifies components that need to be protected. Alternatively, if a component is *Compromised* (and thus not controlled), the relevant properties are *Protectable* and *Unprotectable*, which specify whether a compromised component A can be protected $(Prot(A))$ or not $(\neg Prot(A))$. The difference with the previous case is that a *Vulnerable* component can always be protected, since it is *Controlled*, whereas an *Unprotectable* component refers to a *Malicious* component, such as an external attacker, a malicious provider, or more generally any external component already compromised and that impacts the security properties of other components, and cannot always be reverted to the *Controlled* state.

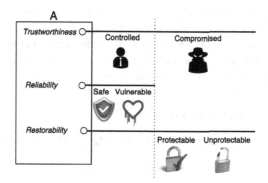

Fig. 1. Security properties

High-Level Properties. Let us introduce FATHoM's high-level properties, which can be defined from the basic ones. We define a component A *assumed trusted*, if it is assumed controllable and safe:

$$assTrust(A) := assContr(A) \land assSafe(A).$$

A component is *assumed vulnerable*, if it is assumed controllable and not safe:

$$assVuln(A) := assContr(A) \land \neg assSafe(A).$$

A component is *assumed untrusted*, if it is assumed not controllable (compromised) but is assumed protectable:

$$assUntrust(A) := \neg assContr(A) \land assProt(A).$$

Finally, a component is *assumed malicious*, if it is assumed not controllable and not protectable:

$$assMalic(A) := \neg assContr(A) \land \neg assProt(A).$$

We represent the rules between these properties and the basic ones in Table 2.

Table 2. Derivation rules between basic and high-level properties in FATHoM

$assTrust(A) \rightarrow assContr(A)$	$assTrust(A) \rightarrow assSafe(A)$
$assVuln(A) \rightarrow assContr(A)$	$assVuln(A) \rightarrow \neg assSafe(A)$
$assUntrust(A) \rightarrow \neg assContr(A)$	$assUntrust(A) \rightarrow assProt(A)$
$assMalic(A) \rightarrow \neg assContr(A)$	$assMalic(A) \rightarrow \neg assProt(A)$

In Table 3 we show the semantics of each combination, and give examples of their occurrence in virtualized systems. Recalling the terms discussed in Sect. 2, which are used frequently in related works, if we compare our nomenclature with these terms, we can see that the combinations of security properties in Table 3 correspond to (from top to bottom): Trusted ($assTrust$), a component that is assumed to be trustworthy; (ii) Vulnerable ($assVuln$), a component that can have bugs and/or can be attacked but is not in the hand of the attacker; (iii) Untrusted ($assUntrust$), assuming that an attacker has full control of this component; (iv) Malicious ($assMalic$), i.e., a component that is compromised by the attacker and cannot be recovered or protected.

3.2 Relations and Derivation Rules

In FATHoM components can have the following relations between them:

$$\mathcal{R} := \{Contr, Threat, Protect, Ign, Contain, Group, Merge\}.$$

Contr defines a binary relation, where $Contr(A, B)$ means that component A controls component B, e.g., when A is at lower virtualisation layer than B, or A is more privileged than B. Therefore, A can (potentially) change B's security properties by attacking or protecting it. This relation is already given to the system, or it can be implied by other relations. *Contr* is transitive.

Threat defines a binary relation, where $Threat(A, B)$ means that component A can threaten (attack) component B. Thus, A may be able to exploit B's vulnerabilities, e.g., when A is a remote attacker and B a reachable server from the Internet, or A is a component at a higher level (e.g., application) and B one at a lower level (e.g., OS). A successful attack must be carried out by a compromised component A against a vulnerable one B. Component A threatens an other component B because of the design of the system, or if A controls B and component A is assumed/derived compromised.

$$Contr(A, B) \wedge (\neg assContr(A) \vee \neg derContr(A)) \rightarrow Threat(A, B)$$

Some examples of these relations, in the context of virtualized systems, are shown in Fig. 2.

As we focus on threat models, we consider the *worst-case* scenario. This means that, for example, if A controls B, and A is assumed not controlled, then we cannot assume B to be controlled. Thus, we consider as not controlled all components that could be compromised within our knowledge. We can now introduce one of the accessory properties from $\mathcal{V_A}$, which is the *can be compromised*

Table 3. Combinations of security properties for components

$assContr$	$assSafe$	$assProt$	Meaning	Examples	High-level property
✓	✓		A component that is assumed not to have been compromised and that cannot be exploited	A micro-kernel OS formally verified, or an app that is protected from integrity attacks from lower levels, or where the attacker has no access	**Trusted** ($assTrust$)
✓	✗		A component that is assumed not to have been compromised but that can be compromised in the future due to a vulnerability	An OS with bugs during the boot, where the attacker has not direct access to it but can, for example, access it remotely	**Vulnerable** ($assVuln$)
✗		✓	A component that is assumed to be compromised and that can be protected	The OS kernel in a VM, assumed to be compromised, and that is protected at run-time through the hypervisor for control-flow integrity attacks	**Untrusted** ($assUntrust$)
✗		✗	A component that is assumed to be compromised and that cannot protected	An external component (the attacker has full control of it) on which the security solution cannot do anything to change its state	**Malicious** ($assMalic$)

property, $derCanBeCompr$, that can be derived from the above relation. We say that B can be compromised, if it is controlled by a compromised component, or if B is threatened by a compromised component and B is vulnerable:

$$((Contr(A, B) \land (assContr(B) \lor derContr(B)))$$
$$\lor (Threat(A, B) \land (\neg assSafe(B) \lor \neg derSafe(B))))$$
$$\land (\neg assContr(A) \lor \neg derContr(A) \lor derCanBeCompr(A)) \rightarrow derCanBeCompr(B).$$

The derived versions of the high-level properties: $derTrust$, $derVuln$, $derUntrust$, and $derMalic$, which are part of $\mathcal{V_D}$, are defined as follows:

$$derTrust(A) := \neg derCanBeCompr(A) \land assTrust(A)$$
$$derVuln(A) := \neg derCanBeCompr(A) \land assVuln(A)$$
$$derUntrust(A) := derCanBeCompr(A) \lor assUntrust(A)$$
$$derMalic(A) := assMalic(A).$$

We represent in Table 4 the derivation rules between derived properties. Finally, the Ign (Ignore) relation, used to ignore components, forces the model to assume a given component as trusted: $Ign(A) \rightarrow assTrust(A)$.

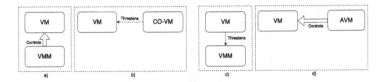

Fig. 2. Examples of *Controls* and *Threatens* relations

Table 4. Derivations rules between derived properties in FATHoM

$derTrust(A) \rightarrow derContr(A)$	$derTrust(A) \rightarrow derSafe(A)$
$derVuln(A) \rightarrow derContr(A)$	$derVuln(A) \rightarrow \neg derSafe(A)$
$derUntrust(A) \rightarrow \neg derContr(A)$	$derUntrust(A) \rightarrow derProt(A)$
$derMalic(A) \rightarrow \neg derContr(A)$	$derMalic(A) \rightarrow \neg derProt(A)$

3.3   Composability

We further introduce the possibility of composing components together, by exploiting three compositional relations: *Contains*, *Groups* and *Merges*. They are respectively used to: (i) enforce consistency among the state of a composite component and the state of its set components; (ii) simplify the description of the threat model, by grouping components together; (iii) abstract from inner components by introducing a new component that summarizes their security states and relations.

   Contain is a binary relation, where *Contain(A, B)* means that A contains B, and all of A's internal components must have the same security property as A. This is useful when an external component always includes an internal one, such as a VM that includes the OS, and the security states need to be coherent among them. This relation is transitive given the assumptions in the internal components, represented in Table 5 (1)–(5). *Group* is a binary relation, where *Group(A, B)* means that A is a new (virtual) component, which groups B (together with, possibly, other components). In this case A is a new component, and *Group* is consistent in terms of *Contr* and *Threat* relations, as shown in Table 5 (6)–(12). The last composability relation is *Merge*, where *Merge(A, B)* means that a new component A is used to consolidate all the internal components (B, and possibly other components) into a new one and merges their states and relations, as represented in Table 5 (13)–(18). The internal components are no longer considered, and assumptions and relations can be now expressed about A. This is useful when we want to consider several, similar, components in a single one with the same properties. The difference between *Groups* and *Merges* is that the *Groups* relation is only used to facilitate the definition of several rules and assumptions on several components together, but the external (virtual) component is not used by the rules, only the internal (real) ones. Instead, *Merges* is used to remove from the model similar components and replaces them by a new (real) one. In this case, the assumptions and the relations are firstly given on the internal component B, and applied to the external one. Note that a

Table 5. The composability rules in FATHoM

$$Contain(A, B) \wedge Contain(B, C) \rightarrow Contain(A, C) \tag{1}$$

$$Contain(A, B) \wedge assTrust(A) \rightarrow assTrust(B) \tag{2}$$

$$Contain(A, B) \wedge assVuln(A) \rightarrow assVuln(B) \tag{3}$$

$$Contain(A, B) \wedge assUntrust(A) \rightarrow assUntrust(B) \tag{4}$$

$$Contain(A, B) \wedge assMalic(A) \rightarrow assMalic(B) \tag{5}$$

$$Group(A, B) \wedge Group(B, C) \rightarrow Group(A, C) \tag{6}$$

$$Group(B, C) \wedge Contr(A, B) \rightarrow Contr(A, C) \tag{7}$$

$$Group(A, B) \wedge Contr(A, C) \rightarrow Contr(B, C) \tag{8}$$

$$Group(B, C) \wedge Threat(A, B) \rightarrow Threat(A, C) \tag{9}$$

$$Group(A, B) \wedge Threat(A, C) \rightarrow Threat(B, C) \tag{10}$$

$$Group(A, B) \wedge Group(C, D) \wedge Contr(A, C) \rightarrow Contr(B, D) \tag{11}$$

$$Group(A, B) \wedge Group(C, D) \wedge Threat(A, C) \rightarrow Threat(B, D) \tag{12}$$

$$Merge(C, A) \wedge Contr(A, B) \rightarrow Contr(C, B) \tag{13}$$

$$Merge(C, A) \wedge Threat(A, B) \rightarrow Threat(C, B) \tag{14}$$

$$Merge(C, A) \wedge assTrust(A) \rightarrow assTrust(C) \tag{15}$$

$$Merge(C, A) \wedge assVuln(A) \rightarrow assVuln(C) \tag{16}$$

$$Merge(C, A) \wedge assUntrust(A) \rightarrow assUntrust(C) \tag{17}$$

$$Merge(C, A) \wedge assMalic(A) \rightarrow assMalic(C) \tag{18}$$

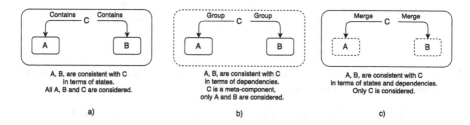

Fig. 3. *Contains* (a), *Groups* (b) and *Merges* (c) Relations

precondition to merge components together is that they are similar, i.e., there are no conflicts. An example of these three relations is shown in Fig. 3.

3.4   Protecting Components

We introduce in FATHoM two versions of the *Protect* relation. This relation is given by the system/designer, and through it we can derive a very important security property *derIsProt*, which defines the property of a component being protected. The first version of *Protect* is a binary relation, where *Protect*(A, B) means that A can protect component B from the threats considered in the model.

The second version is a ternary relation, where $Protect(A, C, B)$ means that component A can protect component B, with the help of a new component C. This relation is reflexive, where $Protect(A, C, A)$ means that component A can protect itself, with the help of a new component C (that enhances A). For the ternary $Protect$ relation, the new component C is inserted in the set of components of A. We show these relations in Fig. 4 (for the sake of readability, we split the ternary relation in two cases, (a) and (c)).

The $Protects$ relations are used to define the $derIsProt$ property, which means that a component is in the state of being $protected$. There are four cases when we can derive that a component is protected, as shown in Table 6. We say that A is protected when it is derived trusted, as shown in (19). We say that A is protected when there exists a controlled component B that protects A (and B can control A), in case A is not safe or protectable, as shown in (20). We say that A is protected when there exists a controlled component B that protects A, with the help of another component C, where B controls A and A is not safe or protectable, as shown in (21). In this case, C is a new component, inserted in the set of components, that is contained in B, and is assumed controlled or is controlled by B. Finally, we say that A is protected when it can protect itself

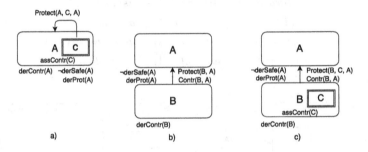

Fig. 4. Rules $Protects$ relation: (a) Using a patch, (b) Using an external component, (c) Enhancing an external component with a patch

Table 6. The four cases when a component is derived protected

$$derTrust(A) \;\rightarrow\; derIsProt(A) \qquad (19)$$

$$
\begin{aligned}
Protect(B, A) \;\wedge\; Contr(B, A) \;\wedge\; derContr(B) \;\wedge\; \\
(\neg derSafe(A) \vee derProt(A)) \;\rightarrow\; derIsProt(A)
\end{aligned}
\qquad (20)
$$

$$
\begin{aligned}
Protect(B, C, A) \;\wedge\; Contr(B, A) \;\wedge\; derContr(B) \;\wedge\; \\
(\neg derSafe(A) \vee derProt(A)) \;\wedge\; Insert(A, C) \;\wedge\; \\
Contain(B, C) \;\wedge\; (assContr(C) \vee Contr(B, C)) \;\rightarrow\; derIsProt(A)
\end{aligned}
\qquad (21)
$$

$$
\begin{aligned}
Protect(A, C, A) \;\wedge\; derContr(A) \;\wedge\; \\
(\neg derSafe(A) \vee derProt(A)) \;\wedge\; Insert(A, C) \;\wedge\; \\
Contain(A, C) \wedge (assContr(C) \vee Contr(A, C)) \;\rightarrow\; derIsProt(A)
\end{aligned}
\qquad (22)
$$

with the help of C, where A is controllable, exploitable or protectable, as shown in (22). In this case, C is a new component, contained in A, assumed or derived controlled by A. Note that with the current rules, a component is derived *Vulnerable* only if it is assumed so. Furthermore, a component is derived *Malicious* iff it is assumed so, using the worst-case rule. However, in some situations, we need to take into account threat models where a component A is assumed to be vulnerable and either (i) it is the target of the protection solution itself or (ii) it is assumed protected by another component (e.g., a vulnerable VMM protected by a trusted module). Hence, it is assumed, and required for the threat model definition, that the component is vulnerable. To limit the cascading effect of this vulnerable component being exploited, we need to check whether it is already protected. This is captured by one of the properties in $\mathcal{V}_A$:

$$derCanBeExpl(A) := derCanBeCompr(A) \wedge assVuln(A)$$

where a component is derived exploitable if it can be compromised and it is assumed vulnerable.

4   Using FATHoM to Define and Analyse a Threat Model

We now discuss the implementation of FATHoM, and how it can be used to define and analyse threat models.

4.1   FATHoM Prototype Tool

We have designed and developed a tool implementing FATHoM (available at http://rissgroup.org/fathom/) that includes in its knowledge base all the general rules discussed so far. The tool is used also to load a template with the components and relations. A graphical interface facilitates the description of the threat model, which is converted into FATHoM language. (An example of a template is described in Sect. 5.) After loading the template, the user can customize some components, and then specify the security states of the components. Finally, the FATHoM tool compiles the threat model (derived from the template and the user choices) and the model's rules into an executable program for XSB[1]. After converting the threat model and the rules for XSB, a designer can query the FATHoM tool to analyse the system: to display those components whose assumed state is different from the derived ones (i.e., a consistency check); to add protection components and exploit the *Protects* relations. At this point, FATHoM re-compiles the updated threat model (i.e., the derived initial model plus the new protection components and relations), and shows the derived and final threat model.

---

[1] http://xsb.sourceforge.net/.

4.2   Definition of the Threat Model

The following steps are used to define threat models within our model: (i) FATHoM loads the *rules* already defined for all domains, i.e., *Controls* and *Threatens*; (ii) the user defines (or imports an existing) *template* that includes the components' *ontology* for the domain of interest (e.g., virtualized system), which defines: the *components* specific to the domain and the *Controls* and *Threatens* relations on these components; (iii) the user selects those components that need to be *Merged* (if any) and those to *Ignore* (if any); (iv) the user can add new components (optional) or new relations in the model to both existing or new components (optional); finally, (v) the user sets, for each component, the assumed value for *Trusted* or *Vulnerable* or *Untrusted* or *Malicious*. In contrast to the current, verbose, definitions of threat models, which often span several pages in research papers, in FATHoM users only need to define the assumed security states for all the components, e.g., through a table, such as Table 7, or through a figure, such as Fig. 5b. Not only is the representation very succinct, but the underlying semantics is also common across all the threat models.

4.3   Derivation and Analysis

Once the model has been defined (and possibly customized), and the values of the assumptions on the security states has been chosen, FATHoM is used to derive the security states. FATHoM allows the developer to analyse the consistency and completeness of the model, and query possible combinations of assumptions to derive a desired target model. In particular, FATHoM allows the designers to check if there are some security states whose assumptions are different from the derived ones. When an inconsistency is found, the developer is asked to only update the inconsistent assumptions. FATHoM also forces the designers to define the security states for all the components. When a security state for a component is not defined, unless the user has specifically chosen to *Ignore* it, a warning is returned. Designers can analyse possible solutions to protect the vulnerable and protectable components in the derived threat model. This can be done by refining the model as follows: (i) the user introduces new protection components in the system, such as a hardware co-processor; (ii) the users specifies which components are used to *Protect* which other components, e.g. the *Vulnerable* ones. Then, FATHoM enables the user to perform the same analyses on the improved model.

5   Use-Cases Analysis: Virtualized Systems

We show an instantiation of FATHoM for virtualized systems including the template we have defined for a use-case scenario.

5.1 Ontology of Components and Relations

The *components* we model in this template are defined at four layers: (i) *virtualization* level: OS, application (App), administrative VM (AVM), co-resident VM (CO-VM), VT-Driver-domain (i.e., a VM that interfaces all the requests to the devices using shared drivers); (ii) *hypervisor* level: VMM, VMM interface; (iii) *firmware* level: BIOS (or UEFI), SMM; (iv) *hardware* level: DMA, Trusted Boot, which can be specialized in static-root-of-trust (SRTM), dynamic-root-of-trust (DRTM), Intel SGX [2], Memory (MEM), which can be refined into RAM and L2-Cache, CPU[2]. We augment these elements with additional ones to consider further threats. In detail, when the virtualized environment is run by an external provider, the trust placed in that provider also needs to be considered [5,7,9,14]. Hence, other components that we introduce are: (i) *physical-access*: a component that defines whether physical access is possible for the attacker; (ii) *actors*: the Cloud service provider (CSP), the tenant and a generic external attacker. Note that for some components, such as actors and physical-access, the only relevant security state is the *Controlled/Compromised* one, which is semantically equivalent to the component being trusted or not, whereas the *Protected/Vulnerable* may not need to be considered. Hence, we will restrict their security states to *Trusted* and *Malicious* only. Furthermore, the actors in the system can be further refined if we consider entities such as the manufacturer of the hardware used by the provider, the developers of the software run by the provider, and, in general, any third-party involved with the Cloud provider [3].

  The template we have defined includes the following *relations*: (i) we *Group* the components at the hardware-, firmware-, hypervisor- and virtualization-level; (ii) any element at lower-levels can *Control* those at higher ones (and physical access *Controls* all the levels); (iii) the Tenant *Controls* the user VM; (iv) the remote attacker *Threatens* all the Virtualization level and VMM; (v) the CSP *Controls* all the VMs, the VMM and lower levels; (vi) the VT-d *Threatens* the VM, VMM; (vii) the AVM *Controls* the VM, VMM; (viii) the Co-resident VM *Threatens* the VM, VMM. These relations used on the previous ontology give rise to the template shown in Fig. 5a.

5.2 Analysis of the Threat Model

Defining the Threat Model and Checking for Inconsistencies. This analysis is used to identify inconsistencies in the threat model's assumptions, by showing the derived security states that are different from the assumed ones. In this use-case, we firstly customize the template depicted in Fig. 5a to adapt it to the description of this use-case. Here, we consider a threat model that assumes the VMM to be *Vulnerable*, the tenant and remote attacker to be *Malicious*, and co-resident VM to be *Untrusted*. The goal, from the point of view of the provider, is to protect the OS from attacks by tenants and remote attackers by

---

[2] Further components that could be considered here are virtualization extensions, chipset, hard-disk firmware.

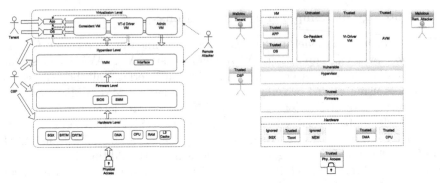

(a) FATHoM Template for Virtualized   (b) Use-Case of Assumptions on a
System: Components and Relations   FATHoM Threat Model

Fig. 5. FATHoM template and initial assumptions

enhancing the VMM to check the integrity of the OS. This use case is adapted
from [13,15]. In particular, we consider that a trusted boot-based solution is
used to protect the loading of the hypervisor. Then, the provided solution will
describe how a new component inside the VMM is used to protect the OS.
In detail, we use the FATHoM compositional rules on the template as follows:
(i) we *Merge* RAM and L2Cache into MEM; (ii) we *Merge* SRTM and DRTM
into a single Tboot component; (iii) we *Merge* BIOS and SMM into a Firmware
component; (iv) MEM and CPU are *Ignored*; (v) SGX is *Ignored*. We then set
the assumptions on the security states as shown in Fig. 5b (the relations are not
shown, since after loading the template we only need to define the assumptions).
This graphical description is then translated in the FATHoM syntax, and then
compiled for XSB. By using these assumptions, and by querying the FATHoM
tool for inconsistencies among assumptions and derived states, FATHoM shows
that the components App, OS, AVM, Co-VM and hypervisor are inconsistent[3].
These components are those whose assumed states is different than the derived
one. In this specific case, FATHoM shows that, by letting the attacker being able
to threaten the hypervisor, he/she can compromise the AVM and Co-VM too, as
well as the OS and App, and this is not consistent with the initial assumptions.
Furthermore, the tenant can compromise the OS. Note that, since in this use-
case we have assumed the VMM to be vulnerable, but protected by a Tboot
solution[4], we need to update the model with the relations to protect the VMM
from Tboot, and check the model again. By querying FATHoM we see that
the hypervisor is consistent with the assumptions, and, hence, we only need to
change the App and OS to "untrusted" to be consistent. We have now an initial

---

[3] For the sake of conciseness, we do not show the complete rules, ontology, assumptions, and analysis in XSB here. All the examples are available at http://rissgroup.
org/fathom/, along with a technical report.

[4] We only focus on static integrity protection.

Table 7. Components and assumptions of the use-cases

Component	Trusted	Vulnerable	Untrusted	Malicious
APP			✓	
OS			✓	
Co-VM			✓	
Vt-Driver	✓			
AVM	✓			
Hypervisor		✓		
Firmware	✓			
Tboot	✓			
DMA	✓			
Physical Access	✓			
CSP	✓			
Tenant				✓
Remote Attacker				✓

consistent threat model, whose instantiation is shown in Table 7. As we can see, the formulation of the threat model is very succinct.

Protecting the Components and Derivation Analysis. On this stable threat model, we then introduce a patch in the VMM to protect the OS[5]. Then, by recompiling the threat model with the new protection component, and its relation(s), we query the FATHoM tool again to check the derived *Protected* components. In this case, FATHoM derives VMM and OS as *Protected* as well.

6   Related Work

Mulval [8] is a logic-based analyser that enables the modelling and reasoning about components' interaction. The main difference with our model is that in FATHoM we define *assumptions* on the security of components, not vulnerabilities or attack paths. Furthermore, our goal is to formalize these assumed security states using a common terminology and ontology, and check its soundness. The *CORAS* method [4] defines a language, and a set of UML-based diagrams, for threat and risk modelling. FATHoM differs from CORAS as it focuses only on threat modelling. Furthermore, FATHoM facilitates the description of the system's assumptions, and follows a worst-case approach, instead of a probabilistic one, and can analyse its soundness. The goals are also different: using CORAS it is possible to implement a risk-evaluation plan, while in our model we depict a static scenario. Similarly, *CySeMoL* [12] is a modelling language

---

[5] The description of the patch is outside the scope of the use-case.

targeted at enterprise architectures, to enable administrators to perform a probabilistic inference analysis. The model includes a set of meta-components to define probabilistic dependencies, attack-paths, preconditions, etc. In FATHoM we are focused on describing the initial security preconditions of the system in an easy and sound way, and to take into account generic attacks. *Nemesis* [6] is a risk-assessment framework to test Cloud systems, by collecting measurements on known vulnerabilities of the system components, modelling the threats and assessing the risk. FATHoM is a framework to define in a consistent way the threat model and used to reason on generic security solutions valid for a set of use-cases. Finally, [1] exploits model checking to verify system-level security properties of interacting VMs, and is focused in particular on distributed access control policies. Even if the context is similar, i.e., virtualized environment, the goal of FATHoM is the formalization and analysis of threat models, rather than the verification of access control policies. In summary, none of the the existing works allows designers to (i) define in a compact way threat models, and (ii) perform custom analysis, e.g. to check their consistency. Most existing tools allow users to perform predefined queries over such a threat model (i.e., to check for vulnerabilities), which is supposed to be consistent. Hence, these approaches and FATHoM are complementary.

7   Conclusion and Future Work

Current threat models lack a common terminology to describe the trusted components, and the relations between them. This gives rise to possible inconsistencies, and incompleteness, of the considered definition. This issue may also impact the assumptions on which a security solution is built upon. In this paper we have proposed FATHoM to describe and analyse threat models and have demonstrated that in real-world scenarios the usability of the FATHoM model is very simple, since it only requires to load an existing template, optionally customize it, and set the assumed values for the security states. We are considering other attacker's goals, such as confidentiality, to be defined in the relations and rules, and other scenarios (e.g., mobile). Finally, the worst-case assumptions underlying our model could be mitigated using probabilistic assumptions on the relations and rules.

Acknowledgement. Supported by FP7 EU-funded project Coco Cloud under grant no. 610853, and EPSRC Project CIPART grant no. EP/L022729/1.

References

1. Alexander, P., Pike, L., Loscocco, P., Coker, G.: Model checking distributed mandatory access control policies. ACM Trans. Inf. Syst. Secur. **18**(2), 6:1–6:25 (2015)
2. Anati, I., Gueron, S., Johnson, S., Scarlata, V.: Innovative technology for CPU based attestation and sealing. In: 2nd Workshop on Hardware and Architectural Support for Security and Privacy, HASP 2013 (2013)

3. Bleikertz, S., Mastelic, T., et al.: Defining the cloud battlefield - supporting security assessments by cloud customers. In: 2013 IEEE Cloud Engineering (IC2E), pp. 78–87, March 2013

4. Brændeland, G., Dahl, H.E.I., Engan, I., Stølen, K.: Using dependent CORAS diagrams to analyse mutual dependency. In: Lopez, J., Hämmerli, B.M. (eds.) CRITIS 2007. LNCS, vol. 5141, pp. 135–148. Springer, Heidelberg (2008)

5. Butt, S., Lagar-Cavilla, H.A., et al.: Self-service cloud computing. In: ACM Conference on Computer and Communications Security, pp. 253–264. ACM (2012)

6. Kamongi, P., Gomathisankaran, M., Kavi, K.: Nemesis: automated architecture for threat modeling and risk assessment for cloud computing. In: Academy of Science and Engineering, USA (2015)

7. Li, M., Zang, W., Bai, K., Yu, M., Liu, P.: Mycloud: supporting user-configured privacy protection in cloud computing. In: Annual Computer Security Applications Conference, ACSAC 2013, pp. 59–68. ACM (2013)

8. Ou, X., Govindavajhala, S., Appel, A.W.: MulVAL: a logic-based network security analyzer. In: 14th USENIX Security Symposium, SSYM 2005, vol. 14, p. 8 (2005)

9. Santos, N., Rodrigues, R., Gummadi, K.P., Saroiu, S.: Policy-sealed data: a new abstraction for building trusted cloud services. In: 21st USENIX Conference on Security Symposium, Security 2012, p. 10 (2012)

10. Sgandurra, D., Lupu, E.: Evolution of attacks, threat models, and solutions for virtualized systems. ACM Comput. Surv. **48**(3), 46:1–46:38 (2016)

11. Shostack, A.: Threat Modeling: Designing for Security. Wiley (2014)

12. Sommestad, T., Ekstedt, M., Holm, H.: The cyber security modeling language: a tool for assessing the vulnerability of enterprise system architectures. IEEE Syst. J. **7**(3), 363–373 (2013)

13. Srivastava, A., Raj, H., Giffin, J., England, P.: Trusted VM snapshots in untrusted cloud infrastructures. In: Balzarotti, D., Stolfo, S.J., Cova, M. (eds.) RAID 2012. LNCS, vol. 7462, pp. 1–21. Springer, Heidelberg (2012)

14. Szefer, J., Keller, E., Lee, R.B., Rexford, J.: Eliminating the hypervisor attack surface for a more secure cloud. In: 18th ACM Conference on Computer and Communications Security, CCS 2011, pp. 401–412. ACM (2011)

15. Xiong, X., Tian, D., Liu, P.: Practical protection of kernel integrity for commodity OS from untrusted extensions. In: NDSS (2011)

Reasoning About Firewall Policies Through Refinement and Composition

Ultan Neville$^{(\boxtimes)}$ and Simon N. Foley$^{(\boxtimes)}$

Department of Computer Science, University College Cork, Cork, Ireland
ultan.neville@insight-centre.org, s.foley@cs.ucc.ie

Abstract. An algebra is proposed for constructing and reasoning about anomaly-free firewall policies. Based on the notion of refinement as safe replacement, the algebra provides operators for sequential composition, union and intersection of policies. The algebra is used to specify and reason about iptables firewall policy configurations. A prototype policy management toolkit has been implemented.

Keywords: Firewalls · Algebra · iptables · Anomalies · Policy-composition

1 Introduction

Firewall configuration management is complex and error-prone, and a misconfigured policy may permit accesses that were intended to be denied or vice-versa. We regard the specification of a firewall policy as a process that evolves. Threats to, and access requirements for, resources behind a firewall do not usually remain static, and over time, a policy or distributed policy configuration may be updated on an ad-hoc basis, possibly by multiple specifiers/administrators. This can be problematic and may introduce anomalies; whereby the intended semantics of the specified access controls become ambiguous.

In this paper, we present a firewall policy algebra $\mathcal{FW}_1$ for constructing and reasoning over anomaly-free policies. The algebra allows policies to be composed in such a way that the result upholds the access requirements of each policy involved; and permits one to reason as to whether some policy is a safe (secure) replacement for another policy in the sense of [11,14]. The proposed algebra is used to reason about iptables firewall policy configurations. A partial mapping for the iptables filter table is given in the algebra. iptables is a command line utility used to define policies for the Linux kernel firewall Netfilter [1]. We focus on stateful firewall policies that are defined in terms of constraints on source/destination IP/port ranges, the TCP, UDP and ICMP protocols, and additional filter condition attributes.

The primary contribution of this paper is an algebra $\mathcal{FW}_1$, that can be used to reason about firewall policies using refinement and composition operators.

Published by Springer International Publishing Switzerland 2016. All Rights Reserved
S. Ranise and V. Swarup (Eds.): DBSec 2016, LNCS 9766, pp. 268–284, 2016.
DOI: 10.1007/978-3-319-41483-6_19

The effectiveness of the algebra is demonstrated by its application to anomaly detection, and standards compliance.

The paper is organised as follows. Section 2 introduces the notion of adjacency, which is at the heart of reasoning about/composing firewall rules that involve IP/port ranges. In Sect. 3 we define datatypes for firewall rule attributes, such as IP/port ranges. Section 4 defines the firewall policy algebra $\mathcal{FW}_1$. In Sect. 5, we use $\mathcal{FW}_1$ to reason about firewall policies in practice. Section 6 describes a prototype policy management toolkit for iptables and presents some preliminary results. Related work is outlined in Sects. 7 and 8 concludes the paper. The Z notation [19] is used to present the algebra and has been syntax- and type-checked using the fUZZ tool.

2   A Theory of Adjacency

A firewall policy is conventionally defined as a sequence of order-dependent rules. A rule is composed of filter conditions and a target action. Filter conditions usually consist of fields/attributes from IP, TCP/UDP headers; with the most commonly used attributes being source/destination IP/port, and network protocol. Target actions are usually *allow* or *deny* [3,8].

Range-based filter condition attributes (IPs/ports) have logical mappings to intervals of $\mathbb{N}$. For example, the port range that includes all ports from SSH up and including HTTP can be written as the interval [22..80]. Consider as part of a running example, a system that is capable of enforcing firewall rules where the filter condition attribute for the rules is destination port range. Then if we had a rule that allowed all ports from SSH to HTTP, it may look like: $(i, [22..80], allow)$, where i is the index of the rule in the policy, [22..80] is the required port range, and *allow* means that network traffic matching this pattern be permitted traversal of the firewall. Suppose we had a second rule, that specifies *allow* everything from Quote Of The Day (QOTD) up to and including FTP Control. Then $(j, [17..21], allow)$, specifies that for the rule at index j; the required port range [17..21] is allowed. Intuitively, we can see that the port ranges for the rules at index i and index j are *adjacent*, and we may want to join rules i and j into a single rule that looks like $(k, [17..80], allow)$. This notion of adjacency becomes more complex when we consider comparing/composing firewall rules comprising $2..n$ filter condition attributes.

2.1   The Adjacency Specification

In this section we define the filter condition attribute relationships of *adjacency*, *disjointness* and *subsumption*. These relationships are at the heart of adjacency, and ultimately the $\mathcal{FW}_1$ algebra.

Let $\mathcal{IV}[min, max]$ be the set of all intervals on the natural numbers, from min up to and including max. Intervals are defined by their corresponding sets.

$$\mathcal{IV}[min, max] == \{S : \mathbb{PN} \mid \exists \bot, \top : S \bullet \forall x : S \bullet min \leq \bot \leq x \leq \top \leq max\}$$

For example, $\mathcal{IV}[1,3]$ gives $\{[1..1],[1..2],[1..3],[2..2],[2..3],[3..3]\}$. For ease of exposition and when no ambiguity arises, we may write an interval as a pair $[\bot..\top]$, rather than by the set it defines. Let *IPv4* define the set of all possible IPv4 address ranges, and similarly, let *Port* define the set of all possible network port ranges, where $IPv4 == \mathcal{IV}[0,2^{32}-1] \wedge Port == \mathcal{IV}[0,2^{16}-1]$.

Adjacency. Two intervals are adjacent if their union defines a single interval. We generalize this to any attribute of type X, whereby for $a,b \in X$, if $a\,\wr_X\,b$, then a and b are adjacent in the set X.

$$
\begin{array}{l}
\boxed{
\begin{array}{l}
\underline{[X]} \\
\_\wr\_ : \mathbb{P}X \twoheadrightarrow (X \leftrightarrow X) \\
\hline
\forall\, a,b : X \bullet \\
\quad a\,\wr_X\,a \wedge (a\,\wr_X\,b \Rightarrow b\,\wr_X\,a)
\end{array}
}
\end{array}
$$

For example, interval $[1..2]$ is adjacent to interval $[3..3]$, thus $[1..2]\,\wr_{\mathcal{IV}[1,3]}\,[3..3]$. It follows for $a,b \in \mathbb{N}$ that $a\,\wr_{\mathbb{N}}\,b \Leftrightarrow (a=b \vee a+1=b \vee b+1=a)$, and given $S,T \in \mathbb{P}X$ then $S\,\wr_{\mathbb{P}X}\,T \Leftrightarrow true$.

Disjointness. Two intervals are disjoint if they don't intersect. Given $a,b \in X$, $a\,|_X\,b$ denotes a and b are disjoint in X.

$$
\begin{array}{l}
\boxed{
\begin{array}{l}
\underline{[X]} \\
\_|\_ : \mathbb{P}X \twoheadrightarrow (X \leftrightarrow X) \\
\hline
\forall\, a,b : X \bullet \\
\quad \neg\,(a\,|_X\,a) \wedge (a\,|_X\,b \Rightarrow b\,|_X\,a)
\end{array}
}
\end{array}
$$

For example, $[1..2]$ and $[3..3]$ are disjoint, thus $[1..2]\,|_{\mathcal{IV}[1,3]}\,[3..3]$. It follows for $a,b \in \mathbb{N}$ that $a\,|_{\mathbb{N}}\,b \Leftrightarrow a \neq b$, and given $S,T \in \mathbb{P}X$ then $S\,|_{\mathbb{P}X}\,T \Leftrightarrow S \cap T = \emptyset$.

Subsumption. An interval I subsumes (covers) an interval J, if $J \subseteq I$. For $a,b \in X$, if $a \overset{X}{\leftarrow} b$ then b covers a in X. The properties of reflexivity, transitivity and antisymmetry define $\overset{X}{\leftarrow}$ as a non-strict partial order over X [5].

$$
\begin{array}{l}
\boxed{
\begin{array}{l}
\underline{[X]} \\
\_\overset{}{\leftarrow}\_ : \mathbb{P}X \twoheadrightarrow (X \leftrightarrow X) \\
\hline
\forall\, a,b,c : X \bullet \\
\quad a \overset{X}{\leftarrow} a \wedge (a \overset{X}{\leftarrow} b \wedge b \overset{X}{\leftarrow} c \Rightarrow a \overset{X}{\leftarrow} c) \wedge (a \overset{X}{\leftarrow} b \wedge b \overset{X}{\leftarrow} a \Rightarrow a = b)
\end{array}
}
\end{array}
$$

For example, $[1..3]$ covers $[3..3]$, thus $[3..3] \overset{\mathcal{IV}[1,3]}{\twoheadleftarrow} [1..3]$. It follows for $a, b \in \mathbb{N}$ that $a \overset{\mathbb{N}}{\twoheadleftarrow} b \Leftrightarrow a = b$, and given $S, T \in \mathbb{P}X$, then $S \overset{\mathbb{P}X}{\twoheadleftarrow} T \Leftrightarrow S \subseteq T$.

For a set X and $S \in \mathbb{P}X$, the flattening function $\lceil S \rceil$ gives the cover-set for the elements of S.

$$\boxed{\begin{array}{l} =[X]= \\ \hline \lceil \_ \rceil : \mathbb{P}X \twoheadrightarrow \mathbb{P}X \\ \hline \forall S : \mathbb{P}X \bullet \\ \quad \lceil S \rceil = S \setminus \{a, a' : S \mid a \overset{X}{\twoheadleftarrow} a' \land a \neq a' \bullet a\} \end{array}}$$

For example, $\lceil \mathcal{IV}[1, 3] \rceil = \{[1..3]\}$. We define a *difference* operator for $S, T \in \mathbb{P}X$, where $S \setminus_{\mathbb{P}X} T$ gives the relative compliment of T in S.

$$\boxed{\begin{array}{l} =[X]= \\ \hline \_ \setminus \_\_ : \mathbb{P}(\mathbb{P}X) \twoheadrightarrow \mathbb{P}X \times \mathbb{P}X \rightarrow \mathbb{P}X \\ \hline \forall S, T : \mathbb{P}X \bullet \\ \quad S \setminus_{\mathbb{P}X} T = \lceil \{a : S; \ c : X \mid c \overset{X}{\twoheadleftarrow} a \land (\forall b : T \bullet \neg (c \overset{X}{\twoheadleftarrow} b)) \bullet c\} \rceil \end{array}}$$

For example, $\lceil \mathcal{IV}[1, 3] \rceil \setminus_{\mathcal{IV}[1,3]} \{[1..1], [3..3]\} = \{[2..2]\}$.

3   Filter Condition Attribute Datatypes

In this section we define the datatypes used to construct the filter condition attributes for the $\mathcal{FW}_1$ policy model.

3.1   The Adjacency Datatype

For a set X, the Adjacency datatype $\alpha[X]$, is the set of all closed subsets of X partitioned by adjacency.

$$\alpha[X] == \{S : \mathbb{P}X \mid (\forall a, b : S \mid a \neq b \bullet \neg (a \wr_X b))\}$$

For example $\alpha[\mathcal{IV}[1, 3]]$ gives $\{\{[1..1]\}, \{[1..2]\}, \{[1..3]\}, \{[2..2]\}, \{[2..3]\}, \{[3..3]\}, \{[1..1], [3..3]\}\}$, and $\alpha[IPv4]$ defines the set of all closed subsets for the intervals of the IPv4 address range partitioned by adjacency.

Adjacency Ordering. An ordering can be placed over Adjacency-sets, and is defined as follows.

$$\models [X] =\!=\!=\!=\!=\!=\!=\!=\!=\!=$$

$\bot, \top : \alpha[X]$

$\mathbf{not} : \alpha[X] \to \alpha[X]$

$\_ \leq \_ : \alpha[X] \leftrightarrow \alpha[X]$

$\_ \otimes \_,$

$\_ \oplus \_ : \alpha[X] \times \alpha[X] \to \alpha[X]$

$\bot = \emptyset \wedge \top = \lceil X \rceil$

$\forall S, T : \alpha[X] \bullet$

$\quad \mathbf{not}\, S = \top \setminus_{\alpha[X]} S \wedge$

$\quad S \leq T \Leftrightarrow (\forall a : S \bullet \exists b : T \bullet a \overset{X}{\twoheadleftarrow} b) \wedge$

$\quad S \otimes T = \lceil \bigcup \{ U : \alpha[X] \mid \forall c : U \bullet \exists a : S;\ b : T \bullet c \overset{X}{\twoheadleftarrow} a \wedge c \overset{X}{\twoheadleftarrow} b \} \rceil \wedge$

$\quad S \oplus T = \bigcap \{ U : \alpha[X] \mid \forall c : U \bullet \exists a : S;\ b : T \bullet a \overset{X}{\twoheadleftarrow} c \vee b \overset{X}{\twoheadleftarrow} c \}$

The elements $\bot, \top \in \alpha[X]$ define the least and greatest bounds, respectively, on $\alpha[X]$, where for any $S \in \alpha[X]$, then $\bot \leq S \leq \top$. Adjacency negation defines a valid complement operator in $\alpha[X]$, where $(S \oplus \mathbf{not}\, S) = \top$ and $(S \otimes \mathbf{not}\, S) = \bot$.

Adjacency Intersection. Under this ordering, the *meet*, or intersection $S \otimes T$ of $S, T \in \alpha[X]$ is defined using subsumption, as the cover-set for the generalized union of all Adjacency-sets, where each element of $(S \otimes T)$ is covered by an element in *both* S and T. Intuitively, this means that the values of the meet are all non-empty intersections of each value in S with each value in T. Under the ordering relation $\leq$, $\otimes$ provides a *greatest lower bound* (glb) operator, and $S \otimes T$ is covered by both S and T, that is $(S \otimes T) \leq S$ and $(S \otimes T) \leq T$.

Adjacency Union. The *join* of $S, T \in \alpha[X]$ is defined using subsumption, as the generalized intersection of all Adjacency-sets, where each element of $(S \oplus T)$ covers an element in *either* S or T. Intuitively, this means that the values of the join are exactly a union of the elements from both S and T. Given the definition of ordering using subsumption, it follows that the Adjacency join provides a *lowest upper bound* (lub) operator. Since $\oplus$ provides a lub operator we have $S \leq (S \oplus T)$ and $T \leq (S \oplus T)$.

Proposition. The poset $(\alpha[X], \leq)$ forms a distributive lattice with compliment operator $\mathbf{not}$. This follows from the definition of $\leq$ as a subsumption ordering/an antisymmetric preorder, the properties of $\mathbf{not}$, the intuitive definition of the meet of $S, T \in \alpha[X]$ as all non-empty intersections of each value in S with each value in T, and the intuitive definition of the join operation as an exact union of the elements from both S and T [18].

Given the adjacency, disjointness and subsumption relations; then for $S, T \in \alpha[X]$, we define $S \wr_{\alpha[X]} T \Leftrightarrow true \wedge S \mid_{\alpha[X]} T \Leftrightarrow S \otimes T = \bot \wedge S \overset{\alpha[X]}{\twoheadleftarrow} T \Leftrightarrow S \leq T$.

3.2   The Duplet Datatype

A duplet is an ordered pair, where the set of all duplets for types X, Y, is defined as $\delta[X, Y]$, where $\delta[X, Y] == X \times Y$. For example, $\delta[\mathcal{IV}[1, 1], \mathcal{IV}[1, 2]]$ gives $\{([1..1],[1..1]), ([1..1],[1..2]), ([1..1], [2..2])\}$, and $\delta[\alpha[IPv4], \alpha[Port]]$ gives the set of all duplets for adjacency-free IP/port-ranges.

Recall the earlier example of the firewall system that supports only destination port range filter conditions. Suppose we want to extend the expressiveness of the policy rules for this system to include a definition for destination IP range. Then $\alpha[\delta[\alpha[IPv4], \alpha[Port]]]$, is the set of all closed subsets of adjacency-free IP/port-range duplets, partitioned by adjacency. Consider two policy requirements, where network traffic is to be allowed to the IP range $[1..3]$ on ports $[1..3]$, and to the IP range $[2..4]$ on ports $[2..4]$. Then modelling this using sets of adjacency-free duplets, we have $S, T \in \alpha[\delta[\alpha[IPv4], \alpha[Port]]]$, where $S ==$ $\{((\{[1..3]\}, \{[1..3]\}))\}$ and $T == \{((\{[2..4]\}, \{[2..4]\}))\}$.

Duplet Disjointness. A pair of duplets are disjoint if the attributes in the first coordinate are disjoint, or the attributes in the second coordinate are disjoint. For $(a_1, b_1), (a_2, b_2) \in \delta[X, Y]$, then:

$$(a_1, b_1) \mid_{\delta[X,Y]} (a_2, b_2) \Leftrightarrow (a_1 \mid_X a_2 \vee b_1 \mid_Y b_2)$$

For example, $\neg (S \mid_{\alpha[\delta[\alpha[IPv4], \alpha[Port]]]} T)$.

Duplet Adjacency. A pair of duplets are adjacent if the attributes in the first coordinate are adjacent, and the attributes in the second coordinate are not disjoint. Thus, we have:

$$(a_1, b_1) \wr_{\delta[X,Y]} (a_2, b_2) \Leftrightarrow (a_1 \wr_X a_2 \wedge \neg (b_1 \mid_Y b_2))$$

For example, $S \wr_{\alpha[\delta[\alpha[IPv4], \alpha[Port]]]} T$.

Duplet Subsumption. A duplet is distinguished from a standard ordered pair, whereby we explicitly define orderings separately in each coordinate. For example, suppose we wanted to join adjacent policies S and T, then under a 'standard' Cartesian product ordering we have $S \oplus T = \{(\{[1..4]\}, \{[1..4]\})\}$. This obviously results in an overly permissive policy, conversely; an overly restrictive policy if we were composing deny rules. A duplet (a_1, b_1) covers a duplet (a_2, b_2) in $\delta[X, Y]$, if a_1 covers a_2 in X, and b_2 covers b_1 in Y. Thus:

$$(a_2, b_2) \overset{\delta[X,Y]}{\leftarrow} (a_1, b_1) \Leftrightarrow (a_2 \overset{X}{\leftarrow} a_1 \wedge b_1 \overset{Y}{\leftarrow} b_2)$$

Then we have $S \oplus T = \{((\{[1..4]\}, \{[2..3]\}), (\{[1..3]\}, \{[1..1]\}), (\{[2..4]\}, \{[4..4]\}))\}$. Thus, the join, or union $(S \oplus T)$ of S and T, defines the adjacency-free coalescence of all duplets from S and T. For reasons of space, we do not give the implementation definition for this operation.

3.3   The Stateful/Protocol Datatype

In this section, we define the network protocols of interest for the model and encode a notion of *state*. The iptables command line utility allows the end-user to specify one (or all) of seven different protocols in a rule [1]. For reasons of space, we focus only on the TCP, UDP and ICMP protocols.

Let *Flags* be the set of TCP flags, where *Flags* ::= syn | ack | fin | psh | rst | urg. The TCP protocol is defined as the set of all sets of pairs of sets of *Flags*, whereby for each pair; the first set contains the flags that are to be examined in a packet-header, and the second set contains the flags that must be set (in a packet-header). In [1], these are referred to as the *comp* and *mask* values for a packet, respectively. Let *TCP* be the set of all sets of comp/mask pairs, where $TCP == \mathbb{P}(\mathbb{P}\,Flags \times \mathbb{P}\,Flags)$. Let [*TypesCodes*] be the set of all valid ICMP Type/Code pairs. For simplicity and reasons of space, we do not consider how the values of *TypesCodes* may be constructed, other than to assume that the usual human-readable notation can be used, such as (8,0) and (17,0) $\in$ *TypesCodes*. The iptables conntrack modules' statelist [1] may be defined as follows. Let *State* be the set of connection tracking states for a packet/connection, where *State* ::= new | established | related | invalid | untracked.

Let *Protocol* define the set of all protocols, given as the set of all duplets over *TCP*, UDP ([0..1]), ICMP ($\mathbb{P}$ *TypesCodes*) and the set of all sets of connection tracking states ($\mathbb{P}$ *State*).

$$Protocol == \delta[TCP, \delta[\{0,1\}, \delta[\mathbb{P}\,TypesCodes, \mathbb{P}\,State]]]$$

Proposition. The *Protocol* datatype forms a product-lattice structure. This follows from the definition of *Protocol* as the product of powerset/binary lattices [5].

4   The $\mathcal{FW}_1$ Policy Algebra

In this section we define an algebra $\mathcal{FW}_1$, for constructing and reasoning about anomaly-free firewall policies. We focus on stateful firewall policies that are defined in terms of constraints on source/destination IP/port ranges, the TCP, UDP and ICMP protocols.

A filter condition is a five-tuple (*s*, *sprt*, *d*, *dprt*, *p*), representing network traffic originating from source IP range *s*, with source port range *sprt*, destined for destination IP range *d*, with destination port range *dprt*, using stateful-protocols *p*. Let *FC* define the set of all filter conditions, where:

$$FC == \delta[\alpha[IPv4], \delta[\alpha[Port], \delta[\alpha[IPv4], \delta[\alpha[Port], Protocol]]]]$$

A firewall policy defines the filter conditions that may be allowed or denied by a firewall. Let *Policy* define the set of all firewall policies, whereby:

$$Policy == \{A, D : \alpha[FC] \mid \forall\, a : A;\; d : D \bullet a \mid_{FC} d\}$$

A firewall policy $(A, D) \in Policy$ defines that a filter condition $f \in A$ should be allowed by the firewall, while a filter condition $f \in D$ should be denied. Given $(A, D) \in Policy$ then A and D are disjoint: this avoids any contradiction in deciding whether a filter condition should be allowed or denied. Given that A and D are also both adjacency-free; then $Policy$ defines the set of *anomaly-free* firewall policies in the sense that they contain no redundancy, shadowing, or other anomalies [4].

Note that $(A, D) \in Policy$ need not partition $\lceil FC \rceil$: the allow and deny sets define the filter conditions to which the policy *explicitly* applies, and an *implicit* default decision is applied for those filter conditions in $\lceil FC \rceil \setminus_{\alpha[FC]} (A \oplus D)$. For the purposes of modelling iptables firewalls it is sufficient to assume *default deny*, though we observe that $\mathcal{FW}_1$ can also be used to reason about *default allow* firewall policies. The policy destructor functions *allow* and *deny* are analogous to functions *first* and *second* for ordered pairs:

$$\begin{array}{|l}
allow, deny : Policy \to \alpha[FC] \\
\hline
\forall\, A, D : \alpha[FC] \; \bullet \\
\quad allow\,(A, D) = A \wedge deny\,(A, D) = D
\end{array}$$

Policy Refinement. An ordering can be defined over firewall policies, whereby given $P, Q \in Policy$ then $P \sqsubseteq Q$ means that P is no less restrictive than Q, that is, any filter condition that is denied by Q is denied by P. Intuitively, policy P is considered to be a *safe replacement* for policy Q, in the sense of [11,14] and any firewall that enforces policy Q can be reconfigured to enforce policy P without any loss of security. The set $Policy$ forms a lattice under the safe replacement ordering and is defined as follows.

$$\begin{array}{|l}
\mathcal{FW}_1 \\
\hline
\bot, \top : Policy \\
\_ \sqsubseteq \_ : Policy \leftrightarrow^{\bullet} Policy \\
\_ \sqcap \_, \\
\_ \sqcup \_ : Policy \times Policy \to Policy \\
\hline
\bot = (\emptyset, \lceil FC \rceil) \wedge \top = (\lceil FC \rceil, \emptyset) \\
\forall\, P, Q : Policy \; \bullet \\
\quad P \sqsubseteq Q \Leftrightarrow ((allow\, P \leq allow\, Q) \wedge (deny\, Q \leq deny\, P)) \wedge \\
\quad P \sqcap Q = (allow\, P \otimes allow\, Q, deny\, P \oplus deny\, Q) \wedge \\
\quad P \sqcup Q = (allow\, P \oplus allow\, Q, deny\, P \otimes deny\, Q)
\end{array}$$

Formally, $P \sqsubseteq Q$ iff every filter condition allowed by P is allowed by Q and that any filter conditions explicitly denied by Q are also explicitly denied by P. Note that in this definition we distinguish between filter conditions *explicitly* denied in the policy versus those *implicitly* denied by default. This means that, everything else being equal, a policy that explicitly denies a filter condition is considered more restrictive than a policy that relies on the implicit default-deny for the same network traffic pattern. Safe replacement is defined as the Cartesian product of Adjacency orderings over allow and deny sets and it therefore follows that $(Policy, \sqsubseteq)$ is a poset.

$\perp$ and $\top$ define the most restrictive and least restrictive policies, that is, for any $P \in Policy$ we have $\perp \sqsubseteq P \sqsubseteq \top$. Thus, for example, any firewall enforcing a policy P can be safely reconfigured to enforce the (not very useful) firewall policy $\perp$.

Policy Intersection. Under this ordering, the meet $P \sqcap Q$, of two firewall policies P and Q is defined as the policy that denies any filter condition that is explicitly denied by *either* P or Q, but allows filter conditions that are allowed by *both* P and Q. Intuitively, this means that if a firewall is required to enforce both policies P and Q, it can be configured to enforce the policy $(P \sqcap Q)$ since $P \sqcap Q$ is a safe replacement for both P and Q, that is; $(P \sqcap Q) \sqsubseteq P$ and $(P \sqcap Q) \sqsubseteq Q$. Given the definition of safe replacement as a product of two Adjacency lattices, it follows that the policy meet provides the glb operator. Thus, $P \sqcap Q$ provides the 'best'/least restrictive safe replacement (under $\sqsubseteq$) for both P and Q.

Policy Union. The join of two firewall policies P and Q is defined as the policy that allows any filter condition allowed by *either* P or Q, but denies filter conditions that are explicitly denied by *both* P and Q. Intuitively, this means that a firewall that is required to enforce either policy P or Q can be safely configured to enforce the policy $(P \sqcup Q)$. Since $\sqcup$ provides a lub operator we have $P \sqsubseteq (P \sqcup Q)$ and $Q \sqsubseteq (P \sqcup Q)$.

Proposition. The set of all policies *Policy* forms a lattice under safe replacement. This follows from the definition of $\sqsubseteq$ as a Cartesian product of two Adjacency lattice orderings.

4.1   Constructing Firewall Policies

The lattice of policies $\mathcal{FW}_1$ provides us with an algebra for constructing and interpreting firewall polices. The following constructor functions are used to build primitive policies. Given a set of adjacency-free filter conditions A, then (Allow A) is a policy that allows filter conditions in A, and (Deny D) is a policy that explicitly denies filter conditions in D.

$$
\begin{array}{|l}
\text{Allow,} \\
\text{Deny} : \alpha[FC] \rightarrow Policy \\
\hline
\forall\, S : \alpha[FC]\; \bullet \\
\quad \text{Allow } S = (S, \emptyset) \wedge \text{Deny } S = (\emptyset, S)
\end{array}
$$

This provides what we refer to as a *weak* interpretation of allow and deny. Network traffic patterns that are not explicitly mentioned in parameter S are default-deny and therefore are not specified in the deny set of the policy. The following provides us with a *strong* interpretation for these constructors:

$$\begin{array}{|l}
\mathsf{Allow}^+, \\
\mathsf{Deny}^+ : \alpha[FC] \to Policy \\
\hline
\forall\, S : \alpha[FC]\,\bullet \\
\quad \mathsf{Allow}^+ S = (S, \mathbf{not}\ S) \wedge \mathsf{Deny}^+ S = (\mathbf{not}\ S, S)
\end{array}$$

In this case ($\mathsf{Allow}^+ A$) allows filter conditions specified in A, while explicitly denying all other filter conditions, and ($\mathsf{Deny}^+ D$) denies filter conditions specified in D while allowing all other filter conditions.

Proposition. A firewall policy $P \in Policy$ can be decomposed into it's corresponding allow and deny sets, and re-constructed using the algebra; for any $(A, D) \in Policy$, since A and D are disjoint then:

$$\begin{aligned}
(\mathsf{Allow}^+ A) \sqcup (\mathsf{Deny}\, D) &= (A, \lceil FC \rceil \setminus_{\alpha[FC]} A) \sqcup (\emptyset, D) \\
&= (A, D) \\
&= (\mathsf{Allow}\, A) \sqcap (\mathsf{Deny}^+ D)
\end{aligned}$$

5 Reasoning About Policies in Practice

Sequential Composition. A firewall policy is conventionally constructed as a sequence of rules, whereby for a given network packet, the decision to allow or deny that packet is checked against each policy rule, starting from the first, in sequence, and the first rule that matches gives the result that is returned. The algebra $\mathcal{FW}_1$ can be extended to include a similar form of sequential composition of policies. The policy constructions above can be regarded as representing the individual rules of a conventional firewall policy.

Let ($\mathsf{Allow}\, A$) $\mathbin{\raise.5ex\hbox{$\scriptstyle{}^\circ_\circ$}} Q$ denote a sequential composition of an allow rule ($\mathsf{Allow}\, A$) with policy Q with the interpretation that a given network packet matched in A is allowed; if it does not match in A then policy Q is enforced. The resulting policy either: allows filter conditions in A (and denies all other filter conditions), or allows/denies filter conditions in accordance with policy Q. We define:

$$\begin{aligned}
(\mathsf{Allow}\, A) \mathbin{\raise.5ex\hbox{$\scriptstyle{}^\circ_\circ$}} Q &= (\mathsf{Allow}^+ A) \sqcup Q \\
&= ((A \oplus allow(Q)), (((\lceil FC \rceil \setminus_{\alpha[FC]} A) \otimes deny(Q)))) \\
&= ((A \oplus allow(Q)), (deny(Q) \setminus_{\alpha[FC]} A))
\end{aligned}$$

which is as expected. A similar definition can be provided for the sequential composition ($\mathsf{Deny}\, D$) $\mathbin{\raise.5ex\hbox{$\scriptstyle{}^\circ_\circ$}} Q$, whereby a given network packet that is matched in D is denied; if it does not match in D then policy Q is enforced. We define:

$$\begin{aligned}
(\mathsf{Deny}\, D) \mathbin{\raise.5ex\hbox{$\scriptstyle{}^\circ_\circ$}} Q &= (\mathsf{Deny}^+ D) \sqcap Q \\
&= (allow(Q) \setminus_{\alpha[FC]} D, deny(Q) \oplus D)
\end{aligned}$$

While in practice its usual to write a firewall policy in terms of many constructions of allow and deny rules, in principle, any firewall policy $P \in$ *Policy* can be defined in terms of one allow policy (Allow $allow(P)$) and one deny policy (Deny $deny(P)$) and since the allow and deny sets of P are disjoint we have $P \,\mathring{,}\, Q = ($Deny $deny(P)) \,\mathring{,}\, ($Allow $allow(P)) \,\mathring{,}\, Q$. We define this as:

$$\_\,\mathring{,}\,\_ : Policy \times Policy \rightarrow Policy$$

$$\forall \mathcal{FW}_1;\ P, Q : Policy \bullet$$
$$P \,\mathring{,}\, Q = (Q \sqcup (\text{Allow}^+ (allow(P)))) \sqcap (\text{Deny}^+ (deny(P)))$$

Let *Rule* define the set of all firewall rules, where $Rule:: = $ allow $\langle\!\langle FC \rangle\!\rangle$ | deny $\langle\!\langle FC \rangle\!\rangle$. We define a rule interpretation function as:

$$\mathcal{I} : Rule \rightarrow Policy$$

$$\forall f : FC \bullet$$
$$\mathcal{I}(\text{allow } f) = \text{Allow}(\{f\}) \wedge \mathcal{I}(\text{deny } f) = \text{Deny}(\{f\})$$

A firewall policy is defined as a sequence of rules $\langle r_1, r_2, .., r_n \rangle$, for $r_i \in$ *Rule*, and is encoded in the policy algebra as $\mathcal{I}(r_1) \,\mathring{,}\, \mathcal{I}(r_2) \,\mathring{,}\, .. \,\mathring{,}\, \mathcal{I}(r_n)$.

Policy Negation. The policy negation of $P \in$ *Policy* allows filter conditions explicitly denied by P and explicitly denies filter conditions allowed by P. We define:

$$\mathbf{not} : Policy \rightarrow Policy$$

$$\forall \mathcal{FW}_1;\ P : Policy \bullet$$
$$\mathbf{not}\, P = (\text{Allow}^+ (deny\, (P))) \sqcup (\text{Deny}\, (allow\, (P)))$$

From this definition it follows that $(\mathbf{not}\ P)$ is simply $(deny\,(P), allow\,(P))$ and thus $\mathbf{not}\,(\text{Deny } D) = (\text{Allow } D)$ and $\mathbf{not}\,(\text{Allow } A) = (\text{Deny } A)$. Note however, that in general policy negation does not define a complement operator in the algebra $\mathcal{FW}_1$, that is, it not necessarily the case that $(P \sqcup \mathbf{not}\ P) = \top$ and $(P \sqcap \mathbf{not}\ P) = \bot$.

5.1   Anomaly Analysis

A firewall policy is conventionally constructed as a sequence of order-dependent rules, and when a network packet matches with two or more policy rules, the policy is anomalous [3,4,8]. By definition, the adjacency-free allow and deny sets of some $P \in$ *Policy* are disjoint, therefore P is anomaly-free by construction. We can however define anomalies using the algebra; by considering how a policy changes when composed with other policies.

Redundancy. A policy P is redundant given policy Q if their composition results in no difference between the resulting policy and Q, in particular, if $P \, \mathbf{;} \, Q = Q$.

Shadowing. Some part of policy Q is shadowed by the entire policy P in the composition $P \, \mathbf{;} \, Q$ if the filter condition constraints that are specified by P contradict the constraints that are specified by Q, in particular, if $(\mathbf{not}\, P) \, \mathbf{;} \, Q = Q$. This is a very general definition for shadowing. Perhaps a more familiar interpretation of this definition is one where the policy P is a specific allow/deny rule that shadows a part or all of the policy with which it is composed. Recall that $(\mathbf{not}(\mathsf{Allow}\, A)) = (\mathsf{Deny}\, A)$ and, for example, in $(\mathsf{Allow}\, A) \, \mathbf{;} \, Q$ all or part of policy Q is shadowed by the rule/primitive policy $(\mathsf{Allow}\, A)$ if Q denies the filter conditions specified in A, that is, $(\mathsf{Deny}\, A) \, \mathbf{;} \, Q = Q$. Similarly, in $(\mathsf{Deny}\, D) \, \mathbf{;} \, Q$ part or all of policy Q is shadowed by the rule/primitive policy $(\mathsf{Deny}\, D)$ if $(\mathbf{not}\,(\mathsf{Deny}\, D)) \, \mathbf{;} \, Q = Q$. Further definitions for shadowing may be constructed using the algebra. For example, an initial interpretation of the generalisation anomaly [3] in the composition $P \, \mathbf{;} \, Q$; is where Q is generalised by P if all of P shadows (specifically) part of Q. We are currently investigating how this and other anomalies can be reasoned about within the algebra.

Inter-policy Anomalies. Anomalies can also occur between the different policies of distributed firewall configurations [4]. In the following, assume that P is a policy on an *upstream* firewall and Q is a policy on a *downstream* firewall.

An inter-redundancy anomaly exists between policies P and Q if some part of Q is redundant to some part of P, whereby the target action of the redundant filter conditions is *deny*. Given some set of filter conditions A denied by P, and some set of filter conditions B denied by Q, if $(\mathsf{Deny}\, A) \, \mathbf{;} \, (\mathsf{Deny}\, B) = (\mathsf{Deny}\, A)$ then there exists an inter-redundancy between P and Q.

An inter-shadowing anomaly exists between policies P and Q if some part of Q's allows are shadowed by some part of P's denies. Given some set of filter conditions A denied by P, and some set of filter conditions B allowed by Q, if $(\mathsf{Deny}\, A) \, \mathbf{;} \, (\mathsf{Allow}\, B) = (\mathsf{Deny}\, A)$, then there is an inter-shadowing anomaly between P and Q.

An inter-spuriousness anomaly exists between policies P and Q if some part of Q's denies are shadowed by some part of P's allows. Again, given some set of filter conditions A allowed by P, and some set of filter conditions B denied by Q, if $(\mathsf{Allow}\, A) \, \mathbf{;} \, (\mathsf{Deny}\, B) = (\mathsf{Allow}\, A)$, then there exists an inter-spuriousness anomaly between P and Q.

5.2   Standards Compliance

RFC 5735 [7], details fifteen IPv4 address blocks/ranges that have been assigned by the Internet Assigned Numbers Authority (IANA) for specialized/global purposes. Some of these address spaces may appear on the Internet, and may be used legitimately outside a single administrative domain, however, while the assigned values of the ranges do not directly raise security issues; unexpected use may indicate an attack [7]. For example, packets with a source IP address from the private address space 172.16.0.0/12, arriving on the Wide Area Network interface of a network router, may be considered spoofed, and may be part of a Denial of Service (DoS), or Distributed DoS attack.

RFC 5735 Compliance. An IP spoof-mitigation compliance policy RFC5735 is defined. Best practice recommendations are implemented for each of the fifteen specialized IP ranges in [7], resulting in one hundred and twenty iptables *deny* rules. In [10], we defined this *deny* ruleset for a firewall management tool, we do not give the definition here for reasons of space. The compliance policy terminates with a final iptables rule that specifies all other traffic be permitted. To model these iptables rules in the algebra, we define some additional filter condition attributes and provide a more formal definition of RFC5735.

An Extended Firewall Policy. An attribute for the iptables filter table chains may be defined as *Chain* ::= input | output | forward. Direction-based filtering may be given as *Dir* ::= ingress | egress, and the set of all sets of interfaces on a machine may be given as $\mathbb{P}$ *Iface*, where for simplicity, we assume elements of *Iface* resemble eth0, wlan0, tun0, etc. Let *AdditionalFC* be the set of all duplets for additional filter condition attributes of interest for this paper, whereby:

$$AdditionalFC == \delta[\mathbb{P}\ Chain, \delta[\mathbb{P}\ Dir, \mathbb{P}\ Iface]]$$

A revised definition for the set of all filter conditions $FC_\mathcal{I}$ is given as:

$$FC_\mathcal{I} == \delta[\alpha[IPv4], \delta[\alpha[Port], \delta[\alpha[IPv4], \delta[\alpha[Port], \delta[Protocol, AdditionalFC]]]]]$$

A revised definition for the set of all policies $Policy_\mathcal{I}$ is given as:

$$Policy_\mathcal{I} == \{A, D : \alpha[FC_\mathcal{I}] \mid \forall\, a : A;\ d : D \bullet a \mid_{FC_\mathcal{I}} d\}$$

The compliance policy RFC5735 $\in Policy_\mathcal{I}$, defines the minimum requirement for what it means for some perimeter network firewall policy to mitigate the threat of IP spoofing for all traffic, in accordance with RFC 5735. Thus, we have for all $P \in Policy_\mathcal{I}$, if $P \sqsubseteq$ RFC5735, then P complies with the best practice recommendations outlined in [7] for IP spoof-mitigation.

6   Encoding and Evaluating Iptables Policies

A prototype policy management toolkit has been implemented in Python for iptables. We reason over $Policy_\mathcal{I}$ policies using $(\S, \sqcup, \sqsubseteq)$; time-based performance-analysis tests were conducted. The test-bed for the experiments was a 64-Bit Ubuntu 14.04 LTS OS, running on a Dell Latitude E6430, with a quad-core Intel i5-3320M processor and 4 GB of RAM. Every experiment was conducted three times; the median result chosen for inclusion in this paper. Overall, the results are promising.

Evaluating Sequential Policy Composition. Two datasets were generated for experimentation. Each dataset consists of iptables policies of size $2^4..2^{11}$. One dataset contains policies where no rule is adjacent to any other rule (other than itself), and the other dataset consists of policies where every new rule is adjacent to the previous rule; to ensure the maximum number of possible rules are generated as a result of composition. The rules all have a target action of *allow*. The implementation parses the system's currently enforced iptables ruleset $\langle r_1, r_2..r_n \rangle$ by chain, and then normalizes each rule to a primitive/singleton policy $\langle \mathcal{I}(r_1), \mathcal{I}(r_2)..\mathcal{I}(r_n) \rangle$. The overall policy for the chain is evaluated as $\mathcal{I}(r_1) \,\S\, \mathcal{I}(r_2) \,\S..\S\, \mathcal{I}(r_n)$. For reasons of space, we give the results for the sequential composition experiments as lists of tuples $(\mathcal{P}, \mathcal{T}(\mathcal{P}))$, where $\mathcal{P}$ is the policy named by the number of iptables rules it was constructed from for the experiment, and $\mathcal{T}(\mathcal{P})$ is the time taken in seconds for the evaluation of the sequential composition of the rules in $\mathcal{P}$. For the adjacent dataset we have $[(2^4, 0.80), (2^5, 2.02), (2^6, 5.13), (2^7, 15.32), (2^8, 51.18), (2^9, 183.42), (2^{10}, 707.15), (2^{11}, 2792.81)]$. We observe that the evaluation time for the sequential composition of 2^9 rules is around three minutes, and $\mathcal{T}(2^{11})$ is approximately forty six minutes. For the non-adjacent dataset, we have $[(2^4, 0.07), (2^5, 0.13), (2^6, 0.29), (2^7, 0.67), (2^8, 1.73), (2^9, 4.98), (2^{10}, 16.09), (2^{11}, 57.81)]$, and we see that for the largest ruleset, 2^{11}, $\mathcal{T}(2^{11})$ is approximately one minute.

Evaluating Policy Union. Experiments were conducted to test policy lub, whereby each policy in the adjacent dataset was split into two policies, where the first policy contains the odd (index) rules from the original policy, and the second policy contains the even (index) rules from the original policy. Then for each $P, Q \in Policy_{\mathcal{I}}$ in this split dataset, the time taken for the operation $P \sqcup Q$ is encoded in the matrix in Table 1. The times taken for composition of policies of equal size are approximately the same as (slightly less than) those for the results given in the adjacent sequential composition dataset. This is highlighted through the diagonal in the matrix, and is as expected; given that we used all *allow* rules.

Table 1. Time taken to compute $P \sqcup Q$ (in seconds)

P \ Q	2^3	2^4	2^5	2^6	2^7	2^8	2^9	2^{10}
2^3	0.65	0.79	0.81	0.99	1.40	2.51	5.73	16.93
2^4	0.79	1.86	2.09	2.32	2.91	4.50	8.83	22.19
2^5	0.81	2.09	4.97	5.45	6.78	9.17	15.50	32.89
2^6	0.99	2.32	5.45	14.70	17.01	21.93	32.29	57.47
2^7	1.40	2.91	6.78	17.01	48.85	58.44	76.94	119.28
2^8	2.51	4.50	9.17	21.93	58.44	179.87	217.34	294.56
2^9	5.73	8.83	15.50	32.29	76.94	217.34	699.11	839.49
2^{10}	16.93	22.19	32.89	57.47	119.28	294.56	839.49	2722.63

Evaluating Policy Compliance. A further dataset consisting of iptables policies of size $2^4..2^{11}$ was generated to test policy compliance. Each policy in this dataset was RFC 5735 compliant by construction. Results are again given as a list of tuples $(\mathcal{P}, \mathcal{T}(\mathcal{P}))$, where $\mathcal{P}$ is the policy named by the number of iptables rules it was constructed from for the experiment, and $\mathcal{T}(\mathcal{P})$ is the time taken in seconds for the evaluation of $\mathcal{P} \sqsubseteq$ RFC5735. We have $[(2^4, 1.07 \times 10^{-3}), (2^5, 1.62 \times 10^{-3}), (2^6, 2.23 \times 10^{-3}), (2^7, 3.50 \times 10^{-3}), (2^8, 5.24 \times 10^{-3}), (2^9, 1.03 \times 10^{-2}), (2^{10}, 2.76 \times 10^{-2}), (2^{11}, 4.95 \times 10^{-2})]$, and we see that for each $\mathcal{P} \in Policy_{\mathcal{I}}$ in this compliance-dataset $\mathcal{T}(\mathcal{P})$ is negligible.

7   Related Work

In [3], a firewall policy is modelled as a single rooted tree, relations between rules are defined on a pairwise basis, and definitions for firewall configuration anomalies are provided. In [4], the work is extended to distributed firewall policies. In [8], a firewall policy is modelled as a linked-list, and in [13] rule relations within a policy are modelled in a directed graph. In [20] Binary Decision Diagrams are used to model firewall rulesets. We model a firewall policy as an ordered pair of disjoint adjacency-free sets, where the set of policies *Policy* forms a lattice under $\sqsubseteq$, and each $P \in Policy$ is anomaly-free by construction. In [3,4,8,13,20] an algorithmic approach is taken to detect/resolve anomalies. We follow an algebraic (as opposed to algorithmic) approach towards modelling anomalies in a single policy, and across a distributed policy configuration through policy composition. In earlier work [12], we developed the algebra $\mathcal{FW}_0$, and used it to reason over host-based and network access controls in OpenStack. In the $\mathcal{FW}_0$ algebra, we focused on stateless firewall policies that are defined in terms of constraints on individual IPs, ports and protocols. In this paper, the algebra $\mathcal{FW}_1$ is defined over stateful firewall policies constructed in terms of constraints on source/destination IP/port ranges, the TCP, UDP and ICMP protocols, and additional filter condition attributes. We argue that $\mathcal{FW}_1$ gives a more expressive means for reasoning over OpenStack security group and perimeter firewall configurations. In [16], *cloud calculus* is used to capture the topology of cloud computing systems and the global firewall policy for a given configuration. This paper could extend the work in [16], given that $\mathcal{FW}_1$ may be used in conjunction with cloud calculus to guarantee anomaly-free dynamic firewall policy reconfiguration, where the ordering relation $\sqsubseteq$ may give a viable alternative for the given equivalence relation defined over 'cloud' terms for the formal verification of firewall policy preservation after a live migration. In [21], a firewall policy algebra is proposed. However, the authors note that an anomaly-free composition is not guaranteed as a result of using their algebraic operators. Our work differs, in that policy composition under the $\sqcap, \sqcup$ and $\,_9^\circ$ operators defined in this paper all result in anomaly-free policies. In [2], an abstract model for Netfilter is proposed, and a language to specify firewall configurations is introduced that is similar to the XML-based access control language supported by Or-BAC presented in [9]. In [17], a formal model of Netfilter is defined, and the properties of reachability and cyclicity within firewall policy configurations are investigated. In [6], a theorem-proving approach is used to reason about firewall policies. The proposed algebra $\mathcal{FW}_1$ is used to reason about and compose anomaly-free policies and therefore we do not have to worry about dealing with conflicts that may arise. Anomaly conflicts are dealt with in composition by computing anomaly-free policies, rather than using techniques such as [15] to resolve conflicts in policy decisions. Encoding a definition for Network Address Translation in $\mathcal{FW}_1$ is a topic for future research.

8 Conclusion

A policy algebra $\mathcal{FW}_1$ is defined in which firewall policies can be specified and reasoned about. At the heart of this algebra is the notion of safe replacement, that is, whether it is secure to replace one firewall policy by another. The set of policies form a lattice under safe replacement and this enables consistent operators for safe composition to be defined. Policies in this lattice are anomaly-free by construction, and thus, composition under glb and lub operators preserves anomaly-freedom. A policy sequential composition operator is also proposed that can be used to interpret firewall policies defined more conventionally as sequences of rules. The algebra can be used to characterize anomalies, such as shadowing and redundancy, that arise from sequential composition. Best practice policy compliance may be defined using $\sqsubseteq$. The algebra $\mathcal{FW}_1$ provides a formal interpretation of the network access controls for a partial mapping to the iptables filter table. $\mathcal{FW}_1$ is a generic algebra and can also be used to model other firewall systems. The results in this paper are described in terms of the algebra $\mathcal{FW}_1$, for stateful firewall policies that are defined in terms of constraints on source/destination IP/port ranges, the TCP, UDP and ICMP protocols, and additional filter condition attributes.

Acknowledgement. This work was supported, in part, by Science Foundation Ireland under grant SFI 10/CE/I1853 and Irish Research Council/Chist-ERA.

References

1. Linux iptables - CLI for configuring the Linux kernel firewall, Netfilter. http://www.netfilter.org/projects/iptables/index.html
2. Adão, P., Bozzato, C., Dei Rossi, G., Focardi, R., Luccio, F.L.: Mignis: a semantic based tool for firewall configuration. In: Proceedings of the 2014 IEEE 27th Computer Security Foundations Symposium, pp. 351–365. IEEE (2014)
3. Al-Shaer, E., Hamed, H.: Firewall policy advisor for anomaly discovery and rule editing. In: Goldszmidt, G., Schönwälder, J. (eds.) Integrated Network Management VIII. IFIP, vol. 246, pp. 17–30. Springer, New York (2003)
4. Al-Shaer, E., Hamed, H., Boutaba, R., Hasan, M.: Conflict classification and analysis of distributed firewall policies. IEEE J. Sel. Areas Commun. **23**(10), 2069–2084 (2005)

5. Birkhoff, G.: Lattice Theory. American Mathemical Society Colloquium Publications, vol. XXV, 3rd edn. American Mathemical Society, Providence (1967)
6. Brucker, A.D., Brügger, L., Wolff, B.: Formal firewall conformance testing: an application of test and proof techniques. Softw. Test. Verif. Reliab. **25**(1), 34–71 (2015)
7. Cotton, M., Vegoda, L.: Special Use IPv4 Addresses. RFC 5735, January 2010
8. Cuppens, F., Cuppens-Boulahia, N., García-Alfaro, J.: Detection and removal of firewall misconfiguration. In: Proceedings of the 2005 IASTED International Conference on Communication, Network and Information Security, vol. 1, pp. 154–162 (2005)
9. Cuppens, F., Cuppens-Boulahia, N., Sans, T., Miège, A.: A formal approach to specify and deploy a network security policy. In: Dimitrakos, T., Martinelli, F. (eds.) Formal Aspects in Security and Trust. IFIP, vol. 173, pp. 203–218. Springer, New York (2005)
10. Fitzgerald, W.M., Neville, U., Foley, S.N.: MASON: mobile autonomic security for network access controls. J. Inf. Secur. Appl. (JISA) **18**(1), 14–29 (2013)
11. Foley, S.N.: The specification and implementation of commercial security requirements including dynamic segregation of duties. In: ACM Conference on Computer and Communications Security, pp. 125–134 (1997)
12. Foley, S.N., Neville, U.: A firewall algebra for openstack. In: 2015 IEEE Conference on Communications and Network Security, CNS 2015, Florence, Italy, 28–30 September 2015, pp. 541–549 (2015)
13. Hari, A., Suri, S., Parulkar, G.: Detecting and resolving packet filter conflicts. In: Proceedings of the IEEE Nineteenth Annual Joint Conference of the IEEE Computer and Communications Societies, vol. 3, pp. 1203–1212. IEEE (2000)
14. Jacob, J.L.: The varieties of refinement. In: Morris, J.M., Shaw, R.C. (eds.) Proceedings of the 4th Refinement Workshop, pp. 441–455. Springer, Heidelberg (1991)
15. Jajodia, S., Samarati, P., Sapino, M.L., Subrahmanian, V.S.: Flexible support for multiple access control policies. ACM Trans. Database Syst. **26**(2), 214–260 (2001)
16. Jarraya, Y., Eghtesadi, A., Debbabi, M., Zhang, Y., Pourzandi, M.: Cloud calculus: security verification in elastic cloud computing platform. In: 2012 International Conference on Collaboration Technologies and Systems (CTS), pp. 447–454. IEEE (2012)
17. Jeffrey, A., Samak, T.: Model checking firewall policy configurations. In: IEEE International Symposium on Policies for Distributed Systems and Networks, POLICY 2009, pp. 60–67. IEEE (2009)
18. Levine, L.: (Lemma 3, Example 6.) Algebraic Combinatorics, Lecture 8, March 2011. http://www.math.cornell.edu/~levine/18.312/alg-comb-lecture-8.pdf
19. Spivey, J.M.: The Z Notation: A Reference Manual. Series in Computer Science, 2nd edn. Prentice Hall International (1992)
20. Yuan, L., Chen, H., Mai, J., Chuah, C., Su, Z., Mohapatra, P.: Fireman: a toolkit for firewall modeling and analysis. In: 2006 IEEE Symposium on Security and Privacy, pages 15, pp. 199–213. IEEE (2006)
21. Zhao, H., Bellovin, S.M.: Policy algebras for hybrid firewalls. Technical report CUCS-017-07, Department of Computer Science, Columbia University, March 2007

CheapSMC: A Framework to Minimize Secure Multiparty Computation Cost in the Cloud

Erman Pattuk[1]([⊠]), Murat Kantarcioglu[1], Huseyin Ulusoy[1],
and Bradley Malin[2]

[1] The University of Texas at Dallas, Richardson, USA
{erman.pattuk,muratk,huseyin.ulusoy}@utdallas.edu
[2] Vanderbilt University, Nashville, USA
b.malin@vanderbilt.edu

Abstract. Secure multi-party computation (SMC) techniques are increasingly more efficient and practical, due in part, to various improvements. For instance, recent research has shown that different protocols that are implemented using different sharing mechanisms (e.g., boolean and arithmetic sharings) can have varying computational and communication costs. Although there are some approaches to automatically mix protocols of different sharing schemes to enhance execution efficiency, none provide a generic optimization framework to discover the least expensive mixed-protocol SMC execution for cloud deployment.

In this work, we introduce a generic SMC optimization framework CheapSMC that can invoke any mixed-protocol SMC circuit evaluation tool as a black box to uncover the cheapest SMC cloud deployment option. To do so, CheapSMC computes one-time benchmarks for the target cloud service and gathers performance statistics for basic circuit components. Relying on these statistics, an optimization layer of CheapSMC invokes several heuristics to find the cheapest mix-protocol circuit evaluation. Subsequently, the optimized circuit is passed to a mixed-protocol SMC tool for actual executable generation. Our empirical results, gathered by running cases studies on large range of complexity in data volume and functions for computation, show that significant cost savings can be achieved via our optimization framework in comparison to the state-of-the-art.

1 Introduction

Over the last couple of years, various two-party secure multi-party computation (SMC) protocols have been proposed to address different secure computation needs, ranging from privacy-preserving face recognition (e.g., [1]) to secure biometric identification (e.g., [3]). In addition, numerous generic two-party circuit evaluation platforms (e.g. [5,12]) have been developed to improve the efficiency of existing secure protocols. Most of these platforms (e.g., [4]) also provide high-level programming language support that can automatically generate circuits from programs written in C-like languages. These recent advances have enabled

© IFIP International Federation for Information Processing 2016
Published by Springer International Publishing Switzerland 2016. All Rights Reserved
S. Ranise and V. Swarup (Eds.): DBSec 2016, LNCS 9766, pp. 285–294, 2016.
DOI: 10.1007/978-3-319-41483-6_20

two-party SMC protocols to be more practical and push towards actual deployment of such technologies.

At the same time, there remain several critical challenges to making these platforms practical. One challenge in particular that has received little attention is performance optimization. Recent research [6] has shown that different two-party SMC protocols can have different computational and communication cost profiles. For example, arithmetic sharing-based circuit evaluation protocols may be better for certain tasks in comparison to Yao's garbled circuit evaluation protocols. On the other hand, Boolean secret sharing-based circuit evaluation techniques can achieve the best performance in certain situations. Based on such observations, it has been shown [6] that the combination of these techniques can perform much better than each in isolation. This begs the question: *How can we find the best combination of two-party SMC techniques for a given task?*

Most of the existing work to date fails to consider the problem of finding the optimal combination of different sharing- based protocols for a given task. Rather, they require the end user to manually specify the specific sub-protocols that must be invoked. There has been some investigation into optimization and automation of the selection process (e.g., [7]), but it is limited in scope with respect to the cost dimensions that the user can choose to optimize. For example, if one party leverages a cloud infrastructure for running the protocol, the network communication may significantly impact the overall cost (in terms of money) paid by the parties. As such, it is clear that we need an optimization framework that can automatically consider communication, computation and monetary costs when searching for the optimal two-party SMC protocol composition.

The goal of this paper is to introduce an optimization framework where the given two-party SMC task can be automatically optimized under a set of predefined cost constraints. In doing so, the optimal (or near optimal) combination of different sharing-based subprotocols (e.g., arithmetic, boolean, and Yao's secret sharing protocols) can be selected automatically. This goal is similar to other automatic task optimization frameworks associated with other systems. In our optimization framework, we especially focus on the cloud setting because it is being widely adopted by organizations in a wide range of application domains [8] due to its flexibility and low initial management cost. In the cloud setting, in addition to minimizing the overall run time of the system, we may need to balance the network traffic, and computation time to achieve overall lowest monetary cost. This makes the problem more challenging because it suggests we need to consider both communication and computation costs in the optimal mixed-protocol circuit generation.

Overview of the CheapSMC. The objective of the system[1] is to make it easier for users to implement and execute SMC protocols, while minimizing the monetary cost of the SMC execution in the cloud. To ease the implementation phase and make CheapSMC extensible to available SMC tools, we partition it into three primary components. First, the *Programming API* acts as the frontend for the users, which enables implementation of SMC protocol using a C++

---

[1] Please see https://arxiv.org/abs/1605.00300 for the full version of our paper.

library. This layer is ultimately responsible for representing the user protocol as a circuit of atomic operations. It should be noted that CheapSMC can be further extended by designing a custom language (e.g., SFDL of *Fairplay* [4]), which uses our *Programming API* in the background. In this work, we do not focus on such integration and instead focus on the optimization aspects.

Second, the *Optimization Module* is responsible for assigning secret sharing schemes (e.g., Arithmetic, Boolean, Yao sharing as in the *ABY* framework [6]; Additively homomorphic, Yao sharing as in the *Tasty* framework [12]) to the nodes in the circuit, such that the total cost of executing the protocol in the cloud is minimized. Finding an optimal solution to this problem is NP-Hard, so this module provides heuristics to find near-optimal solutions.

Finally, the *SMC Layer* implements the *optimized* circuit given an existing SMC tool (e.g., *ABY* or *Sharemind* [5]). We recognize the development of efficient SMC tools is a vibrant research area, such that the design of CheapSMC does not focus on a single SMC tool that could limit its usefulness. Rather, we leverage a given SMC tool as a black box, provided that it is a mixed-protocol SMC tool (i.e., it allows for implementation using different sharing schemes).

CheapSMC relies on several atomic operations (e.g., addition, multiplication, binary xor, as well as binary and) that cover various application scenarios. In Sect. 4, we show the results of applying our system to several case studies, while further applications can be realized using our C++ library. Moreover, the process of optimizing the circuit is decoupled from the circuit generation and other layers, so that proposing a new heuristic and implementing it can be achieved with minimal effort.

2   The Optimal Partitioning Problem

2.1   Problem Definition

Let $\mathcal{S} = \{s_1, \ldots, s_n\}$ be the set of provided secret sharing mechanisms. Then, given a variable x in some domain $\mathcal{I}$, let $[x]_{s_i}$ represent the secret sharing of x using s_i.

Next, we define the set of operations $\mathcal{O} = \{o_1, \ldots, o_k\}$, such that each operation $o_i \in \mathcal{O}$ takes a set of parameters that are secretly shared in s_j and outputs a single variable secretly shared in s_j. Note that the number of inputs that an operation takes is fixed, regardless of the secret sharing scheme. An operation o_i is **supported** in s_j, if there exists an execution protocol that takes the input parameters to o_i and outputs a result secretly shared in s_j. Let $\delta(o_i) \subseteq \mathcal{S}$ represent the secret sharing mechanisms that support operation $o_i \in \mathcal{O}$.

Since an operation can be executed in the cloud environment, one should approximate the monetary cost of performing the protocol execution in a certain setup. In order to achieve this goal, we focus on the processing and network transfer costs of executing a single operation in the pay-as-you-go cloud model. In this computing model, a customer of a cloud provider service is charged a constant amount per unit time for using a particular type of virtual machine (VM), while the prices vary depending on the processing capabilities of the VM.

On the other hand, the monetary cost of transferring a single byte in and out of the VM is fixed based on the VM specifications. The unit cost of network transfer vary as the network capacity of the VM changes.

Under such circumstances, we define the processing and network transfer costs of executing an operation $o_i \in \mathcal{O}$ in the secret sharing scheme $s_j \in \delta(o_i)$ as $P(o_i, s_j)$ and $N(o_i, s_j)$, respectively. Furthermore, we define the processing and network transfer cost of converting a variable that is secretly shared in $s_i \in \mathcal{S}$ to $s_j \in \mathcal{S}$ as $CP(s_i, s_j)$ and $CN(s_i, s_j)$, respectively. Note that defined costs may vary based upon VM specifications.

Given the set of operations $\mathcal{O}$, the parties in the computation (i.e., the server and the client) implement a circuit $\mathcal{C}$ that is represented as a directed acyclic graph (DAG) and consists of m nodes $c_1, \ldots, c_m$. Each node represents a single operation and takes input from other nodes, whereas the number of inputs is decided by the operation. To be more concrete, let $\alpha(c_i) \in \mathcal{O}$ represent the operation that is assigned to the node $c_i \in \mathcal{C}$, while $\beta(c_i) \subseteq \mathcal{C}$ is the set of nodes that supply input to $c_i{}^2$. Furthermore, let $\gamma(c_i) \in \mathcal{S}$ be the secret sharing scheme assigned to c_i. Then the monetary cost of executing a node $c_i \in \mathcal{C}$ is simply:

$$\text{cost}(c_i) = P(\alpha(c_i), \gamma(c_i)) + N(\alpha(c_i), \gamma(c_i)) + \sum_{c_j \in \beta(c_i)} CP(\gamma(c_j), \gamma(c_i)) + CN(\gamma(c_j), \gamma(c_i)) \quad (1)$$

Using the above definitions, the optimal partitioning problem investigated in this paper is formally defined as follows:

Definition 1. *Given the processing and network transfer cost for a set of operations $\mathcal{O}$ using a set of secret sharing schemes $\mathcal{S}$, the cost of conversion between different secret sharing schemes, and a circuit $\mathcal{C} = \{c_1, \ldots, c_m\}$ of m nodes, where each node c_i is assigned an operation $\alpha(c_i) \in \mathcal{O}$, assign a secret sharing scheme to each node c_i, such that the total monetary cost of executing the circuit with the assigned secret sharing schemes is minimal.*

$$\begin{aligned} \text{Given} : &\mathcal{O}, \mathcal{S}, \mathcal{C}, P(o, s) \text{ and } N(o, s) \; \forall o \in \mathcal{O}, \forall s \in \delta(o), \\ &CP(s_i, s_j) \text{ and } CN(s_i, s_j) \; \forall s_i, s_j \in \mathcal{S}, \alpha(c_i) \; \forall c_i \in \mathcal{C} \\ \text{Minimize} : &\sum_{c_i \in \mathcal{C}} \text{cost}(c_i) \; \text{Subject to} : \gamma(c_i) \in \delta(\alpha(c_i)) \; \forall c_i \in \mathcal{C} \end{aligned} \quad (2)$$

The partitioning problem is NP-Hard, and the reduction can be realized via the Integer Programming problem.

3   The Details of CheapSMC

3.1   Architecture

CheapSMC is composed three primary parts: (i) The programming interface (API), (ii) the optimization module, and (iii) the SMC layer. Each part is

---

2 Note that this circuit representation of a computation can be provided by the programming language.

responsible for a different task: The programming interface morphs a user's program into its circuit representation. The optimization module heuristically assigns the secret sharing schemes to each node in the circuit using. The SMC layer generates the executables using state-of-the-art cryptographic primitives and techniques. The user of CheapSMC is expected to provide two inputs: (A) the specifications of the protocol that are going to be executed securely and (B) the unit costs for the operations and secret sharing schemes supported by the SMC framework. As discussed later, we provide a benchmark suite to automatically learn these unit costs for any target cloud service to assist the user.

User Inputs. It is assumed that the user knows the secure protocol for the application for CheapSMC will be invoked. One input to our system is the protocol specification, which can either be implemented using the associated C++ library or via a custom programming language, whose compiler turns the user input to an output compatible with our programming API. Next, the user must input the unit monetary cost of the operations for the hardware specifications that secure executables will work over. We have implemented a set of benchmark applications that can be executed by a user to discover the unit costs of each operation. It should be recognize that this is a one-time operation per tested cloud environment.

Programming API. We implemented an extensible library in C++ that allows a user to implement a secure protocol (e.g., set intersection or biometric matching). We provided several operations in the API that cover a variety of applications. Currently, the set of operations $\mathcal{O}$ include addition (`Add`), subtraction (`Sub`), multiplication (`Mul`), greater (`Ge`), equality (`Eq`), multiplexer (`Mux`), binary xor (`Xor`), and binary and (`And`). There are also two additional operations in the form of input (`In`) and output (`Out`), which allow the programmer to specify secret inputs to the circuit and to learn the outputs of the protocol execution.

As a proof of concept, we provided the interface as a C++ library that can be used to generate cost-optimal SMC executables. The interface can be bound with the compiler of a custom programming language, though which the system user can type the protocol specifications. Next, the compiler can generate the C++ program that uses the CheapSMC programming interface. In any scenario, the programming interface transforms the protocol into the circuit representation (See Sect. 2).

Optimizer. Given the circuit representation of the user protocol and the secret sharing schemes that are provided by the SMC layer, the optimizer module applies one of the heuristics (cf. Sect. 3.2) to assign secret sharing schemes to each node in the circuit. As discussed earlier, this module is responsible for finding the assignment that minimizes the monetary cost of executing the protocol securely.

Due to the fact that the optimal partitioning problem is NP-Hard, finding the optimal assignment may be impractical (even for a circuit of moderate size). As such, we introduced several heuristics (See Sect. 3.2) that are oriented to find a reasonable solution. In the background, CheapSMC applies each heuristic and chooses the one that gives the best result.

SMC Layer. Once the secret sharing schemes are assigned to each node in the circuit, CheapSMC passes the circuit to the SMC layer to generate the SMC executables. It should be recognized that there are several related investigations that provide mixed-protocol SMC tools, including the *ABY* framework by Demmler et al [6], the *TASTY* framework by Henecka et al. [12], and the *Sharemind* framework by Bogdanov et al. [5]. The SMC layer in CheapSMC is responsible for automatically implementing the optimized circuit from such existing tools. Note that since the selected SMC tool provides the low-level implementation of the cryptographic primitives (e.g., oblivious transfer [10,11], multiplication triplets [2], and sharing and reconstructing secret inputs), we focus on optimizing the user protocol using sharing assignments.

3.2   Optimization Heuristics

In addition to two existing heuristics, we developed two new heuristics to solve the optimal partitioning problem. Here, we provide a high-level description of thee heuristics.

Bottom-up Heuristic. The key idea in this heuristic is to assign an *optimal* secret sharing scheme to the nodes in their topological order in the circuit. When a node $c_i \in C$ is ready to be processed, the heuristic first assigns sharing schemes to the nodes that provide input to c_i. Based on the values assigned to the *children*, this heuristic selects the scheme that minimizes the expected monetary cost for c_i.

Top-Down Heuristic. This technique processes the nodes of the circuit in a manner quite the opposite of the Bottom-Up heuristic. Specifically, it assigns secret sharing schemes to the higher-level nodes first and iterates down to the lower levels. The idea in this heuristic is to assign the scheme that minimizes the cost of the current node, given that the schemes for the nodes for which its input to are already known. Now, assume that the secret sharing scheme for the node c_k is set to s_k previously. When assigning the secret sharing scheme for the node c_i, this heuristic takes into account that the result of the node c_i should be converted to s_k. The *optimal* decision is made with this consideration in mind.

Fixed Secret Sharing. In this optimization heuristic, each node in the circuit is assigned the same secret sharing scheme. However, in some SMC tools, certain secret sharing schemes may not necessarily support each single operation (e.g., Arithmetic sharing in *ABY* framework does not support And, Xor, and Mux). In such a case, this heuristic selects one scheme that supports each CheapSMC operation. One common secret sharing scheme that is included in almost all SMC tools and supports each operation is garbled circuit sharing (based on Yao's garbled circuit protocol [13]). Using this heuristic, we can measure the monetary cost of executing the user protocol by a single secret sharing scheme (e.g., pure SMC by garbled circuit sharing).

Hill-Climbing. This heuristic is based on the technique of Kerschbaum et al. [7]. The basic idea is to start by assigning a common secret sharing scheme (e.g., garbled circuit sharing) to each node in the circuit. Next, we check if the total cost can be reduced by changing the current secret sharing scheme of a node. This loop continues until the total cost cannot be improved by any further assignment.

4 Case Studies

4.1 Experiment Setup

We conducted empirical performance evaluations in two scenarios: (1) *Intra-Region*, where the parties are in the same Amazon EC2 region and (2) *Inter-Region*, where the parties are not in same region, for four different Amazon EC2 VM models. We tested each scenario and VM model with four techniques: the three optimization heuristics - (i.e., *Top-down*, *Bottom-up*, and *Hill Climbing*) - and *Pure-Yao*, which assigns Yao-style (i.e., garbled circuit) sharing to each node in the circuit.

In addition to the monetary cost of running CheapSMC, we measure the average running time of the four techniques. As mentioned in Sect. 3.2, our optimization problem can be enhanced by introducing performance constraints (e.g., the expected running time should be less than some threshold t). Given such a performance constraint, the heuristic solver may prune any solution that fails to satisfy the estimated performance constraint.

4.2 Biometric Matching

Biometric matching applications cover a two-party scenario, where (i) the server has a set of private entries and (ii) a client, holding its private entry, wants to learn the closest entry in the server's dataset based on some similarity measure. There are various problems related to this case study (e.g., biometric identification [3], fingercode authentication [9], and face recognition [1,14]). One of the commonly used distance metric is squared Euclidean distance. In this protocol, the server and the client proceed over the server's dataset one by one, which results in the client learning the entry with the minimal distance to its private input. We implemented this case study using our Programming API for a dataset of 30 rows with 5 attributes of 32-bit numbers.

We performed tests on four different Amazon EC2 VM configurations. Detailed information on the specifications of each VM configuration can be found in the full version of this paper.

Table 1 shows the average running time for the *Biometric Matching* case study, two different scenarios, four VM models, and four secret-sharing assignment heuristics. As expected, the performance is much better in the Intra-Region scenario. In all cases, applying any of the heuristics yields lower running times compared to the Pure-GC assignment (i.e., where each node is assigned the Yao

Table 1. The average execution time for the *Biometric Matching* case study in the Amazon EC2 Cloud. The results are for two different scenarios, four different VM models, and four different techniques.

		Execution time (*ms*)			
		Pure-GC	Hill	TD	BU
INTRA	m3.med	1229.481	398.02	**348.43**	416.944
	m3.large	715.5147	355.2913	**321.388**	372.529
	c4.large	577.333	293.544	**256.363**	284.378
	c4.xlarge	561.602	352.197	**292.522**	326.393
INTER	m3.med	**5518.04**	6738.14	6237.37	6749.467
	m3.large	**4801.94**	6096.73	6103.647	6083.193
	c4.large	**8731.577**	35580.13	33267.77	35569.97
	c4.xlarge	9118.693	6916.357	**6381.093**	6826.727

Table 2. The average computational, network, and total cost of running the *Biometric Matching* case study in the Amazon EC2 Cloud. The results are for two different scenarios, four different VM models, and four different techniques.

		Computation Cost ($¢10^{-3}$)				Network Cost ($¢10^{-3}$)				Total Cost ($¢10^{-3}$)			
		Pure-GC	Hill	TD	BU	Pure-GC	Hill	TD	BU	Pure-GC	Hill	TD	BU
INTRA	m3.med	4.78	1.55	**1.36**	1.62	0.00	0.00	0.00	0.00	4.78	1.55	**1.36**	1.62
	m3.large	5.57	2.76	**2.50**	2.90	0.00	0.00	0.00	0.00	5.57	2.76	**2.50**	2.90
	c4.large	3.72	1.89	**1.65**	1.83	0.00	0.00	0.00	0.00	3.72	1.89	**1.65**	1.83
	c4.xlarge	7.24	4.54	**3.77**	4.21	0.00	0.00	0.00	0.00	7.24	4.54	**3.77**	4.21
INTER	m3.med	**27.74**	33.88	31.36	33.93	990.71	189.71	**129.71**	189.71	1018.46	223.58	**161.07**	223.64
	m3.large	**45.75**	58.09	58.15	57.96	990.71	189.71	**129.71**	189.71	1036.46	247.80	**187.86**	247.67
	c4.large	**63.79**	259.93	243.04	259.86	990.71	218.29	**173.27**	218.29	1054.50	478.23	**416.31**	478.15
	c4.xlarge	133.23	101.06	**93.23**	99.75	990.71	189.71	**129.71**	189.71	1123.95	290.76	**222.94**	289.45

sharing). Moreover, our Top-Down heuristic yields the best running time for all VM models. Specifically, it is 15 % better than the Hill Climbing heuristic of Kerschbaum et al [7] in terms performance. For the Inter-Region scenario, we find that Pure-GC performs much better than the other techniques in terms of performance, except for the last model c4.xlarge. Since the physical distance between the two parties is large (i.e., between Tokyo and North Virginia), network latency plays a vital role in the overall performance. And it is shown that Yao sharing is much better than any other solution in high-latency networks. Since our primary optimization objective is to minimize cost (and not to minimize performance) the Inter-Region results are not surprising.

Table 2 shows the monetary cost for the *Biometric Matching* case study with the aforementioned setup. In the Intra-Region scenario, we see that the Top-Down heuristic performs better than any other technique in all VM models. This is due to a better assignment of secret sharing schemes to the nodes in the circuit for this particular case study. Note that the network communication cost within the same region is 0 in Amazon EC2, which is why the network cost in Table 2 is simply 0. In the Inter-Region scenario, the Top-Down heuristic once again delivers the cheapest assignments for all VM models. It performs 30 % better than the Hill Climbing heuristic. In terms of computation cost, we see that Pure-GC performs better due to the reasons discussed earlier (i.e., high network latency). However, in terms of total cost, Top-Down heuristic induces up to 80 % reduction.

5 Conclusion

This paper introduced CheapSMC, an SMC framework that aims to minimize the cost of executing SMC protocols in the cloud. We performed extensive cost profiling for the Amazon EC2 cloud service leveraged the gathered statistics and applied our system two case studies (i.e., biometric matching and matrix multiplication). We evaluated CheapSMC using four VM models and two scenarios (i.e., Inter-Region and Intra-Region). and we showed that the cost of executing SMC using our heuristics is up to 96 % and 30 % less than pure garbled circuit and Hill-Climbing methods, respectively. The evidence suggests that purchasing faster and more expensive VM models from Amazon EC2 do not necessarily reduce the total monetary cost of executing SMC protocols. In general, compute-optimized VMs can result in more expenses, while those which are memory-optimized can produce cheaper SMC executions.

Acknowledgement. The research was supported by grants from the NIH (R01LM009989, R01HG006844, & 1U01HG008701) and NSF (CNS-1111529, CNS-1228198, & CICI-1547324).

References

1. Sadeghi, A.-R., Schneider, T., Wehrenberg, I.: Efficient privacy-preserving face recognition. In: Lee, D., Hong, S. (eds.) ICISC 2009. LNCS, vol. 5984, pp. 229–244. Springer, Heidelberg (2010)
2. Beaver, D.: Efficient multiparty protocols using circuit randomization. In: Feigenbaum, J. (ed.) Advances in Cryptology – CRYPTO '91. LNCS, pp. 420–432. Springer, Heidelberg (1992)
3. Evans, D., et al.: Efficient privacy-preserving biometric identification. In: NDSS (2011)
4. Malkhi, D., et al.: Fairplay-secure two-party computation system. In: USENIX Security (2004)
5. Bogdanov, D., Laur, S., Willemson, J.: Sharemind: a framework for fast privacy-preserving computations. In: Jajodia, S., Lopez, J. (eds.) ESORICS 2008. LNCS, vol. 5283, pp. 192–206. Springer, Heidelberg (2008)
6. Demmler, D., et al.: ABY - a framework for efficient mixed-protocol secure two-party computation. In: NDSS (2015)
7. Kerschbaum, F., Schneider, T., Schröpfer, A.: Automatic protocol selection in secure two-party computations. In: Boureanu, I., Owesarski, P., Vaudenay, S. (eds.) ACNS 2014. LNCS, vol. 8479, pp. 566–584. Springer, Heidelberg (2014)

8. Forbes. Cloud computing: United states businesses will spend $13 billion on it (2014). http://www.forbes.com/sites/tjmccue/2014/01/29/cloud-computing-united-states-businesses-will-spend-13-billion-on-it

9. Barni, M., et al.: Privacy-preserving fingercode authentication. In: ACM workshop on Multimedia and security, pp. 231–240. ACM (2010)

10. Naor, M., et al.: Efficient oblivious transfer protocols. In: SIAM, pp. 448–457 (2001)

11. Rabin, M.O.: How to exchange secrets with oblivious transfer. IACR Cryptology ePrint Arch. **2005**, 187 (2005)

12. Henecka, W., et al.: Tasty: tool for automating secure two-party computations. In: ACM CCS, pp. 451–462 (2010)

13. Yao, A.C.: Protocols for secure computations. In: IEEE ASFCS, pp. 160–164. IEEE (1982)

14. Erkin, Z., Franz, M., Guajardo, J., Katzenbeisser, S., Lagendijk, I., Toft, T.: Privacy-preserving face recognition. In: Goldberg, I., Atallah, M.J. (eds.) PETS 2009. LNCS, vol. 5672, pp. 235–253. Springer, Heidelberg (2009)

Diversifying Network Services Under Cost Constraints for Better Resilience Against Unknown Attacks

Daniel Borbor[1]([✉]), Lingyu Wang[1], Sushil Jajodia[2], and Anoop Singhal[3]

[1] Concordia Institute for Information Systems Engineering,
Concordia University, Montreal, USA
{d_borbor,wang}@ciise.concordia.ca
[2] Center for Secure Information Systems, George Mason University, Fairfax, USA
jajodia@gmu.edu
[3] Computer Security Division, National Institute of Standards and Technology,
Gaithersburg, USA
anoop.singhal@nist.gov

Abstract. Diversity as a security mechanism has received revived interest recently due to its potential for improving the resilience of software and networks against unknown attacks. Recent work show diversity can be modeled and quantified as a security metric at the network level. However, such an effort does not directly provide a solution for improving the network diversity, and existing network hardening approaches are largely limited to handling previously known vulnerabilities by disabling existing services. In this paper, we take the first step towards an automated approach to diversifying network services under various cost constraints in order to improve the network's resilience against unknown attacks. Specifically, we provide a model of network services and formulate the diversification requirements as an optimization problem. We devise optimization and heuristic algorithms for efficiently diversifying relatively large networks under different cost constraints. We also evaluate our approach through simulations.

1 Introduction

Many critical infrastructures, governmental and military organizations, and enterprises have become increasingly dependent on networked computer systems today. Such mission critical computer networks must be protected against not only known attacks, but also potential zero day attacks exploiting unknown vulnerabilities. However, while traditional solutions, such as firewalls, vulnerability scanners, and IDSs, are relatively successful in dealing with known attacks, they are less effective against zero day attacks.

To this end, diversity has previously been considered for a security mechanism for hardening software systems against unknown vulnerabilities, and it has received a revived interest recently due to its potential for improving networks'

© IFIP International Federation for Information Processing 2016
Published by Springer International Publishing Switzerland 2016. All Rights Reserved
S. Ranise and V. Swarup (Eds.): DBSec 2016, LNCS 9766, pp. 295–312, 2016.
DOI: 10.1007/978-3-319-41483-6_21

resilience against known attacks. In particular, a recent work shows diversity can be modeled and quantified as a security metric at the network level [23, 26]. However, the work does not directly provide a systematic solution for improving the network diversity under given cost constraints, which can be a challenging task for large and complex networks. On the other hand, existing efforts on network hardening (a detailed review of related work will be given later in Sect. 2) are largely limited to handling previously known vulnerabilities by disabling existing services.

In this paper, we propose an automated approach to diversifying network services under various cost constraints in order to improve the network's resilience against unknown attacks. Specifically, we devise a model of network services and their different instances by extending the resource graph model; such a model allows us to formulate the diversification requirements and cost constraints as an optimization problem; we apply optimization techniques to solve the formulated problems, and design heuristic algorithms to more efficiently handle larger networks. We evaluate our approach through simulations in order to study the effect of optimization parameters on accuracy and running time, and the effectiveness of optimization for different types of networks. In summary, the main contribution of this paper is twofold:

- To the best of our knowledge, this is the first effort on formulating the problem of network service diversification for improving the resilience of networks, which enables the application of existing optimization techniques and also provides a practical application for existing diversity metrics [23, 26].
- As evidenced by the simulation results, the optimization and heuristic algorithms provide a relatively accurate and efficient solution for diversifying network services while considering various cost constraints. By focusing on zero day attacks, our work provides a complementary solution to existing network hardening approaches that focus on fixing known vulnerabilities.

The remainder of this paper is organized as follows: The rest of this section first builds the motivation through a running example. Section 2 reviews related work. In Sect. 3, we present the model and formulate the optimization problem, and in Sect. 4 we discuss the methodology and show case studies. Section 5 shows simulation results and Sect. 6 concludes the paper.

1.1 Motivating Example

We present a motivating example to demonstrate that diversifying network services can be a tedious and error-prone task if done manually, even if the considered network is of a small size. Figure 1 shows a hypothetical network, which is roughly based on the virtual penetration lab described in [15]. Despite its relatively small scale, it mimics a typical enterprise network, e.g., with DMZ, Web server behind firewall accessible from public Internet, and a private management network protected by another firewall.

Specifically, the network consists of four hosts running one or more services allowing accesses from other hosts. We assume the two firewalls and other host-based mechanisms (e.g., personal firewalls or iptables) together enforce the connectivity described inside the connectivity table shown in the figure. We consider attackers on external hosts (represented as $h0$) attempting to compromise the database server ($h4$), and we assume the network is secured against known vulnerabilities (we exclude exploits and conditions that involve the firewalls).

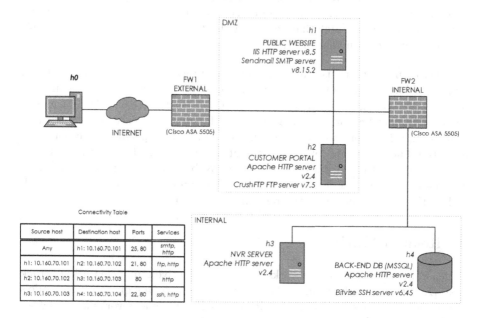

Fig. 1. Example network.

To measure the network's resilience against unknown zero day attacks, we consider the *k-zero day safety metric* [19] (which will be referred to as *k0d* from now on for simplicity), which basically counts how many distinct zero day vulnerabilities must exist and be exploited before an attacker may reach the goal. For simplicity, although the attacker may follow many paths to compromise $h4$, here we only consider the Web servers as the initial targets. We can observe that there must exist at least two distinct zero-day vulnerabilities, one for the Apache servers ($h2$, $h3$, and $h4$) and one for the IIS server[1] ($h1$), and the attacker must exploit both in order to compromise $h4$. Finally, we assume the administrator has the option of replacing those Web servers with either an NGINX 1.9 or a Litespeed 5.0.14 Web server and each replacement will incur a given installation/maintenance cost (we will discuss the cost model in more details later in Sect. 3). Based on above assumptions, consider the following scenarios:

---

[1] If different software are considered likely to share common vulnerabilities, a similarity-sensitive diversity metric may be needed [23,26].

- *Scenario 1:* The administrator aims to render the network as resilient as possible to zero-day attacks (which means to maximize the aforementioned $k0d$ metric).
- *Scenario 2:* He/she aims at the same goal as in above Scenario 1, but under the constraint that the overall diversification cost must be less than a given budget.
- *Scenario 3:* He/she aims at the same goal as in above Scenario 2, but under an additional constraint that at most two Web servers may be replaced.
- *Scenario 4:* He/she aims at the same goal as in above Scenario 3, but under an additional constraint that replacing the IIS web server in the DMZ ($h4$) should be given a higher priority.

Clearly, many more use cases may exist in practice than those listed above, and the solution may not always be straightforward even for such a small network. For example, while the administrator can easily increase the $k0d$ metric value to 4 under Scenario 1 (by having four different Web servers), the optimal solution in other scenarios will critically depend on the specific cost constraints and given budgets. Considering that the attacker may also follow other paths to attack (e.g., starting with SMTP, instead of Web, on h1), the problem becomes even more complicated. This shows the need for an automated approach, which will be the subject matter of the remainder of this paper.

2   Related Work

In general, the security of networks may be qualitatively modeled using attack trees [7,8,16] or attack graphs [2,17]. A majority of existing quantitative models of network security focus on known attacks [1,22], while few works have tackled zero day attacks [19,20,23,26] which are usually considered unmeasurable due to the uncertainties involved [13].

Early works on network hardening typically rely on qualitative models while improving the security of a network [17,18,21]. Those works secure a network by breaking all the attack paths that an attacker can follow to compromise an asset, either in the middle of the paths or at the beginning (disabling initial conditions). Also, those works do not consider the implications when dealing with budget constraints nor include cost assignments, and tend to leave that as a separate task for the network administrators. While more recent works [1,25] generally provide a cost model to deal with budget constraints, one of the first attempts to systematically address this issue is by Gupta et al. [11]. The authors employed genetic algorithms to solve the problem of choosing the best set of security hardening options while reducing costs. Dewri et al. [7] build on top of Gupta's work to address the network hardening problem using a more systematic approach. They start by analyzing the problem as a single objective optimization problem and then consider multiple objectives at the same time. Their work consider the damage of compromising any node in the cost model in order to determine the most cost-effective hardening solution. Later on, in [8] and in [24], the authors extrapolate the network hardening optimization problem as vulnerability analysis with cost/benefit assessment, and risk assessment respectively. In [14] Poolsappasit et al. extend Dewri's model to also take into account dynamic conditions (conditions that may change or emerge while the model is running) by using Bayesian attack graphs in order to consider the likelihood of an attack. Unlike our work, most existing work on network hardening are limited to known vulnerabilities and focus on disabling existing services.

There exist a rich literature on employing diversity for security purposes. The idea of using design diversity for tolerating faults has been investigated for a long time, such as the N-version programming approach [3], and similar ideas have been employed for preventing security attacks, such as the N-Variant system [5], and the behavioral distance approach [9]. In addition to design diversity and generated diversity, recent work employ opportunistic diversity which already exists among different software systems. For example, the practicality of employing OS diversity for intrusion tolerance is evaluated in [10]. More recently, the authors in [23,26] adapted biodiversity metrics to networks and lift the diversity metrics to the network level. While those works on diversity provide motivation and useful models, they do not directly provide a systematic solution for improving diversity, which is the topic of this paper.

3 Model

We first introduce the extended resource graph model to capture network services and their relationships, then we present the diversity control and cost model, followed by problem formulation.

3.1 Extended Resource Graph

The first challenge is to model different resources, such as services (e.g., Web servers) that can be remotely accessed over the network, different instances of each resource (e.g., Apache and IIS), and the causal relationships existing among resources (e.g., a host is only reachable after an attacker gains a privilege to another host). For this purpose, we will extend the concept of *resource graph* introduced in [23,26], which is syntactically equivalent to attack graphs, but models network resources instead of known vulnerabilities as in the latter.

Specifically, we will define an *extended resource graph* by introducing the notion of *Service Instance* to indicate which instance (e.g., Apache) of a particular service (e.g., Web server) is being used on a host. Like the original resource graph, we only consider services that can be remotely accessed. The extended resource graph of the running example is shown in Fig. 2 and detailed below.

In Fig. 2, each pair shown in plaintext is a security-related condition (e.g., connectivity $\langle source, destination \rangle$ or privilege $\langle privilege, host \rangle$). Each exploit node (oval) is a tuple that consists of a service running on a destination host, the source host, and the destination host (e.g., the tuple $\langle http, 1, 2 \rangle$ indicates a potential zero day vulnerability in the *http* service on host 2, which is exploitable

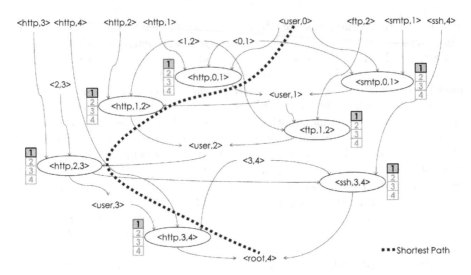

Fig. 2. The example network's resource graph (Color figure online)

from host 1). The small one-column table beside each exploit indicates the current service instance using a highlighted integer (e.g., 1 means Apache and 2 means IIS) and other potential instances in lighter text. The self-explanatory edges point from pre-conditions to an exploit (e.g., from $\langle 1, 2 \rangle$ and $\langle http, 2 \rangle$ to $\langle http, 1, 2 \rangle$), and from the exploit to its post-conditions (e.g., from $\langle http, 1, 2 \rangle$ to $\langle user, 2 \rangle$).

A design choice here is whether to associate the service instance concept with a condition indicating the service (e.g., $\langle http, 2 \rangle$) or the corresponding exploits (e.g., $\langle http, 1, 2 \rangle$). While it is more straightforward to have the service instance defined as the property of a condition, which can then be inherited by the corresponding exploits, we have opted to define this property as a label for the exploit nodes in the graph, because this will make it easier to check the number of distinct services along a path, as we will see later. One complication then is that we must ensure all exploits with the same service and destination host (e.g., $\langle http, 1, 2 \rangle$ and $\langle http, 3, 2 \rangle$) to be associated with the same service instance. Definitions 1 and 2 formally introduce these concepts.

Definition 1 (Service Pool and Service Instance). *Denote S the set of all services and Z the set of integers, for each service $s \in S$, the function $sp(.)$: $S \to Z$ gives the service pool of s which represent all available instances of that service.*

Definition 2 (Extended Resource Graph). *Given a network composed of*

- *a set of hosts H,*
- *a set of services S, with the service mapping $serv(.) : H \to 2^S$,*
- *the collection of service pools $SP = \{sp(s) \mid s \in S\}$,*

– *and the labelling function* $v(.) : E \rightarrow SP$, *which satisfies* $\forall h_s \in S \; \forall h'_s \in S, v(\langle s, h_s, h_d \rangle) = v(\langle s, h'_s, h_d \rangle)$ *(meaning all exploits with common service and destination host must be associated with the same service instance, as explained earlier).*

Let E be the set of zero day exploits $\{\langle s, h_s, h_d \rangle \mid h_s \in H, h_d \in H, s \in serv(h_d)\}$, and $R_r \subseteq C \times E$ and $R_i \subseteq E \times C$ be the collection of pre and post-conditions in C. We call the labeled directed graph, $\langle G(E \cup C, R_r \cup R_i), v \rangle$ the extended resource graph.

3.2   Diversity Control and Cost Model

We employ the notion of *diversity control* as a model for diversifying one or more services in the resource graph. Since we represent the service instance using integers, it will be straightforward to regard each pair of service and destination host on which the service is running as an optimization variable, and formulate diversity control vectors using those variables as follows. We note that the number of optimization variables present in a network will depend on the number of conditions indicating services, instead of the number of exploits (since many exploits may share the same service instance, and hence the optimization variable). Since we only consider remotely accessible services in the extended resource graph model, we would expect in practice the number of optimization variables to grow linearly in the size of network (i.e., the number of hosts).

Definition 3 (Optimization Variable and Diversity Control). *Given an extended resource graph $\langle G, v \rangle$, $\forall e \in E$, $v(e)$ is an optimization variable. A diversity control vector is the integer valued vector $\boldsymbol{V} = (v(e_1), v(e_2), ..., v(e_{|E|}))$.*

Changing the value of an optimization variable has an associated *diversification cost* and the collection of such costs is given in a *diversity cost matrix* in a self-explanatory manner. We assume the values of cost are assigned by security experts or network administrators. Like in most existing works (e.g., [7]), we believe an administrator can estimate the diversification costs based on monetary, temporal, and scalability criteria like (*i*) installation cost, (*ii*) operation cost, (*iii*) training cost, (*iv*) system downtime cost and, (*v*) incompatibility cost. We define the diversity cost, diversity cost matrix, and the total diversity cost.

Definition 4 (Diversification Cost and Diversity Cost Matrix). *Given $s \in S$ and $sp(s)$, the cost to diversify a service by changing its service instance to another inside the service pool is called the diversification cost. The collection of all the costs constraints associated with changing services in S are given as a diversity cost matrix DCM in which the element at i^{th} row and j^{th} column indicates the diversification cost of changing the ith service instance to be the jth service instance. Let $v_s(e_i)$ be the service associated with the optimization variable $v(e_i)$ and $\boldsymbol{V}_0$ the initial service instance values for each of the exploits in the network. The total diversification cost, Q_d, given by the diversity vector $\boldsymbol{V}$ is obtained by*

$$Q_d = \sum_{i=1}^{|E|} DCM_{v_s(e_i)}(\boldsymbol{V}_0(i), \boldsymbol{V}(i))$$

We note that the above definition of diversification cost between each pair of service instances has some advantages. For example, in practice we can easily imagine cases where the cost is not symmetric, i.e., changing one service instance to another (e.g., from Apache to IIS) carries a cost that is not necessarily the same as the cost of changing it back (from IIS to Apache). Our approach of using a collection of two-dimensional matrices allows us to account for cases like this. Also, the concept can be used to specify many different types of cost constraints, which we will examine in the coming section. For example, an administrator who wants to restrict the total cost to diversify all servers running the *http* service can do so by simply formulating the cost as the addition of all the optimization variables corresponding to *http*.

3.3   Problem Formulation

As demonstrated in Sect. 1.1, the *k0d* metric is defined as the minimum number of distinct resources on a single path in the resource graph [19]. For example, a closer look at Fig. 2 shows that the *k0d* value for our example network is 1. That is, an attacker needs only one zero-day vulnerability (in *http* service instance 1) to compromise this network. The dashed line in Fig. 2 depicts the shortest path that provides this metric value.

The *k0d* value can be increased by changing the service instances as long as we respect the available budget of cost. For example, consider a total budget of 78 units, and assume the costs to diversify the *http* service from service instance 1 to 2, 3 or 4 be 78, 12, and 34 units, respectively. We can see that changing $\langle http, 2, 3 \rangle$ from instance 1 to 2 would respect the budget, as well as increasing the *k0d* value of the network to be 2. We may also see that this is not the optimal solution, since we could also replace $\langle http, 2, 3 \rangle$ and $\langle http, 3, 4 \rangle$ with instances 3 and 4, respectively, increasing *k0d* to 3 and still respecting the budget. In the following, we formally formulate this as an optimization problem.

Problem 1 (k0d Optimization Problem).   Given an extended resource graph $\langle G, v \rangle$, find a diversity control vector $\boldsymbol{V}$ which maximizes $min(k0d(\langle G(\boldsymbol{V}), v \rangle))$ subject to the constraint $Q \leq B$, where B is the availble budget and Q is the total diversification cost as given in Definition 4.

Since our problem formulation is based on an extended version of the resource graph, which is syntactically equivalent to attack graphs, many existing tools developed for the latter (e.g., the tool in [12] has seen many real applications to enterprise networks) may be easily extended to generate the extended resource graphs we need as inputs. Additionally, our problem formulation assumes a very general budget B and cost Q, which allows us to account for different types of budgets and cost constraints that an administrator might encounter in practice, as will be explained in the following section.

4   Methodology

This section details the optimization and heuristic algorithms used for solving the formulated diversification problem and describes a few case studies.

4.1   Genetic Algorithm Optimization

The genetic algorithm (GA) is a simple and robust search method and optimization technique inspired by the mechanisms of natural selection. We employ GA for our automated optimization approach because it requires little information to search effectively in a large search space in contrast to other optimization methods (e.g., the mixed integer programming [4]). It also provides a simple way to encode candidate solutions to the problem [6]. While inspired by [7], we focus on service diversification and not on disabling services.

The extended resource graph is the input to our automated optimization algorithm where the function to be optimized (fitness function) is $k0d$ defined on the resource graph (later we will discuss cases where directly evaluating $k0d$ is computationally infeasible). One important point to consider when optimizing the $k0d$ function on the extended resource graph is that, for each generation of the GA, the graph's labels will dynamically change. This in turn will change the value of $k0d$, since the shortest path may have changed with each successive generation of the GA. Our optimization tool takes this into consideration. We also note one limitation here is that the optimization does not provide a priority if there are more than one shortest path that provide the optimized $k0d$ since the optimization only aims at maximizing the minimum $k0d$.

The constraints are defined as a set of inequalities in the form of $q \leq b$, where q represents one or more constraint conditions and b represents one or more budgets. These constraint conditions can be overall constraints (e.g., the total diversity cost Q_d) or specific constraints to address certain requirements or priorities while diversifying services (e.g., the cost to diversify $http$ services should be less than 80 % of the cost to diversify ssh). Those constraints are specified using the diversity control matrix.

The number of independent variables used by the GA (genes) are the optimization variables given by the extended resource graph. For our particular network hardening problem, the GA will be dealing with integer variables representing the selection of the service instances. Because $v(e)$ is defined as an integer, the optimization variables need to be given a minimum value and a maximum value. This range is determined by the number of instances provided in the service pool of each service. The initial service instance for each of the services is given by the extended resource graph while the final diversity control vector V is obtained after running the GA.

The population size that we defined for our tool was set to be at least the value of optimization variables (more details will be provided in the coming section). This way we ensure the individuals in each population span the search space. We ensure the population diversity by testing with different settings in genetic operations (like crossover and mutation). In the following, we discuss several test cases to demonstrate how the optimization works under different types of constraints. For all the test cases, we have used the following algorithm parameters: population size $= 100$, number of generations $= 150$, crossover probability $= 0.8$, and mutation probability $= 0.2$.

Test case A: $Q_d \leq 124$ units with individual constraints per service. We start with the simple case of one overall budget constraint ($Q_d \leq 124$). The solution provided by the GA is $V = [3, 2, 1, 4, 1, 1, 1]$ (represented by label column a in Fig. 3). The associated costs for $V(1)$, $V(2)$, and $V(4)$ are 12, 78, and 34, respectively, and the test network's $k0d$ metric becomes 4 while keeping Q_d within the budget ($Q_d \leq 124$).

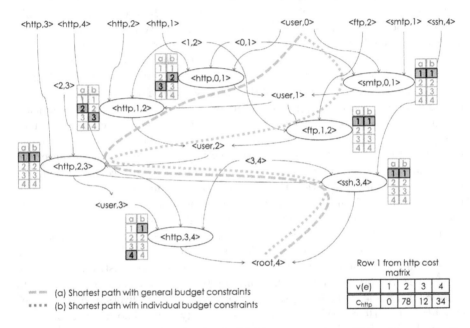

Fig. 3. Test case A: general and individual budget constraints. (Color figure online)

On the other hand, if we assign individual budgets per services, while maintaining the overall budget $Q_d \leq 124$, the optimization results will be quite different. In this case, assume the budget to diversify the *http* services cannot exceed 100 units ($q_{http} \leq 100$); for *ftp*, it cannot exceed 3 units ($q_{ftp} \leq 3$); for *ssh*, it cannot exceed 39 units ($q_{ssh} \leq 39$); finally, for *smtp*, it cannot exceed 50 units ($q_{smtp} \leq 50$). The solution provided by the GA is a V vector where $V(1) = 2$ and $V(2) = 3$, with a cost of 78 and 12 units, respectively. The value of the $k0d$ metric rises to 3 with $Q_d = 90$. This total diversification cost satisfies both the overal budget constraint and each of the individual constraints per service.

From this test case, we can see that even with the minimum requeried budget to maximize the $k0d$ metric, additional budget constraints might not allow to achieve the maximum $k0d$ possible. We can see the result of running the GA for this test case in label column b in Fig. 3.

Test case B: $Q_d \leq 124$ *units while* $q_{http} + q_{ssh} \leq 100$. While test case 1 shows how individual cost constraints can affect the $k0d$ metric optimization, in practice not all services may be of concern and some may have negligible cost. This test case models such a scenario by assigning a combined budget restriction for only the *http* and *ssh* services, i.e., the cost incurred by diversifying these two services should not exceed 100 units.

The solution provided by the GA is $V = [3, 4, 3, 1, 1, 3, 2]$ (lable column a in Fig. 4). Since $V(1)$ to $V(3)$ deal with the *http* service, we can see that the total incurred cost for *http* is $q_{http} = 12+34+12 = 58$ units. Because $V(6)$ and $V(7)$ are the only optimization variables that deal with the *ftp* and *ssh* services respectively, we can see that $q_{ftp} = 8$, and $q_{ssh} = 40$. The value of the $k0d$ metric rises from 1 to 3 by incurring a total cost of $Q_d = 106$ units. The combined *http/ssh* budget constraint of 100 units is also satisfied since $q_{http} + q_{ssh} = 98$ units.

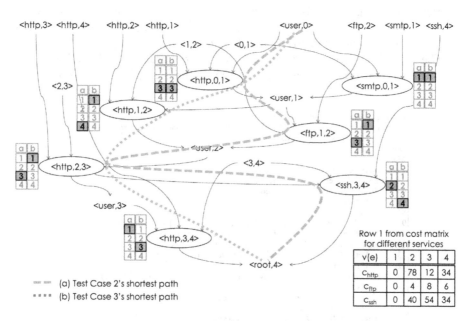

Fig. 4. Test case B and test case C. (Color figure online)

Test case C: $Q_d \leq 124$ *units while* $q_{http} \leq 0.8 \cdot q_{ssh}$. This final case deals with scenarios where some services might have a higher priority over others. The constraint in this test case is that the total incurred cost while diversifying the *http* service should not exceed 80 % of what is incurred by diversifying the *ssh* service.

The solution provided by the GA is $V = [3,1,3,1,1,1,4]$ (see column b in Fig. 4). Here $V(1)$ and $V(3)$ have changed from service instance 1 to 3, while

$V(7)$ have changed from service instance 1 to 4. The incurred cost for the $http$ service is $q_{http} = 12+12=24$ units and for the ssh service is $q_{ssh} = 34$ units. While the value of the $k0d$ metric only rises from 1 to 2, the budget constraints are satisfied.

As seen from the above test cases, our model and problem formulation makes it relatively easy to apply any standard optimization techniques, such as the GA, to optimize the $k0d$ metric through diversity while dealing with different budget constraints.

4.2   Heuristic Algorithm

All the test cases described above rely on the assumption that all the attack paths are readily available. However, this is not always the case in practice. Due to the well known complexity that resource graphs have inherited from attack graphs due to their common syntax [23,26], it is usually computationally infeasible to enumerate all the available attack paths in a resource graph for large networks. Therefore, we design a heuristic algorithm to reduce the search complexity when calculating and optimizing the $k0d$ metric by only storing the m-shortest paths at each step, as depicted in Fig. 5 and detailed below.

The algorithm starts by topologically sorting the graph (line 1) and proceeds to go through each one of the nodes on the resource graph collection of attack

---

Procedure *Heuristic_m-shortest*
Input: Extended resource graph $\langle G, v \rangle$, goal condition c_g, number of paths m,
    diversified diversity control vector, D
Output: $\sigma(c_g)$
Method:
1. **Let** $vlist$ be any topological sort of G
5. **While** all $vlist$ elements are unprocessed
6.   **If** $c \in C_I$ and c is unprocessed
7.   **Let** $\sigma(c) = c$
8.   **Mark** c as processed
9.   **Else if** $e \in E$ (e is not processed) and $(\forall c \in C)((c, e) \in R_r \Rightarrow c$ is processed)
10.   **Let** $\{c \in C : (c, e) \in R_r\} = \{c_1, c_2, \ldots, c_n\}$
11.   **Let** $\alpha(e) = a_1 \cup a_2 \ldots \cup e : a_i \in \sigma(c_i),\ 1 \leq i \leq n$
13.   **Let** $\alpha'(ov(e)) = a_1' \cup a_2' \ldots \cup e : a_i' \vdash a_i,\ 1 \leq i \leq n$
12.   **If** $n > m$
13.   **Let** $\sigma(e) = ShortestM(\langle \alpha(e), | Unique(\alpha'[ov(e)]) | \rangle, m))$
13.   **Else**
15. $\sigma(e) = a_1 \cup a_2 \ldots \cup e : a_i \in \sigma(c_i),\ 1 \leq i \leq m$
16.   **Mark** e as processed
17.   **Else** (c s.t. $(e, c) \in R_i$ and c is unprocessed)
18.   **If** $(\forall e' \in E)((e', c) \in R_i \Rightarrow e'$ is processed)
19.   **Let** $\alpha(c) = \bigcup_{e' \text{ s.t. } (e',c) \in R_i} \sigma(e')$
20.   **Let** $\alpha'(c) = \bigcup_{e' \text{ s.t. } (e',c) \in R_i} \sigma(ov(e'))$
21.   **If** $length(\alpha(c)) > m$
22.   **Let** $\sigma(c) = ShortestM(\langle \alpha(c), | Unique(\alpha'[ov(c)]) | \rangle, m))$
23.   **Else**
24.   **Let** $\sigma(c) = \bigcup_{e' \text{ s.t. } (e',c) \in R_i} \sigma(e')$
25.   **Mark** c as processed
26. **Return** $\sigma(c_g)$

Fig. 5. A Heuristic algorithm for calculating m-shortests paths

paths, as set of exploits $\sigma()$, that reach that particular node. The main loop cycles through each unprocessed node. If a node is an initial conditions, the algorithm assumes that the node itself is the only path to it and it marks it as processed (lines 6–8). For each exploit e, all of its preconditions are placed in a set (line 10). The collection of attack paths $\alpha(e)$ is constructed from the attack paths of those preconditions (lines 10 and 11). In a similar way, $\sigma'(ov(e))$ is constructed with the function $ov()$ which, aside of using the exploits includes value of element of the diversity control vector that supervises that exploit.

If there are more than m paths to that node, the algorithm will use the function $Unique$ to first look for unique combinations of service and service instance in $\alpha'(ov(e))$. Then, the algorithm creates a dictionary structure where the key is a path from $\alpha(e)$ and the value is the number of unique service/service instance combinations given by each one of the respective paths in $\alpha'(ov(e))$. The function $ShortestM()$ selects the top m keys whose values are the smallest and returns the m paths with the minimum number of distinct combination of services and service instances (line 13). If there are less than m paths, it will return all of the paths (line 15). After this, it marks the node as processed (line 16). The process is similar when going through each one of the intermediate conditions (lines 17–24). Finally, the algorithm returns the collection of m paths that can reach the goal condition c_g. It is worth noting that the algorithm does not make any distinction in whether or not a particular path has a higher priority over another when they share the same number of unique service/service instance combinations.

5   Simulations

In this section, we show simulation results. All simulations are performed using a computer equipped with a 3.0 GHz CPU and 8 GB RAM in the Python 2.7.10 environment under Ubuntu 12.04 LTS and MATLAB 2015a's GA toolbox. To generate a large number of resource graphs for simulations, we first construct a small number of seed graphs based on real networks and then generate larger graphs from those seed graphs by injecting new hosts and assigning resources in a random but realistic fashion (e.g., the number of pre-conditions of each exploit is varied within a small range since real world exploits usually have a constant number of pre-conditions). The resource graphs were used as the input for the optimization toolbox where the objective function is to maximize the minimum $k0d$ value subject to budget constraints. In all the simulations, we employ the heuristic algorithm described in Sect. 4.2.

Figure 6 shows that the processing time increases almost linearly as we increase the number of optimization variables or the parameter m of the heuristic algorithm. The results show that the algorithm is relatively scalable with a linear processing time. On the other hand, the accuracy of the results is also an important issue to be considered. Here the accuracy refers to the approximation ratio between the result obtained using the heuristic algorithm and that of the brute force algorithm (i.e., simply enumerating and searching all the paths while

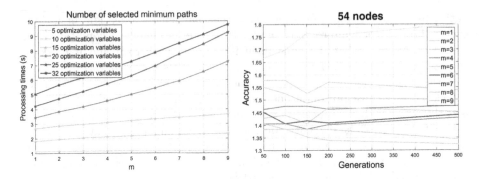

Fig. 6. Processing time.

Fig. 7. Accuracy vs m (parameter of the heuristic algorithm).

assuming all services and service instances are different). For the simulations depicted in Fig. 7, we settled for 50 iterations per graph per m-paths. The diversity control vector provided by the GA is used to calculate the accuracy. From the results, we can see that when m is greater or equal to 4 the approximation ratio reaches an acceptable level. For the following simulations, we have settled with an m value of 6 and 100 generations.

Our simulations also showed that (detailed simulation results are omitted here due to page limitations), when no budget constraints are in effect, using the GA with a crossover probability of 80 %, a mutation rate of 20 %, and setting the number of generations to 50 will be sufficient to obtain good results. However, this is no longer the case when dealing with budget constraints. We have noticed that, by decreasing the crossover probability (and consequently increasing the mutation rate), we can reach a viable solution with less generations. We have therefore settled with a crossover probability of 40 % which provides us with a fast (with less generations) way to converge to viable solutions. Additionally, our

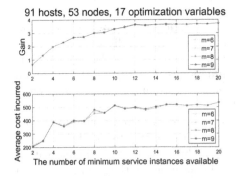

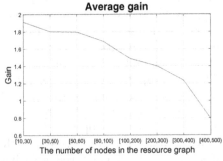

Fig. 8. The effect of the number of available service instances.

Fig. 9. The average gain vs the number of nodes.

experiences also show that, when dealing with a diversity control vector (also known as a chromosome in the GA) of less than 100 variables (genes in the GA), the population size could be equal to the amount of variables in the diversity control vector; when dealing with a bigger number, the population size should be at least twice the amount of variables.

Figure 8 shows the results when the diversity control vector has different numbers of sevice instances to take from (i.e., different sizes of the service pools). In this simulation, we have picked graphs with a relative high difference in the length of the shortest path before and after all services are diversified using the algorithm (the maximum $k0d$ value is 16 and the minimum 3). We can see an increasing gain in the $k0d$ value after optimization, when more service instances are available. However, this trend begins to stall after a certain number (13). From this observation it can be inferred that the number of available service instances will affect the difference between the maximum $k0d$ value possible and the minimum $k0d$, but such an effect also depends on the size of the network (or the extended resource graph) and increasing the number of available service instances does not always help.

In Fig. 9, we analyze the average gain in the optimized results for different sizes of graphs. In this figure, we can see that we have a good enough gain for graphs with a relatively high amount of nodes. As expected, as we increase the size of the graphs, the gain will decrease if we keep the same optimization parameters. For those simulations, we have used a population size of 300, 50 generations, and a crossover fraction of 50 %. It is interesting to note that the decrease in gain is very close to being linear.

Figures 10 and 11 show the optimization results on different shapes of resource graphs. While it may be difficult to exactly define the depth of a resource graph, we have relied on the relative distance, i.e., the difference of the shortest path before and after all services are diversified. There is a relative linear increase in the gain as we increase the relative distance in the shortest path. While this does not provide an accurate description of the graph's shape, it does

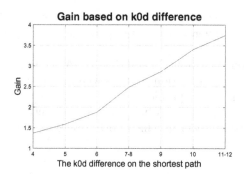
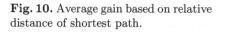
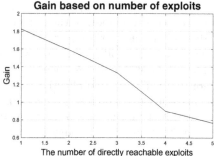

Fig. 10. Average gain based on relative distance of shortest path.

Fig. 11. Average gain based on directly reachable vulnerabilities.

provide an idea of how much our algorithm can increase the minimum $k0d$ for graphs with different depths, as shown in Fig. 10.

Finally, in Fig. 11, we can see the effect of the network's degree of exposure, which is defined as the number of exploits that are directly reachable by the attacker from the external host $h0$. As we increase the degree of exposure, the gain in optimization decreases in almost a linear way. That is, there will less room for diversification if the network is more exposed.

6   Conclusions

In this paper, we have formulated service diversity as an optimization problem and proposed an automated diversity-based network hardening approach against zero-day attacks. This automated approach used a heuristic algorithm that helped to manage the complexity of computing the $k0d$ value as well as limiting the time for optimization to an acceptable level. We have shown some sample cost constraints while our model and problem formulation would allow for other practical scenarios to be specified and optimized. We have tested the scalability and accuracy of the proposed algorithms through simulation results, and we have also discussed how the gain in the $k0d$ value will be affected by the number of available service instances in the service pools and different sizes and shapes of the resource graphs.

We discuss several aspects of the proposed automated optimization technique where additional improvements and evaluations can be done.

- While this paper focuses on diversifying services, a natural future step is to integrate this approach with other network hardening options, such as addition or removal of services, or relocating hosts or services (e.g., firewalls).
- This study has relied on a simplified model by assuming all service instances to be completely different from each another and all service instances are equally likely to be exploited. A possible future research direction would be to model the degree of difference (or similarity) between the different types of service instances.
- We have assumed an abstract cost model in this paper and an important direction is to elaborate the model from different aspects of potential cost for diversifying network resources.
- We will also consider other optimization algorithms, in addition to GA, to compare and potentially use them in hybrid optimization schemes when searching for more efficient and effective solutions to our problem.
- This study relies on a static network configuration. A future research direction would be to consider a dynamic network model in which both attackers and defenders may cause changes in the network.

Acknowledgements. This work was partially supported by the National Institute of Standards and Technology grant 60NANB15D091, by the National Science Foundation grant IIP-1266147, and by the Natural Sciences and Engineering Research Council of Canada under Discovery Grant N01035.

References

1. Albanese, M., Jajodia, S., Noel, S.: Time-efficient and cost-effective network hardening using attack graphs. In: 2012 42nd Annual IEEE/IFIP International Conference on Dependable Systems and Networks (DSN), pp. 1–12. IEEE (2012)

2. Ammann, P., Wijesekera, D., Kaushik, S.: Scalable, graph-based network vulnerability analysis. In: Proceedings of the 9th ACM Conference on Computer and Communications Security, pp. 217–224. ACM (2002)

3. Avizienis, A., Chen, L.: On the implementation of n-version programming for software fault tolerance during execution. In: Proceedings of the IEEE COMPSAC, vol. 77, pp. 149–155 (1977)

4. Azamathulla, H.Md., Wu, F.-C., Ghani, A.A., Narulkar, S.M., Zakaria, N.A., Chang, C.K.: Comparison between genetic algorithm and linear programming approach for real time operation. J. Hydro-Env. Res. **2**(3), 172–181 (2008)

5. Cox, B., Evans, D., Filipi, A., Rowanhill, J., Wei, H., Davidson, J., Knight, J., Nguyen-Tuong, A., Hiser, J.: N-variant systems: a secretless framework for security through diversity. In: Usenix Security, vol. 6, pp. 105–120 (2006)

6. Deb, K.: An efficient constraint handling method for genetic algorithms. Comput. Methods Appl. Mech. Eng. **186**(2), 311–338 (2000)

7. Dewri, R., Poolsappasit, N., Ray, I., Whitley, D.: Optimal security hardening using multi-objective optimization on attack tree models of networks. In: Proceedings of the 14th ACM Conference on Computer and Communications Security, pp. 204–213. ACM (2007)

8. Dewri, R., Ray, I., Poolsappasit, N., Whitley, D.: Optimal security hardening on attack tree models of networks: a cost-benefit analysis. Int. J. Inf. Secur. **11**(3), 167–188 (2012)

9. Gao, D., Reiter, M.K., Song, D.: Behavioral distance measurement using hidden markov models. In: Zamboni, D., Kruegel, C. (eds.) RAID 2006. LNCS, vol. 4219, pp. 19–40. Springer, Heidelberg (2006)

10. Garcia, M., Bessani, A., Gashi, I., Neves, N., Obelheiro, R.: Os diversity for intrusion tolerance: myth or reality? In: 2011 IEEE/IFIP 41st International Conference on Dependable Systems & Networks (DSN), pp. 383–394. IEEE (2011)

11. Gupta, M., Rees, J., Chaturvedi, A., Chi, J.: Matching information security vulnerabilities to organizational security profiles: a genetic algorithm approach. Decis. Support Syst. **41**(3), 592–603 (2006)

12. Jajodia, S., Noel, S., O'Berry, B.: Topological analysis of network attack vulnerability. In: Kumar, V., Srivastava, J., Lazarevic, A. (eds.) Managing Cyber Threats: Issues, Approaches and Challenges. Kluwer Academic Publisher (2003)

13. McHugh, J.: Quality of protection: measuring the unmeasurable? In: Proceedings of the 2nd ACM Workshop on Quality of Protection, pp. 1–2. ACM (2006)

14. Poolsappasit, N., Dewri, R., Ray, I.: Dynamic security risk management using bayesian attack graphs. IEEE Trans. Depend. Secure Comput. **9**(1), 61–74 (2012)

15. Penetration testing virtual labs, September 2015. https://www.offensive-security.com/offensive-securitysolutions/virtual-penetration-testing-labs

16. Ray, I., Poolsapassit, N.: Using attack trees to identify malicious attacks from authorized insiders. In: di Vimercati, S.C., Syverson, P.F., Gollmann, D. (eds.) ESORICS 2005. LNCS, vol. 3679, pp. 231–246. Springer, Heidelberg (2005)

17. Sheyner, O., Haines, J., Jha, S., Lippmann, R., Wing, J.M.: Automated generation and analysis of attack graphs. In: Proceedings of the 2002 IEEE Symposium on Security and Privacy, pp. 273–284. IEEE (2002)

18. Wang, L., Albanese, M., Jajodia, S.: Network Hardening: An Automated Approach to Improving Network Security. Springer Publishing Company, Incorporated, Heidelberg (2014)

19. Wang, L., Jajodia, S., Singhal, A., Cheng, P., Noel, S.: k-zero day safety: a network security metric for measuring the risk of unknown vulnerabilities. IEEE Trans. Depend. Secure Comput. **11**(1), 30–44 (2014)

20. Wang, L., Jajodia, S., Singhal, A., Noel, S.: k-zero day safety: measuring the security risk of networks against unknown attacks. In: Gritzalis, D., Preneel, B., Theoharidou, M. (eds.) ESORICS 2010. LNCS, vol. 6345, pp. 573–587. Springer, Heidelberg (2010)

21. Wang, L., Noel, S., Jajodia, S.: Minimum-cost network hardening using attack graphs. Comput. Commun. **29**(18), 3812–3824 (2006)

22. Wang, L., Singhal, A., Jajodia, S.: Measuring the overall security of network configurations using attack graphs. In: Barker, S., Ahn, G.-J. (eds.) Data and Applications Security 2007. LNCS, vol. 4602, pp. 98–112. Springer, Heidelberg (2007)

23. Wang, L., Zhang, M., Jajodia, S., Singhal, A., Albanese, M.: Modeling network diversity for evaluating the robustness of networks against zero-day attacks. In: Kutyłowski, M., Vaidya, J. (eds.) ICAIS 2014, Part II. LNCS, vol. 8713, pp. 494–511. Springer, Heidelberg (2014)

24. Wang, S., Zhang, Z., Kadobayashi, Y.: Exploring attack graph for cost-benefit security hardening: a probabilistic approach. Comput. Secur. **32**, 158–169 (2013)

25. Yigit, B., Gur, G., Alagoz, F.: Cost-aware network hardening with limited budget using compact attack graphs. In: 2014 IEEE Military Communications Conference (MILCOM), pp. 152–157. IEEE (2014)

26. Zhang, M., Wang, L., Jajodia, S., Singhal, A., Albanese, M.: Network diversity: a security metric for evaluating the resilience of networks against zero-day attacks. IEEE Trans. Inf. Forensics Secur. (TIFS) **11**(5), 1071–1086 (2016)

Reasoning About Privacy Properties of Architectures Supporting Group Authentication and Application to Biometric Systems

Julien Bringer[1], Hervé Chabanne[1,2], Daniel Le Métayer[3], and Roch Lescuyer[1(✉)]

[1] Morpho, Issy-Les-Moulineaux, France
roch.lescuyer@morpho.com
[2] Télécom ParisTech, Paris, France
[3] INRIA, Université de Lyon, Lyon, France

Abstract. This paper follows a recent line of work that advocates the use of formal methods to reason about privacy properties of system architectures. We propose an extension of an existing formal framework, motivated by the need to reason about properties of architectures including group authentication functionalities. By group authentication, we mean that a user can authenticate on behalf of a group of users, thereby keeping a form of anonymity within this set. Then we show that this extended framework can be used to reason about privacy properties of a biometric system in which users are authenticated through the use of group signatures.

Keywords: Privacy by design · Formal methods · Biometric systems

1 Introduction

The privacy-by-design approach promotes the consideration of privacy requirements from the early design stage of a system. As an illustration of the importance of this topic, the General Data Protection Regulation adopted by the European trilogue (the European Commission, the European Parliament and the Council) in December 2015 [7] introduces privacy-by-design and privacy-by-default as legal obligations. Architectural choices have a strong effect on the privacy properties provided by a system. For this reason, the authors of [1] argue that key decisions regarding the design of a system should be taken at the architecture level. They introduce a formal framework for reasoning about privacy properties of architectures. The description of an architecture within this framework specifies the capacities of each component, the communications between them, the location of the computations and the data, and the trust relationships between the stakeholders. A dedicated privacy logic is used to express the privacy properties of the architectures. The use of formal methods enables precise

© IFIP International Federation for Information Processing 2016
Published by Springer International Publishing Switzerland 2016. All Rights Reserved
S. Ranise and V. Swarup (Eds.): DBSec 2016, LNCS 9766, pp. 313–327, 2016.
DOI: 10.1007/978-3-319-41483-6_22

definitions of properties and comparisons between architectures. It also makes it possible to provide a rigorous justification for the design choices.

As a first contribution of this paper, we propose an extension of this formal framework and show that it can be used to reason about properties of architectures supporting group authentication. By group authentication, we mean that a user can authenticate on behalf of a group of users. Several cryptographic primitives have been designed to achieve this goal. Our work provides the formal tools needed to reason about the properties of architectures involving these primitives, especially the guarantees that are provided in terms of privacy.

As a second contribution of this paper, we apply our extended framework to biometric systems. In a biometric system, users are authenticated with their biometric traits. The work of [3] uses the formal framework of [1] to reason about privacy properties of biometric architectures but it cannot deal with group signatures. We show that the extended framework can be used to reason about privacy properties of a biometric system in which users are authenticated by group signatures.

The interest of group signature in the context of biometrics has been shown in different contexts. For example, the biometric system architecture analysed in this paper was proposed in TURBINE [16], a European project which aimed at solving privacy concerns regarding the use of fingerprint biometrics for ID management. The application of this architecture was a pharmacy product research system. Pharmacists, for instance working at their selling desks, authenticate themselves to a pharmacy administration system. Authentication is based on a card owned by the employee, as well as its fingerprint. Thanks to the use of group signatures, a remote server (which does not get the fingerprint) is convinced that a valid enrolled user authenticates without knowing precisely who he is among the set of valid users (aka the employees).

Organization of the paper. Section 2 supplies an overview of the formal framework of [1]. Section 3 introduces our extension of this model. Section 4 presents the biometric architecture we are interested in, describes it within the architecture language of the formal framework, and analyses its privacy properties. Finally, we discuss in Sect. 5 some variants of the biometric architecture, before concluding in Sect. 6.

2   Reasoning About Privacy Properties of Architectures

In this section, we provide an overview of the framework introduced in [1] which is the foundation for our work. The interested reader can refer to [1] for a more complete description of the framework.

This framework relies on a dedicated epistemic logic for expressing privacy properties. Epistemic logics are good candidates to express privacy properties since they deal with the notion of knowledge. However, the standard *possible worlds* semantics for these logics lead to a well-known issue called the *logical omniscience problem* [9]. In a nutshell, any agent knows all the logical consequences of his knowledge. To get around this issue, the authors of [1] adopt an approach based on *deductive algorithmic knowledge* [13]. In this context, each component of an architecture is endowed with its own deductive capabilities.

Architectures are described with a dedicated architecture language. Then the semantics of a privacy property is defined as the architectures in which the property holds.

2.1   A Privacy Architecture Language

First of all, the functionality of a system is described by a set $\Omega = \{X = T\}$ of equations over the following term language.

$$T ::= X \mid c \mid F(X_1, \ldots, X_m)$$

A term T might be a variable X ($X \in Var$), a constant c ($c \in Const$) or F a function applied to some variables ($F \in Fun$).

Then the architecture of a system is described by the following architecture language.

$$
\begin{aligned}
A ::= {}& \{R\} \\
R ::= {}& Has_i(X) \mid Receive_{i,j}(\{St\}, \{X\}) \mid Trust_{i,j} \\
& \mid Compute_G(X = T) \quad \mid Verify_i(\{St\})
\end{aligned}
$$

$$
\begin{aligned}
St ::= {}& Pro \mid Att \quad\quad Att ::= Attest_i(\{Eq\}) \\
Pro ::= {}& Proof_i(\{P\}) \quad Eq ::= Pred(T_1, \ldots, T_m) \\
P ::= {}& Att \mid Eq
\end{aligned}
$$

An architecture A is associated to a set of components $\mathcal{C} = \{C_1, \ldots, C_{|\mathcal{C}|}\}$. In the architectural primitives, i and j stand respectively for C_i, C_j and $G \subseteq \mathcal{C}$ denotes a set of components.

In the above syntax, $\{Z\}$ denotes a set of elements of category Z. $Pred$ denotes a predicate, the set of predicates depending on the architectures to be considered. $Has_i(X)$ denotes the fact that component C_i possesses (or is the origin of) the value of X, which may correspond to situations in which X is stored on C_i or C_i is a sensor collecting the value of X. $Receive_{i,j}(\{St\}, \{X\})$ means that C_i can receive the values of variables in $\{X\}$ together with the statements in $\{St\}$ from C_j.

$Attest_i(\{Eq\})$ is the declaration by C_i that the properties in $\{Eq\}$ hold and $Proof_i(\{P\})$ is the delivery by C_i of a set of proofs of properties. $Verify_i$ is the verification by component C_i of the corresponding statements (proof or authenticity). $Compute_G(X = T)$ means that the set of components G can compute the term T and assign its value to X and $Trust_{i,j}$ represents the fact that component C_i trusts component C_j.

Graphical data flow representations can be derived from architectures expressed in this language. For the sake of readability, we use both notations in the next sections.

All architectures are assumed to satisfy minimal consistency assumptions, in order to restrict the analysis to those which make sense. For instance, if a component sends a variable, we assume that this variable can be sent, computed or received by the component.

Events are instantiations of the architectural primitives (trust relations excepted). Traces are sequences of events, defined according to the following trace language.

$$\theta ::= \mathsf{Seq}(\epsilon)$$
$$\epsilon ::= Has_i(X : V) \mid Receive_{i,j}(\{St\}, \{X : V\})$$
$$\mid Compute_G(X = T^\epsilon) \qquad \mid Verify_i(\{St\})$$

$\mathsf{Seq}(\epsilon)$ denotes an ordered sequence of events ϵ. When instantiating a primitive containing a variable X, the notation $X : V$ means that the variable X receives the value V. Let Val be the set of values that the variables can take. T^ϵ is a term where values have been assigned to variables. The set $Val_\perp$ is defined as $Val \cup \{\perp\}$ where $\perp \notin Val$ is a specific symbol used to denote that a variable has not been assigned.

As for architectures, only traces satisfying consistency assumptions are considered. $\langle \rangle$ denotes the empty trace (with no event).

A trace θ of events is said compatible with an architecture A if each event in θ (except the computations) can be obtained by instantiation of an element of A (*Receive, Verify*, etc.). Let $T(A)$ be the set of traces which are compatible with an architecture A.

Each component C_i is associated with a dependence relation Dep_i. For a variable Y and a set $\mathcal{X}$ of variables, $Dep_i(Y, \mathcal{X})$ – equivalently $(Y, \mathcal{X}) \in Dep_i$ – means that the value of Y can be obtained by the component C_i if it gets access to the value of X, for each $X \in \mathcal{X}$.

Each component C_i is also associated with a deductive system, noted $\rhd_i$, allowing it to derive new knowledge. $\rhd_i$ is defined as a relation between equations $\{Eq_1, \ldots, Eq_n\} \rhd_i Eq_0$, where equations over terms are defined according to the following syntax.

$$Eq ::= Pred(T_1, \ldots, T_m) \mid Eq \wedge Eq$$

By a slight abuse of notations, Eq is an overloaded notation of the Eq definition in the language architecture, where conjunctions of equations are also possible.

Finally, the semantics of an architecture is defined from the traces of events. Each component is associated with a state. Each event in a trace of events affects the state of each component involved in the event. The semantics $S(A)$ of an architecture A is defined as the set of states reachable by compatible traces.

2.2   A Privacy Logic

Privacy properties of architectures are expressed with the following language.

$$\phi ::= Has_i(X) \mid Has_i^{none}(X) \mid K_i(Eq) \mid \phi_1 \wedge \phi_2.$$

The knowledge operator K_i represents the knowledge of the component C_i. The formula Has_i represents the fact that C_i can get access to variable X.

The semantics $S(\phi)$ of a property ϕ is defined as the set of architectures where ϕ is satisfied. The fact that a property ϕ is satisfied by a (consistent) architecture A is defined for each property as follows.

- A satisfies $Has_i(X)$ if there is a reachable state of C_i in which X is not undefined.
- A satisfies $Has_i^{none}(X)$ if no compatible trace leads to a state in which C_i assigns a value to X.
- A satisfies $K_i(Eq)$ if from all reachable states C_i can deduce Eq.
- A satisfies $\phi_1 \wedge \phi_2$ if A satisfies ϕ_1 and A satisfies ϕ_2.

Based on the semantics of properties, [1] introduces a set of deductive rules which can be used to reason about privacy properties of architectures. This deductive system is shown correct and complete with respect to the semantics of the properties.

$A \vdash \phi$ denotes that ϕ can be derived from A – in other words, that there exists a derivation tree such that each step belongs to the axiomatics and the leaf is $A \vdash \phi$. A subset of this axiomatics, useful for this paper, is presented in Fig. (1a).

3   Adding a Group Attestation to the Formal Model

As a first step to extend the architecture language of [1], we introduce the primitive $Attest_G(E)$ where G is a group of components and E a set of equations. This primitive generalizes $Attest_i(E)$ which involves a single component C_i. Section 3.1 defines the semantics of the traces containing these events and Sect. 3.2 extends the set of deductive rules.

3.1   Semantics of Traces

The semantics of a trace is defined by specifying, for each event, its effect on the states of the components.

The state of a component is either the *Error* state or a pair consisting of: (i) a variable state assigning values to variables, and (ii) a property state defining the current knowledge of a component. In the initial state of an architecture A, denoted $Init^A = \langle Init_1^A, \ldots, Init_{|C|}^A \rangle$, the variables are undefined and the knowledge state only contains the trust primitives.

Let σ denote the global state, and σ_i denote the state of component i. The semantics of traces, denoted S_T, is defined recursively over sequences of events.

$$S_T(\langle \rangle, \sigma) = \sigma$$
$$S_T(\epsilon \cdot \theta, \sigma) = S_T(\theta, S_E(\epsilon, \sigma)).$$

$$H1 \frac{Has_i(X) \in A}{A \vdash Has_i(X)} \qquad H2 \frac{Receive_{i,j}(S, E) \in A \qquad X \in E}{A \vdash Has_i(X)}$$

$$H3 \frac{Compute_G(X = T) \in A \qquad C_i \in G}{A \vdash Has_i(X)} \qquad I\wedge \frac{A \vdash \phi_1 \qquad A \vdash \phi_2}{A \vdash \phi_1 \wedge \phi_2}$$

$$H4 \frac{Dep_i(Y, \mathcal{X}) \qquad \forall X \in \mathcal{X}: A \vdash Has_i(X)}{A \vdash Has_i(Y)} \qquad HN \frac{A \nvdash Has_i(X)}{A \vdash Has_i^{none}(X)}$$

$$K1 \frac{Compute_G(X = T) \in A \qquad C_i \in G}{A \vdash K_i(X = T)} \qquad K\wedge \frac{A \vdash K_i(Eq_1) \qquad A \vdash K_i(Eq_2)}{A \vdash K_i(Eq_1 \wedge Eq_2)}$$

$$K3 \frac{Verify_i(Proof_j(E)) \in A \qquad Eq \in E}{A \vdash K_i(Eq)}$$

$$K\triangleright \frac{E \triangleright_i Eq_0 \qquad \forall Eq \in E: A \vdash K_i(Eq)}{A \vdash K_i(Eq_0)}$$

(a) Subset of the axiomatics of [1]

$$K4^+ \frac{\begin{array}{cc} Verify_i(Proof_j(E)) \in A & \forall k \in G : Trust_{i,k} \in A \\ Attest_G(E') \in E & Eq \in E' \end{array}}{A \vdash K_i(Eq)}$$

$$K5^+ \frac{Verify_i(Attest_G(E)) \in A \qquad \forall k \in G : Trust_{i,k} \in A \qquad Eq \in E}{A \vdash K_i(Eq)}$$

(b) Our extended axioms

Fig. 1. Axiomatics

The function S_E, which defines the effect of the events, is defined for each type of event. The modification of a state is noted $\sigma[\sigma_i/(v, pk)]$ the variable and knowledge states of C_i being replaced by v and pk respectively. $\sigma[\sigma_i/Error]$ denotes that the *Error* state is reached for component C_i. A component reaching an *Error* state is no longer involved in any action.

Restricting our attention to the events which contains a group attestation leads us to consider the events $Verify_i(Attest_G(E))$ and $Verify_i(Proof_j(E))$. The semantics of the verification events are defined according to the (implicit) semantics of the underlying verification procedures. In both cases, the knowledge state of the component is updated if the verification passes, otherwise the component reaches an *Error* state. The variable state is not affected. Informally, a verification event containing a generalized attestation statement generates new knowledge only if all possible authors of the attestation are trusted by the verifying component C_i.

$$S_E(Verify_i(Proof_j(E)), \sigma) = \begin{cases} \sigma[\sigma_i/Error] & \text{if the proof is not valid,} \\ \sigma[\sigma_i/(\sigma_i^v, \sigma_i^{pk} \cup new_{Proof}^{pk})] & \text{otherwise,} \end{cases}$$

$$S_E(Verify_i(Attest_G(E)), \sigma) = \begin{cases} \sigma[\sigma_i/Error] & \text{if the attestation is not valid,} \\ \sigma[\sigma_i/(\sigma_i^v, \sigma_i^{pk} \cup new_{Attest}^{pk})] & \text{otherwise,} \end{cases}$$

where the new knowledge new_{Proof}^{pk} is defined as:

$$new_{Proof}^{pk} := \{Eq \mid Eq \in E \ \lor \ (\exists G \subseteq C : (Attest_G(E') \in E \ \land \ Eq \in E'$$
$$\land \ \forall k \in G : Trust_{i,k} \in \sigma_i^{pk}))\}; \quad (1)$$

and the new knowledge new_{Attest}^{pk} is defined as:

$$new_{Attest}^{pk} := \{Eq \mid Eq \in E \ \land \ \forall k \in G : Trust_{i,k} \in \sigma_i^{pk}\}. \quad (2)$$

3.2 Axiomatics

The next challenge to deal with group attestation is the extension of the set of deductive rules and the proof of the correctness and completeness properties still hold. Our axioms for group attestation are presented in Fig. (1b). In the remaining of this section, we show that the correctness and the completeness of the axiomatics still hold with these new axioms.

Correctness. Let A be a consistent architecture and ϕ a property. The correctness theorem states that if there exists a derivation tree for this property ($A \vdash \phi$), then this property holds in the architecture ($A \in S(\phi)$).

The proof is made by induction on the depth of the tree $A \vdash \phi$. Let us restrict our attention to the cases where (K4$^+$) and (K5$^+$) are used. That is, let us assume that $A \vdash K_i(Eq)$, and that the derivation tree is of depth 1. By definition of the set of axioms, such a proof is obtained by application of (K1), (K3), (K4$^+$) or (K5$^+$). Let us focus on the K4$^+$ and K5$^+$ cases.

K4$^+$. Let us assume that $Verify_i(Proof_j(E)) \in A$, $Attest_G(E') \in E$ and $\forall k \in G: Trust_{i,k} \in A$ for some i, j and G. Our goal is to prove that $\forall Eq \in E'$: $A \in S(K_i(Eq))$.

Let us consider a given state $\sigma' \in S_i(A)$. By the architecture semantics, there exists a consistent trace θ', compatible with A, such that $\sigma' = S_T(\theta', Init^A)$. Two cases may happen. Either θ' contains an event $Verify_i(Proof_j(E))$ such that $Attest_G(E') \in E$, and we let $\theta := \theta'$, or it is not. In the latter case, we extend θ' into a trace θ such that θ contains such an event without breaking the consistency of the trace.

In either cases, there exists a trace θ which extends θ' and contains an event $Verify_i(Proof_j(E))$ such that $Attest_G(E') \in E$. Let $\sigma = S_T(\theta, Init^A)$. Since an $Error$ state has not been reached (we have $\sigma' \in S_i(A)$), and since $\forall k \in G$: $Trust_{i,k} \in \sigma_i^{pk}$ by definition of the initial state, then by the semantics of the group attestation (Eq. (1)) we have $\forall Eq \in E: Eq \in \sigma_i^{pk}$.

By the definition of the architectures semantics, we deduce that $\sigma \in S(A)$. The prefix order over the traces together with the definition of the semantics of the trace induce a prefix order over the states, hence $\sigma \geq_i \sigma'$. By the reflexivity of the deductive algorithmic knowledge, we have $\forall Eq \in E': \sigma_i^{pk} \triangleright_i Eq$. By the semantics of the properties, we conclude that $\forall Eq \in E': A \in S(K_i(Eq))$.

K5$^+$. Let us assume that $Verify_i(Attest_G(E)) \in A$ and $\forall k \in G: Trust_{i,k} \in A$. We must show that $\forall Eq \in E: A \in S(K_i(Eq))$. Adaptation of the K4$^+$ to the K5$^+$ case is straightforward, invoking Eq. (2) of the trace semantics instead of Eq. (1).

Completeness. Let A be a consistent architecture and ϕ a property. The completeness theorem states that if the property holds in the architecture ($A \in S(\phi)$), then there exists a derivation tree for this property ($A \vdash \phi$).

The proof is made by induction over the definition of the property ϕ. We restrict our attention here to the knowledge operator K_i. Let us assume that $A \in S(K_i(Eq))$ for a given component C_i and equation Eq. We must show that $A \vdash K_i(Eq)$.

By the semantics of properties, $A \in S(K_i(Eq))$ means that $\forall \sigma' \in S_i(A)$: $\exists \sigma \in S_i(A): \sigma_i^{pk} \triangleright_i Eq$. By the semantics of architectures, $\exists \theta \in T(A)$ such that $(\sigma = S_T(\theta, Init^A)$ and $\sigma_i^{pk} \triangleright_i Eq)$. By the semantics of the traces, this implies one among the following statements: either there exists $Compute_G(X = T^\epsilon) \in \theta$ where $Eq := (X = T)$ and $C_i \in G$ and T^ϵ is obtained from T (by assigning values to variables); or there exists $Verify_i(Proof_j(E)) \in \theta$ where $Eq \in E$; or there exists $Verify_i(Proof_j(E)) \in \theta$ where $Attest_G(E') \in E$, $Eq \in E'$ and $\forall k \in G: Trust_{i,k} \in \sigma_i^{pk}$ and $Eq \in E'$; or there exists $Verify_i(Attest_G(E)) \in \theta$, $Eq \in E$ and $\forall k \in G: Trust_{i,k} \in \sigma_i^{pk}$.

By the compatibility of the traces, we deduce that: either $Compute_G(X) \in A$ where $Eq := (X = T)$ and $C_i \in G$; or $Verify_i(Proof_j(E)) \in A$ where $Eq \in E$; or $Verify_i(Proof_j(E)) \in A$ where $Attest_G(E') \in E$, $Eq \in E'$ and $\forall k \in G$: $Trust_{i,k} \in A$ and $Eq \in E'$; or $Verify_i(Attest_G(E)) \in A$, $Eq \in E'$ and $\forall k \in G$: $Trust_{i,k} \in A$. We conclude that $A \vdash K_i(Eq)$ by applying (respectively) (K1), (K3), (K4$^+$) or (K5$^+$).

4   Modelling a Biometric Architecture Supporting Group Authentication

4.1   A Biometric Architecture Using Group Signatures

Biometric systems involve two main phases: enrolment and verification (either authentication or identification) [10]. Enrolment is the registration phase, in which the biometric traits of a person are collected and recorded within the system. In the *authentication* mode, a fresh biometric trait is collected and compared with the registered one by the system to check that it corresponds to the claimed identity. In the *identification* mode, a fresh biometric data is collected and the corresponding identity is searched in a database of enrolled biometric references.

A group signature scheme [2] is an advanced cryptographic mechanism. It enables a user to sign messages on behalf of a group of users while staying anonymous inside this group. With a (public) verification algorithm, anyone can be convinced, given a group public key, a message, and a signature, that *a certain* member of the group authenticates the message.

The biometric system introduced in [4] aims at achieving some anonymity from the server's point of view. The server is convinced that the authentication was successful for a certain enrolled user, but has no information about which among them. During the enrolment, a biometric reference is registered by the issuer. The issuer derives a user secret key from the biometric template and computes a group secret key, that is, a certificate attesting the enrolment inside the group. The user gets a card containing its biometric reference and the group certificate.

During the verification phase, the terminal gets a fresh capture of the biometric trait and computes a fresh template. A match between the fresh template and the reference is performed by the terminal. In case of success, the terminal derives the user secret key from the reference, produces a group signature thanks to the user secret key and the certificate (both are needed to produce a valid signature), and sends the signature to the server. The server checks the signature attesting that a registered user authenticates. If the signature is valid, the server is convinced of the correctness of the matching. However, it has no access to the biometric templates, neither to the identity of the user who authenticates.

4.2   Description Within the Formal Framework

For the sake of clarity, let us distinguish the biometric system and its formalization. We denote by B_{gs} the biometric system introduced in [4] and A_{gs} its definition within the formal framework, which we present below.

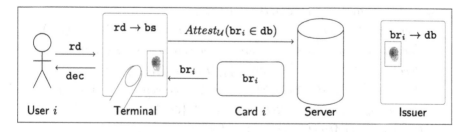

Fig. 2. High-level view of the biometric system architecture using group signatures

Upper case sans serif letters in A_{gs} denote components. Components of the A_{gs} architecture are a set of N enrolled users $\mathcal{U} := \{U_1, \ldots, U_N\}$ (each user U_i owning a card C_i), a server S, an issuer I and a terminal modelled by two components TM and TS. The issuer I enrols the users. The server S manages a database containing the enrolled templates. The terminal is equipped with a sensor used to acquire biometric traits. Formally, the terminal is split into two components TM and TS, corresponding respectively to its two functionalities. The matcher TM, acquires the fresh template and performs the comparison, and the signer TS authenticates on behalf of the group of users. As shown by the variants below, this distinction is motivated by the different trust assumptions a designer may consider.

Type letters denote variables. br_i denotes the biometric reference template of the user U_i built during the enrolment phase. rd denotes a raw biometric data provided by the user during the verification phase. bs denotes a fresh template derived from rd during the verification phase. A threshold thr is used during the verification phase as a closeness criterion for the biometric templates. The output dec of the verification is the result of the matching between the fresh template bs and the enrolled templates br, considering the threshold thr. db denotes the database of the registered biometric templates.

As in [3], we focus on the verification phase and assume that enrolment has already been done. The database db is computed by the issuer from all the references, using the function $DB \in Fun$. A verification process is initiated by the terminal receiving as input a raw biometric data rd from the user. The terminal, more precisely the TM component, extracts the fresh biometric template bs from rd using the function $Extract \in Fun$. The matching is expressed by the function $\mu \in Fun$ which takes as arguments two biometric templates and the threshold thr. The terminal reads in the card the biometric template br. The user receives the final decision dec of the matching from the terminal TM. Then the terminal, here the TS component, attests that the fresh template belongs to the set of enrolled templates.

The complete description of A_{gs} within the architecture language is as follows. Figure 2 sketches this description. When indices i are used, it is assumed that the corresponding primitive exists in A_{gs} for all users. For instance $Has_I(br_i) \in A_{gs}$ implicitly means that $\forall U_i \in \mathcal{U}: Has_I(br_i) \in A_{gs}$.

$$
\begin{aligned}
A_{gs} := \big\{ & Has_I(br_i), Has_{U_i}(rd), Has_{TM}(thr), \\
& Compute_I(db = DB(br_1, \ldots, br_N)), Compute_{TM}(bs = Extract(rd)), \\
& Compute_{TM}(dec = \mu(br_i, bs, thr)), Trust_{S,U_i}, Trust_{S,TM}, Trust_{S,TS}, \\
& Receive_{I,U_i}(\{Attest_{U_i}(br_i \in db)\}, \{\}), Receive_{TM,U_i}(\{\}, \{rd\}), \\
& Receive_{C_i,I}(\{Attest_{U_i}(br_i \in db)\}, \{br_i\}), Receive_{U_i,TM}(\{\}, \{dec\}), \\
& Receive_{TM,C_i}(\{\}, \{br_i\}), Receive_{TS,TM}(\{\}, \{dec\}), \\
& Receive_{TS,C_i}(\{Attest_{U_i}(br_i \in db)\}, \{br_i\}), \\
& Receive_{S,TS}(\{Attest_{\mathcal{U}}(br_i \in db)\}, \{\}), Verify_S(\{Attest_{\mathcal{U}}(br_i \in db)\}) \big\}
\end{aligned}
$$

To complete the description of A_{gs}, it remains to define the dependence relations between the variables. The database is computed from all the references: $\forall j \in \mathcal{C}$: (db, {br$_1$, ..., br$_N$}). Conversely, access to db gives access to all br$_i$: $\forall j \in \mathcal{C}, \mathsf{U}_i \in \mathcal{U}$: Dep_j (br$_i$, {db}). Moreover, $\forall j \in \mathcal{C}, \mathsf{U}_i \in \mathcal{U}$: we also have (bs, {rd}), (dec, {br$_i$, bs}), (dec, {br$_i$, rd}) $\in Dep_j$.

4.3 Trusting a Group of Users

In the biometric system architecture A_{gs}, the group of users is trusted by the server, which is denoted $\forall \mathsf{U}_i \in \mathcal{U}$: $Trust_{S,\mathsf{U}_i}$. However, the formalization does not define which cryptographic primitive is used in the concrete B_{gs} system. Let us discuss this point in more detail.

In a group signature scheme, users are typically not trusted, but a group manager, called the issuer, is trusted. When it enrols a user, the issuer provides a group secret key, aka a membership certificate – concretely, a signature of some secret user-specific data. In other words, it *attests* that the user is enrolled. Then the untrusted user *proves* that it is enrolled (by supplying a zero-knowledge proof of her user secret data and the corresponding membership certificate). In our case, the server does not trust the card, but trusts the issuer of the card. The card contains an attestation that the user was indeed enrolled by the issuer, here a certificate for a group signature, *i.e.*, a group secret key.

The point to be noticed is that we do not model its internal machinery in our formal architecture. We only express the fact that the group is trusted. Whether this trust assumption is justified or not in practice is not part of the reasoning about architecture: it rather regards the justification of the choice of certain primitives to achieve the functionality. With the same trust assumption (all users are trusted), other primitives can be used, as ring signatures [14], where a member authenticates on behalf of a group without group manager.

The use of group signatures is a choice made at the protocol level. Checking the conformity between the protocols and the architecture is out of scope of this paper. This line of work has been initiated in [15].

4.4 Application of the Axiomatics

We now reason about the privacy properties of the A_{gs} architecture from the server point's of view. A_{gs} should enable the server to be sure that a certain enrolled user authenticates, but the authenticated user is anonymous from the server's point of view: $A_{gs} \vdash K_S(\text{br}_i \in \text{db})$. But the server should have no access to the templates: $A_{gs} \vdash Has_S^{none}(\text{br}_i)$.

Regarding the template protection, the statement $A_{gs} \vdash Has_S^{none}(\text{br}_i)$ is shown using rule HN. A subtlety here is the presence of the dependence between the biometric template br$_i$ and the database db. Therefore we first need to show $A \nvdash Has_S(\text{db})$.

$$\frac{Has_S(\text{db}) \notin A_{gs} \qquad \nexists T: Computes_S(\text{db} = T) \in A_{gs}}{\nexists \overrightarrow{X}: (\text{db}, \overrightarrow{X}) \in Dep_S \qquad \nexists j, \nexists S, \nexists E: Receives_{S,j}(S,E) \in A_{gs} \wedge \text{db} \in E}{A_{gs} \nvdash Has_S(\text{db})}$$

Now HN can be applied.

$$\dfrac{\begin{array}{c} (\mathsf{br}_i, \{\mathsf{db}\}) \in Dep_S \qquad A_{\mathsf{gs}} \not\vdash Has_S(\mathsf{db}) \\ Has_S(\mathsf{br}_i) \notin A_{\mathsf{gs}} \qquad \not\exists T\colon Computes(\mathsf{br}_i = T) \in A_{\mathsf{gs}} \\ \not\exists j, \not\exists S, \not\exists E\colon Receives_{S,j}(S, E) \in A_{\mathsf{gs}} \wedge \mathsf{br}_i \in E \end{array}}{A_{\mathsf{gs}} \not\vdash Has_S(\mathsf{br}_i)} \; \mathsf{HN}$$

$$\mathsf{HN} \; \dfrac{A_{\mathsf{gs}} \not\vdash Has_S(\mathsf{br}_i)}{A_{\mathsf{gs}} \vdash Has_S^{none}(\mathsf{br}_i)}$$

$A_{\mathsf{gs}} \vdash Has_S^{none}(\mathsf{bs})$ is also shown by an application of HN.

Since the server trusts the users, an application of $\mathsf{K5^+}$ shows that the server is ensured that some enrolled user authenticates.

$$\mathsf{K5^+} \; \dfrac{Verif_S(Attest_{\mathcal{U}}(\mathsf{br}_i \in \mathsf{db})) \in A_{\mathsf{gs}} \qquad \forall \mathsf{U}_i \in \mathcal{U}\colon Trust_{S,\mathsf{U}_i} \in A_{\mathsf{gs}}}{A_{\mathsf{gs}} \vdash K_S(\mathsf{br}_i \in \mathsf{db})}$$

5   Variants

Several variants [4] of the biometric system B_{gs} can be expressed and analyzed in our formal framework.

5.1   Lowering the Trust on the Group Signing Functionality

If the server trusts the matching functionality TM of the terminal but does not trust its signer functionality TS, then the component TS must supply a proof that some user is enrolled. The architecture, denoted $A_{\mathsf{gs}}^{\mathsf{p}}$, becomes:

$$
\begin{aligned}
A_{\mathsf{gs}}^{\mathsf{p}} := A_{\mathsf{gs}} \setminus \; & \{Receives_{S,\mathsf{TS}}(\{Attest_{\mathcal{U}}(\mathsf{br}_i \in \mathsf{db})\}, \{\}), Trust_{S,\mathsf{TS}}, \\
& Verif_{\mathcal{S}}(\{Attest_{\mathcal{U}}(\mathsf{br}_i \in \mathsf{db})\} \\
\cup \; & \{Receives_{S,\mathsf{TS}}(\{Proof_{\mathsf{TS}}(Attest_{\mathcal{U}}(\mathsf{br}_i \in \mathsf{db}))\}, \{\}), \\
& Verif_{\mathcal{S}}(\{Proof_{\mathsf{TS}}(Attest_{\mathcal{U}}(\mathsf{br}_i \in \mathsf{db}))\})\}
\end{aligned}
$$

An application of the new rule $\mathsf{K4^+}$ enable to prove that the server is ensured that some enrolled user authenticates.

$$\mathsf{K4^+} \; \dfrac{Verif_S(Proof_{\mathsf{TS}}(Attest_{\mathcal{U}}(\mathsf{br}_i \in \mathsf{db}))) \in A_{\mathsf{gs}}^{\mathsf{p}} \qquad \forall \mathsf{U}_i \in \mathcal{U}\colon Trust_{S,\mathsf{U}_i} \in A_{\mathsf{gs}}^{\mathsf{p}}}{A_{\mathsf{gs}}^{\mathsf{p}} \vdash K_S(\mathsf{br}_i \in \mathsf{db})}$$

5.2   Combination with Match-On-Card

In the A_{gs} architecture, the card is a plastic card. The biometric reference is just printed on it, together with a group secret key. To enhance the protection of the reference, a smart-card can be used instead of a plastic card, as in the Match-On-Card (MOC) technology [8,11,12]. The card stores the reference template, and the reference never leaves the card. During a verification, the card receives the fresh biometric template, carries out the comparison with its reference, and sends the decision back. The terminal trusts the smart card for the correctness of the matching. This trust is justified by the fact that the card is a tamper-resistant hardware element.

The A_{gs} architecture in which the plastic card is replaced by a smart-card performing a MOC is modelled as follows. In addition to the comparison, the card also computes the group authentication.

$$A_{gs}^{moc} := \{Has_I(br_i), Has_{U_i}(rd), Has_{TM}(thr), Trust_{TM,C_i}, Trust_{S,U_i},$$
$$Compute_I(db = DB(br_1, \ldots, br_N)), Compute_{TM}(bs = Extract(rd)),$$
$$Compute_{C_i}(dec = \mu(br_i, bs, thr)), Receive_{I,U_i}(\{Attest_{U_i}(br_i \in db)\}, \{\}),$$
$$Receive_{C_i,I}(\{Attest_{U_i}(br_i \in db)\}, \{br_i\}), Receive_{TM,U_i}(\{\}, \{rd\}),$$
$$Receive_{TM,C_i}(\{Attest_{C_i}(dec = \mu(br_i, bs, thr)), Attest_{\mathcal{U}}(br_i \in db)\}, \{dec\}),$$
$$Receive_{C_i,TM}(\{\}, \{bs\}), Receive_{U_i,TM}(\{\}, \{dec\}),$$
$$Receive_{S,TM}(\{Attest_{\mathcal{U}}(br_i \in db)\}, \{\}), Verify_S(\{Attest_{\mathcal{U}}(br_i \in db)\}),$$
$$Verify_{TM}(\{Attest_{C_i}(dec = \mu(br_i, bs, thr))\})\}$$

Using rule HN, it is easy to show that no component apart from I and C_i gets access to br_i.

The terminal should be convinced that the matching is correct: $A_{gs}^{moc} \vdash K_{TM}(dec = \mu(br_i, bs, thr))$. The proof relies on the trust placed by the server in the matching component TM of the terminal.

$$K5^+ \frac{Verify_{TM}(Attest_{C_i}(dec = \mu(br_i, bs, thr))) \in A_{gs}^{moc} \qquad Trust_{TM,C_i} \in A_{gs}^{moc}}{A_{gs}^{moc} \vdash K_{TM}(dec = \mu(br_i, bs, thr))}$$

Regarding the group authentication, an application of $K5^+$ shows that the server is ensured that some enrolled user authenticates.

5.3 Anonymity Revocation

As shown in [4], an additional mechanism can be used to revoke the anonymity of a group authentication if there is any legal need to do so. After the matching phase, the terminal has to encrypt the fresh template under the public key of a specific tracing authority, to sign all messages together, and to send the authentication result to the server. Then, at a later stage, the tracing authority may decrypt the template and check, with an access to the database of the issuer, that the templates were indeed close. This *a posteriori* check ensures a form of accountability which can be requested in certain contexts.

The formal model introduced in [1] includes an additional architectural primitive, called SpotCheck, which can be used to carry out *a posteriori* checks and therefore to describe the above variant. However, the model including the

SpotCheck primitive is proven complete only when all the functions of the term language are at most unary. Since the comparison between templates, an essential operation of biometric systems, is inherently binary, we would then obtain a correct but incomplete system.

We leave for future work the definition of a formal model with *a posteriori* verifications which would be both correct and complete and would not suffer this arity restriction in the term language.

6   Conclusion

In this paper, we have analysed the privacy properties of a biometric system in which users can remain anonymous from the point of view of a remote server, while the server is still convinced that a valid user authenticates. Table 1 sums up the properties of the different architectures considered here. Architecture A_{gs}^{moc} provides the best guarantees in terms of privacy. However, its deployment has a cost, since it requires that each user owns a card with powerful capabilities. Although quite demanding, these assumptions are not out of reach of the current technology [5]. The main variant A_{gs} is more realistic. The choice between A_{gs} and A_{gs}^p depends on the trust placed on each component in a specific deployment. The possibility to express these trust assumptions in a formal way and to study their consequences is one of the main benefits of the framework presented here because it provides rigorous justifications to make well-informed design choices for the architecture of a system.

Table 1. Comparison between architectures

Arch.	Template protection		Trust relations
	Components accessing the reference br_i	Components accessing the query bs	
A_{gs}	I, C, TM, TS	TM	(S, U_i), (S, TS)
A_{gs}^p	I, C, TM, TS	TM	(S, U_i)
A_{gs}^{moc}	I, C	TM, C	(S, U_i), (TM, C_i)

Components are: users U_i, terminal components TM and TS, server S, card C, issuer I. A trust relation (i, j) means that component i trusts component j.

Acknowledgment. This work has been partially funded by the French ANR-12-INSE-0013 project BIOPRIV. Part of this work has been conducted within the Inria Project Lab on Privacy CAPPRIS [6].

References

1. Antignac, T., Le Métayer, D.: Privacy architectures: reasoning about data minimisation and integrity. In: Mauw, S., Jensen, C.D. (eds.) STM 2014. LNCS, vol. 8743, pp. 17–32. Springer, Heidelberg (2014)

2. Boneh, D., Shacham, H.: Group signatures with verifier-local revocation. In: ACM Conference on Computer and Communications Security, CCS 2004, pp. 168–177. ACM Press (2004)
3. Bringer, J., Chabanne, H., Le Métayer, D., Lescuyer, R.: Privacy by design in practice: reasoning about privacy properties of biometric system architectures. In: Bjørner, N., Boer, F. (eds.) FM 2015. LNCS, vol. 9109, pp. 90–107. Springer, Heidelberg (2015)
4. Bringer, J., Chabanne, H., Pointcheval, D., Zimmer, S.: An application of the Boneh and Shacham group signature scheme to biometric authentication. In: Matsuura, K., Fujisaki, E. (eds.) IWSEC 2008. LNCS, vol. 5312, pp. 219–230. Springer, Heidelberg (2008)
5. Canard, S., Girault, M.: Implementing group signature schemes with smart cards. In: Smart Card Research and Advanced Application, CARDIS 2002, pp. 1–10. USENIX (2002)
6. CAPPRIS. Collaborative Project on the Protection of Privacy Rights in the Information Society. Inria Project Lab on Privacy. https://cappris.inria.fr/
7. European Parliament. European Parliament legislative resolution of 12 March 2014 on the proposal for a regulation of the European Parliament, of the Council on the protection of individuals with regard to the processing of personal data, on the free movement of such data. General Data Protection Regulation, Ordinary legislative procedure: first reading (2014)
8. Govan, M., Buggy, T.: Acomputationally efficient fingerprint matching algorithm for implementation on smartcards. In: Biometrics: Theory, Applications, and Systems, BTAS 2007, pp. 1–6. IEEE (2007)
9. Halpern, J.Y., Pucella, R.: Dealing with logical omniscience. In: Conference on Theoretical Aspects of Rationality and Knowledge, TARK 2007, pp. 169–176 (2007)
10. Jain, A.K., Ross, A., Prabhakar, S.: An introduction to biometric recognition. IEEE Trans. Circuits Syst. Video Techn. 14(1), 4–20 (2004)
11. National Institute of Standards and Technology (NIST). MINEXII - an assessment of Match-On-Card technology (2011). http://www.nist.gov/itl/iad/ig/minexii.cfm
12. International Standard Organization. International standard iso/iec 24787 information technology - identification cards - on-card biometric comparison (2010)
13. Pucella, R.: Deductive algorithmic knowledge. J. Log. Comput. 16(2), 287–309 (2006)
14. Rivest, R.L., Shamir, A., Tauman, Y.: How to leak a secret. In: Boyd, C. (ed.) ASIACRYPT 2001. LNCS, vol. 2248, p. 552. Springer, Heidelberg (2001)
15. Ta, V.T., Antignac, T.: Privacy by design: on the conformance between protocols and architectures. In: Cuppens, F., Garcia-Alfaro, J., Zincir Heywood, N., Fong, P.W.L. (eds.) FPS 2014. LNCS, vol. 8930, pp. 65–81. Springer, Heidelberg (2015)
16. TURBINE. TrUsted Revocable Biometric IdeNtitiEs. Collaborative European project 216339 call FP7-ICT-2007-1 (2007). http://cordis.europa.eu/project/rcn/85447_en.html

Trust and Zero-Day Vulnerabilities

Whom You Gonna Trust? A Longitudinal Study on TLS Notary Services

Georg Merzdovnik[1(✉)], Klaus Falb[2], Martin Schmiedecker[1],
Artemios G. Voyiatzis[1,2], and Edgar Weippl[1,2]

[1] SBA Research, Vienna, Austria
{gmerzdovnik,mschmiedecker,avoyiatzis}@sba-research.org
[2] TU Wien, Vienna, Austria

Abstract. TLS is currently the most widely-used protocol on the Internet to facilitate secure communications, in particular secure web browsing. TLS relies on X.509 certificates as a major building block to establish a secure communication channel. Certificate Authorities (CAs) are trusted third parties that validate the TLS certificates and establish trust relationships between communication entities. To counter prevalent attack vectors - like compromised CAs issuing fraudulent certificates and active man-in-the-middle (MitM) attacks - TLS *notary services* were proposed as a solution to verify the legitimacy of certificates using alternative communication channels.

In this paper, we are the first to present a long-term study on the operation of TLS notary services. We evaluated the services using active performance measurements over a timespan of one year and discuss the effectiveness of TLS notary services in practice. Based on our findings, we propose the usage of multiple notary services in conjunction with a semi-trusted centralized proxy approach, so as to protect arbitrarily-sized networks on the network level without the need to install any software on the client machines. Lastly, we identify multiple issues that prevent the widespread use of TLS notary services in practice and propose steps to overcome them.

1 Introduction

Secure communication is a key part of today's Internet applications. The majority of online applications, ranging from e-mail to VPN and browsing the web, rely on SSL and TLS[1] to provide secure communication mechansims such as authenticity, confidentiality, and integrity. TLS 1.2 is, at the time of writing, the most recent version [5], with TLS 1.3 currently in the making. Trust in the TLS ecosystem is distributed over software vendors and an underlying public key infrastructure (PKI) composed of various certificate authorities (CAs). To establish a secure connection, a client verifies the signature of a server's certificate.

---

[1] In this paper we use the term "TLS" to refer to all incarnations of SSL and TLS, if not specified otherwise.

© IFIP International Federation for Information Processing 2016
Published by Springer International Publishing Switzerland 2016. All Rights Reserved
S. Ranise and V. Swarup (Eds.): DBSec 2016, LNCS 9766, pp. 331–346, 2016.
DOI: 10.1007/978-3-319-41483-6_23

If the server's certificate is signed by a trusted certificate authority, the certificate is accepted, otherwise it is rejected. To determine if a CA is to be trusted, the client relies on a so called "trust store", i.e., a list of certificate authorities that it can trust. These trust stores are usually shipped with the application or are included in the operating system. If an attacker gets her hands on one of the private keys of one of these certificate authorities, she is able to issue valid (trusted) certificates for arbitrary-named servers, since the signatures can only be validated against the local trust store. This allows for effective Man-in-the-Middle (MitM) attacks against any kind of targets.

Recent incidents have shown that the subversion of the chain of trust is a viable scenario. Examples include the infamously hacked certificate authorities DigiNotar and Comodo [21], during which their private keys were stolen. Incidents such as the case of Superfish [22] and the Dell eDellroot certificate [31] demonstrate that sometimes even system vendors, like Lenovo or Dell, accidentally introduce vulnerabilities. In these cases, trusted certificate authorities were included in the local trust store of the operating system, which also included the private keys to provide extended functionality, allowing everyone to extract the CA private key and launch unnoticed MitM attacks. For affected users, there is nearly no possibility to distinguish between valid server certificates and those signed by fraudulent CAs, since there are no visible distinction marks and the client's software marks them as trusted.

To solve the problem of multiple valid and trusted certificate chains, several solutions have been proposed recently. These solutions include DANE [15], public key or certificate pinning using HPKP [10], and TLS notary services. The latter are based on the principle of multi-path probing. Figure 1 depicts the usual workflow of such notary services. The idea is to query different "notary" servers if they are presented with the same certificate for a certain communication entity as the client. Therefore, to launch an undetected MitM attack, an attacker would need to intercept as well all the connections to the entity that originate from all the queried notary servers. Since these notary servers are usually spread in different networks around the globe, the risk of an effective, unnoticed MitM attack is highly reduced, even if the certificate is trusted by the local trust store. On the other hand, such a system could reduce the dependability on certificate authorities, since the validation does not have to depend on trusted certificate authorities, but could rely solely on the quorum of a set of notary servers.

DANE is far from being usable in practice as it relies on DNSSEC which is still not widely deployed. Certificate and public key pinning are still supported only by selected applications (e.g., Chrome, Firefox, and some mobile apps [11,27]). On the other hand, TLS notaries are already implemented as browser extensions, thus being usable in practice. However, there is still no complete study on the long-term usage of notary services and how they react to changes in a real-world setting. In this paper we therefore implement a modular system to evaluate notary services in the long term and on a daily basis, independently of the used browsers.

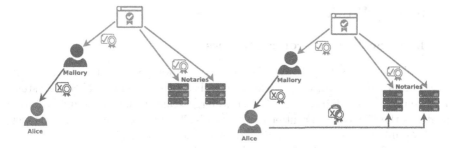

(a) Alice requests a webpage. Mallory intercepts the request and presents a forged certificate.

(b) Alice asks the notaries if they know the certificate.

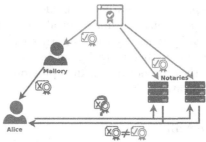

(c) The notaries' responses tell Alice that the certificate is different from what they have seen.

Fig. 1. The usual flow of a request for certificate notary services.

The contributions of this paper are as follows:

- We present a longitudinal study on the effectiveness of three well-known notary services over a one-year period.
- We describe a concept of mapping multiple TLS notaries for transparent end-user protection and an implementation of it as a proxy service.
- We identify problems of combining these services, including lack of widespread adoption and the problem of view inconsistencies.

The rest of the paper is organized as follows: In Sect. 2, we provide the necessary background on TLS and notary services, as well as the related work. In Sect. 3, we describe our concept of a proxy notary. In Sect. 4, we describe our methodology for evaluating the proxy as well as the three TLS notary services independently, whereas our results are described in Sect. 5. We discuss these results in Sect. 6. Finally, Sect. 7 presents the conclusions of this paper and discusses future directions of work.

2   Related Work

2.1   Large-Scale TLS Protocol Studies

The problems with SSL and trusted certificate authorities have been studied for several years, and several large-scale studies that focused on the TLS ecosystem have been conducted lately. One of the first large-scale studies targeting SSL certificates is the Electronic Frontier Foundation's SSL Observatory [9]. Its dataset includes publicly visible SSL certificates available through IPv4.

Holz and Durumeric [7,17] focused on the IPv4-wide analysis of TLS in the context of HTTPS. Mayer et al. [24] and Holz et al. [16] mainly focused on TLS in other application domains, like the e-mail ecosystem. In particular, the recently proposed improvements to port-scanning as well as the open-source release of tools like *zmap* [8] and *masscan* [14] made it easy to collect IPv4-wide information on specific questions. Durumeric et al. also set up a special search engine, Censys [6], which is backed by these Internet-wide scans and allows for deeper analyses. While these studies provide an interesting and valuable view on the TLS ecosystem, they are not designed to provide further information on fraudulently issued certificates.

2.2   TLS Certificate Validation

Several approaches have been proposed in the literature to mitigate the shortcomings of a central point of trust. One method to provide protection against fraudulent certificates is Certificate Pinning which is already distributed in mobile applications [11,27]. However, recent studies showed that many mobile applications incorrectly implement the validation of TLS certificates [11,12]. The Internet Engineering Task Force also proposed the Public Key Pinning Extension for HTTP [10]. This allows a web server to set a special header, which tells the browser to only accept a certain certificate or certificates signed by a specific CA, for the specific server and for a specific amount of time.

Other protection mechanisms have been implemented in the form of browser extensions. Soghoian et al. [29] implemented *Certlock*, an extension that is based on the trust-on-first-use policy to bind the CA to the CommonName of a websites certificate. This method is similar to pinning every certificate on first encounter. Winter et al. [35] provide a system that uses an independent Tor circuit for certificates that issued a browser warning. However, this does not protect against valid but yet malicious certificates. Syverson and Boyce also employ Tor for page verification [30], but they do not rely on probing the same server on the same domain; instead, they host the site again on a .onion address and use this mirror to compare the keys. Holz et al. [18] implemented CrossBear, a system which employs hunter nodes to track down TLS MitM attacks.

TLS certificate notary services can be used to verify a certificate through multiple paths. Wendlandt et al. [34] proposed *Perspectives*, which is based on multiple servers to observe the state of TLS certificates. *Convergence* [23] builds on the same principles as *Perspectives* and provides further methods for trust management. Bates et al. [2] tried to answer the question of what happens if everyone is using the notary service *Convergence*; Fuchs et al. extended the approach of centralized notary servers and implemented *Laribus* [13], a P2P-based approach on notary services. *Laribus* is based on a social graph, which allows users to build notary groups without the need to rely on a central notary server.

3   Methodology and Measurement Setup

To monitor the effectiveness and behavior of different notary services, we set up an automated crawling environment. Figure 2 gives an overview of the overall design.

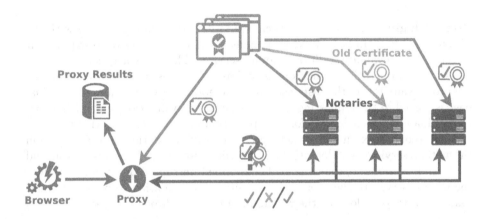

Fig. 2. Overview of our measurement setup.

We implemented the proxy in `mitmproxy` [4], which allowed us to validate certificates through several extension modules. These extension modules implement interfaces to various notary services, which will be described in Sect. 3.2. We used this system to collect daily statistics of these implemented extension modules over a one-year period.

3.1   Data Collection System

The data collection system was implemented in such a way that it is extensible, reusable and can furthermore be used by the end users to evaluate their own browsing session. Therefore the overall data collection consists of three components: (1) a web browser, (2) an intercepting proxy to monitor HTTPS sessions, and (3) proxy plugins to query various notary services.

Browser. To query the different webpages, we utilized `wget` with the proxy settings pointing to our intercepting proxy. While we used a lightweight, GUI-less browser for our periodic scans, any other full-blown browser could be used as well. This makes the validation proxy described in the next paragraph easier to deploy in combination with other systems. End users can use the proxy to secure or evaluate TLS certificates against various notary services without the need to install separate plugins in their browsers.

Intercepting Proxy. To conduct the certificate validation, we implemented an HTTP/HTTPS proxy server in Python 2 using the `mitmproxy` [4] library as a basis. The proxy server acts as an intermediary between the client and the web server. For each encountered HTTPS certificate, the proxy server conducts the certificate validation using the configured notary services.

Proxy Plugins. To make the system extensible, the communication with the notary services is implemented as plugins. This makes it easy to extend our system so as to evaluate additional notary services. The proxy in general supports two modes of operation: synchronous and asynchronous. In synchronous mode, the proxy waits for all the responses from the notary services before the original page is passed to the requesting browser. In case of a validation error, this allows to terminate the page load before the page content is rendered to the user.

The second proxy mode asynchronously collects validation information from the notary services and logs them in the file system for later inspection and analysis. In this mode, the page load cannot be interrupted or terminated, since the page is served to the user without waiting for validation responses. For the evaluation, we only look at the results from the asynchronous mode.

3.2   Notary Services

At the time of our initial analysis of the notary services ecosystem, we identified three services that were in use and also had an active and open infrastructure, namely Perspectives, Convergence, and ICSI. We give a short introduction to the inner workings of these systems in the next paragraphs.

Perspectives. [3] pioneered the *multi-path probing* approach: The system employs multiple independent servers, called *notaries*, which observe publicly-visible web servers and store data about their certificates. When a client contacts a server using TLS, it queries a number of notaries. The notaries reply with information about which certificate the server in question was using in which time period. Using this information, the client can make a more informed trust decision: Do the notaries see the same certificate as the client?

Convergence. [32] was developed by Moxie Marlinspike and builds on the same design principles as Perspectives, but it incorporates other ideas and principles as well. Its central idea is "trust agility", i.e., the users themselves can choose whom to trust and may also revoke their trust. Similarly to Perspectives, Convergence relies on notaries to decide if a certificate is trustworthy or not. However, the decision process is somewhat different. Using a REST web service API, the client sends a request containing the host, port number, and certificate hash to each notary it wishes to query. The server sends one out of five different types of responses, which can be distinguished by the HTTP status code. The possible responses are:

- The notary could verify the certificate.
- The notary could not verify the certificate.
- The notary cannot decide whether to accept or reject the certificate; the client should ignore this notary in its trust decision.
- The client sent a malformed request.
- The server could not perform the request due to an internal error.

This approach makes the implementation of a client rather simple, because the client just has to count the votes collected from the notaries. The protocol is described in more detail in [33]. The user can decide whether decisions are based on majority voting or if an unanimous vote is mandatory in order to accept a certificate.

ICSI Certificate Notary. [19] is a service from the University of Berkeley that monitors certificates. In contrast to the two aforementioned services, the ICSI Certificate Notary passively monitors traffic from multiple Internet sites and builds a database of certificates seen in this traffic.

The database can be queried by clients by issuing a DNS query containing the hash of the certificate. The service responds to the client whether it has observed that certificate in the past, and if it could trace this certificate to a valid root certificate through one of the following responses:

1. ICSI has seen this certificate:
   (a) ICSI can establish a chain of trust to a certificate from the Mozilla root store → ICSI replies 127.0.0.2 to the request.
   (b) ICSI cannot establish a chain of trust → ICSI replies 127.0.0.1
2. ICSI has not seen this certificate or an error (such as a time-out) has occurred → no reply

Note that it is not possible to distinguish between the cases *"a query timed out"* and *"ICSI has not seen this certificate"*, therefore our proxy plugin rejects the certificate in both cases.

4 Data Collection

Our data collection involves periodic TLS certificate validation requests to the set of analyzed notary instances for 1,000 web pages. The scans were conducted daily, and each scan involved queries to the three different notary services for each of the encountered certificates. We conducted the evaluation of the validation proxy in two steps: First, we collected a sample set of pages served through HTTPS. Secondly, we conducted daily scans to validate the corresponding TLS certificates against different notary services and analyzed their responses.

4.1   Sample Selection

To select samples, we initially obtained the list of Alexa Top 1,000,000 sites [1] on November 29, 2013. From this list, we then selected the top 1,000 sites that responded to an HTTPS query within 30 s. This selection represents the websites that attract most of the visits by users, including pages such as Facebook, Twitter, and Google. Many of the selected websites did respond to HTTPS queries, but with an immediate redirection to a (non-secure) HTTP connection. This means that while they do support HTTPS, many users will probably not use it. However, we still included these sites in the evaluation under the assumption that HTTPS is likely to be used in some parts of the website, like the login pages.

4.2   Periodic Scan

Between January 31, 2014 and January 29, 2015, for a period of one year, the collection was conducted daily. For each run of the scan, the proxy server was started and the previously selected URLs were queried, with the different notary plugins enabled. The data returned by the proxy plugins as well as the collected certificates were stored for further analysis. To get a baseline for comparison, we also queried the URLs without using a proxy server. Thus, in one evaluation run, each site from our data set was queried for a total of four times.

For each pair of URL and validation method, the following measurements were taken:

Verdict: Whether the validation method *accepted* or *rejected* the site's X.509 certificate.

Reason: The reason why a certificate was rejected, if it had been rejected. This metric is specific to each validation method.

Validation Time: The entire time the validation process of a certificate took, including querying the notary server(s) and waiting for a response.

5   Results

In the following, we describe our results and findings from the collected dataset. For each notary service, we analyzed how long it took to answer a validation request and also how long it took to react to certificate changes. Furthermore, we studied the availability of these services over the course of one year.

5.1   Certificate Changes

To analyse the functionality of notary services, it is important to observe actual certificate changes. Figure 3 depicts the number of different certificates per website we encountered during the course of our study. In 80 % of the cases, the websites changed at least once their certificate; some 10 % of them changed more than 9 times their certificate within the one year that our study was active.

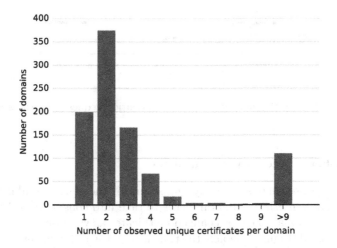

Fig. 3. Number of different certificates observed for each tracked domain

5.2   Validation Time

An important factor concerning notary services from a usability point of view is their response time to validation requests. Therefore, we conducted an analysis of the response time of the various services. With the 1,000 webpages crawled daily for one year, we collected in total more than 350,000 response timing samples per analyzed notary service. Figure 4 summarizes the timing information for the three notary services.

The DNS-based approach of ICSI yields the fastest responses to queries, with the majority (95 %) of answers received in under one second. While about half of the responses for Convergence and Perspectives are also below this mark, response times for these two services have a far higher fluctuation. This can be an issue in the case where the notary services are used to validate certificates before a page is loaded, as it could introduce noticeable page load delays for the users. We note that Convergence usually employs a client cache for fingerprints, in an effort to improve the loading times. We did not implement this caching in our proxy so as to get a comparison of the notary service based on newly-encountered pages.

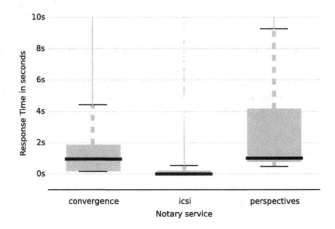

Fig. 4. Response times of notary services to validation requests. Outliers are cut off at 10 s.

5.3 Certificate Acceptance Duration

While the response time is certainly important for the general usability in day-to-day browsing, another temporal factor to take into consideration is the time a notary needs to mark new or changed certificates as valid once they are introduced or updated. Figure 5 depicts the time it took the different services to mark a new certificate as valid after it was changed on the server. Since we conducted daily crawls at a fixed time, the resolution of our scan is also on a daily basis. Therefore, a value of zero days means that the certificate was changed by a server as well as validated by a service within this 24-h time frame. The validations are set in relation to the total amount of certificate changes that we observed during our scanning period. In the case of Convergence we only considered the server we setup ourselves and did not include the official server results, since the latter only responded in error for the majority of our scans.

As depicted in Fig. 5, it takes less time to Convergence so as to adopt to newly-changed certificates, with the majority of certificates seen as valid within the first 24-h time frame. ICSI is only able to validate about 75 % of changed certificates within the same time frame. This fact could be due to the nature of ICSI, which relies on passive information collection, whereas Convergence actively probes servers itself. The relatively low validation rate of Perspectives (45 %) can most likely be accredited to the fact that more and more of the servers failed; in the end, it was not possible to reach a quorum on the validity of a certain certificate. Therefore, some of the changed certificates could not be validated successfully anymore. However, even with these limitations in mind, we can still see the general trend that it takes a longer time for Perspectives to successfully validate certificates compared to the other two services. It takes one day for Convergence and at most three for ICSI to fully synchronize.

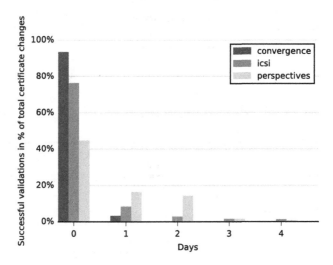

Fig. 5. Time until a newly-seen certificate is marked as validated in percent of the total of observed certificate changes within the period of one year.

5.4 Service Availability

Figure 6 provides an overview on the status of certificate validation of the three notary services during the course of one year. The return state for each of the services is given as a percentage for all the collected service responses. It shows the daily average of responses to the 1,000 page request made by the respective crawler.

ICSI was constantly up and running during our scan. We experienced several problems with both Convergence and Perspectives. The analysis of Convergence was based on two servers. The first one was the official server available at *notary.thoughtcrime.org* and the second one was a server we hosted on an Amazon EC2 instance. The official server became unresponsive in the middle of June 2014.

We encountered a similar problem with Perspectives, where the initially-available servers one after the other shut down or responded in error. As described earlier, the Perspectives validation of certificates operates with a quorum-based approach, in which at least a certain amount of servers must provide a valid response. Due to the fact that more servers answered with an error state, this requirement was no longer met and therefore, from a certain point in time, all certificates were rejected by the system, even if some of the servers still provided a valid response.

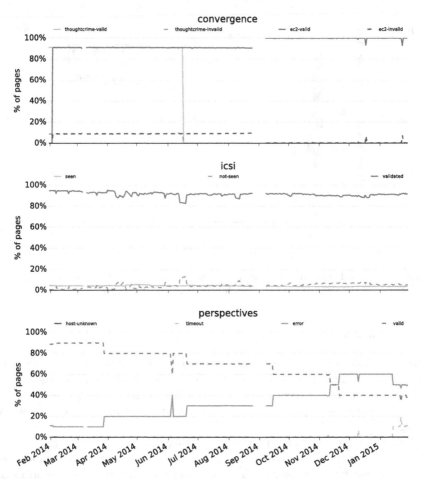

Fig. 6. Timeline of the responses collected from the different services over the course of one year.

6   Discussion

Analyzing notary services on a longitudinal scale reveals several problems and shortcomings that limit the usability of these services. In the following we discuss the observed limitations and possible future directions for the deployment of notary services.

6.1   Response and Validation Times

One problem with notary services is the delay that these services introduce in page requests. As we described in Sect. 3.1, there are two approaches to verify a certificate through a notary: synchronous and asynchronous. Both approaches have positive and negative sides. Since the synchronous method waits for all notary responses before actually requesting the page, it can introduce a significant delay (as shown in Sect. 5.2) in page loading, especially if a notary server times out. On the other hand, the asynchronous method loads the page before it receives all notary responses, therefore leaving a window of exposure before notifying the user that something went wrong.

Another problem is the reaction to legitimate certificate changes, namely how long it takes until a service marks a newly seen certificate as valid. Our study shows that it can take up to several days until a certificate is considered as valid. Until the new certificate is validated and has been seen by all the notary services, it will appear as a MitM attack.

6.2   Adoption and Continuous Operation

For a notary service (or multi-path probing in general) to be useful for actually validating certificates, there are two important factors that need to be met: (i) Services need to be adopted by the users. This means that users have to run their own servers which others can query. For example, if there is only one official server you can query, this defeats the whole concept. (ii) It implies that one has to fully trust this service, which introduces a single point of failure. A single server could just provide wrong answers to the client's queries without a possibility to check these claims, which would be similar to a device-hosted trust store. On the other hand, even if users set up their own servers, the question is how long they can keep them up and running for other clients to use. Therefore, an important factor to consider is that the amount of available servers could fluctuate. The clients need to be informed of failing servers, since this influences the weight of still-running services in the case of majority voting.

Currently it seems that the adoption of these services by users is low. At the time of the writing, the Firefox Add-on for Perspectives has 5,334 users [28] and the plugin for Convergence only 77 users [25]. During our study some of the official servers seem to be discontinued, which does not help to increase the trust in this system. What our insights show is that either the incentive for the users to host their own notary services has to be increased or the system itself has to be adapted. One possible adaption is presented by tofu [20], proposing a P2P-based system in which every client is automatically also a host. While this system may be able to solve the problem of service availability, it could still impose further risks that need to be analyzed in the future.

6.3   Privacy

Beside the technical aspects, there are others to be considered. One of them are possible privacy implications. By using a third-party service to validate certificates, it is easy for its server(s) to collect information about the pages a client visited. Therefore it is possible for the server(s) to build a browsing profile of the specific user. One solution to this problem would be for the users to host their own servers. However, this is not always an option and future research should focus on the possibilities to validate certificates without giving away too much information about the client.

While we do not have solutions to these problems (yet), we still believe that notaries are a viable alternative to increase the overall security of TLS. Thus, they should be studied further so as to improve the current limitations.

7   Conclusion

In this work, we presented a longitudinal study on the availability and functionality of different notary services. We conducted daily scans over a period of one year and analyzed the collected data. We explored the ecosystem of notary services and analyzed their behavior on a large scale. To conduct this study, we developed a new proxy-based system to transparently query different notary services for increased protection against MitM attacks and gave an overview on the inner workings of these notary services. Lastly, we discussed the results of our study in the context of the available notary services. We described the problems and pitfalls that can arise by using the existing systems.

Existing notary services have the problem that the initial request for an unknown page can introduce extra latency, since the notary has to query the server for the certificate. With the rise of fast, Internet-wide scanning solutions, there are several projects that analyze the TLS landscape. One of these projects is scans.io [26] which hosts a regularly-collected dataset of TLS certificates. Censys.io [6] provides a search engine over the scans.io datasets. Future research could evaluate the possibilities to use these data sources either as alternative initial data providers to bootstrap notaries or to wrap the data into a separate notary service.

Acknowledgements. This work has been carried out within the scope of "u'smile", the Josef Ressel Center for User-Friendly Secure Mobile Environments, funded by the Christian Doppler Gesellschaft, A1 Telekom Austria AG, Drei-Banken-EDV GmbH, LG Nexera Business Solutions AG, NXP Semiconductors Austria GmbH, and Österreichische Staatsdruckerei GmbH. Additionaly the research was funded by the Austrian Research Promotion Agency (FFG) through the BRIDGE 1 grant P846028 (TLSiP) and the COMET K1 program.

References

1. Alexa. Alexa top domains. http://www.alexa.com/topsites
2. Bates, A., Pletcher, J., Nichols, T., Hollembaek, B., Butler, K.R.: Forced perspectives: evaluating an SSL trust enhancement at scale. In: Proceedings of the Conference on Internet Measurement Conference, IMC 2014, pp. 503–510. ACM, New York (2014)
3. CMU. Perspectives project (2016). http://www.perspectives-project.org/
4. Cortesi, A.: mitmproxy, February 2016. https://mitmproxy.org/
5. Dierks, T., Rescorla, E.: The Transport Layer Security (TLS) Protocol Version 1.2. RFC 5246 (Proposed Standard), August 2008. Updated by RFCs 5746, 5878, 6176

6. Durumeric, Z., Adrian, D., Mirian, A., Bailey, M., Halderman, J.A.: A search engine backed by Internet-wide scanning. In: Proceedings of the 22nd ACM SIGSAC Conference on Computer and Communications Security, pp. 542–553. ACM (2015)
7. Durumeric, Z., Kasten, J., Bailey, M., Halderman, J. A.: Analysis of the HTTPS certificate ecosystem. In: Internet Measurement Conference (2013)
8. Durumeric, Z., Wustrow, E., Halderman, J.A.: ZMap: fast Internet-wide scanning and its security applications. In: Usenix Security, vol. 2013 (2013)
9. Eckersley, P., Burns, J.: An observatory for the SSLiverse. Talk at Defcon 18 (2010)
10. Evans, C., Palmer, C., Sleevi, R.: Public key pinning extension for HTTP (HPKP). RFC 7469 (Draft) (2015)
11. Fahl, S., Harbach, M., Muders, T., Baumgärtner, L., Freisleben, B., Smith, M., Eve, W.: Mallory love Android: an analysis of Android SSL (in) security. In: Proceedings of the ACM Conference on Computer and Communications Security, pp. 50–61. ACM (2012)
12. Fahl, S., Harbach, M., Perl, H., Koetter, M., Smith, M.: Rethinking SSL development in an appified world. In: Proceedings of the ACM SIGSAC Conference on Computer & Communications Security, pp. 49–60. ACM (2013)
13. Fuchs, K.-P., Herrmann, D., Micheloni, A., Federrath, H.: Laribus: privacy-preserving detection of fake SSL certificates with a social P2P notary network. EURASIP J. Inf. Secur. 2015(1), 1–17 (2015)
14. Graham, R.D.: Masscan: Mass IP port scanner (2014). https://github.com/robertdavidgraham/masscan
15. Hoffman, P., Schlyter, J.: The DNS-Based Authentication of Named Entities (DANE) Transport Layer Security (TLS) Protocol: TLSA. RFC 6698 (Proposed Standard), August 2012. Updated by RFC 7218
16. Holz, R., Amann, J., Mehani, O., Wachs, M., Kâafar, M.A.: TLS in the wild: an Internet-wide analysis of TLS-based protocols for electronic communication. CoRR, abs/1511.00341 (2015)
17. Holz, R., Braun, L., Kammenhuber, N., Carle, G.: The SSL landscape: a thorough analysis of the X.509 PKI using active and passive measurements. In: Proceedings of the ACM SIGCOMM Conference on Internet Measurement Conference, pp. 427–444. ACM (2011)
18. Holz, R., Riedmaier, T., Kammenhuber, N., Carle, G.: X.509 forensics: detecting and localising the SSL/TLS men-in-the-middle. In: Foresti, S., Yung, M., Martinelli, F. (eds.) ESORICS 2012. LNCS, vol. 7459, pp. 217–234. Springer, Heidelberg (2012)
19. ICSI. ICSI certificate notary (2016). http://notary.icsi.berkeley.edu/
20. Jones, R.: tofu:// - the web security protocol which should have been, October 2013. https://gun.io/blog/tofu-web-security/
21. Leavitt, N.: Internet security under attack: the undermining of digital certificates. Computer 44(12), 17–20 (2011)
22. Lenovo. Superfish vulnerability, October 2015. https://support.lenovo.com/at/de/product_security/superfish
23. Marlinspike, M.: SSL and the future of authenticity. In: Black Hat USA (2011)
24. Mayer, W., Zauner, A., Schmiedecker, M., Huber, M.: No need for black chambers: testing TLS in the e-mail ecosystem at large. CoRR, abs/1510.08646 (2015)
25. Kazantsev, M.: Convergence extra Firefox Add-on, April 2016. https://addons.mozilla.org/en-US/firefox/addon/convergence-extra
26. U. of Michigan. Scans.io - Internet-Wide scan data repository, February 2016. https://scans.io/

27. Oltrogge, M., Acar, Y., Dechand, S., Smith, M., Fahl, S.: To pin or not to pin–helping app. developers bullet proof their TLS connections. In: 24th USENIX Security Symposium (USENIX Security 2015), pp. 239–254 (2015)

28. Schaefer, D.: Perspectives Firefox Add-on, April 2016. https://addons.mozilla.org/en-US/firefox/addon/perspectives/

29. Soghoian, C., Stamm, S.: Certified lies: detecting and defeating government interception attacks against SSL (Short Paper). In: Danezis, G. (ed.) FC 2011. LNCS, vol. 7035, pp. 250–259. Springer, Heidelberg (2012)

30. Syverson, P., Boyce, G.: Genuine onion: Simple, fast, flexible, and cheap website authentication. In: Proceedings of the 9th Workshop on Web 2.0 Security and Privacy (W2SP) (2015)

31. Thomas, L. P.: Response to concerns regarding eDellroot certificate (2015). http://en.community.dell.com/dell-blogs/direct2dell/b/direct2dell/archive/2015/11/23/response-to-concerns-regarding-edellroot-certificate

32. Thoughtcrime Labs. Convergence (2016). http://www.convergence.io/

33. Thoughtcrime Labs. Convergence notary protocol (2016). https://github.com/moxie0/Convergence/wiki/Notary-Protocol

34. Wendlandt, D., Andersen, D.G., Perrig, A.: Perspectives: Improving SSH-style host authentication with multi-path probing. In: USENIX Annual Technical Conference on Annual Technical Conference, ATC 2008, pp. 321–334. USENIX Association, Berkeley (2008)

35. Winter, P., Köwer, R., Mulazzani, M., Huber, M., Schrittwieser, S., Lindskog, S., Weippl, E.: Spoiled onions: exposing malicious tor exit relays. In: De Cristofaro, E., Murdoch, S.J. (eds.) PETS 2014. LNCS, vol. 8555, pp. 304–331. Springer, Heidelberg (2014)

Runtime Detection of Zero-Day Vulnerability Exploits in Contemporary Software Systems

Olgierd Pieczul[1,2(✉)] and Simon N. Foley[2]

[1] Ireland Lab, IBM, Dublin, Ireland
olgierdp@ie.ibm.com
[2] Department of Computer Science, University College Cork, Cork, Ireland
s.foley@cs.ucc.ie

Abstract. It is argued that runtime verification techniques can be used to identify unknown application security vulnerabilities that are a consequence of unexpected execution paths in software. A methodology is proposed that can be used to build a model of expected application execution paths during the software development cycle. This model is used at runtime to detect exploitation of unknown security vulnerabilities using anomaly detection style techniques. The approach is evaluated by considering its effectiveness in identifying 19 vulnerabilities across 26 versions of Apache Struts over a 5 year period.

1 Introduction

Contemporary software is routinely constructed from a myriad of components and frameworks. With the emphasis on rapid construction and reuse comes a tacit acceptance that it is neither practical nor expected that a programmer should fully understand the minutiae of every component included with their application. As a consequence, its not unusual for the programmer to focus on understanding their application at the level of the business logic, while hoping that abstraction neatly deals with the complex interoperation of its underlying components. However, these underlying components often require particular configuration and usage patterns in order to operate securely. These component requirements may be ignored by the programmer, through ignorance or as a result of coding error in the application. A programmer, while focused on using an external software component to implement one task may overlook that the application is implicitly enabled to perform another, unexpected task. Flaws can also occur within the components themselves, for similar reasons; the component developer may not have anticipated all possible use-cases. A consequence of what can be described as "dark code" [11] or "the dark side of the code" [16], is that while the programmer expects certain program execution paths, other, unexpected paths may be possible and give rise to a security vulnerability.

The software industry's approach to software vulnerabilities includes security quality assurance processes such as code reviews, static analysis and penetration testing. However, it is rarely possible to cover the subtleties of all of the

S. Ranise and V. Swarup (Eds.): DBSec 2016, LNCS 9766, pp. 347–363, 2016.
DOI: 10.1007/978-3-319-41483-6_24

numerous components and their inter-operation. In addition, during application development, third-party components are not routinely reviewed or tested for vulnerabilities. Some of the security vulnerabilities that gained notoriety in recent years, such as Heartbleed and Shellshock, were deployed for many years before they were discovered, despite being used by large number of consumers.

Our position is that many software vulnerabilities can be attributed to programming errors that enable unexpected software behavior. Runtime verification [5] of software execution against a specified expected behavior can help identify unexpected behavior in the software. For small applications, limited requirements on expected behavior can be specified a priori, for example as a temporal proposition [5]; however, this does not scale when the requirement is to constrain emergent behavior across large complex systems of interoperating components. An alternative strategy, used by anomaly detection techniques [4,6,7,17], is to learn a behavioral reference profile from system logs of past/normal behavior and use this profile at runtime to check behavior. However, practical application of this approach has tended to generate profiles with limited expressiveness [18] for relatively small and uncomplicated software components [14], such as sendmail or lpd, observed though system calls [7]. The practical challenges of applying these techniques to contemporary enterprise software, such as dealing with scale and alignment with software release processes have not been considered.

The contributions of the paper are as follows. The anomaly-detection model proposed in [15] is extended to incorporate the notion of scope which provides an effective way of dealing with scale in contemporary application systems. Based on this model, an implementation framework is developed whereby existing software testing techniques are adapted to generate profiles of expected behavior that can be used for runtime verification. The approach has been evaluated by considering its effectiveness in identifying code vulnerabilities across the 26 versions of Apache Struts over the past 5 years. Of significance is the result that anomaly-detection/run-time verification techniques would have been quite effective in identifying exploits of these zero-day vulnerabilities, prior to their discovery. To the best of our knowledge this is the first successful construction of profiles used to detect vulnerabilities in large-scale enterprise software.

The paper is organized as follows. Section 2 uses an example of contemporary software development—a microblog application implemented with Struts—to illustrate how easy it is for the programmer to unwittingly introduce a programming flaw/security vulnerability. Section 3 reviews and considers the challenges of applying techniques for anomaly detection to contemporary software systems and describes our proposed approach. Section 4 discusses the evaluation of the approach and Sect. 5 provides the conclusion.

2   Contemporary Software Development

Contemporary software is implemented using a variety of high-level programming languages, software frameworks and third party components. While application-level code may appear straightforward, enabling rapid and low-cost application development, its underlying system is a complex arrangement of inter-dependent software whose behavior can be difficult for a programmer to fully comprehend. There are a great many examples whereby misunderstanding of contemporary software systems leads to errors in the application code that can be exploited as security vulnerabilities. We consider this problem using a simple example that runs through the paper.

2.1 A Micro-Blogging Application

A micro-blogging social networking application provides an online facility for users to post short text messages and share them with others. The application provides a web interface and REST API for integration with various types of clients, including desktop browsers and mobile devices. The application is built using Apache Struts, a popular Model-View-Controller framework for J2EE. Struts abstracts application logic from HTTP request processing flow by encapsulating it into objects called *actions*. For example, Fig. 1 shows how the action responsible for posting a new micro-blog message is implemented in just a few lines of code. Actions can be mapped to specific URL paths, such as /api/post. Struts can separately handle routine tasks, including parameter validation, authentication, session handling and CSRF protection, before passing parameter values to the action as associated by their setters. This facilitates the separation of business logic from HTTP processing concerns. Thus, rather than dealing with low-level operations such as accessing parameters by name, the developer need only implement a public setter. This makes the code re-usable, easier to maintain, document and test.

```
class PostAction extends ApiAction {
    private String message;
    public void setMessage(String msg) {
        this.message = msg;          StrutsActionProxy: PostAction.<init>
    }                                ServletInterceptor: ApiAction.setSession()
    public void execute(){           ParametersInterceptor: PostAction.setMessage("Hello")
        String userId = getUser().getId();   DeprecationInterceptor: PostAction.execute()
        datastore.add(userId, message);      PostAction: PostAction.getUser()
    }                                PostAction: ApiAction.getSession()
    public User getUser() {          PostAction: User.getId()
        return getSession().get(USER);   PostAction: Datastore.add("lucy", "Hello")
    }
}
```

Fig. 1. Micro-blog application code and trace

Application behavior can be traced as a sequence of the underlying Java method calls. For example, invoking the application using /api/post?message=Hello results in the included trace fragment. Each method includes a reference to its calling class. In the above, Struts creates an instance of PostAction, which is provided with its session and parameter data and is in turn executed, and the return value sent as response.

2.2   An Unexpected Vulnerability

While the implementation of the micro-blog post action appears straightforward, it can be easy for a developer to overlook subtleties in the interoperation between the application code and the underlying Struts framework. The code in Fig. 1 contains one such oversight, that results from how the getUser method operates with Struts, and results in a security vulnerability. Suppose that this method was not intended to be a part of the action's interface, rather, it is implemented by the programmer as a means to provide convenient access to the user object from the session. The method returns a User object, which is a container for various user attributes, such as name and identifier and accessor methods. The combination of a public getter for the User object and public setters for the object makes it possible to manipulate user information request parameters. For example, an attacker Alice can invoke /api/post?message=Hello&user.id=frank in order to modify the user-id stored in the session to Frank and submit a message on Frank's behalf. A fragment of the execution trace in this case is:

```
StrutsActionProxy: PostAction.<init>
ServletConfigInterceptor: ApiAction.setSession()
ParametersInterceptor: PostAction.setMessage("Hello")
ParametersInterceptor: PostAction.getUser()
PostAction: ApiAction.getSession()
ParametersInterceptor: User.setId("frank")
DeprecationInterceptor: PostAction.execute()
PostAction: PostAction.getUser()
PostAction: ApiAction.getSession()
PostAction: User.getId()
PostAction: Datastore.add("frank", "Hello")
```

The Struts ParametersInterceptor parses and interprets the user.id attribute as an instruction to set the id property of the user property. This results in a sequence of operations equivalent to getUser().setId("frank"). This oversight by the developer illustrates how easy it can be to program an unexpected execution path that compromises security. Accessing object fields though a chain of getters and setters is a useful and documented feature of Struts. However, it can come as a surprise to a programmer, who is focused more on application-level development, that something as intuitive as implementing a getter for the current user results in a security vulnerability.

This problem is further highlighted by an almost identical vulnerability (CVE-2014-0094) that was found within Struts itself. Even though the consequences of exposing a public getter may have been clear to the Struts developers, it is easy to overlook the fact that every Java object (and therefore, every Struts action) also contains a getClass method. This results in an unintended exposure of an action's Class object, accessed through request parameters [2]. Unfortunately, even after the problem was discovered, the implemented remedy was incomplete. The initial remedy black-listed the class parameter, however, it did not consider uppercase parameters (such as Class). Eventually, three more vulnerabilities were reported on incomplete remedies before the issue was believed addressed.

The micro-blogging application is one example of how programming error can result in a security vulnerability whose identification and prevention require an in-depth understanding of the underlying systems. However, given the complexity of contemporary systems, our position is that there will always be some aspect of the behavior that the programmer does not fully understand. For example, a study of developers by Oliveira et al. [13] found that 53 % of its participants knew about a particular coding vulnerability, however they did not correlate it with their own programming activity unless it was explicitly highlighted.

3   Security Vulnerabilities and Anomaly Detection

The use of anomaly detection in software execution has tended to focus on relatively small-scale homogeneous applications. However, the microblogging example illustrates that even very simple contemporary applications are in fact large systems of interconnected components. This section considers the key challenges encountered in applying anomaly detection techniques to contemporary application software. For reasons of space, but without loss of generality, the discussion is focussed on a common enterprise scenario of a web application/service built on a high-level software platform (Java) and an MVC framework (Struts).

3.1   Abstraction and Scope

The activity of an application is observed as a sequence of events, such as a system log. These observations can be made at different levels of abstraction. For example, the micro-blogging application activity could be observed as a series of high-level user actions, such as posting or viewing a message. At a lower level of abstraction the actions can be observed as HTTP calls to the application server. Further lower levels describe the activity of the application code and its libraries, Java virtual machine, operating system, and so forth. The objective is to use the observed activity/log of the system to build a behavior reference model for use in anomaly detection. The challenge is determining a level of abstraction that enables anomalous execution paths to identify security vulnerabilities.

Security vulnerabilities occur at different levels of abstraction. Building reference models from observations of low-level interactions, such as operating system calls [4,7,12] or Javascript [17] calls has been shown to be quite effective in detecting specific exploits on the application, such as buffer overflow vulnerabilities or cross-site scripting. However, the anomalous execution path in the micro-blog example cannot be detected at a level of abstraction comparable with [4,7,12,17] as observing the sequence of calls to the database looks the same as valid behavior. While one may think of this anomaly as occurring at a higher level of abstraction, making observations based on HTTP requests is not sufficient in this case (although we note that there are other anomalies that can be characterized at this high-level). An analysis algorithm is proposed [15] that discovers a level of event abstraction that provides good anomaly-detection accuracy in transaction-like behaviors; it has proven quite effective in discriminating actions that remain static from the parameters that can change within a transaction.

In our experiments we found that observing (Java) application behavior in terms of its method calls and permission checks is the most effective in distinguishing the un-expected execution paths that lead to software vulnerabilities.

However, in practice it is unrealistic to base anomaly detection on every underlying method call invoked as a consequence of executing an application. For example, the few lines of the microblog application Java code in Fig. 1 generate tens of thousands of method calls. Therefore, the *scope* of observation is restricted to methods that belong to the specific component(s) of interest. Section 2 considers detection of vulnerabilities in the microblog application code and, therefore, restricts the observed scope to just those methods that belong to this application's Java package. In the experiment described in Sect. 4 the focus is on detecting vulnerabilities in the code that implements Apache Struts and therefore the scope is the 2400 methods defined within Struts packages.

3.2 Generating Baseline Activity

A baseline of observed activity must be obtained in order to build the behavior reference model for the software component. In order to be applicable to an enterprise environment, the method of establishing baseline activity has to be systematic, repeatable and aligned with application development/deployment lifecycle. Most importantly, the baseline generation must provide sufficient coverage for the normal/expected behavior of the application.

A common position is that a satisfactory baseline can be obtained as a recording of "normal" activity obtained though monitoring application operation in its target environment [6,7,17]. However this has practical limitations for enterprise software; in particular, the system must run over a period of time in order to generate a baseline with sufficient coverage. As the software industry adopts faster and more automated delivery approaches and software releases are as frequent as on daily basis, building a (normal) baseline based on observation of application in production is impractical. It would not only require the application to be active for a significant length of time without anomaly detection, it also may be impossible to obtain a sufficient baseline before it becomes obsolete.

We argue that is more appropriate to obtain the baseline and corresponding behavioral model during the software testing phase. In [16] it is suggested that unit tests might be used to generate the necessary system logs. Such a baseline is useful if the required scope and level of abstraction is consistent with the unit tests. Notwithstanding coverage, unit tests are typically constructed for a specific component, in isolation, and may only be suitable for relatively simple components or utility libraries An alternative approach is using functional and/or integration tests to also generate the baseline. Enterprise software is often subjected to extensive testing, usually highly automated and with controlled coverage. Traces resulting from such software tests may provide a reliable and systematic baseline model. However, as with unit tests, the functional test coverage is usually built only to a certain satisfactory level but is rarely complete. Additional coverage may be obtained using fuzz testing or application scanners that automatically exercise application in order to perform non-functional types of testing such as security or performance. The application scanners often use functional test execution as its starting point and then extend the coverage by exploring the application further in automated fashion.

In our experiments we found that using an application scanner allows the application system to be explored in a comprehensive, un-biased and repeatable manner and was the most effective for our task. The application scanner explores the application extensively to discover its structure, parameters, cookies and so forth, and also engages in a series of tests in an attempt to discover security vulnerabilities. While the scanner interacts via high-level requests to the application's external interfaces, a system log/trace of the consequent low-level actions is generated. If the scanner does not discover any security vulnerabilities then it is this log that provides the baseline of expected activity.

3.3 Behavioral Reference Model

A number of approaches can be used to infer a reference model of system behavior based on observed past activity, with varying complexity and precision. Statistical models [8] probe various system characteristics periodically to establish a baseline of metrics. Such models, while useful for simple intrusion detection, are not sufficiently rich to detect anomalous software execution. Sequence-based techniques have been designed to infer acceptable behavior/policies for anomaly detection [7,15] and process mining [1]. Strengths and weaknesses of existing techniques have been studied [3,18] and expected properties of the reference model discussed [6,14].

In many applications, activity may be contained in finite and separate units of work, where a sequence of operations that have clear beginning and end and, in general, follow some repeatable pattern is performed. Application behavior may contain multiple such transaction-like work units. For example, observing the micro-blogging application at a method call level, can be modeled as a collection of different kinds of transaction behaviors, such as posting a message or reading a message. Activity observations related to invocations of the same transaction are similar and activity related to invocations of different transactions substantially different. For this type of activity, rather than merging all transactions into a single set of short-range correlations [7], the reference model should be able to express units of activity separately from each other [15], thus at increased precision and reduced chance for mimicry attack [19].

Correlations between sequences of operations and their target values can be used to discover repeating patterns of behavior and [15] uses this to develop an automated technique to partition a system trace into a collection of behavioral norms. In our experiments we use these *behavioral norms* [15] to provide a reference model for anomaly detection. A collection of behavioral norms is generated, from baseline activity log of Java events, for a given scope and level of abstraction, each corresponding to a sequence of method calls parameterized by common target attributes. The approach is not unlike process mining [1] or sequence call monitoring [6], however, behavioral norms can be used to provide a more precise model for system-level behavior.

3.4 Runtime Verification and Application Integration

While traditional logging may be useful for retrospective detection of anomalous behavior, integrating runtime verification/anomaly detection with the application provides the ability to interrupt application execution before the anomalous operations are executed. Contemporary software platforms provide integration techniques such as Aspects that may be suitable for easy and non-disruptive enablement of execution monitoring and runtime verification.

The trapping and monitoring of application execution is implemented using Runtime Verifier, a customized Java Security Manager. Its purpose is to intercept permission check requests, such as the permission to open a file, connect to server or execute a process. According to its mode of operation, this manager may log the events, check that event execution is compliant with a norm-model provided, and if required, prevent the execution of anomalous event sequences.

While the Java Security Manager is a natural integration point for monitoring and controlling application execution, it is limited to those methods that have explicit permission checks such as input/output operations or security related activity such as access to cryptographic keys. An arbitrary off-the-shelf component might not have been programmed with its own permissions. In this case it is insufficient to rely on the Security Manager, and therefore, a Java Aspect was developed that can intercept specific method calls that match programmer-specified pattern. For example, in the case of the micro-blog application, the aspect was configured to intercept method calls that are provided by classes of the application. The aspect, on intercepting a method call, invokes the Security Manager, which in turn forwards the call details as an event to the Runtime Verifier runtime. This is depicted in Fig. 2.

   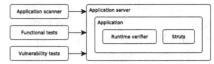

Fig. 2. Java Runtime Verifier   **Fig. 3.** Experiment setup

Using a security manager in the implementation of the Runtime Verifier permits control over application execution. Permissions and identified method calls are checked prior to execution, and thus can be validated for compliance with the behavioral model at runtime, and prevented, if considered anomalous.

4 Experimental Evaluation

The previous section outlined our implementation of Java application-level anomaly detection based on behavioral norms: checking that the actual execution of an application is compliant with a model of expected behavior that was generated during software development. Our thesis is that unknown security vulnerabilities in software components can be identified as runtime anomalies arising from unexpected execution paths.

Testing this thesis using a catalog of vulnerabilities hand-crafted for the purpose, may provide insight, but their design can be contrived/cherry-picked and is not an effective evaluation of whether the approach would work 'in the wild'. We therefore decided to test the thesis against an application that used a well-established and popular enterprise-scale software component that has a history of security vulnerabilities. In particular, the objective is to test whether vulnerabilities reported against earlier versions of software can be identified as anomalies, while those same anomalies are not reported against later versions of the software in which the corresponding vulnerability has been remedied.

In the following we considered the vulnerability history of 26 versions of Apache Struts over a five year period, starting with version 2.3.1, released in December 2011, to version 2.3.24.1, released in September 2015.

4.1   Experiment Setup

Figure 3 outlines the key elements of the experimental setup. In order to evaluate Struts behavior in its typical environment, we developed a small Struts-based web application based on the micro-blogging program described in Sect. 2. The application makes conventional use of Struts, with a standard configuration including default interceptor stack and properties.

The application system is built automatically and the experiment is carried out separately for each version of Struts. Experiment characteristics, such as execution times and sizes, were comparable for the different versions of Struts. Experiments were orchestrated by Apache Maven and each iteration for a different Struts version comprised of two phases. In the first phase, a trace of the application system's execution is generated and from which the behavioral model is built for the given version of Struts. In the second phase the effectiveness of anomaly checking based on the generated behavioral model is verified.

4.2   Building Behavioral Models

A commercial application security scanner was run against the micro-blogging web application. The scanner configuration was standard and not tailored in any particular way for Struts. The same scanner configuration was repeatedly used against each deployment of the application with a different version of Struts. In each experiment, the scanner interacts with the micro-blogging web application, black-box testing an extensive collection of known vulnerabilities and misconfigurations. The Runtime Verifier was deployed with the application and used to build/check the behavior models in each experiment.

In our experiment, we consider the behavior of Struts, in terms of how it is used by the application. Therefore, the Runtime Verifier (Sect. 3.3) was configured to intercept all method calls within the Struts packages scope, that is org.apache.struts2.*., corresponding to 460 distinct methods that are used in the context of the micro-blogging web application. A single scan experiment resulted in 8963 HTTP requests to the micro-blogging web application URLs with a range of inputs, taking 8 min to complete. In monitoring the execution of the application during this scan, the Runtime Verifier generates a 237 megabyte baseline trace containing 2.76 million Struts events (in scope), which is analyzed, and a set of behavioral norms is generated within approximately a further 5 s, running on a mid-range computer. The norms are sequences of method calls, such as ⟨..., UrlHelper.encode, UrlRenderer UrlProvider.getAnchor, UrlRenderer UrlProvider.isPutInContext, ...⟩, represented as tri-grams.

Figure 4 plots an example of the number of distinct norms (transactional behavior patterns) generated, against the number of HTTP requests made by the scanner to the application deployed with Struts version 2.3.1. From the start of the scan, as the number of requests increase, the number of norms resulting from the requests rapidly increase initially, and then appear to stabilize after a period. This graph suggests that our scan size of 8963 requests is adequate, after which no new norms are identified. Similar results were achieved for the other versions of Struts. Having generated a behavioral norm model for a given version of Struts and included it with the Runtime Verifier in the application deployment, the second phase of the experiment involves testing the effectiveness of using the model to detect vulnerabilities for that version of Struts.

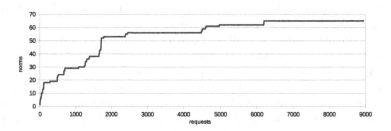

Fig. 4. Growth in behavioral norms (transactional patterns).

4.3   Vulnerability Tests

At the time of writing and based on the Common Vulnerabilities and Exposures (CVE) entries in the National Vulnerability Database, there are 19 vulnerabilities known to the general public for the 26 versions of Struts under study. For each vulnerability, the CVE advisory was studied alongside the vulnerable Struts code and the remediated version of the code, and an attack vector exploiting the vulnerability was developed. Of the 19 vulnerabilities, attacks for the 18 listed in Table 1 were developed; we could not find enough information to reproduce the vulnerability identified in CVE-2012-4386. For each vulnerability, we implemented an automated test case which attempts to exploit the vulnerability and verify that the exploitation was successful.

For example, CVE-2013-2115 is a vulnerability that allows a remote attacker to execute arbitrary OGNL code via a crafted request. It affects Struts JSP tags for rendering URLs. Using the tag is convenient and relieves the developer from having to manually map actions to URLs and passing parameters, thus further separating application logic from low-level details. In order to render a URL for a search action, including the current page's parameters, the developer can use: `<s:url action="SearchAction" includeParams="all">`. The tag is evaluated to `/api/search?name=Frank`. However, the code for processing the tag suffers from a security vulnerability. An attacker may add a request parameter by including OGNL code and that code will be evaluated when processing the tag. For example, the official security advisory for this vulnerability (CVE-2013-2115) describes that an attacker may append `x=$ {@java.lang.Runtime@getRuntime().exec('cmd')}` to the page parameters. The OGNL code, enclosed in `${}` is evaluated and custom Java code is executed by the application. However, the attack results in activity caused not only by an unexpected Struts execution path, but also by the injected code involved in creating a process and accessing a file binary. Rather than injecting malicious code that results in significantly different behavior, each test case attempts to inject benign code that simply sets a variable that can be subsequently checked to determine the success of the attack. The objective of each test is to generate the minimal behavior needed to explore the path of the attack, but it does not engage in subsequent behavior that might be easily recognized as anomalous in its own right. In this way the test case is intended to represent a worst-case scenario for anomaly detection.

In many cases developing the vulnerability test cases required some effort. A number of the vulnerabilities are not clearly described in their respective advisories and sometimes the details are intentionally undisclosed. For example, CVE-2013-4310 (discussed below in this paper) is described as allowing "to bypass security constraints under certain conditions". In order to prepare the test case for this vulnerability it was necessary to understand its nature though analysis of source changes of Struts.

Vulnerability Test Results. Table 1 contains[1] the outcome of testing each of the 18 reported vulnerabilities against each of the 26 versions of Struts. Each table cell contains three outcomes. The first indicates whether it was reported that the particular version of Struts was indeed affected (+), or not (−) by the vulnerability. The second outcome specifies whether the execution of the attack for that vulnerability was successful (+), or not (−). The third outcome, specifies whether th Runtime Verifier detected anomalous behavior during execution of the test case (+), or not (−). For example, the outcome +++ means that the version had the reported vulnerability, that the attack test case successfully executed and that anomalies were detected (true positive).

---

[1] Presented as a table, keeping in mind Edward R. Tufte's (2004) observation that *"small non-comparative highly labeled data sets usually belong in tables"*.

Table 1. Attack Outcomes on different versions of Struts.

CVE ID	2.3.1	2.3.4	2.3.14	2.3.14.1	2.3.14.2	2.3.15	2.3.15.1	2.3.16	2.3.16.1	2.3.16.2	2.3.16.3	2.3.20	2.3.24	2.3.24.1
2015-5209	+++	+++	+++	+++	+++	+++	+++	+++	+++	+++	+++	+++	+++	---
2015-1831	---	---	---	---	---	---	---	---	---	---	---	+++	---	---
2014-7809	++-	++-	++-	++-	++-	++-	++-	++-	++-	++-	++-			
2014-0116	+++	+++	+++	+++	+++	+++	+++	+++	+++	+++	--+	--+	--+	--+
2014-0113	+++	+++	+++	+++	+++	+++	+++	+++	+++	--+	--+	--+	--+	--+
2014-0112	+++	+++	+++	+++	+++	+++	+++	+++	+++	---	---	---	---	---
2014-0094	+++	+++	+++	+++	+++	+++	+++	+++	---	---	---	---	---	---
2013-4316	+++	+++	+++	+++	+++	+++	+++	---	---	---	---	---	---	---
2013-4310	++-	++-	++-	++-	++-	++-	++-	---	---	---	---	---	---	---
2013-2251	+++	+++	+++	+++	+++	+++	---	---	---	---	---	---	---	---
2013-2248	+++	+++	+++	+++	+++	+++	---	---	---	---	---	---	---	---
2013-2135	+++	+++	+++	+++	+++	---	---	---	---	---	---	---	---	---
2013-2134	+++	+++	+++	+++	+++	---	---	---	---	---	---	---	---	---
2013-2115	+++	+++	+++	+++	---	---	---	---	---	---	---	---	---	---
2013-1966	+++	+++	+++	-++	---	---	---	---	---	---	---	---	---	---
2013-1965	+++	+++	+++	-++	---	---	---	---	---	---	---	---	---	---
2012-4387	+++	+++	---	---	---	---	---	---	---	---	---	---	---	---
2012-0393	+++	---	---	---	---	---	---	---	---	---	---	---	---	---

vulnerable   attack successful   anomalies   not vulnerable   attack failed   no anomalies

Note that some outcomes were identical for different versions of Struts, and in the interest of saving space.

Considering CVE-2013-2115, the URL tag vulnerability described above, we see from Table 1, that the attack test-case successfully exploited this vulnerability, and was detected as an anomaly, for all versions 2.3.1 – 2.3.14.1 publicly announced to be vulnerable (+++). A closer examination of the execution trace fragment, generated from the attack test case,

```
DefaultUrlHelper DefaultUrlHelper.translateAndEncode
DefaultUrlHelper DefaultUrlHelper.translateVariable
OgnlInvoke invoke
ServletUrlRenderer ComponentUrlProvider.getAnchor
ServletUrlRenderer ComponentUrlProvider.isPutInContext
```

identifies the anomaly as OGNL code used in rendering the URL. Examining execution traces may help identify that part of the code that is responsible for the vulnerability. Indeed, a study of subsequent versions of the Struts source code that repair the vulnerability reveals that the issue was attributed to `translateVariable` that invoked OGNL processing. In the repaired code, the method was removed as unnecessary. Carrying out the same test-case on subsequent non-vulnerable versions results in an unsuccessful attack and no anomalous behavior (---), which is as expected. The corresponding trace fragment for those versions shows that no OGNL code execution—the root cause of the vulnerability in previous versions—was observed in the context of URL rendering:

```
DefaultUrlHelper DefaultUrlHelper.encode
ServletUrlRenderer ComponentUrlProvider.getAnchor
ServletUrlRenderer ComponentUrlProvider.isPutInContext
```

Some tests executed with unanticipated outcomes. A surprising result --++, indicates a successful attack, with the anomaly detected, for Struts version 2.3.14.1 for which no vulnerability was reported in CVE-2013-1965 and CVE-2013-1966. A closer examination of these two vulnerabilities confirms that, contrary to publicly available information, version 2.3.14.1 is indeed vulnerable.

False Negatives. In most cases, Table 1 reports that the anomaly detection identified successful attacks on vulnerable versions, while unsuccessful attacks on non-vulnerable versions were not identified as anomalous. The table, however, reports two vulnerabilities with a false negative result (++), that is, a successful attack on a vulnerable version for which anomalous behavior was not observed.

One false negative arises from CVE-2014-7809: a CSRF vulnerability caused by a predictable token generated using a weak generator. It allows an attacker, knowing a previous value of a token, to predict the value of the next token and to use it to perform an attack. Although the attack is caused by a simple coding error, we argue that it does not arise from an unexpected path of code execution. A CSRF attack as a request using a token generated by the attacker results in exactly the same behavior as a legitimate request made by the user. As such, it can not be detected as an anomaly in the execution path.

Another false negative arises from CVE-2013-4310, which reports an ability to bypass security constraints. Our investigation discovered that this vulnerability is only applicable to applications that have a somewhat unusual security mechanism. As mentioned in Sect. 2, actions in Struts are the basic unit of an application's business logic and are normally mapped to specific URL paths (such as /api/post). Struts offers an alternative addressing through URL parameters with action prefix, such as /api/other?action:post. The vulnerability describes a scenario when a security control, implemented outside struts, based on specific URL pattern is bypassed using the alternative addressing. It could be argued such scenario does not really describe a Struts vulnerability, but rather a faulty security control that documented feature of Struts allows to facilitate. In our experiment, the attack exploiting CVE-2013-4310 was undetected because the application we implemented included use of action: prefixes. Addressing actions though parameters was considered a normal behavior of the application and, when executed during the attack, did not cause anomalous behavior.

False Positives. In two instances, the test cases result in false positives, that is, anomalous behavior is detected for an unsuccessful attempt to exploit non-vulnerable version (+). This outcome is observed for CVE-2014-0114 and CVE-2014-0116 in versions where these vulnerabilities are repaired. They are variants of the problem discussed in Sect. 2 where the internal state of an application can be modified through a chain of getters and setters, and in this case, though crafted cookies. A study of the attack test-cases reveals that the anomalous behavior is related to the special treatment that Struts gives to particular cookie names. The original vulnerabilities were repaired by adding a blacklist of disallowed cookie names (such as starting with class). Thus, processing a normal cookie results in a behavior that is different to processing a cookie with blacklisted name. However, in its standard configuration, the application scanner does not generate a request involving a Struts black-listed cookie and, therefore, the generated model of expected behavior does not include an execution path corresponding to the security processing of a blacklisted cookie. Thus, the test-case, while not an attack, is flagged as an anomaly.

Overall, this part of the experiment indicates that all vulnerabilities that could be attributed to unintended code execution path in struts were successfully detected. It also shows that, with one exception of black-listed cookies, in non-vulnerable versions, where malicious request is properly handled by the application no anomalous behavior is reported.

4.4 Functional Tests

On generating an expected model of behavior (for a given version of Struts) we check that its norms are sufficiently complete by engaging a further standard application scan and confirm that no anomalies are identified. This confirms that 'normal' expected behavior is properly recognized by the Runtime Verifier. However, for the purposes of the evaluation, we are interested in confirming that the anomaly detection can also discriminate between attacking behavior that exploits a vulnerability versus other behavior that executes code in the region of the vulnerability, but does not actually exploit the vulnerability. To this end, a suite of functional tests were developed to check this ability to discriminate.

For example, the URL tag vulnerability CVE-2013-2115 described in Sect. 4.3 involves passing a crafted value through a URL parameter. The test calls an application using an additional parameter but without OGNL code. Some vulnerabilities require more advanced test cases. For example, the attack test-case for CVE-2013-2251 involves passing a crafted string through a Struts-specific request parameter, allowing indirect action addressing. We developed two further functional test-cases that check this particular functionality. First uses the indirect addressing, but with a correct action name, and checks that the requested action was called. Second has an incorrect action but checks whether the application replied with expected/corresponding error. The purpose of these tests is to check whether the anomaly detection actually reacts to a genuine vulnerable path of execution or whether the path from related valid functionality is flagged as an anomaly. By making sure that the functionality is exercised we can distinguish between these two cases, exercising particular functionality normally (even if in error scenario) and during the attack.

Overall, we developed 19 test cases that explore non-attacking behavior in the region of the 18 vulnerabilities. The outcome-score of each test is similar to the vulnerability tests and represented using two values. The first outcome value reports whether the test was successful, that is whether the tested functionality worked correctly. Note, that because we have also tested an application's response to an incorrect request, a successful outcome may mean that the application correctly responded to an incorrect value, such presentation of an error page. The second outcome value reports whether an anomaly was detected during execution of the test. Most of the test outcomes are indicating a successful test with no anomalies. However, in two cases the outcome indicates test failure with no anomalies is observed. These are the test cases for indirect action addressing using `action:` prefix. The test fails for all versions from 2.3.15.2. This is because, as a response to CVE-2013-4310, this functionality was disabled.

4.5 Experiment Insights

The application scanner may trigger an unexpected behavior, which if unattended to, becomes part of the model used in runtime verification. However, this phenomenon was not observed during our experiments. Furthermore, we assume that any vulnerability identified during scanning will be remediated by modifying the source code and the scan repeated.

Anomaly detection/prevention adds a performance overhead that should be considered. In order to integrate anomaly detection with the application we used a Java Security Manager and AspectJ. These tools are routinely used for implementing security mechanisms and their performance impact has been investigated [9,10]. During the Struts experiment, the average time to process an HTTP request from the scanner to the application took $4950\,\mu s$ without instrumentation. With the Anomaly Manger enabled for runtime verification, the average time increased by $3.85\,\%$ to $5140\,\mu s$. However, the increase depends on how much of application activity is covered by runtime verification: in the experiment this was limited to the Struts library.

Part of our experimental setup involved inspecting the codebases of different versions of Struts in order to identify the vulnerable code and implement the attack tests. In carrying out this detailed code-level review we observed a number of programming phenomena across the different versions. In particular, the phenomena that some generic functionality of Struts allows for a specific execution scenario that compromised security. The otherwise harmless features, such as addressing actions, setting their parameters and evaluating expressions, when used in a particular way allowed unintended operations. For example, five vulnerabilities exploit the feature that allows setting action properties through HTTP parameters and accessing sensitive objects such as session or class loader.

Overall, we observed that the majority of the programming issues relate to rather simple programming errors. In particular, while a general functionality was implemented, a specific, unexpected execution pattern was not considered nor handled by the code. In some cases, such as accessing the class loader via parameter (CVE-2014-0094), we conjecture that the developers were surely aware that accessing properties though parameters can be a security risk. Some specific parameters, such as session object, were black listed but others that are less obvious, such as class, were not. In other cases, when a vulnerability was identified in one part of the framework it was not immediately correlated to another part that was also vulnerable [2]. For example, the fix for CVE-2014-0094 addressed class loader manipulation though request parameters but did not provide the fix for the same attack using cookies. Our analysis of Struts vulnerabilities would seem to confirm other studies [13] that indicate that developers tend to repeat security errors even when they are aware of particular vulnerability.

5 Conclusion

We argue that many of the security vulnerabilities that are caused by programing error can lead to unexpected execution paths that can be detected using anomaly detection techniques. However, applying such techniques to contemporary, enterprise software is not trivial and poses a set of challenges such as selecting the scope and abstraction level of software monitoring, establishing a base line behavior and choosing suitable behavioral model.

We propose a methodology for putting anomaly detection into use for contemporary software components and apply it to Apache Struts as a part of large scale application. Our experiments demonstrate that it is possible to learn a sufficiently rich model of the application's expected use of Struts such that it can be used to detect anomalies in its subsequent use of Struts. Indeed, results indicate that all 16 execution path-related vulnerabilities identified over 26 versions of Struts over 5 years are effectively identified as anomalies. While the experiments were comprehensive, they are limited to Struts vulnerabilities. Nevertheless, we believe the results point to the potential of using anomaly detection techniques in contemporary software and that further research on this topic is worthwhile.

Acknowledgement. This work was supported, in part, by Science Foundation Ireland under grant SFI/12/RC/2289.

References

1. van der Aalst, et al.: Workflow mining: Discovering process models from event logs. IEEE Trans. Knowl. Data Eng. **16**(9), 1128–1142 (2004)
2. Ashraf, Z.: Analysis of recent struts vulnerabilities in parameters and cookie interceptors, their impact and exploitation. IBM Security Intelligence portal (2014). Accessed 21 May 2015
3. Chandola, V., Banerjee, A., Kumar, V.: Anomaly detection for discrete sequences: a survey. IEEE Trans. Knowl. Data Eng. **24**(5), 823–839 (2012)
4. Creech, G., Hu, J.: A semantic approach to host-based intrusion detection systems using contiguous and discontiguous system call patterns. IEEE Trans. Comp. **63**, 807–819 (2014)
5. Delgado, N., Gates, A.Q., Roach, S.: A taxonomy and catalog of runtime software-fault monitoring tools. IEEE Trans. Softw. Eng. **30**(12), 859–872 (2004)
6. Forrest, S., Hofmeyr, S., Somayaji, A.: The evolution of system-call monitoring. In: Proceedings of the Annual Computer Security Applications Conference (2008)
7. Forrest, S., Hofmeyr, S.A., Somayaji, A., Longstaff, T.A.: A sense of self for unix processes. In: IEEE Symposium on Security and Privacy (1996)
8. Helman, P., Liepins, G.E.: Statistical foundations of audit trail analysis for the detection of computer misuse. IEEE Trans. Softw. Eng. **19**(9), 886–901 (1993)
9. Herzog, A., Shahmehri, N.: Performance of the java security manager. Comput. Secur. **24**(3), 192–207 (2005)
10. Hilsdale, E., Hugunin, J.: Advice weaving in AspectJ. In: Proceedings of the 3rd International Conference on Aspect-Oriented Software Development (2004)
11. Holzmann, G.J.: Code inflation. IEEE Softw. **32**(2), 10–13 (2015)
12. Maggi, F., Matteucci, M., Zanero, S.: Detecting intrusions through system call sequence and argument analysis. IEEE Trans. Depend. Secur. Comput. **7**, 381–395 (2010)

13. Oliveira, D., et al.: It's the psychology stupid: how heuristics explain software vulnerabilities and how priming can illuminate developer's blind spots. In: Proceedings of the Annual Computer Security Applications Conference (2014)
14. Patcha, A., Park, J.M.: An overview of anomaly detection techniques: existing solutions and latest technological trends. Comput. Netw. **51**(12), 3448–3470 (2007)
15. Pieczul, O., Foley, S.: Discovering emergent norms in security logs. In: 2013 IEEE Conference on Communications and Network Security (SafeConfig) (2013)
16. Pieczul, O., Foley, S.: The dark side of the code. In: Christianson, B., Švenda, P., Matyáš, V., Malcolm, J., Stajano, F., Anderson, J. (eds.) Security Protocols 2015. LNCS, vol. 9379, pp. 1–11. Springer, Heidelberg (2015). doi:10.1007/978-3-319-26096-9_1
17. Raman, P.: JaSPIn: JavaScript based Anomaly Detection of Cross-site scripting attacks. Master's thesis, Carleton University (2008)
18. Tan, K.M.C., Killourhy, K.S., Maxion, R.A.: Undermining an anomaly-based intrusion detection system using common exploits. In: Proceedings of the 5th International Conference on Recent Advances in Intrusion Detection (2002)
19. Wagner, D., Soto, P.: Mimicry attacks on host-based intrusion detection systems. In: ACM Conference on Computer and Communications Security (2002)

Author Index

Printed in the United States
By Bookmasters